THE LINCOLN FILENE CENTER FOR
CITIZENSHIP AND PUBLIC AFFAIRS

TUFTS UNIVERSITY

PUBLICATIONS

in

POLITICS AND GOVERNMENT

Franklin Patterson
General Editor

Ideology

PUBLISHED FOR THE CENTER

and World Affairs

By John S. Gibson

THE LINCOLN FILENE CENTER
FOR CITIZENSHIP
AND PUBLIC AFFAIRS

TUFTS UNIVERSITY

BY HOUGHTON MIFFLIN COMPANY · BOSTON

ABOUT THE AUTHOR

John S. Gibson, Associate Professor of Government and Senior Associate Director of the Lincoln Filene Center for Citizenship and Public Affairs, Tufts University, has devoted years of study to world affairs and political ideologies. A graduate of Oberlin College, he received his doctorate in international relations from Columbia University and has taught courses in political philosophy and international relations at a number of colleges and universities. His extensive experience as a teacher, administrator, author, and participant in international conferences has given him a broad perspective on our contemporary "war for the minds of men."

Dr. Gibson first developed the materials on which this book is based in a series of fifteen television programs which have been viewed by hundreds of thousands of students. In 1962, he collaborated with a group of skilled teachers and the Lincoln Filene Center in the preparation of a teacher's guide on ideology and world affairs which is now in use throughout the United States. As a response to the favorable reception of the educational television programs and the teacher's materials, Dr. Gibson was prompted to write *Ideology and World Affairs.*

Preface

The theme of *Ideology and World Affairs* has been woven into a number of educational projects sponsored by the Lincoln Filene Center at Tufts University and other agencies with which I have been associated, such as the World Affairs Council of Boston and THE 21 INCH CLASSROOM at WGBH-TV in Boston. The teacher's resource unit, also entitled *Ideology and World Affairs* and published by the Lincoln Filene Center, includes many of the central concepts presented in this book. It also contains hundreds of suggestions for effective teaching and enthusiastic learning about the ideas, ideals, and ideologies which have such an impact upon world affairs. To further enrich student understanding, there are questions and a short bibliography for each chapter, starting on page 352 of the present book.

Because there have been so many teachers, students, and consultants who have contributed toward the past and present projects and programs of the Lincoln Filene Center dealing with ideologies and world affairs, it would be exceedingly difficult to express appreciation to all who made this book possible. Some seasoned scholars, academic associates, and warm friends of the author deserve special mention, although they bear none of the responsibility for whatever shortcomings may characterize this undertaking.

Professor Philip Mosely of Columbia University, Professor James Vance Elliot of Tufts University, and Professor Andrew Gyorgy of Boston University provided scholarly insights and suggestions. I have been privileged to work with the commissioners of education of the nine Northeastern states and with the Nine States Coordinating Council in relating the concepts of this book to many kinds of classroom activities.

Dr. William J. Reid of Hyde Park High School, Boston, Dr. Karlene Russell, State Curriculum Coordinator in Vermont, and Dr. Thomas J. Curtin, Deputy Commissioner of Education in

v

Massachusetts, have been valuable consultants and sources of wisdom. I have profited greatly from the years of experience and inspired guidance from the twenty-three teachers with whom I worked in the preparation of the teacher's resource unit, *Ideology and World Affairs.*

My colleagues, Franklin Patterson and Wyman Holmes, have been a constant source of moral and intellectual support. Miss Sandra Saba performed the manuscript typing chores with speed, accuracy, and patience. Mrs. Wyman Holmes performed a superb task in editing the manuscript. She was assisted by Miss Miriam C. Berry of the Lincoln Filene Center. Finally, I cannot begin to express the debt I owe to my parents, Mr. and Mrs. Carl B. Gibson, to whom I dedicate this book.

John S. Gibson, Senior Associate Director

THE LINCOLN FILENE CENTER FOR
CITIZENSHIP AND PUBLIC AFFAIRS

Contents

PICTURE ACKNOWLEDGMENTS

The photographs, listed in order of appearance, are credited
as follows:

Labor union meeting	Wide World Photo
Church services	Wide World Photo
Berlin	Bruce MacAllister from PIX
Supreme Court Building	
Mussolini	Wide World Photo
Duvalier	Wide World Photo
Neo-nazism	Wide World Photo
Franco and Salazar	Wide World Photo
Berlin Wall	German Information Service
Red Chinese trial	LIFE Magazine © 1953 Time Inc.
Mboya	Wide World Photo
Shah of Iran	from Black Star
Sukarno and Khrushchev	Wide World Photo
Nasser and Tito	Wide World Photo
Ben Bella	from Black Star
Touré	from Black Star
CARE, Colombia project	Freelance Photographers Guild, Inc.
Women reading, Ghana	© Marc Riboud, Magnum
Colombian farmers	Standard Oil Company (N.J.)
Guinea elections	by Marc & Evelyne Bernheim from Rapho Guillumette

Introduction

The educational world in recent years has witnessed many changes, innovations, and stimulating approaches to helping students cope with the crucial issues of our era. Of great importance has been the increasing maturity and sophistication in teaching about communism. A decade ago, American students received little, if any, education on the nature of international communism and the profound implications of the war for the minds of men in which we are all engaged. Today, thanks to the contributions of many dedicated teachers, inquiring students, and enlightened public opinion, schools and colleges throughout the United States are including unit and course work dealing with the problems of communism and related issues.

The Lincoln Filene Center at Tufts University, along with such other agencies as the 21 INCH CLASSROOM program of educational television in the New England area and the World Affairs Council of Boston, has devoted much of its energy to expanding the quality and quantity of programs in the area of ideology and world affairs. Through educational television programs for students, teacher training programs at four colleges and universities, teacher's resource units, and frequent workshops for both students and teachers, the Lincoln Filene Center has attempted to provide solid educational leadership in teaching about communism, democracy, and other ideologies. This book, *Ideology and World Affairs*, is a logical outcome of this concerted effort.

Several distinguishing characteristics of the Center's programs in ideology and world affairs should be mentioned. In the first place, we have attempted to define our terms carefully. We are concerned with the *ideology* of the state, which is a fusion of a nation's way of life, way of governing, and guide to political action. Secondly, we have attempted to explain *why* communism, as an ideology and guide to action for Communist states, seeks to impose its way of life and way of governing on all nations. In the third place, we oppose not only communism but other brands of totalitarianism as well, such as fascism and nazism and their contemporary stepchildren. We have felt that, while many fine books and courses of study do an excellent job in dealing with the threat of communism, the past and present menace of right-wing dictatorships is too often forgotten.

In the fourth place, we are deeply concerned with authoritarian ideologies in the Afro-Asian world, which often stand in the middle between democracy and totalitarianism. We have not viewed the world, in other words, as one neatly divided between communism and democracy. We are anxious that students examine what can be done to channel contemporary authoritarianism ultimately toward democracy. Finally, we view democracy itself as an ideology. We are not only *against* totalitarianism; we are *for* democracy as a way of life, a way of governing, and a guide to political action. We conceive of democracy as an ideology which can and must be advanced in world affairs through effective practice of democracy as a way of life and through effective foreign policies as well.

These, then, are some central themes of this book, and of the other materials developed by the Lincoln Filene Center in its constant effort to make citizenship education more meaningful than ever in American life. The Center and this book are deeply committed to the belief that a genuine feeling for and practice of democratic citizenship is the best means whereby the values of democracy can be protected and projected in a troubled but challenging and exciting world.

Franklin Patterson, Director
THE LINCOLN FILENE CENTER FOR
CITIZENSHIP AND PUBLIC AFFAIRS

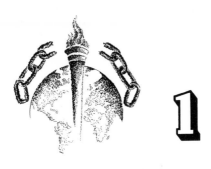

World Ideologies: Their Impact on Men and Nations

Ideas are unseen but dynamic forces guiding the destinies of men and nations.

The power of the democratic idea moved the pen of Thomas Jefferson, shook the throne of England, and brought forth the Declaration of Independence.

Hitler's ideas, born of resentment and hatred, plunged a world into war before his "Thousand Year Reich" collapsed in flames.

The burning idea of nationalism and the human commitment to national freedom have brought Kenya, Malaysia, and more than fifty other former colonies into the international community as sovereign nations since 1946.

The revolutionary guerrilla fighters in the jungles of Southeast Asia today are driven forward by the Communist myth and the distant dream of a "classless society."

These ideas which encourage men to build or kill, to free or enslave, to live in peace or to die in war are great motivating forces in the unfolding drama of mankind. They are beliefs rooted in the minds of men and entangled with their emotions. They are intensely human, sometimes idealistic, sometimes passionate, sometimes destructive. But they are powerful mainsprings of action and reaction, especially in the pulsating calm and crisis of world affairs.

When these ideas or convictions in the minds of men relate to

national ways of life and ways of governing, we call them
ideologies.

1. What Are the Characteristics of an Ideology?

An ideology is a complex and powerful manifestation of the
basic purpose of a state.[1] It is a core of beliefs connecting the
way of life of the people of a state with their way of governing.
It also serves as a guide for the state's pursuit of its goals of
national policy. An ideology gives expression to the central political, social, and economic values of any one state. It expresses
the personality of the state and is the state's blueprint for action
in the cooperation and conflict among nations.

Democracy, totalitarianism, and *authoritarianism* are the three
basic ideologies, or "isms." Their roots penetrate the depths of
all civilizations. In the course of history, totalitarianism and
authoritarianism have been more widely practiced than democracy. Totalitarianism, in particular, has constantly challenged
the right of men to pursue a free way of life and to govern themselves in a democratic manner.

Ideology as a Way of Governing

We tend to view an ideology first of all in its political context
and to relate it to a particular style of governing.

In a democracy. *Democracy* is considered to be an ideology
of governing in which the consent of the governed prevails.
Lincoln's expression — a government of, by, and for the people —
is a superb definition of democracy as a way of governing.

In a totalitarian state. *Totalitarianism* in its many forms is
an ideology characterized by the rule of the few rigorously imposed upon the many. Twentieth-century totalitarianism, such
as communism or Hitler's nazism, is identified with a strict dictatorship, a police state, and the regimentation and ideological
indoctrination of the society.

In an authoritarian state. *Authoritarianism* is a non-demo-

---

[1] By "state" we mean *nation-state,* such as France, Chile, Japan.

cratic method of governing, one with little regard for a genuine multi-party system and elections which really count. Authoritarian governing, however, lacks the rigid and dictatorial control found in totalitarianism. Like the governments of Sukarno's Indonesia or Ayub's Pakistan, authoritarian systems lie midway between democracy and totalitarianism, and can veer in either direction.

Although an ideology is basically a way of governing, it is also a way of life. We should not lose sight of this second vital dimension of any ideology.

Ideology as a Way of Life

Two great political philosophers, Aristotle of ancient Greece and Montesquieu of eighteenth-century France, wrote extensively on relating ways of life to ways of governing. They both held that the way people in any society live or should live will be closely related to how they are or should be governed, or how they do or should govern themselves. Implicit in all styles of governing, therefore, are certain assumptions about human nature and ways of living.

In a democracy. We associate the principles of freedom, human rights, equal justice under law, and the brotherhood of man with the democratic way of life. We believe that these values can be protected and enriched only by democratic governing. Accent on economic and social progress, high standards of education, and equality of opportunity also characterize the democratic style of life.

In a totalitarian state. Totalitarianism, on the other hand, implies total control by a few over all the people in the totalitarian state. Totalitarianism assumes that the majority of human beings do not know what is best for them and that those in control do. Totalitarianism in any of its variations, such as communism or nazism, denies that individuals have any basic rights. It claims that people, like sheep, should be subjected to firm controls. Totalitarianism, like democracy, may well stress economic progress and high educational standards. But it does so, not to provide a better way of life for the people, but as a means to the end of a strong state. The principle of the totalitarian way

(Continued on p. 5)

DIAGRAM OF CONTEMPORARY IDEOLOGIES

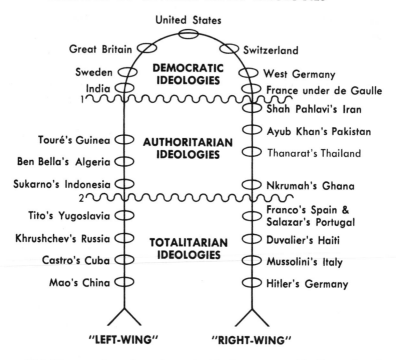

United States

Great Britain

Sweden — **DEMOCRATIC IDEOLOGIES**

India

1

Touré's Guinea — **AUTHORITARIAN IDEOLOGIES**

Ben Bella's Algeria

Sukarno's Indonesia

2

Tito's Yugoslavia

Khrushchev's Russia — **TOTALITARIAN IDEOLOGIES**

Castro's Cuba

Mao's China

Switzerland

West Germany

France under de Gaulle

Shah Pahlavi's Iran

Ayub Khan's Pakistan

Thanarat's Thailand

Nkrumah's Ghana

Franco's Spain & Salazar's Portugal

Duvalier's Haiti

Mussolini's Italy

Hitler's Germany

"LEFT-WING"   **"RIGHT-WING"**

This diagram shows how the major ideologies in world affairs related to each other in the early 1960's. Any ideological chart such as this is subject to change because the ideologies found in the governing systems of states may move in different directions. (The governments of Hitler and Mussolini have been included to indicate the location of extreme "right-wing" totalitarianism.) The diagram demonstrates the variations among the ideologies in each of the three major ideological systems (democracy, authoritarianism, and totalitarianism). It shows authoritarianism to be in the middle, between democracy and totalitarianism. Line 1 separates democratic ideologies from those of an authoritarian nature, and Line 2 divides authoritarianism from totalitarianism. Lines 1 and 2 are wavy, indicating that the divisions among the three major ideological systems are not always clear and precise.

"Right-wing" ideologies stress nationalism and the supremacy of the state, while "left-wing" ideologies tend toward socialism and communism. Democracies lie in the center, between the extremes of right-wing and left-wing ideologies. Democracy in Great Britain is to the left of the United States, due to a proportionately higher degree of government control of the economy. De Gaulle's France is to the

4

of life, therefore, is that the governed exist to serve the state. A totalitarian way of life thus follows naturally from the totalitarian scheme of governing.

In an authoritarian state. Authoritarianism lies at various points between democracy and totalitarianism in the way of life led by its people as well as in its style of governing. As has been pointed out, "Authoritarianism (within a state) denies its subjects the freedom and responsibility of political choice and action, while still leaving them some degree of freedom and self-expression in non-political matters."[1]

Ben Bella's Algeria, Nasser's Egypt, Franco's Spain, Shah Pahlavi's Iran, Ayub Khan's Pakistan, and Sukarno's Indonesia are all contemporary examples of authoritarianism. Most authoritarian states are located in Asia and Africa, where poverty and illiteracy make democracy as a way of life and governing exceedingly difficult. Most Latin American countries are afflicted with similar economic and social maladies. These harsh conditions need not be permanent. Much can be done to develop democratic patterns of living and governing in the Afro-Asian world. The democratic states have an obvious interest in channeling contemporary authoritarianism into the mainstream of democracy.

On the other hand, authoritarianism can flow into the abyss of totalitarianism. Some authoritarian rulers, whether by design or in despair, may step down the totalitarian path or be lured there by the pied piper of totalitarianism. Khrushchev and Mao Tse-tung work hard at playing this piper's tune, and there is no guarantee that another Hitler might not appear to draw some authoritarian rulers into the right-wing totalitarian camp. The ideological middle ground of authoritarianism holds great potential gains or perils for the future of democracy.

[1] William Ebenstein, *Totalitarianism: New Perspectives.* New York: Holt, Rinehart and Winston, Inc., 1962, p. 14.

---

right of the United States, largely because of the ardent nationalism to be found in President de Gaulle's outlook on governing.

Where would the governing systems of other states belong on this diagram?

Other Aspects of Ideologies

The gulf between idealism and realism. Ideologies are usually formulated in idealistic terms. Their practice in ways of living or ways of governing, however, is seldom if ever in accord with their lofty claims.

Communism in the printed word or in the flowery speeches of its advocates may appear to some as the ideal solution for all the troubles of mankind. But an inspection of communism in practice reveals oppression, regimentation, and a crushing conformity to the will of the rulers. Read the Soviet Constitution of 1936. Scan the many "rights and freedoms" guaranteed to the Soviet people. But the exercise of these rights is completely controlled by the Communist Party. The Soviet citizen may have "freedom to speak," but he may not speak up against the Communist regime.

We may well describe democracy in glowing terms. In actual practice, however, ways of life and governing within a democracy do not always attain the heights of the democratic ideology. Patterns of discrimination, a poor turnout at the polls on election day, or abuse of public office hardly live up to the democratic ideals.

Variations within ideologies. The ideology of any state is not uniformly embraced in thought or action by all of its citizens. Distinct patterns of non-democratic behavior can be found in America. Many people behind the Communist "Iron Curtain" undoubtedly yearn for human freedom.

Nevertheless, all contemporary states embrace some variation of one of the three major ideologies. There are, for instance, several brands of democracy, such as the English constitutional monarchy, the American separation-of-powers system, and the centralized regime of De Gaulle's Fifth Republic in France. Variations of totalitarianism run from the strict regimentation found in Communist China to the moderate dictatorship of Tito in Yugoslavia. The spectrum of authoritarianism extends from the leftist government of Sukarno in Indonesia to the democratically inclined rule of Ayub Khan in Pakistan. (See diagram, page 4).

Some "isms" aren't ideologies. Some other "isms," such as *capitalism, Marxism,* and *nationalism,* are frequently referred to as ideologies. These and other concepts are doctrines which properly belong within the framework of the three general ideologies. They do not contain all the elements of an ideology itself. *Capitalism* is an economic system and doctrine generally found within a democratic state. It is characterized by an open and free market for the exchange of goods and services and by strong limitations on governmental control of the economy, as in the United States. But capitalism is not "a way of governing," a vital part of an ideology.

Marxism is the basic economic, social, historical, and political *philosophy* of Karl Marx, the founder of modern communism. As reinterpreted by Lenin, it has provided the philosophical foundation for totalitarian communism. On the other hand, some principles of Marxism have influenced in part such democratic socialist movements as the Labor Party in Great Britain and the Social Democratic Party in Germany.

Nationalism is the intense identification people have with the nation of their origin or the place in which they live. It is therefore a sentiment and guide to action to be found in varying degrees in all states. Nationalism is not an ideology, however, because it tells us nothing about the way of life or governing within any state. It has been a profound force in the evolution of the modern states. But it can be incorporated within the framework of any ideology, unifying the people of the state and serving as a guide to action in world affairs.

2. What Is the Relation of Ideologies to World Affairs?

The ideological crisis — and promise — of our times revolves around the way ideologies operate in world affairs. An ideology helps to determine not only how a country is governed and how its people live. It is often a state's philosophical road map — a set of principles and aims — which guides its relations with other countries. Will it seek domination over other countries by force or conquest or will it desire to live peacefully with them? Will the state start a conflict or will it seek cooperation among the nations of the world? What *are* its aspirations in its conduct of foreign policy?

The three major ideological systems — democracy, totalitarianism, authoritarianism — differ in their approaches to other countries and therefore in the ways they influence world affairs. The impact of these ideologies on world affairs — and of world affairs on the states embracing these ideologies — may lead mankind toward a magnificent future or toward total chaos.

What Are the Goals of a Nation's Foreign Policy?

All countries seek to further their security and well-being. Certain interests are common to every state. These interests include the territory of the state, the people, their values and institutions, and the state's tangible resources. The goal of any state's foreign policy is to further the *security* and *well-being* of its central interests. *Security* means a basic protection of these interests from internal corrosion or subversion and from external attack. *Well-being* means that the basic interests of the nation — its people, institutions, and resources — are maintained in a healthy condition and encouraged to grow and flourish.

The foreign policy of the United States, for instance, strives toward the security of our nation in world affairs and toward having international relations which will further the prosperity and well-being of our central interests.

Factors which help determine a nation's concept of security and well-being. Each state differs in deciding what it must do to further its security and well-being. Today, American security in world affairs is furthered by extending economic assistance to other nations. Our well-being, among other things, calls for importing many foreign goods which are necessary for our high standard of living. But some other states may see the matter differently. Communist China views its security in terms of seeking to dominate other nations. The well-being of the Bolivian people in South America is defined in terms of the world market for Bolivia's tin.

Certain factors determine a state's foreign policy — what it wants and needs from other states to further its goals of security and well-being. Some of these factors derive from the history and geography of the state, the nature of its physical resources, the cultural foundations of the state, the pressures of world politics, and the ideology of the state. In addition, objectives pursued by the leaders of the state and the opinions of the people themselves help each nation to determine its own sense of security and well-being at any one time.

The historical development of any state will be a strong element in its behavior in world affairs. There is much in Russian history, for instance, to shape the Soviet outlook on security and well-being today. The geographical location of England has influenced its relations with the continent of Europe over the ages. Natural resources, such as oil and uranium, do much to shape the requirements for security and well-being for some nations. Democratic states, such as the United States, define national goals through the free interplay and consensus provided by public opinion and democratic governing processes.

The cultural aspects of the Islamic religion bear heavily on the Arab states' views about the well-being of their peoples. Leaders such as President Johnson and Premier Khrushchev do much to mold the aims of security and well-being. A state will be particularly security conscious if faced with imminent attack by another, while in times of ease and calm in world affairs, more emphasis may be placed on advancing national well-being.

What Is the Nature of International Relations?

No nation is self-sufficient. States must have relations with each other just as individuals do within any national society, such as the United States. No nation has all it wants and needs within its own territory to attain its goals of security and well-being. No state is self-sufficient. Each nation, therefore, *must* have relations with some other states to gain the security and well-being it desires. The give-and-take, buying and selling, bargaining and grabbing among all states constitutes the essential nature of international relations.

There is no international government. Within a nation, there is a government to assist people to associate in an orderly manner. In world affairs, however, there never has been any inter-

national government to allocate to each state the things it wants
and needs for its security and well-being. Thus the relations
among states are conducted in a somewhat chaotic manner,
largely because nations have never been able to agree on a stable,
legal, and orderly process which might provide general security
and equal opportunity for well-being for all of them.

When most states respect each other's security and national
well-being in the marketplace of world affairs and when their
needs are supplied within a legal framework of give-and-take
and good will, a condition of peace and progress usually exists
in world affairs. When, however, negotiations and good relations
between states break down and when some states want territory,
or control over people or resources from other states and employ
threats or force to attain their aims, the result is tension and
possibly war.

How Does the Ideology of a State Affect its Foreign Policy?

Ideology plays a key role. The ideology of any state plays a
key role in defining the kind of security and well-being toward
which a state aspires. Most nations view the idea of security
and human well-being in terms of their basic convictions about
ways of life and ways of governing. Today, the democracies
want security so that they may further the comparative levels
of social and economic well-being enjoyed by their peoples.
Many totalitarian states, however, do not feel secure unless they
dominate others. Some of them define their security in terms
of goals that can be achieved only by reshaping the entire world
in their own pattern. Ideology defines the way in which states
interpret the motivations and public actions of other states. Thus,
while ideology is not the sole factor which determines what
states do in the global arena, it does play a powerful role in
shaping each nation's goals of foreign policy.

When the ideology of any state is responsible for that state's
attempt to dominate other nations in order to advance its own
security and well-being, the security and well-being of most
other states are seriously affected. It is true that most nations
do not have ideologies which call for unwarranted demands on
other states. But if one nation is convinced that its way of life

is superior to others and that its security in the long run demands that it impose this way of life on other nations, tension is never absent and may lead to sharp crises and wars.

Totalitarianism challenges international relations. The totalitarian ideology often seeks to burst out of the confines of its territorial limits and force its ways of life and governing upon other states. For example, the leaders of communism — whether in Russia, China, or elsewhere — are convinced that the world inevitably will be united, peacefully or by force, through the Communist ideology. The major Communist states believe that their idea of well-being, the classless society, should be imposed upon all other states. The nazism of Hitler viewed security as German domination, and well-being as the supremacy of the "Aryan" race in the conduct of all facets of a nation's life and in ruling all "inferior races."

Some dictatorships, however, such as General Stroessner's in the South American state of Paraguay, entertain no ambitious designs on other states and seek only to maintain their patterns of totalitarianism over their own people. In such states, the dictators usually concentrate on security and well-being for themselves and their small bands of followers, ignoring the wishes and rigidly controlling the rest of their countrymen.

Many democracies of the West were imperialistic and dominated much of Africa and Asia from the sixteenth century to recent times. Although Western political and economic colonialism is now almost entirely a matter of the past, the era of imperialism demonstrates how some nations can have one ideology at home and impose another brand of ideology on states abroad. The essence of modern democracy, however, is in the long run incompatible with imperialism because it proclaims the goal of the freedom of all states along with the expansion of human progress and well-being.

The United Nations hails the "sovereign equality" of all states and opposes intervention by itself or any state into the "domestic jurisdiction" of other states. No state has the authority to dictate to another state what its ideology should be. Any state, however, can attempt to influence the shaping or altering of ideologies of other states through peaceful and legal means. But when a state with an imperialistic ideology uses force in the pursuit of its interpretation of security and well-being, firm measures must be employed by those who are the targets of domination. This, then, is the central problem and challenge of our time. Democracy must respond to this challenge with its own ideological conviction — in which security and equality for all nations and the values of freedom and human rights are supreme.

3. Why Are Ideologies so Important Today?

Because of the war for the minds of men in which we find ourselves today, the impact of ideologies on the lives of all of us is stronger than ever. But in our study of history and world affairs, the true significance of ideas and ideologies is frequently overlooked.

The Significance of Ideologies, Past and Present

Ideology and history. All too often we study history by memorizing names of statesmen and dates of wars and treaties. We learn that Peter the Great of Russia lived from 1672 to 1725, that the Peloponnesian War in ancient Greece lasted for twenty-seven years, and that the Treaty of Versailles, signed on June 28, 1919, brought World War I to a formal close. But, what kind of a government and society did Peter the Great envisage for Russia? What differing ways of life and governing lay behind the hot and cold war between Athens and Sparta? What were some of the fundamental political ideas and passions which mixed with the ink on the Treaty of Versailles?

Names and dates, times and places are the parts of the icebergs of great events which we can see clearly above the waters of history. The ideas, ideals, and ideologies which lie unseen beneath the surface provide the foundation, determine the form, and shape the destiny of men and nations.

During the past two centuries, ideas have played decisive roles in the seesaw of cooperation and conflict among nations. The crumbling of age-old traditions and the magnetism of national freedom in the eighteenth century helped to produce an independent United States and launched the French Revolution. The stirring sentiment of nationalism had a profound impact on the European states in the nineteenth century. During the past five decades, the totalitarian ideologies of fascism, nazism, and communism have fueled the fires of national and international turmoil. These threats to national independence and freedom, however, have made all of us deeply aware of the powerful relationship between the ideologies and the foreign policies of all nations.

Ideology and current events. In viewing world affairs today, we focus attention on such *tools* or instruments of policy as arms, rockets, missiles, money, and foreign aid. Public pronouncements of rulers and diplomatic conferences are always in the headlines. We give much too little consideration, however, to the ideas and ideologies behind the behavior of nations.

Ideology provides the foundation for policy-making. A policy is a decision stemming from a basic ideology. When the United States rushed troops to Korea in 1950, perfected the Polaris missile, sponsored the tour of the musical, *Porgy and Bess,* throughout the Soviet Union, orbited John Glenn in space, and devised the Alliance for Progress, it was transforming its ideological convictions into action. As we believe, so we do.

Three Reasons Why Ideologies Loom so Large Today

The cold war between communism and democracy, the powerful voice of public opinion in all nations, and the ideological dilemmas in world affairs of the new states all demonstrate the dramatic role played by ideologies on the global stage.

The cold war. The ambitions of international communism are crystal clear — control of the world. Freedom-loving peoples can effectively respond to this challenge in many ways. Their governments can employ the material elements of policy, such as arms and foreign aid, in providing the common defense for democracy and in promoting the general welfare so vital to advancing democracy in world affairs. But when all is said and done, the clash of ideologies is the important issue in the cold war. Two ways of life oppose each other. Two diametrically different ways of governing compete with each other, along with two different economic systems.

The deep cleavage between these different ways of life—including ways of producing and distributing wealth — and ways of governing, lies at the root of the epic struggle between the forces of democracy and of totalitarianism. Furthermore, it will be largely a matter of ideological conviction and persuasion which will determine the outcome of this gigantic duel. Premier Khrushchev believes this — and he also is convinced that the Communist camp will be the winner. "We will bury you!" he has told us. He intends to accomplish this goal through the effective use of Communist ideology and Soviet power in every action and policy of the Soviet Union. Our response cannot help but be mainly ideological in nature. Khrushchev has made the cold war one in which the clash of ideologies is the main issue. Democracy's success in winning the cold war is in direct proportion to its ability to meet the ideological challenge of communism and to take the initiative for the democratic ideology in world affairs.

The powerful role of public opinion. Public opinion in all countries must be taken into consideration by national leaders in the shaping of their domestic and foreign policies. Only a few decades ago, the principal decisions in world affairs were made by the leaders of states and their diplomats. For the most part, the people within the state had little or no influence in directing the course of national policy. Today, the man in the street or the field or the jungle wants to be heard.

Public opinion of a political nature is particularly important in the democracies, where governing is based upon the consent of the governed. Because technological advances have made the world much smaller, the pressures of world events now affect every nation, no matter how remote. In the democracies public opinion about the issues of war and peace plays a lively political role. Effective foreign policy in the democracies must rest upon a broad public consensus on the wisdom of key policies. Decisions behind United States foreign policy, such as the 1963 nuclear test-ban agreement, the billions of dollars which we pour into foreign aid each year, and a firm stand in Berlin, all require strong support from American voters. They also call for a deep conviction in and commitment to the democratic ideology.

In the totalitarian state, the rulers must persuade or force their peoples to accept the ideology, whatever it may be. The Communist Party controls Russian opinion by monopolizing the press, radio, and television, and by indoctrinating students in the schools. It does not dare to permit any other set of beliefs to compete with the Communist doctrine, fearing that its hold on public opinion might crumble. Should the Russian people become exposed to the real facts of world affairs and begin to formulate their own political opinions, the towering Communist pyramid of power might well collapse.

The new nations. More than one billion people living in the newly sovereign states of Africa and Asia have emerged from the shadows of colonial rule during the past fifteen years. They are now shaping their own ideological convictions as they grapple with the vast problems of nation building.

All states have some kind of ideology. In which direction will the evolving ideologies of the Afro-Asian world go? Will totalitarian communism penetrate and dominate these states? Will the present patterns of authoritarianism found in many of these countries harden into some form of totalitarianism other than communism? Or can the forces of democracy plant their seed, cultivate it carefully, and witness during the decades to come a steady growth of the democratic ideology in Africa and Asia?

The desire of modern man to play a role in world affairs and to identify himself with the destiny of his country makes him much more aware of the ideology which binds him to his nation. He knows what terrible instruments of war can be employed to extend an ideology or to defend ideological convictions. He knows that he is involved in the crisis of his time whether he likes it or not.

4. What Is Our Role in the War for the Minds of Men?

The Challenge

You and I are deeply involved in an era of prolonged crisis, marked by a massive war for the minds of men. The Premier of the Soviet Union, Nikita Khrushchev, tells us that the forces of communism "will conquer the world by this mighty weapon (communism) and not by a hydrogen bomb." We did not seek this challenge. But we must recognize the broad dimensions of the monumental conflict between the democratic and totalitarian ideologies.

The Preamble of the United Nations Educational, Scientific, and Cultural Organization (UNESCO) declares that "since wars begin in the minds of men, it is in the minds of men that the defenses of peace must be constructed." Herein lies the challenge and the opportunity.

The Response

Before us lies an unprecedented chance to expand the horizons of human liberty and social progress or complacently to permit the tides of totalitarian communism to sweep over all of us. The greatest task of our generation is to put our minds and energies to work in meeting and surmounting the thrust of international communism and any other totalitarian challenge to freedom. If we are to respond effectively to preserve the democratic way of life and governing, we must understand the nature and magnitude of the Communist threat.

But we must do more. We must not merely defend the democratic ideology. By personal example and official policy, we must advance the ideology of freedom in world affairs. We must fortify ourselves with a knowledge and genuine appreciation of democratic values and institutions. Democratic beliefs must be stated positively. We must know what we are *for* as well as what we are *against*. And we must practice what we believe. Can there be any greater task before us?

The understanding of ideologies and world affairs is particularly essential to a democratic society, which prides itself on government by consent of the governed. To give their consent in a positive and responsible manner, citizens of the democracy must be able to make decisions which will enable democratic societies to survive and grow vigorously in this complex world.

Thomas Jefferson wrote to a friend in 1820:

> I know of no safe depository of the ultimate powers of the society but the people themselves, and if we think them not

enlightened enough to exercise their control with a wholesome discretion, the remedy is not to take it from them but to inform their discretion by education.[1]

Today, education about ideologies and world affairs is of vital importance to the security, well-being, and even to the survival of the people of every country on earth.

---

[1] Saul Padover (ed.), *Thomas Jefferson on Democracy.* New York: Mentor Books, 1946, pp. 89-90.

The Nature and Evolution of Democracy

"You always talk about this 'Communist threat.' You Americans say you don't want the communists to control us. You are against this. All right. But what are you *for?*"

A young man in Indonesia is talking to a member of our Peace Corps. Suppose this question were addressed to you, as a representative of the United States in a foreign country. What would you say?

The Indonesians, most of them, have very little education. They do not share your own heritage of liberty and your belief in the natural rights of man. Their standard of living is low. Their economy is largely state-controlled, and their foreign policy takes a neutral position in the cold war. How can you bridge the gap between your country and theirs? You have to answer the question somehow. How would you explain what you are *for?*

Would you talk about democracy as a way of life or as a way of governing? Could you explain in simple terms that it is actually both? How would you describe the feeling of excitement and suspense that exists during a Presidential campaign, the ease with which anyone can voice a political opinion, and the pride with which you vote? Dozens of examples might come to mind of the way you live, and you might wind up saying that freedom, fairness, and friendliness are all intertwined in the democratic system of governing and way of life. But those are vague words. And what about some of the ugly things that happen in your country which seem neither free nor fair nor friendly? Whatever you might say, the explanation would not be easy.

1. What Is the Nature of Democracy?

It is never easy to define democracy.

The word itself comes from the Greek, *Demokratia,* which is made up of *demos,* the people, and *kratos,* rule. The theory and practice of people ruling themselves is *Demokratia.* All the implications that naturally follow from the principle of *self-rule* constitute the essence of democracy.

People come first. The way of life in a free and "open" society begins with basic convictions about the dignity and freedom of man. In order to guarantee human freedom, government must stem from the will of the people and be limited in scope and power. Governing must be directly controlled by the people or must be conducted by their freely elected representatives, responsible and responsive to them.

Democracy as a way of life and governing thus arises from the ideas ingrained in *Demokratia.*

Democracy as a Way of Life

Democracy as a way of life is indispensable to democracy as a way of governing.

Government by the consent of the governed assumes that the way of life of the governed is one of freedom in which economic and social progress can flourish.

Freedom of the individual. The keystone of democracy is the supreme importance of the human being. Each person has a "right" to a full and meaningful life and a "right" to exercise the inborn attributes of liberty.

The American Declaration of Independence states clearly that "life, liberty, and the pursuit of happiness" are the central and inalienable human rights. These rights, "natural" to every human being, provide the essence of democracy as a way of life. From these basic ingredients of democracy flow other rights, such as the freedoms to speak, to publish, to worship, and to associate with others — all found in the First Amendment to the United States Constitution.

These are *positive* rights which express the very promise and purpose of the human being. Too frequently we think of democratic rights as "freedom *from* this" or "freedom *from* that." Freedom *from* is a negative approach to democracy. It implies that democracy is a way of life which seeks to release itself from some dominating force. Democracy, however, is a natural and positive expression of the fundamental dignity and value of the human being. It should be viewed, therefore, in a positive manner, especially in world affairs.

Respect for the rights of others. Human beings must live together. In the democratic society each individual must respect the innate liberty of others in order to enjoy his own liberty.

The democratic society is characterized by the individual's right to pursue happiness — whatever gives him meaning and enjoyment in life. This right is confined only by the necessity to respect another's right to the pursuit of similar goals. The principal limitation upon the exercise of individual freedom is the well-being of the society itself. We are free to buy a car of any make or size we like, but we are not free to drive it in a manner which might injure others. Freedom of speech does not mean one can maliciously yell "Fire" in a crowded theatre. "Freedom to publish" cannot be used to damage the rights or dignity of others by means of the printed word. Exercise of the freedoms of democracy, in other words, must always take the rights of others into consideration.

Diversity, not uniformity. Democracy as a way of life implies diversity rather than uniformity. As a matter of fact, the rich diversity found in democratic societies expresses the inner meaning of the democratic ideology. You and I may belong to different religious faiths, have different national backgrounds, possess different racial characteristics, live in different social classes, and possess vastly different degrees of economic wealth. And yet we are united through our citizenship and through belief in and commitment to the theory and practice of democracy.

"Pluralism," or differences among members of the democratic society, is expressed in the many kinds of groups and organizations which exist in the United States. Look at the many kinds of churches in small towns and large cities. Note the number of nationality organizations, such as the Italian-American Club or the Chinese Benevolent Association, found throughout the United States. The Yellow Pages of the phone book list numerous associations to which people belong and through which they can pursue their own brand of human happiness.

Fundamental to democracy is the idea that despite human differences, especially those of an economic nature, each man values the rights of others, and each joins in the protection and enhancement of the well-being of all. The American motto, occasionally forgotten, is *e pluribus unum* — unity through diversity. This simply means that, despite all the colorful political, economic, social, and religious differences in our society, we stand together on basic goals and democratic procedures. Consider how all our differences are tossed around in the heat and excitement of an American political campaign. But note how we close ranks after the election! Respect for diversity is indispensable to the democratic creed.

A large middle class. The majority of people in democracies belong to what is frequently called the "middle class." A democratic ideal, in other words, is that great extremes of wealth or poverty do not belong in a society to which the well-being of all is fundamental. The flow of free enterprise, accompanied by laws and programs which assist the less fortunate, promotes the strength of the great democratic middle class. This rough approximation to equality of economic opportunity among democratic peoples blurs harmful class distinctions, generates pride in one's own economic pursuits, and elevates standards of living. The white-collar worker joins the blue-collar laborer in the common cause of making democracy work, and both belong in the same broad middle class.

Democracy as a Way of Governing

To enable members of the democratic society to enjoy their way of life, a democratic way of governing is necessary. Governing involves the exercise of power by officials within the state. They shape the national policy which strives toward the secu-

The true role of labor unions is to protect the rights of workers. Under communism, ideologically, the worker is all-important. Actually, he exists to serve the state. Communist labor unions function mainly as government representatives. In the democracies, however, unions really do represent the workers, protecting their rights of organization and promising them equality of opportunity.

Many of the early colonists came to America in search of religious freedom. The right to worship as one desires is a natural right to which all human beings are entitled. It is one of the basic freedoms of a democracy. In the United States everyone — whether Christian or Jew or member of a minority religion — shares this freedom. Right, worshipers at the Jewish ceremony of Yom Kippur. Below, a congregation participating in the service at an Episcopal church.

The contrast between the democratic way of life and life under totalitarianism is illustrated by this photograph of the two parts of Berlin. The modern buildings to the left are in West Berlin. They reflect the booming economy and freedom of the individual characteristic of West Germany. East Berlin, to the right, presents a striking contrast. Its barrenness serves as a grim reminder of World War II, its inadequate housing reveals the communists' concentration on heavy industry and their disregard for human rights and well-being.

The concept of equal justice is one of the most precious rights of man. In a democracy every person — regardless of who he is, regardless of his crime — has the right to trial by jury. "No person . . . shall . . . be deprived of life, liberty, or property, without due process of law . . ." reads our Constitution, and our courts are devoted to protecting this right.

rity and well-being defined by the over-all ideology of the state. The governing process has five basic elements:

1. the people of the state — the governed
2. the authoritative officials who determine policy — the governors or rulers
3. a procedure to place some people in public office — the political process
4. the legal structure through which official decision-making takes place — the government
5. the national policy of the state working toward national security and well-being, divided between:
   a. regulation in varying degrees of the people within the state — domestic policy
   b. relations between the state and other states — foreign policy

All ways of governing, whether democratic, totalitarian, or authoritarian, contain these five elements. The manner in which these elements fit together, however, varies considerably among the three major ideologies. Let us see how democracy copes with the governing process.

People of the state. The first element of the governing process is the people of the state, or the governed. If democratic peoples are to enjoy their democratic way of life, they must govern themselves. It is here that democracy as a way of life and democracy as a way of governing are joined.

But democracy has no mystical force which guarantees freedom. People must continually work for their freedom in order to possess and retain it. No one revolution, such as ours in 1776, will guarantee the enjoyment of liberty to succeeding generations. Each generation must till the soil of freedom just as a farmer preserves and renews his life-giving earth.

People govern themselves either by *direct democracy*, in which all participate in the governmental decision-making, or through *representative democracy*, in which elected representatives of the people produce national policy in the interests of the people. Direct democracy is not feasible in modern societies because, with the exception of small-town direct democracies (such as some New England town meetings), the conduct of government by all is a numerical impossibility.

The democratic society must choose some of its own members to represent the rest in making the crucial decisions which protect all members of the society. Some men and women must be willing to serve as governing officials. The others who are qualified to vote must have the wisdom to choose those who will best serve the interests of all.

Two things are demanded of the citizens of a democracy if self-government is going to work well:

1. They must be *well-informed* about the major aspects — the

A NATION'S GOVERNING PROCESS

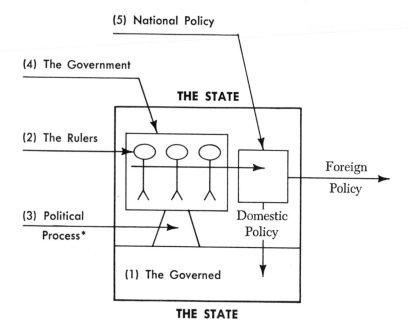

A democracy's political process rests upon the consent of the governed. Such is not the case in a totalitarian state. Nevertheless, the totalitarian state will have *some* kind of a process whereby some people come to occupy positions as rulers. Usually the political process in such a state is monopolized by the totalitarian party (such as the Communist Party).

political and economic issues — and the leaders of public life.

2. They must *participate*: (a) by voting, (b) by contributing to political parties, and (c) by expressing their views to officeholders.

Participation in the political process is meaningless without a fundamental understanding of the issues which affect the entire society.

The rights and obligations of democratic peoples are inseparable. One reason why we put such emphasis on freedom of speech, assembly, and the press is that only through these can citizens be well-informed. The right to vote and to petition are essential to effective participation in government. The heart of democratic ideology (the rights of man) is closely related to the lifeblood of democratic practice (information and participation). We might compare this to the way in which physical exercise stimulates the flow of blood to the heart and brain. We often forget this relationship of ideology to political practice, just as we forget the close relationship of mind and body.

Officials in government. Those who hold public office comprise the second element of the governing process. In the American democracy, some are *elected* by the people, such as the President, members of Congress, and officials at the state and local levels of government. Some are *appointed,* usually by the President, such as cabinet officers and key members of the many agencies of government in the Executive branch. Others are *career officials,* gaining office by virtue of competence and experience in governing, such as officials in the Civil and Foreign Service. The latter two categories of officeholders are under the jurisdiction of the President.

Officeholders in a democracy fill the positions which are defined in the Constitution and by law. The elected officials in particular are those who have been entrusted by the electorate with the responsibility to make decisions which reflect the political desires of the democratic society. They are responsible and should be responsive to the people.

In theory, a public office in a democracy is a public trust. This theory is not always practiced. Some officeholders take advantage of their positions to advance their own interests. But the vast majority of people in public office honestly attempt to serve the public well. They are, after all, part of the entire democratic society and share the expectations of those whom they govern.

Placing people in public office. The procedure of elevating some of the people in the society into elective positions of authority in government is the third element in the governing process. This procedure, which we call politics, is found in practically all countries but varies considerably in accordance with ideological convictions. Fundamental to the political procedure in a democracy are periodic elections and competing parties.

There is a basic agreement in the democratic state about goals. In America, we all want progressively higher standards of living as well as security against the Communist challenge. There will be differences, however, about how to achieve these goals. Periodic elections provide the mechanism for candidates sponsored by political parties to compete for the backing of the majority. Once in public office, public officials attempt to translate the will of the majority into public policy, as best they can. In the next election, the electorate can decide whether to retain these officials or to replace them by others, who may represent them better. In a democracy, there must be an assurance of the "next election" in order to give the people a chance to vote for a change if they desire it.

Political parties, two or more, are likewise indispensable to democracy. This is true even if one party's candidates keep getting elected to office for a long period of time. Parties tend to represent different points of view on how the policy of the state should be formulated and applied. Parties sponsor the candidates. They also do much to inform and educate the public. Parties and elections go hand in hand. One without the other renders the democratic process impossible. Both provide the means for governing by consent of the governed.

Those voted into public office represent the views of the majority who cast ballots for them at any particular election. What of the minority? Naturally, minority views about public policy, as reflected in the political party which loses in any one election, can be voiced with the hope that the minority party might influence public opinion and win in the next election. In

November, 1960, the defeated Republican Party did not retreat to Canada with a view to organizing an army, attacking America, and seizing power. Instead, they immediately began to focus their sights on the Presidential elections of 1964.

The many organizations and associations which represent the pluralism found in democratic societies frequently play a political role as well. They serve as important voices for their members in attempting to influence the shaping of national policy. The AFL-CIO is an organization of millions of laboring men which seeks laws benefiting the trade unions. The American Legion and other veterans' organizations serve the social interests of their members and also press for legislation to support the needs of those who served in the armed forces. The National Association of Manufacturers, the Parent-Teacher Associations, and the American Medical Association, among many others, are organizations which manifest the pluralism in American society and also express their views to political parties and officials in government.

These organizations are frequently referred to as "pressure groups," but they have a definite right to participate in the mainstream of political action. The First Amendment of the Constitution provides for such organizations to "petition the Government for a redress of grievances." If, for instance, farmers in some industrial districts do not have representatives in government who speak for their interests, they have farm organizations which do. If laboring men in Midwestern states find themselves represented in Congress by men who have the farmers' interests more at heart, the AFL-CIO will give them strong support. The over-all political process in the democracy, therefore, provides many points of access to ensure the governed a voice among those who make official decisions in their behalf.

The government. The fourth element in the governing process is the government itself. A government is a structure in which officials use the authority vested in them to make decisions in shaping the national policy of the state. Governments have specific positions or "offices" which are filled, in the democracy, by elected or appointed officials.

These positions in the United States include the "office of the President," seats in the Congress, and nine judicial positions on the Supreme Court. Positions in government and the powers accompanying them are defined by the national Constitution and by other laws and by tradition. These positions and the government itself remain fixed (unless changed by amendment or new laws or by the formation of a new governmental structure). The people who occupy the positions come and go. The actual *structure* of government will tend to vary among democracies. The two principal types are the American separation-of-power government (with three distinct branches) and the English parliamentary government.

The United States Government is organized so that its powers are not concentrated in any one branch or person. This separation of power acts as a check on those who are elected or appointed to public office. The American Congress must approve the amount of money which the President wants to spend and must then appropriate the necessary funds. The President appoints members of the Supreme Court, and the Senate reviews and confirms, or may reject, his nominations. The Court, in turn, decides whether legislation passed by Congress squares with the Constitution.

The enjoyment of the freedoms of democratic living is possible only if limitations are placed upon those who govern. If all governmental power were in the hands of one or a few and if there were no specific limitations on the exercise of power, the public would have no assurance that their basic rights and freedoms would endure.

It is true that the majority (or "government") party in the British House of Commons, headed by the Prime Minister, has broad powers. But the force of tradition in England is great, and serves as a limitation on undue or coercive exercise of power by the Prime Minister of Great Britain. For instance, tradition holds that the Prime Minister must call for a national election if it is clear that the House of Commons opposes his policies.

The democratic idea of government is rooted in this sharing and limitation of power. It is assumed that the people, or the "governed," have the wisdom and the capacity to govern themselves in many areas of human behavior. Totalitarianism simply does not make this assumption.

A "structure" of government, as such, tells us little about the ideology behind it. Some totalitarian states, such as the Soviet Union, have constitutions, "democratic" structures of government, and elections. But in such states these elements of democratic governing are a mere façade. The theory and substance of democratic governing is absent.

In the American democracy, national policy is *formulated* by the Executive branch, led by the President. It is *implemented* through legislation by the Legislature, or the Congress. Policy is then *applied* at home and abroad by the Executive branch, and it is also *interpreted* by the Judiciary, or the Supreme Court and subordinate courts.

This separation of power in the shaping of national policy also provides for the resolution of major differences among the three branches of government. Legislation on civil rights or foreign aid thus reflects the give-and-take of many minds and political groupings. It also represents a consensus on national security and well-being within the constitutional framework.

National policy. The final element of the governing process is national policy, which emerges from the decisions made by those who hold public office. That area of national policy which is largely concerned with internal matters such as labor and agriculture is *domestic policy*. The aim of domestic policy in a democracy is to expand opportunities, so that all may enjoy a happy life in the midst of economic and social progress, security, and well-being. National policy which is concerned with relations with other states in the world is *foreign policy*. The aim of the democracy's foreign policy is to provide for the basic security of the state's national interests and to expand the horizons of democracy in world affairs.

Thus the democratic *way of governing* comes full circle back to the people who enjoy the democratic *way of life*. If the national policy of the state does not further the security and well-being of the society and its way of life, the voters can install new officeholders who might do a better job.

National policy is preferable to the idea of a separate "domestic" policy and "foreign" policy of the state. The mutual impact of these two parts of the total national policy upon each other necessitates our viewing them together. In the last analysis, both domestic and foreign policy seek to further national security and well-being.

Relating domestic policy to foreign policy within the framework of national policy is particularly important in discussing the role of ideology in world affairs. This is because many states attempt to project abroad their way of life and of governing, as practiced within the society. The democracy seeks to promote self-government in other states, while the totalitarian state, such as the USSR, hopes to impose its own way of life and governing upon other states.

If the people in a democracy are to make wise judgments, they must have the political knowledge necessary to an understanding of national policy, and they must participate in the machinery of self-government. To protect their democratic ideology, they must play the game of politics, and play it well. The benefits of the democratic way of life imply an obligation to its way of governing.

Democracy is the most difficult style of governing which any society can embrace. It demands more of its people than any other form of governing. On the other hand, it permits a freer exercise of the human spirit and behavior than does any other kind of governing. The hands and voices which shape national policy in the democracy are many and varied, and thus this policy represents a high degree of national consensus on the requirements for national security and well-being.

By tracing the evolution of the democratic ideology, we can understand some of the difficulties which democracy has encountered in making its way in the world, and some of the reasons why our ideology is not more widespread today.

2. How Did Democracy Evolve?

The Beginnings of Democracy

The democratic ideology as we know it today evolved within the framework of some Greek city-states over 2500 years ago.

In Greece. The city-state of Athens, about the size of Rhode Island, serves as the classic example of Greek democracy, although a number of other sovereign Greek city-states also had democratic regimes.

The Athenian democracy was limited, both as a way of life and of governing. Only adult, male citizens of Athens could vote and hold office, and the democratic process was denied to women, non-citizens, and slaves.

Direct democracy was practiced in Athens, with all eligible male citizens participating in the shaping of governmental policy. Despite its limitations and even some of its later imperialistic activities, the Athenian democracy served its citizens well and provided an important precedent for the development of subsequent democratic states.

The limited nature of the Athenian direct democracy was far removed from the representative, universal suffrage of the twentieth century. Nevertheless, one very important lesson emerges from the Athenian democratic experience which democratic societies should never forget.

The Athenians considered democracy to be a privilege which demanded responsibility and sacrifice. The male Athenian citizen had to be *well-informed* about public issues and *participate* in governing when called upon to do so, by appointment or by elections. If a citizen of Athens were ignorant about public affairs or reluctant to serve in office, he would be penalized or even expelled from the city for a long period of time.

In 431 B.C., Athens and its allies became involved in the long Peloponnesian War with totalitarian Sparta and those city-states associated with the grim Spartan dictatorship. In this war which lasted twenty-seven years, there were many causes of conflict, and the ideological issue of democracy versus totalitarianism was not of least importance. The ultimate victory of Sparta over Athens in 404 B.C. provides plenty of food for thought. There are striking parallels between that struggle and today's war for the minds of men.

One of the greatest Athenian leaders was Pericles (495?-429 B.C.). Shortly after the beginning of the Peloponnesian War, he delivered his famous "Funeral Oration," in which he had many important things to say about the nature of democracy in Athens.

It is true that we are called a democracy, for the administration is in the hands of the many and not of the few. But while the law secures equal justice to all alike in their private disputes, the claim of excellence is also recognized; and when a citizen is in any way distinguished, he is preferred to the public service, not as a matter of privilege, but as the reward of merit. . . . Our city is thrown open to the world, and we never expel a foreigner or prevent him from seeing or learning anything which the secret if revealed to an enemy might profit him. We rely not upon management or trickery, but upon our hearts and hands. . . .

An Athenian citizen does not neglect the state because he takes care of his own household; and even those of us who are engaged in business have a very fair idea of politics. We alone regard a man who takes no interest in public affairs, not as a harmless, but as a useless character; and if few of us are originators, we are all sound judges of policy.[1]

This famous speech can be compared in many ways with Lincoln's eloquent expression of the democratic creed in the Gettysburg Address. It is part and parcel of the core of the democratic ideology.

Under the Romans. Sparta did not remain in power for long. During the following century, waves of totalitarianism in various forms swept over Greece and some other parts of the ancient world. Democracy was left in the dust. The Roman Republic (506-27 B.C.) had some democratic structures of governing, but was basically ruled by the wealthy Roman aristocrats.

During the second century before Christ, the teachings of Greek Stoic philosophy began to penetrate Roman thinking. The stoics believed in such ideals as a universal natural law and the brotherhood of man. Greek Stoics such as Panaetius (185-110 B.C.) and Polybius (203-120 B.C.) stimulated Roman education and thought. A great Roman student of Stoic ideas, Marcus Tullius Cicero (106-43 B.C.) declared in his famous orations that a universal law does indeed exist which can be understood by human reason and which provides the foundation for all human justice. He held that all man-made laws must be based upon the principles of universal natural law. Although the dictator-

---

[1] Carl Cohen (ed.), *Communism, Fascism and Democracy: Their Theoretical Foundations.* New York: Random House, 1962, pp. 424, 425.

ship of Julius Caesar had buried the Roman Republic by 45 B.C., the Stoic ideas and the philosophy of Cicero endured.

With Augustus Caesar, the Roman Empire took shape and presided over the ancient world for some five centuries. Some of the great Roman emperors permitted the Stoic ideas to flourish. Principles such as human reason and compassion did much to liberalize the great system of Roman law during the early centuries of the Empire.

One of the great Roman emperors, Marcus Aurelius (121-180 A.D.) wrote and spoke extensively about the virtues of Stoic philosophy. Succeeding emperors returned to harsh and inept rule, however, in contrast to the ideals of natural law and human reason.

The Empire, which had been decaying from within while suffering invasions from without, came to an end in the West in 476 A.D., but the Roman Law lived on and was later to exert strong influence in the shaping of political doctrines and legal systems in Europe.

Democracy in the Middle Ages

Contributions of the church. The central ideas of the democratic ideology lay buried for centuries. The European system of feudalism was grounded in the belief of natural human inequality. Nevertheless, the doctrines of the Christian Church contributed substantially to the flow of democratic ideas. The Church fused Judaic moral law and the Stoic principle of the universality of man with Jesus' teachings about the equality of man before God. The Church claimed that men must be protected from the extremes of unjust rule, and it was almost the sole center for learning and education. The contributions of Saint Thomas Aquinas (1226-1274) to Christian theology in the mid-thirteenth century served as a vital force in advancing the idea of the value of human life on this earth. His *Summa Theologica* and other works did much to further the doctrine of natural law (and later of natural rights) of man.

Constitutionalism in England. In England, a slow but steady evolution of constitutional principles took place during the mediaeval era. By the beginning of the thirteenth century the seeds of the common law and the jury system were well planted.

The Magna Carta, that feudal document forced upon King John by his leading barons in 1215, placed distinct limitations upon the exercise of governmental powers by the King. The "Great Charter" recognized the fundamental "law of the land" with which the king was compelled to comply. The weakening of arbitrary rule, and the expansion of political powers arising from the first parliaments of 1265 and 1290, were, in the light of history, earmarks of evolving constitutionalism. This era, while generally void of the basic conditions which permit the growth of democracy, was characterized by the unfolding of a law "higher" than kings and emperors.

Taken together, the revealed law of God, the law of nature and reason, and the traditional laws of the land contributed toward the all-important democratic principle of rule by law rather than rule solely by the whims of men. It took hundreds of years for this concept to be fully accepted in the West, but we can trace the limitations on unfettered human rule to the Middle Ages.

The Emergence of Modern Democratic Theory

The Renaissance opened the eyes of men to the meaningful life on this earth, and the Reformation of the sixteenth century greatly accelerated the growth of the modern sovereign state. As the secular political powers of the Church receded, most of the states, such as Spain, France, and England, became unified under powerful kings. These kings, in turn, declared that they ruled "by the divine right of God" rather than under authorization from the Christian church.

In all of these states, however, there were religious minorities who could not and would not subscribe to the religious convictions of the "divine right" monarchs. Protestants questioned the "divinity" of the Catholic king in France. In England, Catholics disagreed with the Protestant monarchs' claim that their authority to rule came directly from God. Jewish peoples in all of these states likewise found it difficult to accept the thesis of the "divine right" of the monarch.

Government by contract and human rights. A new idea of

a contract between a king and his people came into being. Political theorists and groups representing religious minorities in the Western European states began to claim that rulers should be bound by a contract or agreement with the people.

Men began to talk about human rights. They claimed that these rights should be enjoyed regardless of the religious faith of the ruler or the people in a state. They related the rights of man to the contractual idea of government, pointing out that the right to rule should come from the people and the natural law.

Theories of John Locke. The English political philosopher, John Locke (1632-1704) was largely responsible for a clear statement of the relationship between the human rights of man and the contractual theory of government, both of which go to the very heart of democratic doctrine. Locke wrote his famous *Second Treatise on Civil Government* in 1690, two years after King James II was forced off the English throne in the "Bloodless Revolution."

Locke declared that men have basic and inalienable rights of life, liberty, and property. Because these rights are "natural" and therefore inborn or innate, they do not stem from rulers or governments. Governments, indeed, exist to protect and preserve these rights.

The state is designed to serve man. Man is not the puppet of the state. If rulers do not provide security and well-being for men, Locke wrote, then the people have the "right" to break the contract with their rulers and find other rulers who can perform the proper function of governing — securing the rights of man. He held that this ideological scheme was rooted in the law of nature which, as Cicero had pointed out, was fundamental to the existence and purpose of man himself.

In thus rationalizing the eviction of King James II, Locke constructed the ideological framework for democracy which still serves us well today. His writings promoted the increase in power of the English Parliament which, through processes of elections and majority rule, placed even greater limitations on the arbitrary rule of the few.

Modern democracy as we know it today was by no means the immediate result of these historical events in England at the end of the seventeenth century. The landed gentry continued to dominate Parliament for the next 150 years. The right to vote was limited to property owners. The masses of the people did not enjoy full political, economic, and social freedoms for a long time. But the British trend toward democracy and the philosophy of John Locke both found fertile soil in America and France during the eighteenth century and contributed to the expansion of the democratic ideology.

Democracy in America

The British colonies in America, although under the rule of English kings, furthered the democratic cause.

Early forms. Long before Locke's time the *Mayflower Compact* of 1620 provided for a government by contract. The *Fundamental Orders of Connecticut* (1638-1639) became the first written constitution of the New World. The direct democracy of the town meetings, the representative democracy found in the various governments of the colonies, broad public education, rising standards of living, expanding religious tolerance, and emerging freedoms of speech, press, and public assembly all took shape between 1607 and 1776.

The colonies of America were governed within the framework of charters from England which gave experience in governing under some sort of constitutional limitation. During the 1760's, however, rule by Great Britain became increasingly arbitrary and violated what Americans considered to be their own proper rights. Great Britain's smashing defeat of France during the "Seven Years' War" prompted the government of King George III to clamp down on the American colonies. The views of John Locke were voiced by many American patriots. Speeches by Samuel Adams in Massachusetts and Patrick Henry in Virginia, among many others, expressed in the American style what Locke had written years before. The writings of Tom Paine popularized the cause of revolution.

The Declaration of Independence. Ties with Great Britain were formally severed in 1776. The immortal Declaration of Independence closely followed Locke's thesis about the rights of man, the right of breaking the governmental contract, and the obligation to establish a new government which would "provide new Guards for their (the people's) future security."

The Declaration of Independence is not merely a document which formally broke off governmental relations with Great Britain. It contains the essence of the democratic theory of governing and the basic assumptions of the democratic way of life. It confirms the thesis that men have a right to be free and to rule themselves. It expresses the authentic revolution of mankind, a revolution from oppressive and arbitrary rule which is alien to the basic nature of the human being.

The Declaration still has a dramatic ring today. It is a magnificent expression of national and human liberty. As Lincoln said at Gettysburg, "our forefathers brought forth a new nation." They also drew up a document which has never lost meaning for all who cherish national freedom and human rights.

The Constitution. The Constitution, our basic organ of government, rests upon Locke's contractual theory of government, and the separation-of-powers doctrine of the French theorist, Baron de Montesquieu (1689-1755). Although it has been amended extensively and broadly interpreted by the Supreme Court, the Constitution remains as a majestic bulwark of and for democratic governing.

Look carefully at the Preamble to the Constitution. Among other reasons for the establishment of the United States Government is the promise to "secure the blessings of liberty" and "provide for the general welfare." This is American security and well-being, goals of our national policy. Our security is to protect and further our rights, and our well-being is to advance the economic and social horizons and equality of opportunity for all.

Democracy in France

The political writings of Locke also had a great impact upon French political thinking. During the eighteenth century, they were woven into the fabric of French revolutionary theory and action. They greatly influenced such enlightened French philosophers as Montesquieu, Diderot, and many others who wanted to replace the "divine right" rule of the Bourbon kings with a constitutional monarchy. The more radical equalitarian ideas of Jean Jacques Rousseau (1712-1778) added a new fervor to revolutionary ferment. One may question the contribution to democratic ideology of the French Revolution of 1789, especially since it was followed by the authoritarianism of Napoleon and the return to power of later French monarchs and emperors. However, the French doctrine of liberty, equality, and fraternity added to the foundations of democratic ideology. The essential justice of the Napoleonic code would have been impossible without the prior French Revolution.

Interrelation of Political Democracy and Economic Democracy

Growth of free enterprise. The liberation of political systems from royal control was paralleled by a new economic freedom. Mercantilism or state economic controls began to give way to free market economics as advocated by the French "physiocrats" of the eighteenth century. Adam Smith in his *Wealth of Nations* (1776) elaborated upon principles of *laissez-faire*, or free-enterprise capitalism. He based his economic theory on the laws of nature, much as political theory of his times sought the law of nature as the proper basis of democracy.

The so-called Utilitarians of the early nineteenth century in Great Britain, led by Jeremy Bentham (1748-1832), advocated the greatest happiness for the greatest number. Nevertheless, the formative years of the industrial revolution were characterized by the exercise of the economic power of a small minority. It was this minority which enjoyed and practically monopolized the privileges of economic well-being.

Broadening economic opportunity. During the latter half of the nineteenth century, governments in the democracies gradually began to place controls on those economic titans who claimed that economic domination went hand in hand with political democracy. In England, T. H. Green argued that governments had an obligation to broaden equality of opportunity for all people. He called this "positive freedom." It was pointed out that concentration of wealth in the hands of a few people was hardly compatible with the theory of democracy that sought equality of opportunity for all. Slowly but surely the idea began to grow that excesses of wealth and poverty would prevent the growth of the large middle class which is so essential for political and economic stability in any democracy.

In the United States and in other democracies, the government began to regulate certain areas of the economy toward the end of the nineteenth century. This was not for the purpose of sheer governmental tinkering or control. The objective was to broaden economic opportunities for all. The Interstate Commerce Commission, established in 1887, sought to prevent excesses of unfair competition and monopoly in such areas of transportation as the railroads. The aim of the Sherman Anti-Trust Act of 1890 was to reduce the harsh effects of big business monopolies in such industries as oil and steel, so that smaller businesses could also have the opportunity to compete for trade and profits.

The twentieth century has witnessed the increased use of governmental power to bring economic democracy and opportunity more into harmony with political democracy. The Progressive Movement in America, Theodore Roosevelt's "Square Deal," and Woodrow Wilson's "New Freedom" spearheaded this drive. The relation between the capitalistic economies of the democracies and the authority of government to regulate them, however, involves many compromises and provides many debatable issues.

Present-day problems. Does strong governmental control over the economy in such areas as social security, national health programs, various forms of commerce, and agriculture smack of socialism? Or, is democracy as a way of life and a way of governing compatible with centralized government controls over the society and the economy? Is there genuine democracy in such states as Sweden and Israel, where the governments exercise strong controls over the economic activities of the people? Or does this mean that democratic freedoms, political and economic, are continually being chipped away in favor of state controls?

Fortunately, these are issues for the voters themselves to decide. In any event, it is evident that the brand of political democracy of the late eighteenth century has been radically altered by the technological revolutions of the nineteenth and twentieth centuries. Vast increases in population, accompanied by demands for wider distribution of society's wealth, have introduced new problems which affect all of us. The fantastic

strides in standards of living, made possible through the technological revolutions in industry and agriculture and through the
emergence of a kind of welfare capitalism, have greatly broadened the economic and social base of democracy.

This unprecedented record of human well-being deflates the
Communist claim that capitalism and democracy bring oppression to the masses. And yet, the strength of the great middle
class and the open path to political and economic opportunity
must be maintained if we are to keep on striking that delicate
balance between individual freedoms and the well-being of the
democratic society as a whole.

Our Heritage of Democracy

The cause of democracy made tremendous strides during the
period of the great revolutions at the end of the eighteenth
century. But the actual governmental powers in the democracies
remained for some time in the hands of the wealthy and the
privileged. The American *Federalist Papers,* written by Hamilton, Madison, and Jay, urging the adoption of the Constitution
in the United States (1787 and 1788), strongly supported this
aristocratic concept of democracy.

The Constitution itself contains no provisions for contending
political parties. But political parties grew in America and
Great Britain, and during the nineteenth century the less-prop-
ertied classes progressively got more voting privileges. These
privileges were accompanied by the right to contend for and to
participate in government offices. The franchise was expanded
in the West early in the twentieth century, when women received
voting and officeholding rights.

Many people — some famous and some unknown — have contributed mightily to the democratic edifice during the past one
hundred and eighty years. Thomas Jefferson described the
American democratic experiment in terms which could be uni-
versally accepted. Abraham Lincoln viewed the Civil War as
a monumental trial for the unity of the democratic state and
for the very idea of democracy itself. Woodrow Wilson saw
democracy as having a vital mission in releasing millions from
authoritarian bondage throughout the world. The stirring affir-

mations of democracy voiced by Winston Churchill and Franklin Delano Roosevelt during World War II, when democracy was in such grave peril, retain their power to move us today. Thousands have died in war and millions have labored in peace to uphold the cause of democracy. In many ways, Dwight D. Eisenhower, as General and President, made valuable contributions to democracy. President Kennedy gave the supreme sacrifice to the cause of freedom.

Democracy has been furthered by the advent of the many new and sovereign states following World War II, especially with the independence of India, the world's most populous democracy, in 1947. Outside of the Western states, however, the growth of democracy has been slow. After all, most of the nations in the West have enjoyed a common heritage of freedom, along with widespread educational opportunities, the full flowering of science, and many wise leaders.

Many other societies have not been as fortunate. The scourge of war and totalitarian domination have made it impossible for many millions of human beings to participate in the exercise of liberty until recently. In many nations crippling economic and social conditions have made it extremely difficult for millions of human beings to do more than eke out a bare existence. The democratic creed may be wholly meaningless to those who must spend all their days struggling to find enough to eat. A poverty-stricken family in Iran or a destitute farmer in Ecuador cannot be very excited by the noble words of the democratic ideology.

Democracy has indeed come far since the days of Athens, or of Locke, or Jefferson. But it has far to go as well. We cannot take our democratic ideology for granted. We cannot assume that our freedoms are "automatic," requiring no hard work to sustain them on our part. We cannot assume that democracy will "naturally" encompass the world without our lifting a finger to open the vistas of freedom to others. You and I can breathe the air of freedom, but over two billion people on our earth do not enjoy this privilege. The future of democracy depends on our practicing it better in our daily lives, on improving its function as a way of governing, and on increasing and elevating its role in world affairs.

Democracy and Foreign Policy

When a ship is in trouble at sea, the captain issues commands. He does not wait to take a vote among his crew in order to decide upon a course of action which will bring them all safely into port.

The democratic ship of state has a far more difficult problem as it attempts to steer through the stormy waters of international relations. The captain of the ship cannot ignore the many voices which offer advice on how best to chart the course. The ship of democracy has enemies which would like to attack and sink it. It is not always welcome in some of the ports it would like to enter.

1. Can Foreign Policy Be Made in a Democratic Manner?

Basic Problems

The fundamental principles of democracy and the problems of foreign policy are not always comfortable with each other. Foreign policy churned out by a democratic government must necessarily reflect the views of the many rather than the will of the few. It must have toughness to withstand the threat from totalitarianism, and still retain elements of caution and reserve. It should seek to extend the ideology of democracy in world affairs, even though many states do not possess the necessary foundations for democracy as a way of life and way of governing.

In both the *making* of foreign policy and in the *goals* sought by foreign policy, the democracies attempt to preserve and strengthen the democratic doctrine. But our democratic way of governing, which relies on the election of policy makers to public office, on our free institutions and freedom to hold different and often clashing opinions, and on the separation of powers between the Executive branch and Congress, presents real difficulties in the conduct of our foreign relations. *E pluribus unum* is vital to the whole scheme of democracy, but it certainly can cause many trials and tribulations in advancing national security and well-being in world affairs.

We hesitate, too, to extend our way of life and governing to other peoples because we believe that each state should choose its own form of government. This is a fundamental concept in democracy. Then how can the promotion of the democratic ideology be an objective of foreign policy, especially in areas of the world where democracy either does not exist or is present only in embryonic form? Do we stand aside and watch a revolution in Cuba turn towards communism because we believe that each state should choose its own system of government? Should we limit ourselves to helping Iran defend itself against the Communist threat and not seek to promote democracy there?

We are speaking here of the United States. Parliamentary democracies, as in Great Britain and elsewhere, face different problems in the actual making of foreign policy. There, the division between the executive and legislative functions is much less distinct. But the fundamental problem remains.

How can the democratic ideology and the shaping of foreign policy combine to strengthen democracy at home and promote its cause in world affairs?

De Tocqueville's View

One of the most penetrating and lucid critics of the making of foreign policy in a democratic state was the French scholar Alexis de Tocqueville. His famous book, *Democracy in America,* written in the 1830's, is full of remarkable insights about the weaknesses, as well as the strengths, of democracy. He noted that:

> . . . in the conduct of their foreign relations, (the) democracies appear to me to be decidedly inferior to other governments. . . . Foreign politics demand scarcely any of those qualities which are peculiar to a democracy; they require, on the contrary, the perfect use of almost all those in which it is deficient. (Democracy) cannot combine its measures with secrecy or await their consequences with patience.[1]

De Tocqueville declared that an aristocracy could perform foreign policy functions much better than a democracy. But that comment offers no solution for us. What are some of the problems of making foreign policy in a democratic manner, and what can be done about them?

The Making of Foreign Policy

Responsibility of the Executive branch. We have seen that national policy in the United States is formulated by the Executive branch, implemented through legislation by the Legislative branch, and returned to the Executive branch for its final approval. Then the President and his subordinates apply the policy at home and abroad. Only on rare occasions does the Judiciary concern itself with foreign affairs, and state governments in the United States have no official role in foreign policy affairs, except in very minor instances.

The Constitution vests in the President the primary responsibility for the conduct of foreign policy. As part of his broad executive powers, the President is Commander-in-Chief of the Armed Forces, negotiates treaties and other agreements with foreign nations, and appoints and receives representatives (ambassadors and ministers) to and from other states. The President and his subordinates in the Executive branch, therefore, must devise policies designed to advance national security and well-being in the United States' relations with other countries. In

---

[1] Alexis de Tocqueville, *Democracy in America.* New York: Vintage Books, 1945, vol. 1, p. 243.

performing the massive task, a number of measures are taken which are fairly secret in nature. Much of the work is carried out by Presidential appointees and members of the Civil and Foreign Service, people who are responsible to the President, not directly to the electorate. Is this procedure compatible with the basic principles of democracy?

"Closed" aspects of foreign policy. The democratic creed would seemingly call for policy to be made in the open and for nothing to be concealed from the public. But many of the crucial issues of foreign affairs do not lend themselves to continuous public scrutiny. Assessments of military requirements and strategies, reports by ambassadors to the President on sensitive issues in foreign lands, and confidential negotiations leading up to an important treaty are not matters for blazing headlines or the klieg lights of television. Information gathered by the Central Intelligence Agency is not shouted from the rooftops. Furthermore, full exposure of all steps of foreign policy *making* would be of great value to those who seek to destroy democracy.

Sooner or later, however, all the confidential stages in the making of foreign policy are revealed to the public eye. As foreign policy goes through the machinery of Congress, whatever secrecy may becloud it is viewed carefully by Senators and Representatives, officials close to the public at large. And when a policy is put into effect at home or abroad, it generally loses its once-secret nature.

Some critics decry any element of secrecy in foreign policy making as alien to democracy. And some Congressmen argue that they are not kept fully informed in the President's shaping of foreign policy. Nevertheless, some of the openness of democracy must be sacrificed if our national security is to be furthered in world affairs.

The foreign policy experts. A claim might also be made that the thousands of experts in the Executive branch who assist the President and his leading officials in the making of policy take the democratic train off the track. These people are appointed to their government positions on the basis of their experience and degree of specialization. They are not elected by the voters and thus are not always sensitive to public opinion on foreign policy issues. After all, the President, aside from the Vice President, is the only *elected* official among the four-and-a-half million members of the Executive branch of government. He is responsible to the voters, but the many experts who do the bulk of the detailed work in making policy are responsible only to the Chief Executive. Is the role of these non-elected officials contrary to the idea that policy in a democracy should be shaped by those whom the voters elevate to public office?

The scope of foreign policy in our times is increasingly complicated and complex. Our first Secretary of State, Thomas Jefferson, could get along with only a few clerks in his office. Secretary of State Rusk or Secretary of Defense McNamara, as President Johnson's principal assistants in the formulating of foreign policy, could not possibly give guidance and advice in the policy-making process without relying on their many experts. Practically all fields of thought now have a bearing on foreign policy making. Wisdom is needed from specialists in political science, economics, sociology, chemistry, physics, languages, and agriculture, to name only a few.

Think of the many kinds of specialists who must pool their thinking in drawing up American proposals for a nuclear test-ban agreement. Experts in economics, agriculture, and science must shape United States policy toward the European Common Market. Linguists must give constant attention to communications with other nations, and scientists are indispensable in coordinating research on weapons with policy proposals. The specialist in public relations copes with the problem of presenting American policies to peoples in other lands.

These public servants who provide the brain power so necessary to the making of effective foreign policy are fully dedicated to the democratic ideology. The fact that they are selected because of experience and training and not elected is no violation of the democratic doctrine. Their actions come under Congressional surveillance, and their over-all supervision by the President brings their participation in the machinery of government fully within the design of democracy. Without them, policy would be void of the depth it requires if it is to perform its tasks effectively abroad.

Foreign Policy and the Congress

The foreign policy *made* by the Executive branch travels the long mile up to Capitol Hill for *implementation* by Congress. The Constitution requires the President to submit most of his proposed policy to the Congress for the necessary legislative action before he can *apply* policies at home and abroad.

The President does possess some foreign policy powers which he can exercise without Congressional approval. He can dispatch troops to a crisis area in the world, as did President Truman in Korea on June 26, 1950. He can issue proclamations which strongly influence the course of international relations, such as President Eisenhower's warnings to Premier Khrushchev about Berlin. He cannot do these things, however, without at least the implied support of Congress, and all of his policies would be in jeopardy if he did not justify them to Congress.

Authority of Congress. All Presidential appointees to key foreign policy positions in the Executive branch and to ambassadorial posts abroad must be approved by the Senate. All treaties negotiated by the President must receive a two-thirds vote of the Senate before he can put them into effect. Congress has full authority to approve and appropriate funds necessary for the conduct of foreign affairs, such as those used in foreign aid and for the support of the armed forces. Only Congress can declare war. It also has wide powers to oversee and investigate the activities and procedures of the Executive branch.

The President and his experts in the Executive branch may *propose* a major policy, such as a foreign-aid program, which they feel will further the security and well-being of the United States in world affairs. But this program must be submitted to the Congress, both for approval and for the necessary funds. And here is the big problem in the shaping of foreign policy. When a specific foreign policy proposal enters the Congressional arena, such as the annual foreign-aid program, men and women in Congress may not always see eye to eye with the President. They agree on the goals of policy, but frequently disagree on the means toward these goals.

Congressional attitudes on foreign policy. In Congress, the pulse of democracy beats quickly. The men and women there directly represent the voters in the 50 states (the Senate) and in the 435 Congressional constituencies in the 50 states. Not all Congressmen are experts on foreign policy, and they must make decisions on many other areas of national policy as well. They are exposed to the demands of many pressure groups and organizations, and they reflect many different approaches to the conduct of foreign policy. They may often have their own special or constituent interests in mind which on occasion can conflict with the President's convictions as to what is required for the national interest. Frequent clashes are bound to take place between political forces and the substance of foreign policy.

A certain Congressman may feel that the voters in his district want federal spending cut, and therefore he may be inclined to reduce foreign-aid expenditures. Another Congressman may disagree with the Secretary of State or the Secretary of Defense and may alter proposals submitted to him dealing with specific policies advocated by these officials. In 1951 and 1952, some members of Congress sought to hamstring foreign policy, largely because of their distrust of Secretary of State Acheson. A Congressman may feel that the President is too weak in foreign affairs or else that he is exercising too much power. President Kennedy was accused of weakness in his Cuban policies, and President Franklin D. Roosevelt was charged with being a dictator. As a result, the Congressman may strongly oppose the President's request for funds or demand that he spend more money on certain programs, such as planes or rockets.

As representatives of the people, Senators and Representatives have every right and duty to make their voices heard and their power felt on foreign policy issues. On the other hand, their own special interests may seriously challenge policies which the President feels are in the national interest. Their perspective on world affairs may not have the breadth and depth of the officials in the Executive branch. Of course, the President and his advisers aren't always right, and they frequently benefit from Congressional surveillance and criticism of policy. Some feel that Executive-Legislative conflicts over foreign policy may seriously damage the potency of American foreign policy, but all of this is democracy in action.

The views of Walter Lippmann. Walter Lippmann, a veteran writer on political affairs, believes that democracy penetrates too deeply into the processes of the foreign policy. He finds that this is especially true when members of Congress feel they have to cater to the opinions of voters on foreign policy matters in order to remain in office. He writes that:

The unhappy truth is that the prevailing public opinion has been destructively wrong at the critical junctures. The people have imposed a veto upon the judgments of the informed and responsible officials. They have compelled the governments, which usually knew what would have been wiser, or was necessary, or was more expedient, to be too late with too little, or too long with too much, too pacifist in peace and too bellicose in war. Mass opinion (as reflected in Congress) has acquired mounting power in this century. It has shown itself to be a dangerous master of decisions when the stakes are life and death.[1]

Lippmann adds that "the people have acquired power which they are incapable of exercising, and the governments they elect have lost powers which they must recover if they are to govern."[2] People in the democracies, as De Tocqueville pointed out, are impatient and demand immediate results in foreign affairs, an area where "immediate results" are difficult to achieve.

The "Churchill Case." An episode in the British House of Commons almost thirty years ago points up the tumultuous clashing of politics and public opinion with a foreign policy decision.

In 1935, Winston Churchill advocated in the House of Commons that the Royal Air Force should be rapidly increased in numbers and strength to offset Hitler's build-up of the German Air Force, the Luftwaffe. Prime Minister Baldwin, however, declared that the R.A.F. was more powerful than the Luftwaffe, and that there was no need to build more planes as Churchill suggested. Later, after the British elections of 1935, Baldwin admitted that the power of the Luftwaffe exceeded that of the R.A.F. and that he had known this when Churchill spoke up on

[1] *The Public Philosophy*, copyright 1955 by Walter Lippmann, by permission of Atlantic—Little, Brown and Company, p. 20.

[2] *Ibid.*, p. 14.

the matter. He added that he could not admit this to the British people before the election. If he had, his party might have lost the election because the British people wanted peace and did not want to support any warlike measures such as a plane-building program.[1]

Prime Minister Baldwin catered to the British people's understandably peaceful inclinations. He did this instead of assuming vigorous leadership by declaring that Great Britain must balance German power to prevent the Luftwaffe from devastating the nation in case of war. He placed a higher value on his political interests than on the clear needs of the national interest. Such instances, declares Lippmann, show how democracy can choke itself.

Democracy and Foreign Policy Are Compatible

But this is only one side of the picture. The record of the democracies in the making of effective foreign policy, while hardly perfect, is vastly better than that of totalitarian states. In the latter, only a few men make the basic decisions. They frequently become impressed with their own infallible judgment, as did Hitler, and therefore forget about other important factors which must enter into policy making. Hitler, for example, did not care whether the United States entered World War II because he was convinced that we would play no effective part in it.

There is a distinct advantage in having foreign policy go through many hands. The continuous political debate between the Executive and Legislative branches is essentially sound. Policy arising from the decision-making process in a democracy provides for a high degree of national consensus, so important in gaining public support for the state's mission in world affairs. A foreign-aid bill debated in and out of Congress reflects the national will better than would a bill devised by only a few officials. The cooperation between the two major political parties in the United States in the shaping of major foreign policies since World War II has, on the whole, reflected a fundamental and

[1] Winston Churchill, *The Gathering Storm.* Boston: Houghton Mifflin Company, 1948, p. 123 and p. 216.

positive agreement in our democracy on the ends and means of our foreign relations.

Nothing is more essential to wise policy making in a democracy than an enlightened public opinion if policy is to advance the security and well-being of all. It is the essence of democracy that the people participate in the processes of governing. If they do so in ignorance, however, they imperil democracy. Well-informed public participation lends firm support to the making of policy in the Executive branch and fortifies the crucial role which the Congress must play in its implementation of policy. Moreover, responsible public opinion restrains public officials. They are less apt to permit private, special, and narrow political interests to influence their judgment.

2. Should a Democracy Seek to Extend the Democratic Ideology?

Should the foreign policy of a democracy, especially that of the United States, be limited to doing what is necessary to protect its own national security and well-being? Or, should democracy's foreign policy take the offensive as well? Should we seek to extend the ideology of democracy among states where it is weak or non-existent?

Does not logic dictate that the democracies can gain security and well-being for their peoples only if they strive, through peaceful means, to strengthen democracy where it exists, plant its seeds where it is not to be found, and cultivate its growth with positive and vigorous policies throughout the world? The most effective defense for democracy is a vigorous offense. Indeed, defense and offense can be the same thing.

We have seen that democracy as a way of life permits the exercise of the freedom that is fundamental to the very meaning of the human being. But economic and social conditions which have nourished the growth and expansion of democracy in Western civilization, for the most part, have not been abundant in the non-Western world. Democratic governing also demands a great deal — such as education and enlightenment, participation and patience, give-and-take, and tolerance — from those who live within its confines. Is it, then, possible or desirable to further the ideology of democracy in lands whose history, culture, economic and social conditions, and ambitious rulers seem to combine to form a gigantic obstacle to advancing the theory and practice of democracy?

The *ideal* of furthering democracy can hardly be questioned. The *realities* of democracy taking the offensive in world affairs are difficult indeed. This is especially true today, when the totalitarian threat of communism often keeps democracy on the defensive.

Difficulties Encountered in the Past

A brief look at some pages in American history will provide us with a perspective on the vital task of advancing democracy through example, policy, or both.

To states aspiring to freedom and independence, the United States Declaration of Independence shines like a beacon. Our Constitution has been viewed as a model for organizing the powers of government in a number of states, especially in the Western hemisphere. Thus our philosophical origins and structure of government have often served as a mighty example and force in extending the democratic ideology.

The neutrality question. In 1792 and 1793 the revolutionary institutions of France were gravely threatened by the armed forces of the European monarchies. This gave rise to an exceedingly important question. Was the United States obligated to extend assistance to France? Some American statesmen, such as Thomas Jefferson, argued that because France had lent valuable assistance to the United States during the Revolutionary War and because of the treaty of alliance, America had an obligation to aid France in defending its newly won liberties.

At the urging of Alexander Hamilton, however, President Washington declared on April 22, 1793, that America would take a neutral position in the European conflict. In defending this action, Hamilton contended that the United States would place itself in great jeopardy if it allied itself with the French cause. He added that the role of America in world affairs should be considered in terms of its fundamental power (which was then militarily weak) and not by the yardstick of helping a friendly country, or of extending democracy.

This attitude was amplified by Washington in his famous "Farewell Speech" of September 17, 1796, when he called upon the United States to "steer clear of permanent alliances" with other states. Jefferson later came to support this point of view. The Monroe Doctrine of 1823 was based upon the principle that American security was best insured by maintaining comparative isolation from "the quarrels of Europe." Few realized, however, that the Doctrine was intertwined with the balance of power in Europe and that the British Navy was to provide the backbone for shoring up President Monroe's warning to Europe against acquiring new colonies in the Western hemisphere. Great Britain was strongly opposed to the European states' reconquering their lost colonies in South America, and thus backed fully America's "stay out" message to Europe.

The United States continued to serve the interests of democracy in world affairs by example rather than specific action. The life and speeches of Lincoln, for instance, inspired and influenced many to support the cause of democracy. The rise of American imperialism at the end of the nineteenth century prompted many Americans and others to question the compatibility of democracy with the policies of domination.

The tradition of isolation. Woodrow Wilson was the first President who put the aims of American foreign policy in terms of advancing democracy in world affairs. Wilson gave considerable thought to relating the principles of democracy to acts of foreign policy. In recognizing new governments of other states, he felt that any government which came to power by means of revolution should be denied recognition by the United States unless it took steps to establish its democratic legitimacy through free elections. This view was very different from those of Wilson's predecessors and did not take account of the fact that the American government was conceived in revolution. Wilson also declared that "just government rests always upon the consent of the governed and there can be no freedom without order based upon law and upon public conscience and approval."[1]

[1] Quoted by James Reston, *The New York Times,* July 27, 1962.

As the European nations became embroiled in World War I in 1914, Wilson called for American neutrality. As time went on, however, and as the European balance of power no longer provided protection for American security, this nation found its shipping attacked and its neutrality violated. More and more Americans came to view the European conflict as one between the forces of German aggression and the democracy of the Allies. When the United States joined forces with Britain and France in April, 1917, Wilson said that the war in which his nation was now involved was one to make the world "safe for democracy." He added that peace could be maintained only "by a partnership of democratic nations."

Wilson concluded this message by saying that:

> We shall fight for democracy, for the right of those who submit to authority to have a voice in their own governments, for the rights and liberties of small nations, for a universal domination of right by such a concert of free peoples as shall bring peace and safety to all nations and make the world at last free.[1]

When Wilson traveled to Europe in December, 1918, to attend the Paris Peace Conference, he was convinced that he was bringing with him the principles of the successful democratic experiment of the New World to the tired, monarchial system of the Old. He thought his democratically oriented "Fourteen Points," proclaimed on January 8, 1918, would serve as a solid foundation for the organization of the peace. He felt, too, that democratic constitutions and structures of government should be implanted in the defeated states, Germany in particular, and in such newly formed states as Czechoslovakia and Yugoslavia. Wilson's foreign policy and his vision of the democratic ideology were truly intertwined.

Disagreement among the democracies. Most of the leaders of the victorious European states did not share Wilson's view that the aim of the war had been to further the principles and ideology of democracy. They thought it somewhat presumptuous of Wilson to suggest to them how the peace should be organized. The French Premier, Georges Clemenceau, in refer-

[1] Address to Congress on April 2, 1917, asking for a declaration of war against Germany. *Congressional Record,* 65th Congress, 1st Session, p. 104.

ring to the "Fourteen Points," noted that the good God himself had only ten. These leaders did concede some points to Wilson, such as the organization of new states in Europe along lines of nationality. But they sought and gained a vindictive peace, especially with Germany. The League of Nations which Wilson proposed as his fourteenth point became a reality, but its provisions deviated from Wilson's original proposals.

Many of the European states did adopt constitutions and establish democratic structures of government. But in the 1920's and early 1930's these new democracies in Central and Eastern Europe, with the important exception of Czechoslovakia, fell one by one under authoritarian and totalitarian patterns of governing. Unfortunately, Wilson and others had stressed democracy as a way of governing and had given insufficient consideration to democracy as a way of life. There was little or no tradition of democracy in the states of Central and Eastern Europe, and the economic and social conditions there, especially in the 1920's, could not support a democratic way of life. In this area, the democratic dream of Woodrow Wilson collapsed.

Even during his lifetime Wilson witnessed a tragic failure of his high democratic ideals. Because of political considerations, lack of understanding, and a sincere belief in traditional isolationism, the majority of the American people turned their backs on Wilson's desire to further democracy in world affairs. The United States refused to join the League of Nations and reverted to comparative isolation after 1920. Perhaps Wilson was far ahead of his times. On the other hand, a greater emphasis on political realities at home and abroad might have enabled him to merge the goals of the democratic ideology with foreign policy.

World War II Challenged Democracy

Growth of totalitarianism. In the conduct of American foreign policy in the 1920's and 1930's, little attention was devoted to furthering the ideological goals of democracy. In 1922 Mussolini rose to power in Italy, in 1933, Hitler in Germany. The Japanese invaded Manchuria in 1931. These events cast a new light on world affairs. The Soviet Union's aspirations toward world revolution, while toned down during most of the 1930's, did not escape the eye of those who understood the goals of communism. By 1937 dictatorships in Germany, Italy, and Japan cast an increasingly threatening shadow. A number of Americans began to wonder about the possible effect of these new patterns of totalitarianism on America's future place in the world.

In October of 1937, President Roosevelt, deeply disturbed over the growth of totalitarianism in Europe, felt it was time for action by the democracies. He suggested that the democratic states "quarantine" the Fascist and Nazi aggressors in order to prevent the spread of totalitarian creeds beyond the borders of Italy and Germany. Containment of Japanese aggression was included as well.

The American people, disillusioned about the capacity of the United States to influence the politics of Europe, did not see what effect changes in the balance of power in Europe had upon their own security and well-being, although there had always been a close relation between European affairs and American security. The history of the Monroe Doctrine was forgotten.

The European democracies chose the easy path of appeasing the dictators rather than mobilizing their strength as a bulwark against the tide of aggression. Lack of unity among the democracies only invited the forces of totalitarianism, led by Hitler, to fill the vacuum. The League of Nations fell into disuse, and democracy was totally on the defensive when war came on September 1, 1939. The lessons of the 1930's should most assuredly not be forgotten in meeting the totalitarian challenge of today.

Meaning to democracy of the war. President Roosevelt viewed World War II as one in which the democracies were struggling to defend themselves against the totalitarian onslaught. The ultimate purpose of the war was not conceived in terms of bringing democracy to all nations. The President and Prime Minister Churchill did agree in August, 1941, that the "right of all peoples to choose the form of government under which they shall live" should be "restored to those who have been forcefully deprived"[1]

---

[1] Winston Churchill, *The Grand Alliance.* Boston: Houghton Mifflin Company, 1950, p. 435.

of their independence by aggressors. This did not mean, however, that governing by consent of the governed was to be introduced in all states.

Roosevelt felt that the free nations should strive to create *conditions* which ultimately would promote the expansion of the democratic ideology. He declared in 1941 that "in future days, which we seek to make secure, we look forward to a world founded on four essential freedoms (freedom of speech, and worship, and freedom from want and fear)." Roosevelt focused his sights upon laying the foundations for democracy as a way of life rather than pursuing the Wilsonian approach of bringing democratic structures of governing to societies not yet prepared for them.

Extending Democracy in the Post-War World

The United Nations Charter of 1945 provided a framework for the maintenance of international peace and security on the one hand and for promoting economic and social conditions for human welfare and progress on the other. Largely because the Communist bloc of states, led by the USSR, did not subscribe to the basic beliefs and purposes of the world organization, the United Nations has not been able to function in the manner intended by its authors. Therefore, the democracies united in organizations such as the North Atlantic Treaty Organization in order to protect themselves against aggression and to contain the spread of militant, totalitarian communism. Having learned the lessons of the 1930's, they seek to protect and defend democracy through unity rather than to permit the forces of totalitarian communism to swallow them one by one, as Hitler did to so many of them.

Most of the time, effort, and money which the democracies have devoted to foreign policy since 1945 has been directed to containing the spread of communism. But the democracies have realized that their ideology is not preserved and strengthened by purely defensive measures. They have frequently seized the offensive and have sought to expand the democratic doctrine as an alternative to the challenge of communism, especially among the Afro-Asian states. The democracies have tried to create the economic and social conditions which can provide the soil for the growth of democratic patterns of living rather than emphasizing solely democratic structures and ways of governing.

The economic and social programs of the Western states and the United Nations, accompanied by understanding diplomacy and effective political guidance, have done much to reduce hunger, poverty, disease, and illiteracy around the world. With rising standards of living and a genuine desire for the good life of the twentieth century may well come a demand by the people of Afro-Asia and of Latin America for ways of freedom and patterns of governing which are increasingly democratic.

Expanding the democratic ideology by concentrating first on creating the conditions for democratic living is no mere idealistic scheme. It can and does work. But as Alexander Hamilton said many years ago, idealism must be accompanied by the realities of power. The power of the democracies must balance the power of the forces of communism. The extension of democracy would be infinitely easier were it not for the Communist challenge of our times, which seeks not only to conquer the Afro-Asian world and Latin America but to eliminate all vestiges of existing democracy as well.

Communism is the main threat to democracy. But other forms of totalitarianism endanger democracy as well. If we hope to broaden the sphere of democracy, we should know much more about the nature and purpose of totalitarian systems.

The Evolution of
Communist Ideology

1. What Are the Roots of Modern Communism?

The Myth and Promise of Totalitarianism

"The history of all hitherto existing society is the history of class struggles."[1]

"With the removal of this chief cause (exploitation of the masses), excesses will inevitably begin to 'wither away' . . . with their withering away, the State will also wither away."[2]

In these two sentences, Karl Marx and Nikolai Lenin stated the underlying *myth* and *promise* of the Communist ideology.

The *myth* is that the history of all mankind has been shaped by the clashing of economic classes. The *promise* is one of ending this conflict by producing, ultimately, a classless, communal society.

Modern communism, a totalitarian ideology, is based largely upon the philosophy of Karl Marx, the ideas and political action of Nikolai Lenin, the iron dictatorship of Joseph Stalin, and the strategic twists and turns of Nikita Khrushchev. To it, Mao and the Chinese communists have added some features of their own.

The myth of communism presents a neat explanation of history

---

[1] Cohen, *op. cit.*, p. 90.

[2] From Hook's *World of Communism*, copyright 1962, used by permission of D. Van Nostrand Company, Inc., Princeton, New Jersey, p. 22.

and human behavior. Its promise for the future is attractive to a great many people who find life oppressive. This is the *idealism* of communism.

The *realism* of communism presents a different picture. The Communist way of life is harsh, and its way of governing stern. Because the forces of communism seek to dominate all non-Communist states, this brand of totalitarianism is the gravest challenge in our era to advancing the cause of democracy in world affairs.

Communism is a "left-wing" variety of contemporary totalitarianism, while ideologies such as Mussolini's fascism or Hitler's nazism represent the "right-wing" approach. Totalitarianism of any variety, however, involves total control by the few over the whole life of any society where it prevails.

A totalitarian ideology has a distinct *myth* and *promise*. The myth is the core of the ideology. It is some distorted explanation of the social nature of man or of history, and lays claim to being the sole "truth." Hitler's supremacy of the "Aryan" race, and Marx's interpretation of history as an unfolding of clashes between opposing economic classes of people, or *dialectical materialism,* are the central myths of nazism and communism. The promise is the great reward which will come to those who are the true believers of the myth. Hitler promised world domination by the Aryan race. Communism promises to end human exploitation by means of the "classless society."

Other Characteristics of Totalitarianism

In the totalitarian state the dictator exercises control through the sole official party, which is the organized vanguard of the ideology. The party dominates the government, and no competing political organizations are permitted. The dictator and the party hold a monopoly in interpreting the myth and therefore are the sole leaders in the march toward the promise. The masses are indoctrinated through propaganda to accept the creed, and, so far as possible, any point of view disputing the "truth" of the myth is absolutely forbidden. Conformity of the masses to the totalitarian ideology is reinforced by secret police and by the threat of severe penalties for deviating from the party's ideological guideline.

All totalitarian ideologies have built-in enemies, or "scapegoats." Jews were Nazi scapegoats, while "capitalists" perform this function for all communists. Scapegoats provide a convenient explanation for anything that goes wrong within the state, and all the masses are told to be hostile toward these enemies who presumably seek to subvert the totalitarian state and its creed.

Many people in totalitarian societies believe in the myth and the promise of the ideology, because, in most instances, they are denied any opportunity to learn any different point of view. They grow into maturity convinced of the "truth" of the ideology, which is constantly drilled into them by the dictator and his party. Many feel that by being a true believer in the ideology, the promised pot of gold at the end of the mythical and glittering rainbow will someday be theirs.

Most totalitarian ideologies are expansionist. The dictators regard it as their duty to impose the myth and promise of their creed on other nations. They want to destroy the scapegoats at home and abroad, and crush any opposition to their ideology of domination. Such is the objective of international communism. We are the enemy. We are the prime target of communism, as its leaders seek to dominate the world.

Some Important Landmarks

The communal way of life probably existed even before man learned to write. Some American Indian tribes lived in a communal manner, and even the great Greek philosopher, Plato, advocated a form of communism for the rulers of his ideal state, the philosopher kings.

Sir Thomas More preached communism in his famous book, *Utopia*, written in 1516. During the Cromwell period in England in the middle of the seventeenth century, some proposals by the so-called "Levellers" called for the common ownership of property. Many other writers and theorists in history have also felt that communalism might correct some of the inequalities of society. Karl Marx, the founder of modern communism, borrowed heavily from others.

The American and French revolutions at the end of the eighteenth century and the advent of the industrial revolution gave rise to new waves of political and economic thought. Many radical views were aired by those who sought to revolutionize all aspects of life.

One of the earliest advocates of reform was François (Gracchus) Babeuf (1760-1797) who, during the latter stages of the French Revolution, demanded that economic equality accompany political equality. Babeuf's ideas gradually turned toward communism. He and his followers sought to overthrow the French government, the Directory, but he was captured and executed. His doctrines gained some acceptance among radicals and were perpetuated in a number of secret societies.

In the Western European states, Britain, and the United States during the first half of the nineteenth century, the industrial revolution brought hundreds of thousands of men and women to the large cities to find employment. The working and living conditions of the laborers were incredibly miserable, but they had no political representation and no legal right to bargain with their employers. Wealth and political power were concentrated in the hands of the few. Government was not expected to provide for the welfare of the poor. Novels such as Charles Dickens' *Hard Times* vividly describe the human hardships caused by early capitalism.

The "Utopian Socialists"

A group of men, dubbed "utopian socialists," demanded reform. Social innovators such as Claude Saint-Simon (1760-1825) and Charles Fourier (1772-1837) of France, and Robert Owen (1771-1858) of England sought in various ways to bring about measures of economic and social equality. They condemned the abuses of private property and advocated communal approaches to production and to living as well.

Owen's cotton mill in New Lanark, Scotland, which emphasized clean and decent conditions for the factory workers, was widely acclaimed. Fourier and Owen inspired the establishment of several communal settlements in the United States. Brook Farm in West Roxbury, Massachusetts, was admired by some of America's leading literary figures, while Owen's settlement at New Harmony, Indiana, gained fame as well. These experiments in social and economic idealism failed. But the work of these and other men represented efforts to cope with the severe human problems of early capitalism.

2. How Did Marx Mold Modern Communism?

Early Life and Ideas

Karl Marx (1818-1883) was the most influential architect of the Communist ideology. He applied a revolutionary interpretation of history to his analysis of the economic and social conditions of mid-nineteenth century Europe. He produced, as a result, the philosophical foundation of modern communism.

Born at Trier in the German Rhineland in 1818, Marx received a sound education. At the University of Berlin he was attracted to various radical social theories and programs for action then in circulation, and after he finished his education, he began to edit a succession of left-wing publications. He sought new opportunities for spreading his emerging doctrines by moving to Paris in 1843.

At the University of Berlin Marx had been deeply influenced by the philosophy of George Wilhelm Hegel (1770-1831). A strong German nationalist, Hegel provided Marx with the basic structure of modern communism, the "dialectic," or the clash of opposites to produce something new.

In Paris Marx met and began his lifelong friendship and close collaboration with Friedrich Engels (1820-1895), the son of a wealthy German capitalist. The writings of Marx and Engels were closely intertwined. Each complemented the other. Although we tend to discuss Marx more than Engels, there is no doubt that the latter contributed many important ideas to the body of thought we call Marxism. Both were asked by the subversive Communist League to prepare a platform and program for the party. In February, 1848, Marx and Engels published the *Communist Manifesto*, which set forth the philosophic tenets of communism.

Marx also borrowed heavily from the ideas of some utopian socialists, and he and Engels were close observers of the abuses of early capitalism. Marx felt that the miserable conditions of the workers gave them a distinct class consciousness which would make them a powerful revolutionary force. The biological theories of Charles Darwin were later to influence him greatly, especially Darwin's theories about the evolution of man and other organisms. But the dialectic process of history and the economic behavior of men, as Marx saw them, were the keys to his outlook on the world in 1848.

The Communist Manifesto

Two central concepts of this revolutionary program combine to provide the essence of Marxist theory — the principle of the "class struggle" and the economic causation of all human activity.

Dialectical materialism. Marxism has at its foundation the concept of *dialectical materialism*, which Marx claimed to be the sole "scientific explanation" of all history. The debt to Hegel is clear, although a German philosopher, Ludwig Feuerbach (1804-1872), was really the first to convert Hegel's dialectic of abstract ideas into one of material, economic factors. The dialectic consists of a thesis or force which produces an antithesis or counterforce. The clash of the two results in a synthesis which, in turn, is confronted by a new antithesis. This clash produces a new synthesis, and thus the dialectic moves on and on, with continual clashes and always a new synthesis. History, according to Marx and Engels, moves in this dialectic manner. The contending economic classes, at any one time, form the thesis and antithesis.

According to Marx, there has always been an exploiting class (thesis) and an exploited class (antithesis) at any juncture in history. These two classes conflict, because the exploited class never receives what it deserves in return for its work. Motivated by dire conditions of its existence, the exploited class rises up, overthrows the exploiting class, and emerges as a new class (a synthesis). The new class, however, exploits others and thus causes another exploiting class to come into existence (a new antithesis). Another clash takes place and produces a new synthesis. History is pushed forward by this continuous conflict based upon the economic nature of man and the production processes in which he works and through which he produces material goods.

At the time of the writing of the *Manifesto*, the contending classes were the capitalist owners of the factories and other means of production (the bourgeoisie), and the factory workers (the proletariat). The former were the thesis, and the latter, the antithesis in "dialectical" terms.

Labor theory of value. Marx declared that the proletariat of the new industrial era were devoting long hours and hard work to producing the goods which were sold by the bourgeoisie. The workers, by their labor, give *value* to the goods they make and the services they perform. This is Marx's *labor theory of value*, borrowed from several English economic thinkers of the eighteenth century.

SIMPLIFIED DIAGRAM OF MARX'S PRINCIPLE OF SURPLUS VALUE

John Jones works ten hours a day in an English textile factory, owned by Mr. Brown. During this ten-hour period, Jones produces $8.00 worth of textiles. Through his labor, he makes cloth which has a value of $8.00, and which is sold by Brown. But Jones is paid only $.20 an hour, or $2.00 a day — mere subsistence wages. According to Marx's idea of surplus value, Jones's labor is worth $.60 an hour for Brown, who derives a total of $6.00 surplus value each day from Jones's work.

	Hour	Day
TOTAL VALUE PRODUCED	$.80 x 10 hours	$8.00
WAGES	.20 x 10 hours	2.00
SURPLUS VALUE	$.60 an hour	$6.00 a day

Thus the owners of the factories and those who control finance get all the profits. The laborers receive a subsistence wage for their labor, but the goods sold by the owners bring in profits which are not shared with those who, in Marx's view, gave the goods value in the first place. By extracting this "surplus value" or profit from the fruits of the workingmen's labor, a crushing form of exploitation is imposed upon the proletariat by the bourgeoisie.[1]

Call for revolution. The *Manifesto* is a clarion call for another dialectical clash. The proletariat must rise up, overthrow the bourgeoisie, abolish private property in the means of production, and bring human exploitation to an end. In words which have vital meaning today, Marx and Engels concluded the *Manifesto* in this manner:

> The Communists disdain to conceal their views and aims. They openly declare that their ends can be attained only by the forcible overthrow of all existing social conditions. Let the ruling classes tremble at a Communist revolution. The proletarians have nothing to lose but their chains. They have a world to win. Workingmen of all countries, unite![2]

The immediate purpose of the *Manifesto* failed. Workingmen did not unite and had little or no inclination toward rebellion based on Marx's prescription. However, a revolution did break out in Paris shortly after the publication of the *Manifesto*. It was inspired to a great extent by radical ferment. It failed, however, and Marx was forced to leave France following the conservative reaction to the European revolutions of 1848. He fled to London where he remained for the rest of his life. Writing in the British Museum, Marx elaborated upon his theories, especially in his famous work, *Das Kapital* (the first volume of which was published in 1867). He also busied himself with furthering his beliefs in many ways.

Stages in communism. Marx and Engels saw three basic stages in the advent of communism:

1. Overthrow of the bourgeoisie by the proletariat.

---

[1] Marx's concept of surplus value was set forth in detail in his book *Das Kapital* ("Capital").

[2] Cohen, *op. cit.*, p. 110.

2. Dictatorship of the proletariat.
3. Classless society.

In the *Manifesto*, Marx and Engels set forth ten specific measures which would be introduced during the "dictatorship of the proletariat," among them "abolition of property in land," "a heavy progressive or graduated income tax," abolition of all right of inheritance, concentration of economic and financial power in the hands of the state, and equal obligation of all to work. This is the transitional stage of socialism. Public ownership of the means of production and the distribution of rewards in accordance with the work performed bring exploitation to an end. There are no owners of property and none who are oppressed. There is no "surplus value" or profits because the fruits of labor are equally distributed. Because the "classless society" emerges, there can be no further class warfare. The dialectic thus comes to an end.

Finally, as people learn how to live in this classless, communal "utopia," the state "withers away." No further organs of coercion or control are required. The millennium has been reached in which the saying would apply, "from each according to his ability, to each according to his needs."

Some Fallacies of Marxism

History, of course, is infinitely more than a series of class struggles. Man has been motivated by many things in addition to his economic sentiments or class position. History is made by men, contrary to the views of Marx. Some revolutions may have had economic foundations, but Marx ignores the political, social, and nationalistic factors which have produced civil and international wars.

Also, there is no dictatorship *of* the proletariat, only one *over* the proletariat, as evidenced in Communist states today. Some governmental regulation or even ownership of the means of production may be necessary in some states at some times. In no country has complete state control of an economy been able to meet the needs of the people on an equal basis. No Communist government has "withered away." No society has so far ruled itself without some exercise of political authority. And what evidence does Marx give for the ending of the dialectic, hence, of all social revolution, with the establishment of the Communist utopia?

Another criticism of Marx, however, arises from the fact that he and Engels trace all human behavior to material, economic factors. They leave no room whatever for any relationship between human beings and the Deity of a religious faith. For Marx and Engels, there is no such thing as natural law. There are only the tangible, material elements that enter into economic productivity. Marx was an atheist, and the true believer of communism must likewise reject all explanations for human activity other than the "scientific and historic truths" of dialectical materialism. "Religion," said Lenin, "is the opium of the people." Most of Marx's theories depart from the realities of human history and defy the teachings of the great religions and the nature of man himself.

On the other hand, Marx did make important contributions to the study of economics and history. His writings caused many to consider the importance of economic factors in the shaping of political events and social changes.

The International Workingmen's Association

During the 1850's and 1860's, Marx's writings began to circulate among a number of theorists and social reformers. The first international organization to promote the doctrines of Marx and other socialists, the International Workingmen's Association, was organized at London in 1864 under Marx's leadership. Its first Congress met in Geneva in 1866. The I.W.M.A. brought many radical and social reformers together and did much to promote the founding of socialist and labor parties in a number of European states. Internal dissensions on the meanings and interpretations of Marxist and other radical thought, however, contributed to the collapse of the I.W.M.A. in 1874, in Philadelphia.

Democratic Socialism Evolved from Marxism

The question of what is basic and what can be revised in the doctrines of Marxism troubled Karl Marx himself during the later years of his life. There is evidence that, before his death in 1883, Marx began to feel that non-violent means might be a possible route to the goals set forth in the *Communist Manifesto,* because of the spread of parliamentary institutions, democratic political parties, and universal education. During the 1880's and 1890's, this less belligerent approach gained considerable ground. Perhaps the most important of the "revisionists" of dogmatic Marxism was Eduard Bernstein (1850-1932), a prominent German socialist. He held that the "class struggle" would not become as violent or universal as Marx had assumed, that world revolution was not necessary, and that the central elements of Marxism, such as state ownership of the means of production, could be brought about by peaceful and gradual means. This view finally prevailed within the framework of the emerging trade-union movement and among the European socialist parties which sought to use democratic, parliamentary procedures to advance some of the teachings of Marxism. Jean Jaurès in France, among others, was instrumental in advancing this idea of "democratic socialism." Most of the revisionists accepted the basic premises of Marx's theories but rejected his ideas of violent revolution.

There were many economic and social reformers who rejected the atheism implicit in dialectical materialism. While they retained their belief in socialism, they combined it with their Christian heritage to form such parties as the Christian Socialists.

Today, the Social Democrats in Germany and in Scandinavia, the Socialist Party in France, and other socialist groups throughout the world trace their basic origins to Marxism. "Democratic socialism" is compatible with the theory and practice of democracy.

The word "socialism" has been applied to all kinds of political theories and thus should be carefully defined whenever it is used.[1] During the nineteenth century, Marx's communism was generally identified with the word socialism, but when the

[1] Some of the ways "socialism" is used are: Union of Soviet *Socialist* Republics (totalitarian communism); the National *Socialist* Party (the right-wing totalitarianism of the nazis in Germany); the principle of democratic *socialism* advocated by various parties within the Western democracies.

Bolshevik Revolution took place in Russia late in 1917, the Bolsheviks called themselves communists. The distinction between communism and democratic socialism has been fairly clear since that time. Communists generally consider democratic socialists as among their worst enemies because the latter are viewed as traitors to the "only true dogma" of Karl Marx as reinterpreted by Lenin.

3. How Did Lenin Bring Revolutionary Communism to Power in Russia?

If Marx were alive today, he would probably be amazed at the many different ways in which his writings have been interpreted and applied. A conflict similar to the one now being waged between the Russian and Chinese leaders took place among the Russian Marxists over sixty years ago. The struggle led to Lenin's founding a new and extreme revolutionary party, the Bolsheviks, and paved the way for its seizure of power in Russia in 1917.

Vladimir Ilyich Ulyanov (1870-1924), better known to history as Nikolai Lenin, converted the philosophy of Marx into modern communism. As the son of a school official, Lenin's comfortable family life during his early years was certainly not responsible for his becoming one of the most powerful revolutionists in history. But his brother Alexander became involved in a plot to assassinate Czar Alexander II in 1887, was captured, and then executed. This event left an indelible mark on Lenin. It started him on a thirty-year march toward revolution in Russia.

Threads of Reform and Revolt in Russia

Russia was passed by while the great liberalizing movements were reshaping the life and thought of Western Europe. There was no Renaissance or Reformation in Russia, no philosophy of the rights of man, or belief in natural law. Czar Peter the Great (1672-1725) had tried to bring some Western influences into his country, but at best, they only reached a few members of his court. The iron rule of the Czars and Czarinas of Russia left little room for human freedoms or democratic patterns of governing. The society was feudalistic, and the vast majority of Russians lived amidst extreme poverty and human oppression.

Some Russian Army officers were exposed to the freer way of life in the West during their stay in France after the defeat of Napoleon in 1815. In 1825, they organized a rebellion against the new Czar, Nicholas I, but their efforts failed dismally. Life became more oppressive for the masses of Russians, especially for the peasants, during the following decades. Slowly, a ground swell of angry protest began to rise from the troubled sea.

Some groups preached liberalism, and others spoke in hushed tones of revolution. Alexander II, who succeeded Nicholas in 1855, was more humane than his predecessors. He emancipated the Russian serfs in 1861 and introduced measures of local self-government in Russia in 1864. His advisers, however, warned him against further liberalizing measures and also persuaded him to crack down on the expanding liberal and radical movements of thought.

In the 1870's strong currents of protest against the way of life and the way of governing in Russia led to the formation of the secret revolutionary organization called "Land and Freedom," which sought the sharing of all the land among the peasants as its goal and the overthrow of the Czar and his government as the means to this end. Land and Freedom was followed by the terroristic "People's Will," to which Lenin's brother belonged. The People's Will, dissatisfied with the slow pace of reform and convinced of the necessity of revolution, assassinated Alexander II in 1881.

This action made the new Czar, Alexander III, even more determined to impose a harsh totalitarian rule upon the Russian people and to destroy all revolutionary movements. Lenin's brother and the People's Will, convinced there was no middle ground for the introduction of reforms, plotted to assassinate the Czar in 1887. Their failure persuaded Lenin to take up the torch of revolution.

Lenin Joins the Revolutionary Movement

Lenin was only beginning his political education in 1887. The theories of Marx appealed to him, as did the doctrines of socialism. But how could he translate Marxism and socialism into governmental power in Russia? Should his deeply felt hostility toward the Czar's government call for terror to try to overthrow the regime? Or were there other steps toward advancing the socialist cause?

Plekhanov and the Social Democrats. There were a number of Russian radicals who had absorbed the writings of Marx and who also disagreed with the People's Will on the use of revolution and terror to bring down the government and erect the flag of socialism. One of these Marxists was George Plekhanov (1857-1918), who agreed to some extent with the Western European "revisionists" of Marxism. He felt that the path to socialism lay first in working to secure political freedoms for the people and in advancing industry in Russia. Plekhanov was exiled from Russia in 1882. Nevertheless, he was influential in launching a number of Marxist "Social Democratic" groups in his homeland.

Lenin was attracted to Plekhanov's social democratic movements following the execution of his brother. By the time he took his law degree in 1891, he was a confirmed Marxist and a prominent Social Democrat. As a result of his subversive activity, Lenin was arrested by the Czar's police and exiled twice to Siberia. But he slowly moved toward a position of leadership among the Social Democrats.

The size and number of Plekhanov's Social Democratic groups or cells had grown, and workers' strikes, though forbidden by the Czarist police, had also become more frequent. The first "Congress" of Marxist groups met in 1898, and gave birth to the Russian Social Democratic Workers Party. The Party, like all other anti-Czarist groups, was an underground, subversive movement. The *Spark*, the Party revolutionary newspaper, was first published in 1900 in Leipzig, Germany. About this time, however, Lenin began to doubt seriously whether Marxism and the socialist beliefs of the Social Democrats could be furthered by political education of the masses. He began to reject the idea of working toward popular support and gave increasing attention to another approach, put forth in 1902 in a small pamphlet entitled *What Is to Be Done?* Here we have the core of modern communism.

Lenin's theories. Lenin believed that only a small group of professional revolutionists, highly centralized and tightly disciplined, could bring the revolution and the classless society to Russia. The broad masses could not understand Marxism. They required leadership. There was no parliament which could provide a channel for introducing Marxism into the Russian government. Terror could not be used indiscriminately, but harsh means must be employed by the revolutionary leaders should the occasion arise. The dedicated, determined few must lead the masses to revolution. In this way, Lenin set the conspiratorial tone which has existed to this day in the Communist Party. Like Hitler's *Mein Kampf* of 1924, Lenin's *What Is to Be Done?* of 1902 served as a blueprint for ideological theory and action, and as a handbook for totalitarianism.

The Party split of 1903. At a meeting of the Russian Social Democratic Party in London in 1903, Lenin fiercely pressed his views against those who desired to have the Social Democrats pursue their socialist objectives in a more peaceful manner, as in Germany. A temporary majority sided with Lenin and immediately were tagged "Bolsheviks" (Bolsheviki — members of the majority), while the moderates were named "Mensheviks." This event laid the framework for the conspirational, disciplined structure of the Bolshevik (later Communist) Party.

The 1905 Revolution Produces Some Reforms

Russia's defeat by Japan in 1904 and 1905 resulted in severe economic and social disorders in the major Russian cities. Strikes mushroomed, and crowds milled through the capital of St. Petersburg, demanding affirmative action by the Czar.

On "Bloody Sunday," January 9, 1905, a great crowd of people swarmed to the Czar's Palace, believing that the "Little Father," as they still called him, would listen to their grievances. But the Czar's police fired into the crowd, killing and wounding many of the unarmed petitioners. The reaction was violent and disastrous for the Romanovs. A full-scale revolution began that day. The ground swell of discontent became the overpowering wave of the Russian Revolution.

"Bloody Sunday" was the signal for many of the radical exiles to come back to Russia, Lenin among them. They had high hopes of seizing power. Many workers' councils, or "soviets," sprang up throughout the European part of Russia. This first attempt at revolution was short-lived because the radicals lacked unity and effective power. In order to bring an end to strikes and protests, the Czar promised political reforms and consented to a weak but representative parliament, the *Duma*.

The first Duma convened in 1906. At first Lenin forbade his fellow Bolsheviks to play any role in this new organ of government, for which he had no use. The Mensheviks did participate in subsequent Dumas, hoping that their peaceful approach to socialism would gain acceptance. The radicals in Russia began to side with the Mensheviks, because they hoped that the Duma might bring parliamentary democracy and social reforms to Russia. The ranks of the revolutionary Bolsheviks began to shrink. The appeal of terror and revolution was fading. Lenin returned to exile in Switzerland, leaving only a few thousand hard-core Bolsheviks in Russia. Their cause appeared lost.

The Revolutions of 1917

The Russian Dumas might possibly have paved the way for governmental liberalization in Russia had it not been for World War I. Russia's entry into the war strengthened the power of Czar Nicholas II as the nation, together with France and Britain, opposed Germany and Austria-Hungary. Russia was not prepared for war. The army was poorly armed and was often led by inept officers. The economy was unable to support a war. In 1914 and 1915 conditions within Russia went from bad to worse, and the numerous defeats of the Russian armies at the front depressed national morale.

The Czar's court at the capital in Petrograd (the name was changed from St. Petersburg in 1914) became increasingly isolated. The influence of Rasputin, a corrupt mystic who virtually controlled the Empress while the Czar was at the front, aroused disgust and alarm even in the upper ranks of society. The fabric of Russian society began to come apart in 1916, and the revolutionaries found, at last, the path to power.

The March Revolution. Food shortages and low morale brought about strikes during the early part of March, 1917. The Duma urged the Czar to make concessions, but he refused. On March 12th, Petrograd was seized by workers, and the Duma appointed a provisional government. The abdication of the Czar on March 15th brought to an end over 300 years of rule by the Romanov dynasty. In July, 1918, eight months after the Bolshevik Revolution, Nicholas II and his family were executed by a small band of Bolsheviks.

In exile in Zurich, Switzerland, Lenin was thrilled with news of the March Revolution. But his burning desire to return to Russia and convert the "peoples'" revolution to the Bolshevik cause was frustrated. How could he travel through the enemy territory of Austria or Germany to reach his homeland? The German government, however, concocted an ingenious plan. Why not help Lenin get back to Russia, in order to undermine the provisional government and its ability and will to continue the war with Germany. The Germans therefore transported Lenin and his small band of exiles across Germany and on to Finland. From there, he took a train to Petrograd, arriving in the capital on April 16, 1917. Greeted by his loyal Bolshevik followers and other radicals, he cried: "Long live the International Social Revolution!" Lenin's battle cry of 1917 and the ideas behind it continue to challenge the world today.

The November Revolution. During the next six months, Lenin and his fellow Bolsheviks worked intensely to overthrow the Provisional Government. That Government had decided to continue the now unpopular war with Germany and to postpone major reforms in Russia until the dust settled. In July, 1917, it came under the leadership of Alexander Kerensky, a moderate, who sought desperately to ward off the Bolshevik threat. The simplicity of Lenin's appeal for *peace, bread,* and *land* brought increasing numbers flocking to the Bolshevik banner. Leon Trotsky and other close associates of Lenin pushed the leftist Bolshevik cause forward with fantastic zeal, while the Russian Army's General Kornilov sought to organize a right-wing military dictatorship. Kerensky, fighting these two extremes, progressively lost power. Finally, the carefully organized Bolshevik forces struck. On November 7th, they seized power in Petrograd. The Provisional Government and Kerensky were overthrown. Bolshevism, now renamed communism, came to power.

The Bolshevik Revolution of November (the "October" Revolution according to the pre-1918 Russian calendar) was immediately followed by a flurry of decrees handed down by Lenin's new government. Within a few months, private landholding was forbidden (land was now in the hands of the "people"), banks were nationalized, stern measures were taken against the Russian Church, and the Cheka or secret police was organized to "discourage opposition" to the new government. The Bolshevik Revolution dashed all hopes for the evolution of democracy when Lenin's soldiers forced Kerensky's new "Constituent Assembly" to disband in January, 1918. The dictatorship *over* the proletariat became a fact.

Foreign and Civil War, 1918-1920

Withdrawal from World War I. Lenin was committed to ending the war with Germany. He had no choice, for the German armies were moving steadily toward Petrograd. In Russia, the will to fight the "imperialist" war was gone. Leon Trotsky (1879-1940), Lenin's Commissar for Foreign Affairs, entered into negotiations with German military leaders and, after protracted talks, the Soviet government accepted humiliating peace terms. Under the Treaty of Brest-Litovsk of March, 1918, Russia gave up control of over one million square miles and 62 million people. Germany was now free to turn its armies in the East against those of the Allies to the West in France. Russia's exit from the war hardly endeared the new Communist government to the leaders of Britain, France, and the United States.

Civil war. War now had a new meaning in Russia. Lenin was confronted with a civil rebellion which was to continue for some three years. The White Army held large parts of European Russia and Siberia. The Red Army also met with widespread but unorganized resistance from among much of the peasantry and from among the non-Russian nationalities. Troops from thirteen Allied nations, including Britain and the United States, entered Russia and gave token assistance to the anti-Soviet side in the armed struggle. This token effort by the Allies in 1918 and 1919 has always been held up to the Russian people as clear evidence that the Western states used armed force to try to defeat communism and that they might do so again.

The Red Army, under Leon Trotsky, crushed the civil rebellion by 1920. Although the new Communist government was an outcast in world affairs, Lenin was master in his own house.

Lenin's Domestic and Foreign Policies

Compromise at home. The new "house of socialism," however, was in considerable disrepair. Civil war and muddled "socialist" policies and governmental decrees left economic chaos in their wake. Early experiments with government ownership of the means of production met with dismal failure.

In March, 1921, Lenin introduced a "New Economic Policy," or the NEP. This program restored private enterprise in agriculture and retail trade, while the government retained full control of industry, banking, and foreign trade. Almost all the cultivable land was placed in the hands of the peasants and they were free, after paying taxes, to use or sell whatever they could produce. Under this compromise with Socialist principles, production had been restored by 1927 to its 1913 level.

International failure. Lenin's expectations in world affairs were radically altered. In 1914, he was bitterly disappointed when workingmen chose to fight for their countries rather than rise up in revolution against their governments. After the Bolshevik Revolution, he had hoped that socialists in other states would follow Russia's lead and rise in revolution to produce more "dictatorships of the proletariat." Radical movements were on the march in some states. A short-lived Communist revolt terrified Berlin in January, 1919. The communist Béla Kun took power in Hungary in March, 1919, and maintained dictatorial rule until he was overthrown in July. But on the whole, Communist sympathizers met with little success in encouraging revolution in other states. The masses remained loyal to their respective nations. A "proletariat class consciousness," cutting across national boundaries, simply did not materialize.

Trotsky pushed hard for the new Soviet state to take leadership in spreading the revolution, but it became evident to Lenin that conditions in Europe were not ripe for such a radical course. Following Lenin's death in 1924, Stalin stripped Trotsky of political power. Lenin did manage to move the idea of "international communism" forward, with the organization of the Comintern or the "Third International" in 1919. The Comintern brought together in periodic congresses representatives of Communist parties of other states, and served as an agency through which the Kremlin line was to be transmitted to and applied by these parties. But it was clear to Lenin that Communist principles and ideology had to be consolidated in Russia before the global mission of communism could be pursued.

When Lenin died on January 21, 1924, the new Soviet state was in firm control of most of the former Russian Empire, but the major decisions about the shape and purpose of the new "socialist" society were still in the future.

Lenin's Contributions to Communism

Lenin was the mainspring of the Bolshevik Revolution and the author of Russian communism. His fierce ambition to promote the Communist cause led, at staggering costs, to the establishment of the first Communist state, the USSR (Union of Soviet Socialist Republics). How closely did Lenin conform to Marx's ideas? What did he contribute to Communist doctrine?

Importance of the Party. Lenin authored the idea of the Communist Party both in theory and action. His pamphlet, *What Is to Be Done?*, emphasized the Party as the agency which was needed to convert the Marxist theory of dialectical materialism into a program of action. He believed that an organized force was required to guide the dialectic in the desired direction. Serving as the spearhead of the Communist movement, the Party would command the strict adherence to Communist principles by those dedicated few who were its members. It would lead the rest in bringing about revolution and establishing the dictatorship of the proletariat.

Lenin had the support of only 23,000 Bolsheviks in April of 1917. This small core of followers multiplied to some 230,000 during the following six months in time to bring about the November Revolution. This indicates that the power of communism should never be calculated in terms of numbers of Party members. The small, fervent, indoctrinated group, taking advantage of political, economic, and social chaos, disseminating effective and deceitful propaganda, and promising great rewards for the future, characterizes Communist revolutionary activity today as well as in 1917. The Party is the key to power. From the small numbers of Bolsheviks in 1917, the forces of communism have moved steadily forward until today they control over one billion people.

The Party was all important to Lenin. It was the instrument of revolution and the supreme organ of state power in applying the dictatorship of the proletariat. All governing apparatus in the state was under Party control. In marching toward the international Communist empire, all Communist parties would follow the banner of the Communist Party of the Soviet Union. Much of the visionary side of Marx, therefore, flowed into concrete programs for action under Lenin's Communist Party. For Lenin, the Party became the mainspring of Communist action in the drive to crush capitalism, whereas for Marx, capitalism contained the seeds of its own destruction.

Communism through revolution. While hiding out in Finland during the summer of 1917, Lenin wrote a book titled *State and Revolution*. This short work is a testament to Lenin's profound hatred of democratic socialism. It is largely concerned with what happens to the state following a successful Communist revolution and seizure of power. In it, Lenin violently rejects the idea that the "capitalist state" can peacefully "wither away" in the march toward socialism. This is his answer to those who argued that the "withering away" concept of Marx and Engels meant that capitalism could *evolve slowly* into socialism instead of being destroyed through *revolution*. Lenin declares that only revolution can pave the way for socialism, and eventually communism, because only revolution can create a dictatorship of the proletariat. Communist leaders presumably wipe out all opposition and both force and educate the people to accept the Communist way of life. Revolution is thus fundamental to the advent of communism. According to Lenin, the socialist society described by Marx can be introduced in no other way.

Condemnation of capitalism. Lenin and other communists

place all opponents in the enemy camp. Here are to be found capitalists, all adherents to Western democracy, the democratic socialists, and many others. In his work *Imperialism: The Highest Stage of Capitalism,* written in 1916, Lenin lumps all opponents together as capitalists or lackeys of the capitalists. He views Western leaders, or "capitalist ruling circles," as exploiters of the downtrodden. The capitalist states, Lenin wrote, have dominated the non-Western parts of the world and thus clash with each other in their quest for domination. This march toward imperialism produced World War I, he added, and thus represented the highest and final stage of capitalism. Capitalist states make war inevitable, because they must fight each other in order to gain markets and raw materials. In so doing, they create chaos and disorder. This is to the advantage of the communists, however, because they can step in and seize power in the midst of the ruins produced by greedy capitalists and war.

War certainly made the Bolshevik rise to power possible in Russia in 1917, and the same might be said about the Communist victory in China by 1949. Communists have traditionally predicted and welcomed the scourge of war because the resulting impoverishment and instability produce conditions which they can exploit to their advantage. But the main lesson which emerges from Lenin's *Imperialism* is that the communists thrive on a lack of unity among those who oppose them. Lenin is correct when he notes that great opportunities exist for the Communist movement when the capitalist (democratic) states disagree among themselves.

Lenin molded the Communist Party out of the early Bolsheviks, enabled it to survive, and led it to power. He is viewed by today's communists as the messiah of the ideology. His influence in furthering the Communist ideology as a way of life and way of governing surpasses all others, with the possible exception of Marx. He advanced the *myth* of Marx's dialectical materialism by leading the Bolsheviks to revolution in Russia. He held out the *promise* of the classless society but could not deliver it. Khrushchev still dangles this promise of the ideology before today's communists.

4. How Did Stalin Consolidate Communist Totalitarianism?

Between Lenin's death in 1924 and Khrushchev's rise to the chairmanship of the Communist Party in 1953, the twenty-nine years of Josef Stalin's dictatorship overshadowed the Russian people.

Stalin's March to Power

Stalin (Josef Vissarionovich Djugashvili, 1889-1953) was born in Georgia, a Soviet republic south of the Caucasus Mountains. He became interested in Marxism while studying for the priesthood, and after joining the Social Democratic movement, fought intensely for the cause of a Russian revolution. This was followed by a long exile in northern Siberia. After the March, 1917, revolution, Stalin returned to Petrograd and plunged into Bolshevik efforts to overthrow the government. He was a member of the first Politburo, the highest organ of the Communist Party, after the November revolution, and became General Secretary of the Communist Party in 1922.

In 1922 Lenin was dying, and knew it. As he saw the reins of power slipping from his hands, he became alarmed at the ruthless way in which his associate, Stalin, was building up his personal control over the Communist Party. One of Lenin's last acts was to send his colleagues a written warning against Stalin's ambitions to establish a personal dictatorship. Stalin discovered this last "testament" of Lenin's and put an immediate halt to its circulation. Its full contents were not revealed to Soviet citizens until Khrushchev delivered his monumental indictment of Stalin in February, 1956.

Upon Lenin's death in 1924 Stalin, joined by two other Communist leaders, Kamenev and Zinoviev, assumed power in the Soviet Union. Stalin continually but deceitfully presented himself as Lenin's chosen heir. By playing different groups of leaders against each other, he rapidly built up his own party machine and eventually removed, suppressed, or killed those who opposed him. Kamenev and Zinoviev were fired in 1927, although Kamenev later resumed close relations with Stalin. Both of these two associates of Stalin were executed in 1936 for plots against the dictator. Stalin gradually eased Trotsky from power, forced him out of the Party, and exiled the veteran communist from the Soviet Union in 1929. Trotsky finally found refuge in Mexico, where he was murdered in 1940 under orders from Stalin. By 1928, Stalin held complete power over the Party, and therefore over the Soviet state.

Five-Year Planning Launched

Stalin abruptly ended the New Economic Policy, and in 1928 launched the first of the famous "Five-Year Plans," an economic blueprint for production, distribution, and even consumption. The first Plan was ambitious in its promotion of heavy industry. It also subjected millions of peasant families to the regimented system of the new collective farms. The better-off farmer class, the Kulaks, opposed the introduction of the state-organized communal rural settlements. Because of this, millions of these farmers were exterminated or deported. What idealism there was in communism became submerged in Stalin's insatiable quest for total power.

Under Stalin's close direction, a constitution for the USSR was put into effect in 1936. This "Stalin Constitution" provided for a government with a democratic front, but all of the organs of government are, in reality, totally subservient to the dictates of the Communist Party and its self-appointed top leadership.

Stalin Defines His Dictatorship

The effective functioning of the "dictatorship of the proletariat" calls for annihilating all enemies within and making progress toward dominating other states on the outside. Stalin continued to find many who opposed his policies within the USSR. Between 1934 and 1939, his henchmen executed many thousands of government officials and army officers, including more than half of Lenin's Bolshevik Central Executive Committee of 1917. These purges vastly reinforced Stalin's personal domination of Russia.

Stalin's power was now supreme. Was it not time, therefore, to permit the dictatorship of the proletariat to "wither away" and bring forward the classless society?

In a famous letter to "Comrade Ivanov" on February 2, 1938, Stalin said that the "bourgeoisie" have been liquidated within the Soviet Union, and that "Socialism has already been built in essence. We call this the victory of Socialism or, to be more exact, the victory of socialist construction in one country." But, Stalin added, the external threat of the capitalists remains.

> . . . since we live not on an island but in a system of states, a considerable number of which are hostile to the country of Socialism (the USSR), thus creating the danger of intervention and restoration, we say openly and honestly that the victory of Socialism in our country is not yet complete.[1]

Stalin pointed out that the dictatorship of the proletariat cannot "wither away" until the capitalist encirclement is overcome. To bring this about, Stalin told Comrade Ivanov that

> . . . it is necessary to strengthen and consolidate the international proletarian ties between the working class of the USSR and the working class of the bourgeois countries.[2]

Socialism was victorious now in the vanguard nation, the Soviet Union, Stalin claimed. If Communist parties in other states follow the Soviet Union's lead, the "capitalist encirclement" will be broken, the "dictatorship" can then "wither away," and all can march toward the classless society. This is why Stalin demanded strict obedience by Communist parties in other countries. They must, he asserted, make the defense of the Soviet Union their main purpose. They must accept the Soviet "line," work to overthrow their own governments, and identify themselves thoroughly with Soviet leadership and policies. This is why a member of a Communist party anywhere cannot be loyal to his own state.

[1] *The Strategy and Tactics of World Communism*, Committee on Foreign Affairs, 80th Congress, House Document No. 619, Sup. I. Washington, D.C.: Government Printing Office, 1948, p. 151.

[2] *Ibid.*, pp. 151, 152.

World War II

Russia's stand. Others were pursuing goals of world domination in the late 1930's. The power of Nazi Germany was felt throughout Europe, and Stalin realized he now had to make some compromise with the non-Communist states. After carrying on prolonged negotiations with Germany and also with France and Britain, he signed a non-aggression pact with Nazi Germany on August 24, 1939. Shortly after the outbreak of World War II on September 1, 1939, the USSR annexed 40 percent of Poland. Later, after the bitter "Winter War," Stalin also annexed an important part of Finland's territory and seized Latvia, Estonia, and Lithuania. On June 22, 1941, the Nazis launched their own attack against the Soviet Union. Hitler's troops entered the suburbs of Moscow in December, 1941. Russia was now associated with Britain and, after the Japanese attack on Pearl Harbor, with the United States in the fight against Germany. The immediate defense of the Soviet state became more important than the longer term ideological goal of expansion and domination.

Massive material aid from the United States began to arrive in Russia, greatly strengthening the Soviet capacity to withstand the might of Hitler's armies. Russia's great victory at Stalingrad was followed by Soviet counteroffensives during 1943. The revived Red Army forced the Germans to retreat from Russian soil.

Communist take-over in Eastern Europe. Rushing across Eastern Europe in 1944 and early 1945, the USSR imposed Communist-dominated regimes on the Eastern European states, in spite of many promises which Stalin had made to the contrary. From 1945 to 1948, these Communist governments, upheld by the power of the Red Army, assumed control in this entire area and labelled themselves "Peoples' Republics." Yugoslavia was the only Eastern European state which broke away from Stalin's grasp. After splitting with the Soviet Union in June, 1948, Yugoslavia developed a Communist system of its own, independent of Moscow control.

Stalin Resumes the Cold War

As an ally of the Western states during World War II, the USSR conveniently disbanded the Comintern (1943) and promised an ending of all revolutionary aspects of the Communist movement. The West tended to believe Stalin's assurances of future good will and consequently was unprepared for the resumption of his hostility to the West. Thus the "cold war," which rose to the fore in 1945 and 1946, was only a revival of the deep tensions which had existed before.

The unwillingness of the Soviet Union to relax its control of Eastern Europe, its open support of Communist parties in all other states, its constant maneuvers to undermine the effective functioning of the United Nations, and its refusal to reach any agreement on peace treaties for Germany and Austria all led to the West's taking affirmative measures to meet the Communist threat. In 1947, these events launched the challenge and response between the Western and Communist blocs which have dominated world affairs since that time. Stalin was the driving force of the hostility toward the West. During his reign, communism seized power in China and marched to aggression in Korea in 1950. The dictatorship in Russia tightened each year and had reached extreme heights when Stalin died on March 5, 1953.

Importance of Stalin

The supreme instrument of Stalin's rule was his complete dictatorship. Through his firm controls of the Party and therefore of the government, and through bringing the entire economy under Party-state control, he constructed a massive apparatus of rule. The dictatorship over the proletariat, rather than withering away, dominated all life within the USSR.

Stalin advanced communism in the world by speeding up the growth of Communist parties in other states and by compelling them to follow the policies of the Soviet Union. He held to Lenin's decisive idea that a clash would take place sooner or later between the Communist and Western blocs of states and that the forces of communism would emerge as the victors. Shortly before he died, however, he began to develop another approach by declaring that tension and possibly warfare among the non-Communist states would offer new opportunities for communism to seize power.

At the 19th Congress of the Communist Party in October, 1952, he confirmed the doctrine which Lenin had set forth in *Imperialism: The Highest Stage of Capitalism*. Stalin felt that new policies might be pursued by the Soviet Union in trying to eliminate the "capitalist encirclement." The regime of Khrushchev has acted on this suggestion.

5. How Has Khrushchev Redefined Communism?

Kremlin Intrigue After Stalin's Death

A dictator cannot bequeath his power. In the totalitarian state, politics is a process of constant struggle, especially at the highest levels. At the time of Stalin's fatal stroke, at least a half dozen Soviet leaders, all veteran communists, were possible contenders for power. Vyacheslav Molotov (1890-   ) was one of the few left who had played a key role in the November, 1917, revolution. A devoted follower of Stalin, he had been Premier of the Soviet government from 1930 to 1941, and Foreign Minister from 1939 to 1949. Lavrenti Beria (1899?-1953) was head of the Secret Police (the MVD) and thus in a good position to rise to the heights of power. There were two Party warhorses, Nikolai Bulganin and Anastas Mikoyan, and the younger Georgi Malenkov was Stalin's principal henchman in Party affairs. Finally, there was Nikita Khrushchev (1894-   ), who was quite close to Stalin and was then serving as the Secretary of the Moscow Committee of the Communist Party.

The struggles for power at the top of the Soviet pyramid can be vicious and violent. There was a mutual agreement among Communist leaders in March, 1953, that leadership should be exercised in a collective manner. Although Malenkov was named Premier and First Secretary of the Party, the real struggle for power took place behind the scenes. Beria was assassinated in July after an unsuccessful bid for power. By the fall and winter of 1953, the pieces began to fall into place when Khrushchev took over as First Secretary (September 7, 1953). By a clever manipulation of the strings of control, Khrushchev eased Malenkov out of his position as Premier by February, 1955, and replaced him with Bulganin. During the next three years, Khrushchev proceeded to consolidate his position thoroughly as head of the Party and the government.

Khrushchev Rises to Power

Born in Central Russia of a poor family, Nikita Khrushchev received little formal education as a young man. He fought for the Communist cause in the civil war, and then devoted all of his energies toward advancing Party activity in Moscow and the Ukraine. Slowly but surely, Khrushchev climbed the ladder of Party power during the next few decades, always giving strong support to the dictatorial policies and purges of Stalin and carrying them out with great zeal. Although he ripped the memory of Stalin apart in 1956, Khrushchev declared in 1937 that:

> Stalin is hope, he is expectation, he is the beacon that guides all advanced and progressive mankind. Stalin is our banner! Stalin is our will! Stalin is our victory![1]

Khrushchev became a member of the Party's highest organ, the Politburo, in 1939. He is now credited with playing a key role in the epic battle at Stalingrad in 1942, although earlier Soviet versions of this crucial period omit reference to Khrushchev's "valor" and "heroism." (History is constantly rewritten in the USSR to highlight the "previous" achievements of current Russian leaders and to destroy the image of those who have fallen from glory.) Following the war, Khrushchev's star continued to rise as a loyal follower of Stalin.

Trials and Tribulations of the New First Secretary

Deviation from his predecessors. As the new First Secretary

[1] © 1961 by Pocket Books, Inc. Reprinted by permission of Pocket Books, Inc. From *Conquest Without War*, edited by N. H. Mager and Jacques Katel; a Trident Press Book, p. 27.

of the Party, Khrushchev began to develop some ideas which differed considerably from Stalin's inflexible views. Khrushchev felt the need for coming to terms with Marshal Tito in Yugoslavia, whose brand of "national communism" Stalin had violently condemned. He began to disagree with the Stalinist idea that the world was divided into only two blocs of states, the Communist group led by the Soviet Union and the "capitalist" bloc with the United States as its principal member. Stalin believed that a clash between the two was inevitable, and that even if World War III were the result, the Soviet Union would still emerge victorious. Khrushchev began to realize that a third World War, one in which weapons of mass annihilation would be used, would bring destruction to all. Thus Khrushchev slowly veered away from the "inevitable conflict" idea of Lenin and Stalin, and started to press for other means to advance the cause of communism. In particular, he has advocated "peaceful coexistence" with the Western states as a more or less prolonged period of competition for supremacy.

Khrushchev developed further Stalin's concept, reaffirmed in 1952, that the rising third bloc of states, the new neutralist nations in Africa and Asia, should be the prime targets for Communist expansion. He urged that more emphasis be placed on aid, trade, and cultural offensives in these states in order to tie them closely to Soviet policy and eventually to help Communist movements to seize power. The aim of communism was to remain the same, but the means and stages to this end would vary considerably from Stalin's idea of "final and decisive conflict."

Khrushchev did not reveal these emerging ideas immediately. But the pattern gradually became clear as he sought to put them into practice. Because some in the Kremlin, such as Molotov, could not tolerate any deviation from Stalin's views, a sharp struggle among the key Communist leaders took place between 1955 and 1957, ending in victory for Khrushchev.

Attack on Stalin's image. The First Secretary visited Yugoslavia in 1955 in an obvious attempt to bring about a reconciliation with Marshal Tito. He tried to draw Tito back into the Communist fold led by the Soviet Union. This act raised the eyebrows of the old Stalinists in the Kremlin, especially when Khrushchev suggested that Stalin had been responsible for this split in the Communist camp. Likewise, Khrushchev and Bulganin met with Western leaders, including President Eisenhower and Prime Minister Eden, in July, 1955, the first such session of world leaders since the Potsdam Conference ten years earlier. Then, in a long speech at the Twentieth Congress of the Communist Party of the Soviet Union on February 25, 1956, Khrushchev delivered a violent attack on Stalin.

This secret speech against the "cult of the individual" tore into the core of Stalin's years of leadership. Khrushchev claimed that Stalin's policies of self-glorification were "alien to Marxism and Leninism and not consonant with the principles of Party leadership and the norms of Party life." In this address, Khrushchev ripped apart the "excesses" of Stalin's rule as he sought support for his own ideas on communism.

Challenge and response. News of this remarkable tirade gradually leaked out. Some Stalinists in Russia and elsewhere began to quake, while some other communists were furious with Khrushchev for "dethroning" Stalin. Most of the people in Eastern Europe who were living under Stalinist leaders began to feel a breath of fresh air. If Khrushchev could get along with the "national communism" of Tito's Yugoslavia and if the Soviet leader violently condemned some elements of Stalinism, why couldn't others in Eastern Europe seek somewhat looser ties with the USSR?

These questions flowed into action. Nationalistic uprisings in Poland in June and October of 1956 were followed by the revolution in Hungary, starting on October 23, 1956. After some resistance, Khrushchev reconciled himself with the Polish demand for additional freedoms. But the Kremlin leader felt that he could not tolerate any further challenges to Soviet control of Eastern Europe. Soviet tanks poured into Budapest on November 4, 1956, and crushed Hungary's effort to establish an independent government in a Soviet satellite.

During the latter part of 1956 and early 1957, Khrushchev sought to gain support for his "de-Stalinization" policies. He toned down the idea that an armed clash with the Western states was inevitable, and he devoted considerable attention to winning friends and influencing peoples in the Afro-Asian world. All of these acts prompted the devoted followers of Stalin in the Kremlin, led by Molotov, to an attempt to drive Khrushchev from power. At a meeting of the Party Presidium (the old Politburo) in June, 1957, Khrushchev was voted out of the Presidium. He insisted, however, that the larger Central Committee of the Party must approve this action. Calling to his side the power of the army led by Marshal Zhukov (whom he later purged), Khrushchev managed to muster overwhelming support in the Central Committee to defeat the designs of Molotov, Malenkov, the old Bolshevik Kaganovich, and others who were lined up against him. He cast these men from Party power and placed them in positions where they would be unable to thwart his anti-Stalinist policies. From that point on, Khrushchev advanced to new heights of power and assumed the Premiership of the Soviet government in 1958.

Since that time, Khrushchev has proceeded against the Stalinist interpretation of the Communist ideology voiced by the Communist leader of China, Mao Tse-tung. At the Twenty-second Soviet Party Congress in October, 1961, Khrushchev gained unanimous acceptance of a new Program of the Communist Party of the Soviet Union, the first such broad program set forth by the Party since 1918. The new Program calls "for the building of a Communist society." Khrushchev declared that socialism has now been firmly established in the Soviet Union, and the continuous march toward communism, to be led by the Soviet Union, lies ahead.

> The supreme goal of the Party is to build a communist society on whose banner will be inscribed: From each according to his ability, to each according to his needs.[1]

Today Khrushchev, as Premier of the Soviet Government and First Secretary of the Communist Party of the USSR, presides over the destinies of 225,000,000 people and directs the activities of slightly more than 10,000,000 Communist Party members in his nation. The Soviet leaders claim that there are 88 Communist groups in the world, with over 41,000,000 members. The split between Soviet communism and the communism

---

[1] Herbert Ritvo, *The New Soviet Society*. New York: The New Leader, 1962, p. 23.

preached and practiced by the leaders in China raises questions as to whom communists in the world owe loyalty. But all strive toward the same goal, world domination.

Mao Tse-tung and some other communists have made important contributions to the evolution of the ideology. But the basic structure of communism provided by *Marx*, the Communist Party and the November, 1917, revolution brought about by *Lenin*, the strengthening of the Soviet state at tremendous human costs by *Stalin*, and the revisions in theory and practice produced by *Khrushchev* all add up to international communism as we know it today.

Summary

The history of the past hundred years has proved that the predictions of Marx about class conflict and the inevitable revolution were wrong. Lenin did bring about a dictatorship, but it is one *over* the proletariat and not *of* the proletariat. Stalin intensified this dictatorship rather than permitting it to "wither away." Khrushchev has tried to reconcile communism with the tremendous flaws which have appeared in its theory, but he is convinced of the inevitable triumph of Communist ideas in the end.

In Russia, the Party is in complete power. This domination is grounded in the belief that Communist leaders have the keys to power in their access to and interpretation of the *myth* of the "scientific truths of Marxism-Leninism." The *promise* is set forth in the Party's motto, "Everything for the sake of man, for the benefit of man." In truth, this totalitarian ideology seeks to dominate man everywhere and to destroy all vestiges of the genuine liberties of mankind. And yet, communism has marched steadily forward since its initial victory in Russia in 1917. At that time, there were slightly over 200,000 Bolsheviks. Today, the forces of communism control well over one billion people on the face of the earth. Communists everywhere are convinced that the "inevitable triumph" of the "proletariat" over all is a certainty. They may be right, unless non-communists everywhere redouble their efforts to prevent the further spread of this international conspiracy against the dignity and freedom of man.

Communist Ideology and Soviet National Policy

"Practice gropes in the dark unless revolutionary theory throws a light on the path,"[1] said Stalin in a lecture at Sverdlov University in 1924. Khrushchev, in spite of his severe criticisms of the dictator who ruled Russia for almost thirty years, would no doubt agree with him on this score.

Practice and theory, policy and ideology, are closely intertwined in communism. The theory of revolutionary communism lies behind all major facets of Soviet policy.

All states, the Soviet Union included, seek security and well-being at home and abroad for their national interests, although states differ in defining "security and well-being." "Security and well-being" for the USSR is a Communist world. This is the *goal*. The *means* used by the government in the Kremlin to advance toward this goal reveal Communist theory in action.

1. How Is Soviet Policy Made?

Russian national history and the enduring qualities of the Russian national character are vital roots of Soviet national policy. From the mid-fifteenth century, the Russian state expanded its rule from its center in Moscow. Under Peter the

[1] *Strategy and Tactics, op. cit.*, p. 5.

Great at the end of the seventeenth century and Catherine the Great in the eighteenth, Russia moved into an imperialistic stage. The expansive tendencies of the Czars were generally held in check by England. During the past two centuries, Russia aspired toward the control of Eastern Europe, the traditional path of aggression upon Russia from the West. The Czars sought warm-water ports and supremacy in the Turkish Straits area, which would give them an outlet to the Mediterranean. Russia exerted its power in Asia as well, and pressed on into Manchuria late in the nineteenth century. Much of the Soviet imperialism we see today has its parallels in the expansionist foreign policies of the Czars.

The Russian people, as we have seen, were not exposed to the humanizing forces of the Western Renaissance and the doctrines of the inherent rights of man. The liberating influences which did so much to mold democracy as a way of life and governing in the West never penetrated the closed society of Russia. The Russian people have always been accustomed to strong government. They have traditionally been suspicious of the foreigner and have feared invasion from without. The authoritarian system as a way of life and governing has deep roots in Russian history. Communism alone does not explain why Russians act like Russians.

The Goal of National Policy

In domestic affairs. The goal of Soviet national policy is to fulfill the *promise* of communism — the classless society. The Soviet Union considers itself the spearhead of the movement to bring the promise to all men and nations. The aims of Soviet national policy and communism are, therefore, identical. Although the "classless society," on a national or international level, is an idealistic, utopian goal, the realistic threat by the forces of communism is a very concrete one.

Khrushchev claims that *domestic policies* within his nation have brought about socialism and that the USSR is now marching toward the goal of communism. His Party Program, adopted by the Twenty-second Congress in 1961, concludes with this declaration:

Under the tried and tested leadership of the Communist Party, under the banner of Marxism-Leninism, the Soviet people have built socialism. Under the leadership of the Party, under the banner of Marxism-Leninism, the Soviet people will build the Communist society.[1]

The Program describes how "socialism" has been implanted in the Soviet Union, although this brand of socialism is a far cry from the "democratic socialism" advocated by the socialist parties in the Western democracies. The Program also sets forth the idealistic goals of a "classless society," although little is said about the "withering away" of the state. Khrushchev explains this away by doing what all of his predecessors have done, by making revisions or new interpretations of the writings of Marx and Lenin. Whoever holds power in the Kremlin also possesses the keys to the ideological myth of communism. Mao Tse-tung of China, however, claims *he* has a few keys as well!

In foreign affairs. The goal with respect to the *policies* of the Soviet Union is to promote the triumph of communism in all states, by any and all means. Khrushchev leaves no doubt as to the identity between the goals of Soviet foreign policy and those of communism. He declares that:

> We live at a time when new millions upon millions of people are coming under the great banner of Marxism-Leninism. Marxism-Leninism is our main weapon. We will conquer the capitalist world by using this mighty ideological weapon and not the hydrogen bomb.[2]

Furthermore, he seems to be in a hurry. "In the short time I still have to live, I would like to see the day when the communist flag flies over the whole world."[3]

Promotion of security and well-being. Most states are fairly secure if they are not confronted by a threat of imminent invasion from other states. This is not enough for the Soviet Union. Internal security means the eradication of all elements opposing communism within the Soviet Union, and Khrushchev feels, on

[1] Ritvo, *op. cit.*, p. 251.

[2] Mager and Katel, *op. cit.*, p. 51.

[3] *Ibid.*, p. 97.

the whole, that this objective has been reached. External security means eliminating the democratic (or "capitalist") governments and bringing all nations under the Communist banner.

The external security goal can be clarified if we remember that Lenin and Stalin viewed the world as divided into two blocs of states — the communists and the "capitalists." The aims of Communist ideology and Soviet foreign policy, therefore, were to crush the bourgeois bloc, release the peoples now under the "control" of the capitalistic ruling circles, and proceed toward the classless society. Lenin declared in 1919 that:

> We are living not merely in a state but in a system of states and the existence of the Soviet Republic side by side with the imperialist states for a long time is unthinkable. One or the other must triumph in the end. And before that end supervenes, a series of frightful collisions between the Soviet Republics and the bourgeois states will be inevitable.[1]

Lenin left no doubt that, in his view, the proletariat bloc would emerge supreme from this violent struggle, a position obviously in conformity with the conviction of all communists that history is on their side.

However, Khrushchev recognizes a *third* bloc of states in world affairs. These are the new states in Africa and Asia. Today, this area of the world is a key target in the Communist design for domination.

To communists, people can enjoy well-being or a full and meaningful life only when all "exploitation" has come to a halt. Class warfare can end only with the classless society in which no exploitation can deprive a person of the fruits of his labor. This is a myth, because it ignores so much about the nature of human exploitation, especially as found in Communist states. But its very simplicity has force to those who have known nothing but abject poverty and oppression.

The ideology of Marx and Lenin, communists claim, is the sole route to the classless society and well-being for all. Khrushchev declares that the peoples of the Soviet Union are well on the way toward this goal, although those who enjoy genuine freedom would strongly dispute this claim. The fact remains

[1] *Strategy and Tactics, op. cit.,* p. 19.

that the Communist goal of well-being for all will be realized only with a world Communist empire. The well-being of communism is only another way of saying totalitarianism.

Function of the Governing Process

Perhaps the most important aspect of the Soviet governing process is the fact that each twist and turn in the making of national policies is guided by the dictates of the Communist Party, or rather by its self-appointed top leadership. Compare this governing process with that shown in the diagram on page 24.

The people. The Russian and other Soviet peoples play a very small role in the governing process. They must give at least surface evidence of supporting the government and the Party, and probably the majority of Soviet citizens really do believe in the myth and promise of Communist ideology. Those who do not have learned to keep their sentiments to themselves. The Russian people are accustomed to stern governmental control. Thus many may find a totalitarian way of life hardly unusual or burdensome. The thought-control imposed upon them by Soviet rulers prevents their giving much consideration to other ways of life. With few exceptions, anyone in Russia over eighteen years old has the right to vote; but there is only one slate of candidates for which to vote, that submitted by the Communist Party. The purpose of official propaganda is to make the people accept, if not like, the policies conducted on their behalf.

Political parties. Politics in the Soviet Union are naturally Communist politics. There is only one party, although in some Communist states the Communist Party may go under other names, such as the Romanian Workers' Party or the East German Socialist Unity Party.

The government. The government of the Soviet Union, as we have seen, is defined in the Stalin Constitution of 1936. The structure of the government starts at the bottom with local "soviets" or councils and works up to district soviets, regional soviets, and to the Supreme Soviet of each of the fifteen Russian "Republics." These, in turn, lead to the Supreme Soviet of the USSR, or the principal governing organ (see diagram, page

THE SOVIET UNION'S INTERLOCKING LEADERSHIP*

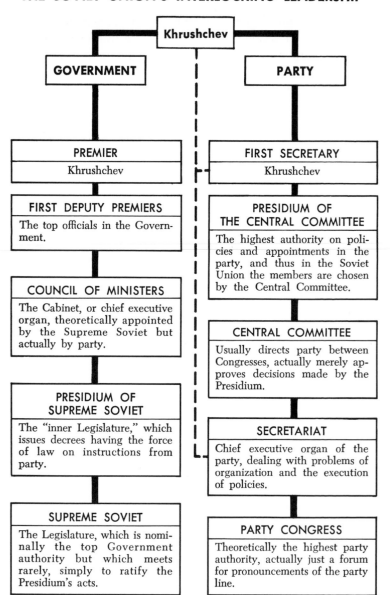

Khrushchev

GOVERNMENT | **PARTY**

PREMIER
Khrushchev

FIRST DEPUTY PREMIERS
The top officials in the Government.

COUNCIL OF MINISTERS
The Cabinet, or chief executive organ, theoretically appointed by the Supreme Soviet but actually by party.

PRESIDIUM OF SUPREME SOVIET
The "inner Legislature," which issues decrees having the force of law on instructions from party.

SUPREME SOVIET
The Legislature, which is nominally the top Government authority but which meets rarely, simply to ratify the Presidium's acts.

FIRST SECRETARY
Khrushchev

PRESIDIUM OF THE CENTRAL COMMITTEE
The highest authority on policies and appointments in the party, and thus in the Soviet Union the members are chosen by the Central Committee.

CENTRAL COMMITTEE
Usually directs party between Congresses, actually merely approves decisions made by the Presidium.

SECRETARIAT
Chief executive organ of the party, dealing with problems of organization and the execution of policies.

PARTY CONGRESS
Theoretically the highest party authority, actually just a forum for pronouncements of the party line.

*THE NEW YORK TIMES, May 12, 1963.

100). The Supreme Soviet is divided into two parts or "houses," the Soviet of the Union and the Soviet of Nationalities. The "steering committee" of the Supreme Soviet is the Presidium, headed by a Chairman who is considered the "Chief of State" of the Soviet Union. The Supreme Soviet also has a Council of Ministers. The head of the Soviet government, the Premier, is the Chairman of the Council of Ministers.

The main function of this government apparatus is to give rubber-stamp approval to policies devised by the Communist Party leaders and to apply these policies at home and abroad. Although the Party dictates the substance of policy, the Supreme Soviet does meet briefly to discuss the policies put before it for approval. The members of the Council of Ministers have wide authority in managing their departments and in carrying out orders but practically no authority in determining the policy which guides them.

Government officials. The rulers or government officials at the top are key members of the Communist Party. Thus they can hardly object to Party control in the performance of their governmental functions in this interlocking governing system.

National policy. The product of the governing process, Soviet national policy, seeks to further the doctrines of communism as originated by Marx, refined by Lenin, consolidated in Soviet power by Stalin, and reinterpreted by Khrushchev. It consists of orders, directives, laws, and processes devised by the high echelons of the Party and poured through the official machinery of government. Convictions about the myths and promises of communism are driven into the minds of the Russian peoples by policies within the USSR. The foreign-policy goal of Soviet national policy is to gain world domination in order that the Communist version of security and well-being may be achieved. In every respect, this all adds up to totalitarianism.

Role of the Communist Party in Policy-Making

This brief view of the governing process of the Soviet Union tells us little about how Russia actually is ruled. The real power, of course, lies within the framework of the Communist Party of the USSR. Those at the top of the Party pyramid direct the affairs of the Party and the government. The Party's primary units or cells, located at the base of the organization, may have only a few or, in some cases, hundreds of members. These cells are scattered throughout the Soviet Union and carry out Party orders at the grass-roots level. They also send delegates to higher Party organs at the district, regional, and republic levels, and finally to the All-Union Party Congress. Delegates are elected to higher positions through outwardly secret ballots, although the real selection is determined at the top.

The All-Union Party Congress has convened twenty-two times since 1918, and at its most recent meeting (1961), 4,799 delegates were in attendance, each one representing about 2,000 Party members. Between sessions of the Congress, the Central Committe of the Party conducts Party affairs. The Central Committee has 175 regular members and 155 alternate or non-voting members. The Committee, in theory, chooses the Presidium of the Party which, in theory, selects a First Secretary. In fact, the First Secretary dominates the 10-man Presidium. The Presidium selects the Central Committee. In rare instances, the Committee can play a vital role in Party affairs, as its support of Khrushchev in June, 1957, indicates (see page 92). The Secretariat of the Party or the "office force" is another high Party organ.

Although there are approximately 225 million people in the Soviet Union, only slightly over 10,000,000 of them belong to the Communist Party. Millions more are in deep sympathy with the theory and practice of communism. However, they simply do not want to accept all the obligations of Party membership. It is by no means an easy matter to become a member, and once a person enters the Party's ranks, his duties are numerous, and his dedication to Party leadership must be unquestionable. On the other hand, Party membership is a great honor, a real status symbol. Party members receive many benefits, such as first-class housing and transportation. The Party, in accordance with Lenin's principles set forth in *What Is to Be Done?*, is comparatively small and select; its members are highly dedicated to their cause.

The vast majority of high *government* officials are members of the Party Presidium or the Central Committee. It is interesting to note that about one fourth of the Supreme Soviet of the government are *not* Party members, although in principle and inclination they fully support the Party. This honor is bestowed on a Soviet citizen by the Party as a reward for some significant achievement. An outstanding performance on the assembly line, in the army, or in running a school may lead to a seat in the Supreme Soviet.

At the highest levels, in the Party Presidium and on down to the Central Committee, issues and proposed policies are discussed at length, and then when agreement is gained, a unanimous decision is announced. Outsiders know nothing about official deliberations by the heads of the government. Without doubt, much debate takes place, especially within the Presidium. But no minority position is revealed to the public except through later Party purges. When a decision is announced, it represents unanimity — or "democratic centralism."

2. What Means Are Used to Further Soviet Policy?

As we have seen, the Communist Party shapes Soviet national policy, which is the spearhead of world communism. Communist China disagrees with this view on two counts. Communist leaders in China dispute the Russian *claim* of leadership over the international Communist movement as well as the kinds of policy which the USSR employs in world affairs to advance the Communist ideology. Mao Tse-tung does not consider the Chinese Communist Party to be subordinate to the Soviet Union. He also insists on taking a "hard" line with all non-Communist states in opposition to Khrushchev's policy of peaceful coexistence. Soviet foreign policy is beamed at the gigantic stage of world politics and at the furtherance of communism within each separate state.

Use of Communist Slogans

The Soviet Union has set itself up as the champion of the common man. One definite keynote of Soviet foreign policy is its attempt to identify its action in world affairs with things all people want. The USSR constantly declares that communism will bring peace, prosperity, and progress for all peoples, that it holds out only good will for all men, and that its goals in world affairs are in harmony with the goals of the masses of people in each state. It is only the dastardly "ruling circles" in non-Communist states who oppose the will of the common man, according to the Kremlin rulers. The USSR manipulates the symbols of peace, progress, and prosperity and, through well-organized propaganda techniques, persuades many to follow the Soviet pied piper.

Peace to the Soviet Union, however, can exist only when there are no class contradictions, and this means only when the bourgeois capitalist states have finally been eliminated. In the Communist view, a constant state of cold or hot war must exist between the two blocs until the classless society triumphs.

Progress consequently means any progressive action toward the goals of Communist domination. Progress is, of course, important to everyone. But the Communist version of progress actually adds up to an undermining of the most basic values of human beings — their dignity, their faith, and their freedom. It is "progress" toward complete regimentation.

Prosperity is something else we all want, and naturally the Soviet Union claims that its policies are guaranteed to deliver prosperity to all peoples. But Communist ideology tells us that prosperity can only be found in a "classless society." As long as there are non-Communist states in existence, the dictatorship of the proletariat must continue. In reality, the Communist idea of prosperity is thus equated with a continuation of totalitarianism.

Communism supports the "masses" and claims that the masses are always held down by "ruling circles" and "imperialist warmongers" in those states where communism does not prevail. The "ruling circles" are the exploiters. They, according to Communist ideology, are Wall Street, the De Gaulles, and the Erhards. Thus the masses must rise up and rid themselves of these exploiters and move on to the classless society. Apparently, the communists really believe that their efforts, policies, and propaganda eventually will persuade Mr. Common Man everywhere that only communism can rid the world of exploitation, oppression, poverty, and war.

Premier Khrushchev declared in an address to the Supreme Soviet of the USSR on December 12, 1962, that:

Mankind wants to build its future not on rubble, not on smoldering ruins, but on the material foundation already created by the work of many generations. . . . This is why we address the peoples with the call to intensify their actions in defense of peace, to step up the struggle against imperialist warmongers. The peoples are a great force in the struggle for peace; they can and must say their decisive word.[1]

And thus the myth and promise of Communist ideology make their bid for the minds of men.

Application of Varied Strategies

The alternating currents of world affairs demand different strategies of policy for any nation. *Strategy* is the application of an ideology to the broad world situation. The strategy of a state's foreign policies in world affairs is an attempt to accommodate the security and well-being of the state with current trends in world politics. The Soviet Union is no exception. For purposes of guile and subversion, the USSR generally seeks to identify its policy with things desirable to most men. Nevertheless, its foreign policies have had to fluctuate over the years in order to further the security and well-being of the Soviet state and world communism. The many shifts in the strategy of Soviet foreign policy over the years, particularly during the Khrushchev regime, are only accommodations which the USSR must make with the facts of international life. But the Communist goal remains constant — domination. We can detect six broad periods of Soviet strategy in world affairs.

In the past. There were five periods of strategy between the triumph of communism in Russia and the period that began after Stalin's death.

1. 1917-1933. During the first part of this period, the USSR was virtually isolated from world diplomacy. The period of civil war and foreign intervention (1917-1920), which followed three years of Czarist Russia's failures in World War I (1914-1917), left the new Communist state exhausted. The goals of world revolution ingrained in Communist ideology shocked and alarmed

[1] *The Present International Situation.* New York: Cross-Currents Press, 1963, p. 7.

statesmen of other states. By necessity and by repudiation, Lenin's Russia was a wallflower in the slow dance of nations after World War I. The power and opportunity to promote the goals of communism were absent, but not the determination.

Starting in 1928, Stalin turned to an intense dictatorship and developed the massive program of economic totalitarianism with the Five-Year Plans. He crushed all external evidences of opposition to him within the Soviet Union and slowly but surely directed the organization of Communist parties in other nations.

2. *1933-1939.* By 1933, all major states had recognized the Soviet government and were carrying on political and commercial relations with it. United States recognition of Stalin's government in November, 1933, completed this process, and in 1934 the USSR also entered the League of Nations. In these years Stalin talked sweetly in favor of peace and disarmament. He directed Communist officials throughout the world to play down revolution and emphasize cooperation with all kinds of liberal causes and in "popular front" organizations. Some came to consider communism a reasonable and even friendly movement. How could it be subversive if it sought peace and good will? Few took the trouble to dip below the surface and really understand the long-range goals of the Communist movement.

This strategy paid off. The security and well-being of the USSR were certainly furthered. Communist parties everywhere swelled in ranks. Was not the Communist Party the enemy of fascism and war? Stalin entered into defensive alliances with such capitalist nations as France and Czechoslovakia, and many believed that the Soviet goal of world revolution was a matter of the past. Secretly, however, Stalin continued to plot the course of revolution. He directed Party members everywhere to remain loyal to the policies of the USSR and to prepare for the day when the forces of communism, led by the Soviet state, would rise up, seize governments, and hasten the "inevitable" triumph of the ideology.

3. *1939-1941.* The march of Hitler and Mussolini toward aggression in the late 1930's posed a grave threat to the Soviet Union. Stalin was ignored by British and French leaders, who preferred to appease Hitler in the Munich "settlement" of September, 1938. The Communist dictator therefore launched secret

negotiations with Hitler and signed a non-aggression pact with Nazi Germany on August 26, 1939. Stalin considered this contradictory change in strategy vital to the security of his nation.

Actually, this pact was advantageous to both Stalin and Hitler because it gave each the assurance that the other would not attack in pursuing their different aggressive designs. It also enabled Stalin to annex the eastern part of Poland and to regain control over Latvia, Estonia, and Lithuania, which Russia lost to Germany in 1918. Moreover, it gave Stalin a green light to launch its "Winter War" against Finland, in which Russia finally overcame stiff Finnish resistance and annexed an important part of Finland's territory.

On the other hand, the Pact was most embarrassing to communists throughout the world. They had advertised themselves as the fiercest enemies of Hitler. Now, because they were compelled to support Soviet foreign policy, they had to explain why Stalin's association with Hitler was good for the Communist movement and for the entire world.

4. 1941-1945. The fourth major strategic shift of Soviet foreign policy began suddenly on June 22, 1941, when Hitler invaded the Soviet Union in total disregard of the non-aggression pact of 1939. This immediately joined Britain and Stalin's Russia in the common fight against Hitler. The United States entered into this unusual association following the Japanese attack on Pearl Harbor. The "Big Three," as they were labelled, bore the heavy responsibility for crushing Hitler. To "prove" his good intentions toward the West during this honeymoon, Stalin disbanded the Comintern in 1943. This action caused many in the West to believe that the revolutionary ambitions of Soviet foreign policy had been abandoned.

Stalin was now depicted in Western publications as a fine man who would participate in full partnership with all other states in maintaining international peace and security. Many in the West viewed this strategic shift as a departure from the ultimate goal of world domination when it was, in reality, dictated by Soviet national interests. The period between 1941 and 1945 brought the two competing blocs in world affairs closer together than ever before. With the victory over Germany in May, 1945, however, the USSR was ready to get down to the business of resuming its march toward world domination.

5. *1945-1955.* The fifth period in the evolution of Soviet foreign policy in world affairs was a "return to normalcy." With an "iron curtain" (so labelled by Churchill in March, 1946) pressed down upon the Communist-controlled states in Eastern Europe and revived activity among Communist parties throughout the world, Stalin at last was prepared to press the goals of communism with deadly earnestness. The gates of the new "cold war" were thrown wide open in 1946 and Soviet foreign policies sought to break the "capitalist encirclement," to subvert democratic government, hamstring the United Nations, and press on toward global domination. This period was characterized by the Berlin blockade of 1948-1949, by the Communist invasion of South Korea in 1950, and by many other attempts to subvert or seize legitimate governments in other states, among them Iran, Greece, and Guatemala. Stalin died in 1953, but Stalinist policies generally remained in effect until 1955.

Under Khrushchev. The sixth period of Soviet strategy is characterized by Khrushchev's adaptability to the world situation.

In 1955, Khrushchev launched a spring thaw, marked by his trip of Communist reconciliation to Tito in Yugoslavia. Since that time, the Kremlin leader has blown hot and cold, speaking and acting softly at one time, abruptly changing course and spewing forth threats and challenges at another.

For many, the alternating freeze and thaw of Soviet policies are quite confusing. Fear of World War III grips men and nations when Khrushchev flexes his nuclear muscles, and hope for world peace surges forth when he says:

> The ice of the cold war has already not only shown signs of a crack but has started to crumble. I believe that by joint efforts we will reach the objective and will really melt the ice and create normal conditions of life for our peoples and good friendly relations between our states.[1]

But if it is realized that the goal is always the same, and

[1] Khrushchev's toast to President Eisenhower, September 16, 1959. *The New York Times,* September 17, 1959.

that Khrushchev swings back and forth in a strategic manner much more flexibly than did his predecessors, the current policies of the Soviet Union will not seem so unusual or contradictory. What explains the sweet and bitter nature of Khrushchev's outlook on world affairs at large?

Khrushchev admits that a nuclear World War III would largely destroy the material achievements of the Soviet Union. In his view, this would be a tremendous setback to the expansion of communism. He feels that he can approach the goal of world-wide communism by more flexible, varied, and clever means than those on which Stalin relied. His actual military policies vary between threats and retreats in his attempt to rattle the saber without actually using it. Khrushchev seeks "peaceful coexistence" with his enemies, until the time is reached when he feels he can knock down the bastions of freedom without firing a shot.

Many fluctuations of Soviet policy in recent years stem from internal political problems confronting Khrushchev within the Kremlin and in the total Communist camp. Some "hard-line" Stalinists, such as friends of the deposed Molotov, Mao Tse-tung of China, and others in Eastern Europe, take serious issue with the Premier's views on flexible foreign policies. Advocates of the old, firm Stalinist policies dislike Khrushchev's backing away from the idea that a "violent conflict" with the Western states is a necessary prelude to the "inevitable" Communist triumph. The Stalinists consider this position as an unforgivable compromise with the foundations of Marxist-Leninism.

Khrushchev turns to words of Lenin as justification for this particular approach:

> The strictest loyalty to the ideas of communism must be combined with the ability to make all the necessary practical compromises, to "tack," to make agreements, zigzags, retreats, and so on, in order to accelerate the coming into power.[1]

Khrushchev occasionally takes a hard line in world politics to demonstrate to his colleagues that he is just as firm as Stalin. His strategies reflect his attempt to soothe the ruffled ideological feelings in the Kremlin, Peking, and elsewhere. Khrushchev forgets the deceptive words of peaceful coexistence when other

[1] *Strategy and Tactics, op. cit.*, Supp. 1, p. 59.

occasions require toughness. The sore point of Berlin, the American U-2 flight over Russia in the spring of 1960, and evidences of weakness in the West bring out the hard line in Khrushchev's policies as he constantly tries to formulate new strategies.

Khrushchev devotes much more attention to the Afro-Asian world than did his predecessors. This third bloc of "neutralist" states, which Stalin largely ignored, makes the drive toward world domination all the more complicated. Lenin and Stalin concentrated on the two-bloc approach, the proletariat led by the USSR against the bourgeois camp led by the United States. For them, international politics could be reduced to the stresses and strains between these two hostile groupings.

In seeking to subvert the new nations of Africa and Asia, Khrushchev must maintain firmness on the one hand and an overall soft line on the other. Since he cannot blow soft and hard at the same time, he must alternate between conciliation and toughness. If Khrushchev had only the West to contend with, perhaps his policies would be more consistent. But his ambition to win over the third bloc keeps him from striking a steady course in world affairs.

Activities of Communist Parties

The role of Communist parties. If we find variety in Communist *strategy* in the total arena of world politics, the fantastic array of *tactics* and tools of policy used by the Soviet Union to advance the Communist cause among and within the nations of the world is almost overwhelming in its variety.

Tactics involves the application of specific instruments of policy in each state in order to further the Communist movement throughout the world. The tactic of sabotage, or the destruction of important military or economic installations, is used in many Afro-Asian and Latin American states where the Communist party seeks to wreak havoc with unstable governments, making it impossible for a new democratic or neutralist regime to consolidate itself in power.

Closely related to sabotage is the tactic of unconventional warfare. This Communist tactic differs substantially from the use of organized armed forces because it is aimed at the control of the civilian populations in the towns and villages of the target country and not specifically at military targets or direct warfare with the enemy. Communist unconventional warfare in Southeast Asia has done much to undermine legitimate governmental institutions in that area.

Official Soviet policy deals with representatives of governments throughout the world, while undercover hustlers of Soviet policy seek to strengthen Communist movements in each state. Thus we have *open* Soviet policy and the *underground* movement as well. A typical Soviet embassy in any nation will have diplomats on the one hand, working in view of all. Through other channels, subversive agents manipulate and direct the Communist party operations in that country. Their operations vary, but the goal is the same.

Stalin said that the Party is the "main guiding force" of Communist states, all of them led by the Communist Party of the USSR. Under Stalin, of course, the Soviet Party was considered the vanguard of world communism, and parties in all states, with rare exceptions, took orders from the Kremlin without question. Khrushchev's claim to exclusive leadership is now challenged by the leaders of Communist China. The Russian Communist Party, however, exercises a great measure of control over the destinies and policies of communism in most states.

The foreign policy of the Soviet Union is the main force which seeks to further the goals of communism in world affairs. Party members in any state must support this policy. The exceptions, of course, are those Communist movements which look to China for leadership. But in all cases, party members throughout the world must advance the cause of international communism and not the national values or desires of their countrymen. Perhaps the main exception is the national Communist movement in Yugoslavia.

The tactics of Soviet policy are directed toward furthering communism in each state in accordance with the particular situation of the party in each state. Communist parties exist in all states, and in one of three forms: (1) as the dominant and usually the only party in the state, as in the USSR, China, and the Eastern European satellites, (2) as a legal political party in non-Communist states, as in France, Italy, and India, and (3) as an illegal organization in non-Communist states where the open operations of the Party are prohibited, as in Spain, the United Arab Republic (Egypt), and Brazil. Nationally, the Communist Party of the United States is a legal entity, but it has been subjected to many crippling restrictions and is illegal in many individual states.

In states where the party is dominant. In those nations where the Communist party is in complete control of the government and the society, a mixed pattern of loyalties emerges, which confuses the whole Communist movement. The Eastern European satellites bow to the Soviet Union, with the exception of tiny Albania, which is ideologically wedded to Communist China. Tito's Yugoslavia is independent of China and Russia, and Castro's Cuba seems to be steering a course of partial independence, despite its need for Soviet strategic and economic support. The Communist Korean Workers' Party in North Korea takes its cues from Communist China. The Workers' Party of North Vietnam draws support from both the Chinese and Soviet parties. Outer Mongolia, however, sides with the Soviet Union. One thing is quite clear. The leaders in the Kremlin no longer have a monopolistic control over the world Communist movement as they did in the days of Stalin.

In exchange for support in the ideological contest with Communist China, Khrushchev has greatly relaxed Soviet control over the Eastern European "Peoples' Republics." Actually, this liberalization began with Khrushchev's "de-Stalinization" program in 1955, and it has noticeably increased since that time. While these satellites remain under the protection of the Russian umbrella, they also press forward with attitudes and policies somewhat independent of the Kremlin's over-all line.

Poland is the real maverick. About 80 percent of Polish agriculture remains in private hands, a distinct snub to the glories of collectivity down on the farm. The Polish government, under the reins of Party leader Wladyslaw Gomulka, conducts about 40 percent of its trade with states outside the Communist bloc, and receives some economic aid from the United States as well. Romanian trade with the outside world is about 30 percent of its total. The Romanian government strongly refuses to abide by Soviet directives on economic integration among members of the Eastern European bloc. Hungarian leader Janos Kadar is making life a bit easier for his people these days. De-Stalinization is even moving ahead cautiously in Czechoslovakia. These Communist-dominated states now seek to expand their trade with the West, partly to offset the rigidities of Soviet economic planning. East Germany still clings to the Kremlin, for de-Stalinization would put an end to Ulbricht's puppet regime. Nevertheless, the old fixed mosaic of Eastern Europe, once in the firm mold of Kremlin domination, is now much less rigid than in Stalin's time.

This is not to say, of course, that genuine ideological change is afoot in Eastern Europe. The tides of democracy are not surging in. Totalitarianism remains in control of these states, as do police-backed regimes, controls over the press, radio, and education, and votes for the Soviet line in the United Nations. Khrushchev, however, has given the satellites a lump of sugar to secure their continued support for his policies. As a result, these Communist states are demanding more lumps as time goes by. How long the Soviet Premier's supply of sugar remains is a most intriguing question.

Legal Communist parties in non-Communist states. Nearly all democratic states, such as Italy, France, and India, permit Communist parties to function in the open as legitimate political parties. In such states, as well as in those where the party is outlawed, the party is viewed by itself and the Soviet Union as the nucleus of a future government for the state. Each Communist party member in non-Communist states must identify himself with this revolutionary cause.

Communist tactics in states where the party may operate legally are under the over-all direction of the Communist Party of the Soviet Union. Some tactics are exercised in the open, and others are conducted underground. In France, for example, the Communist party attempts to identify itself with the masses of the people, openly supports the USSR, and openly condemns the forces of democracy and the states of the West. The *public tactics* of legal parties in non-Communist states are varied and flexible.

Participation in parliaments. A communist in parliament is not a legislator but an agitator for the Communist cause. He answers, not to his constituency, but to the Central Committee of his own Communist party. The Communist party runs candidates for election to parliament; once elected, these party members must seek to undermine the legislature itself. Communist doctrine on this matter is clear.

> It is only possible to speak of utilizing the bourgeois State organizations (such as legislatures) with the object of destroying them. . . . On all important political questions, the (Communist) parliamentary faction shall get preliminary instructions from the Central Committee of the Party.[1]

A communist in a democratic parliament is a contradiction in terms. He does not believe in parliamentary government. He merely uses it in order to destroy it.

Communists serving in parliaments must follow party orders, seek to use the parliament to advance the Communist cause, aspire toward overthrowing the democratic parliament, and then establish a Communist dictatorship of the proletariat. This tactic was successfully applied by the Communist party in Czechoslovakia, in its seizure of power in February, 1948.

United fronts. Communists and party members are instructed to seek influence or control over non-Communist groups. This applies to all types of organizations, political parties, labor unions, and especially various kinds of youth groups. Doctrine on this Communist tactic is as follows:

> The tactics of the United Front imply the leadership of the Communist vanguard in the daily struggles of the large masses of workers for their vital interests. . . . The most important thing in the tactics of the United Front is and remains the agitational and organizational unification of the working masses.[2]

Workers' organizations and trade unions are choice targets for the united front tactic. Communists everywhere consider themselves "proletariat" and constantly seek to draw all workingmen to their side. Lenin's views on bringing unions into the Communist camp still apply today.

[1] Hook, *op. cit.,* p. 66.
[2] *Ibid.,* p. 68.

We . . . must resort to all sorts of stratagems, maneuvers, illegal methods, evasions, and subterfuges, only so as to get into the trade unions, to remain in them, and carry on communist work within them at all costs.[1]

In 1936 the communists gave their support to a "united front" government in France, which led to a crippling right-wing reaction. Communist "united front" activities in Brazilian labor unions are particularly active today. Between 1945 and 1947, in the aftermath of the resistance to Hitler and the Soviet-Western alliance, Communist parties played a leading role in the governments of France and Italy.

Propaganda. The cloak of legality offers the Communist party unusual opportunities in the area of propaganda. Most parties have their own newspapers, such as *L'Humanité* in France and the *Worker* in the United States. Soviet radio, television, books, and pamphlets advertise the Communist approach to national and international affairs. Propaganda is particularly important for the Communist movement under Khrushchev, who declares that:

We shall win only through the minds of men. We must rest on the position of coexistence and non-intervention. It is not necessary to whip people along this road . . . but communism eventually will be in force all over the world.[2]

If Khrushchev really believes in the non-violent approach to the goals of communism, gaining control over the minds of men through propaganda is of prime importance.

Provocation. Communism thrives on instability. Communists therefore seek to provoke or benefit by any unstable situation in countries where they operate. Fomenting strikes, stirring up riots, organizing protest movements, disrupting all kinds of organizational meetings, playing on fear, rivalries, and ignorance are all tactics of provocation.

In some non-Communist states legal Communist parties engage in many other tactics as well. Subversion, sabotage, and other more violent tactics are carried on to advance the cause, depending on the opportunities offered.

[1] *Ibid.*, p. 55.
[2] *The New York Times,* November 8, 1960.

Illegal Communist parties. In many states, the Communist party is banned by law, and therefore it operates as an underground organization. Party cells meet in secret to carry out a number of tactics. Directives come from Moscow and sometimes from the Soviet Embassy.

In such states, party members, following orders from above, carry on the subversive work of communism. They participate in all kinds of organizations, especially those which have some mission of protest. They weave their doctrines, wherever and whenever possible, within the framework of left-wing and nationalist political groups, youth and peace movements. They support mass protests and back all underdogs. They help to provoke strikes and spread malicious gossip. They engage in corrosive propaganda when given the opportunity. Communist party members coordinate their underground activity quite frequently with major moves by the Soviet Union in world affairs. These agents of subversion take great pains to conceal their motives and to disguise their real identity. This greatly hampers the activities of those who do have legitimate protests on such matters as discrimination in housing or racial prejudice.

In some countries, such as Greece, the Communist party is outlawed but operates under the label of another party. The left-wing E.D.A. in Greece functions in the open, is communist-controlled, and attracts about 15 percent of the Greek voters. Through E.D.A., Soviet policy works hard to undermine Greece's government and to sever ties between Greece and NATO.

Whether operating in the open or underground, communists are well-trained in carrying out missions of espionage and sabotage, as we have seen. As masters in all aspects of spying, party members cleverly pursue their tasks in states where legal avenues to gaining information are closed to them.

Sabotage is not employed with great frequency by underground party members. However, should a major international crisis or war arise between the forces of communism and the free world, the long training of party cadres in the techniques of sabotage would come into play. Unconventional warfare, by no means confined to states where the party is an illegal entity, is another underground activity.

This list of Communist party tactics in states where the party is banned by law is by no means complete. In these states, the party must employ tactics which have as their objective the subverting or undermining of all economic, social, political, and even religious organs of legitimate stability. The objective is to get the ideology across, to cause people to lose confidence in their rulers and institutions, to increase the power of the party, to coordinate its activities with the international Communist movement, and to aspire toward the seizure of power in the name of the Communist Party.

There is no clear line between tactics the party employs in states where it may function legally and those used where the party works under clandestine conditions. The legal party must know how to operate underground, and the illegal party must know how to push its activities in all phases of society where it carries on its activities. A directive of the Second Congress of the Third International, still-standing operational procedure, is quite clear on this matter:

> Every legal communist organization must know how to insure for itself complete preparedness for an underground existence, and above all for revolutionary outbreaks. Every illegal communist organization must, on the other hand, make the fullest use of the possibilities offered by the legal labor movement, in order to become, by means of intensive party activity, the organizer and real leader of the great revolutionary masses.[1]

All of these party movements seek power. In some cases, rise to power may come about with only a limited use of force, as in Czechoslovakia in 1948. In others, the route to power might be long and difficult, as in Communist China and North Vietnam, where unconventional warfare was particularly successful. In all cases, the local Communist party looks to the day when it will control the state in which it is located and march with the Soviet Union or Communist China, or both, to the world Communist empire.

[1] Hook, *op. cit.*, p. 62.

Other Means Used to Promote Communism

All states employ instruments or tools of policy in order to strive toward their goals in world affairs. In both the world arena and in each state, the Soviet Union uses diplomacy, propaganda, trade, aid, and armed might within the framework of its strategies and tactics in its drive toward the Communist goal of domination.

Diplomacy. Diplomacy for the Soviet Union is an instrument of policy deeply rooted in the ideological cause of communism. This is as true of Russian diplomacy in such a world arena as the United Nations as it is of Soviet dealings with officials in each nation. The history of diplomacy, of course, does not reveal absolute honesty among all diplomats. But Soviet diplomacy is simply another tool serving the Communist cause. Its history is crammed with deceit, lies, and the dishonoring of treaty commitments.

The first real act of diplomacy under the Communist regime in Russia was Lenin's making public all secret treaties entered into by the Czar's government before 1917. Then, the Soviet government negotiated the Treaty of Brest-Litovsk in March, 1918, a treaty which Lenin declared would be broken by his government as soon as possible. From that point on, the Soviet record in international negotiations is strictly in line with the strategy of the moment and the tactics necessary in any particular country.

Stalin said that:

> Words must have no relations to actions — otherwise what kind of diplomacy is it? Words are one thing, actions another. Good words are a mask for concealment of bad deeds. Sincere diplomacy is no more possible than dry water or wooden iron.[1]

The dictator bore this out when he evaded the fulfilment of the many agreements he made with Western leaders during World War II, especially the Yalta arrangements of February, 1945, dealing with Eastern Europe. Khrushchev would appear on the surface to be somewhat more honest in diplomatic dealings, at

[1] David J. Dallin, *The Real Soviet Russia.* New Haven: Yale University Press, 1947, p. 71.

least with respect to treaty negotiations. But diplomacy, negotiations, treaties, agreements, and other varieties of international communication are subordinated to the goal of expanding communism and are means of striving toward it.

Propaganda. Official Soviet propaganda is of special importance to the USSR in view of its avowed aim of winning the world over by peaceful rather than military means.

The USSR uses all types of media, such as radio, newspapers, pamphlets, books, and of course diplomats. The United Nations, for example, is considered by the USSR to be an important platform for spinning its propaganda web. According to careful estimates, Kremlin leaders spend about two billion dollars annually for official propaganda. The United States Information Agency's budget is around 120 million dollars a year. The Soviet Union has many more official employees throughout the world pressing Soviet views. Moscow broadcasts twice as many hours of radio programs as does the United States' *Voice of America*, and in many more languages. The record of Soviet book publication for propaganda purposes far exceeds that of the West. In 1962, the USSR published and distributed around the world more than forty million copies of some 1800 books and pamphlets in thirty-four languages. The United States Information Agency assisted American publishers to print and circulate about five million books in 1962. The USIA also collected over 700,000 books contributed by American citizens for distribution overseas. Lenin's works receive greater circulation throughout the world than does the Bible.

Soviet propaganda is closely coordinated with the particular strategy it is pursuing at any given time. If the USSR is engaged in a "thaw" in world affairs, the propaganda is sweet and low. If threats are employed, it takes on a strident tone. Propaganda is well-timed with such events as conferences and launchings of satellites and coordinated closely in any particular nation with the activities of the Communist party in that state. The Kremlin propaganda masters frequently use lies, such as claiming that Americans use germ warfare in Southeast Asia. On the other hand, they cleverly play up American sore points, such as race controversies and the U-2 flight over Russia. Russian state-controlled propaganda is malicious, deceitful, and powerful, and it is closely harmonized with all official actions of Soviet policy in international relations.

Foreign aid. In his attempt to win over peoples, Khrushchev launched a foreign-aid program in the Afro-Asian world. Since 1955, the USSR has allocated over seven billion dollars to nearly 30 selected countries. The purpose of this aid program is, of course, not merely to advance the interests and well-being of its recipients. Aid to the United Arab Republic (UAR), Indonesia, India, or Cuba has an intense political purpose behind it — that of winning support for Soviet policy, of weakening Western influence, of presenting the Soviet model of industrial development — all with the ultimate goal of spreading support for communism. Other propaganda devices are coordinated with Soviet aid programs to make certain that the full value is received for Soviet "assistance" to the needy state.

Trade. Soviet foreign trade has increased substantially during the Khrushchev era. The USSR and its Eastern European satellites associated in the COMECON, the economic grouping of Communist states (excluding Yugoslavia and the pro-China bloc), export annually over five billion dollars' worth of goods and services to other nations. Yearly imports add up to almost five billion dollars in products, and the members of COMECON engage in an annual trade with each other of over nine billion dollars each year. Studies reveal that the Soviet Union usually comes out ahead in its trading with its Eastern European satellites.

The most important aspect of Soviet trade as a tool of foreign policy is its distinctly political nature. Trade in the USSR, unlike most non-Communist states, is completely conducted by the government. Export and import prices, conditions of trade, and the kinds of goods and services bought and sold are all matters, for the most part, of advancing Soviet power. The Soviet Union uses trade to take advantage of the troubles of others and to influence people everywhere. For Americans, world trade is primarily a matter of concern for *private* companies and is not a *public* instrument of policy.

The political, state-controlled nature of Soviet trade permits the rulers in the Kremlin to sell products well below world market prices, should this be advantageous to political relationships. Soviet oil sold to Italy is a good example. England's refusal to buy Icelandic fish following a dispute in 1952 over fishing in territorial waters led to an immediate Soviet offer to purchase this leading Icelandic export. Within six years, the Soviet bloc was taking about a third of Iceland's total world trade. A by-product of this event was Iceland's request to the United States to withdraw some of its armed forces stationed in Iceland. The UAR has mortgaged its cotton crop to Russia for years to come in return for Soviet assistance on Aswan Dam. Following the collapse of Cuban-American relations in 1960, the USSR scooped up Cuban sugar exports at prices well below what the United States had paid in years gone by.

This is not to say that Soviet trade with other nations is always dictated by sheer political maneuver. But the Soviet government, steered by ideological directives, completely controls the internal economy and trade in Russia as well. Thus the USSR is in a unique position to manipulate its world trading in such a manner as to further its political objectives. Soviet trade is often determined by political requirements and opportunities rather than a profit motive or prudent economic management.

Armed force. The entire military apparatus of any state is an instrument of policy, largely designed to provide security for the state's national interests. It is sometimes used to advance the ideology of the state as well. Whether any one nation's military forces and capacity are defensive or offensive is a question as old as history. The Soviets naturally claim that theirs is strictly defensive, and yet they call for the ultimate worldwide triumph of their doctrine!

For many years, the military arsenal of the USSR was quite weak, and during the 1930's, strategy called for disarmament because the Soviet Union was hardly prepared for war at that time. Before and during World War II the Red Army slowly but surely was built up. Over eleven billion dollars of American assistance between 1941 and 1945 did much to help the Soviet Union wage war. The Soviet armies carried Communist governments into the Eastern European states in 1944 and 1945, and Russian military power has kept them there ever since. Soviet threats to use this power were invaluable in the installation of a Communist government in Czechoslovakia in 1948, and Soviet tanks were called in to put down the Berlin uprising of 1953 and the Hungarian Revolution of 1956. Khrushchev continues a vast military build-up in conventional arms and nuclear weapons as a massive force supporting other Soviet instruments of policy in world affairs and Communist tactics in all states.

Khrushchev relies heavily on threats to unleash this mighty force:

> I want to be understood correctly: we do not want to frighten anyone, but we can tell the truth — now we have such a stock of rockets, such an amount of atomic and hydrogen warheads, that if they attack us we could wipe our potential enemies off the face of the earth.[1]

The Soviet army, navy, and reserves add up to about four million men. All Communist states have military forces adding up to over twenty million men. Russian nuclear power is undoubtedly great, and most assuredly Khrushchev has the power to back up military threats whenever and wherever he uses them. The military is a powerful instrument of Soviet policy, although Khrushchev in all probability would be hesitant to use it other than as a threat or a goad.

Naturally, there are many other instruments of policy in the Soviet arsenal. Russia makes clever use of cultural offensives in dispatching its films, ballet corps, works of its writers, and compositions of its "proletarian" musicians throughout the world. The pronouncements of Khrushchev and other Soviet leaders are instruments of policy in themselves. Soviet educational institutions seek to indoctrinate young men and women from other countries who receive liberal grants to study in Moscow. All of the instruments of official policy are coordinated with Communist party activity throughout the world. This vast network of pathways to the goals of communism is in constant operation, above ground and underground.

---

[1] Mager and Katel, *op. cit.*, p. 228.

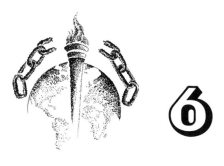

Communist Ideology and the Western World

Back in the days when Marx and Engels penned their *Communist Manifesto*, capitalism was the key object of Communist hatred. Now, democracy is the deadly enemy. Capitalism has changed a lot since 1848, so the communists have some difficulty pinpointing their grievances against this economic system. In the days of Marx, the economy was in the hands of a small number of men who manipulated production and reaped the rewards. But no nation today has the kind of economic system described by Marx. The welfare capitalism in the democratic states of the mid-twentieth century provides for a partnership between private enterprise and government, for the benefit of all citizens. The prosperity of the working man in the democracies is a fact which communists do not like to admit. So they have shifted their antagonism to democracy.

Capitalism and democracy have come a long way since the middle of the nineteenth century, and so has communism. When Russia monopolized the leadership of the world Communist movement under Stalin, the West, not merely "capitalism," became the objective which the forces of communism had to conquer.

The goal of international communism remains fixed. But who speaks for communism, and what means will Communist states use to defeat their prime enemy, the democratic West? There are now two contenders for the voice of international communism and two different sets of means to achieve the common goal. How this conflict within the Communist camp is resolved may spell the difference between war and peace in our time.

The Soviet Union, led by Khrushchev, wants to avoid a major war with the West, fears the potential destructiveness of nuclear weapons, urges "peaceful competition" with the West, and aspires toward "peaceful coexistence" with the democratic states until they can be defeated by means other than war.

Communist China, led by Mao Tse-tung, sees a violent conflict with the West as necessary. Mao apparently is not afraid of a nuclear war. He derides "peaceful competition" and "peaceful coexistence" with the West. To him, these Khrushchev policies are treason to the ideology of communism (see Chapter 8).

1. What Does Khrushchev's "Peaceful Coexistence" Mean?

Cannot peaceful coexistence with the Soviet Union and other Communist states reduce world tension, smooth over the idea that communism is out to dominate us, and bring about a cozy world of international peace and security? Khrushchev, most certainly, would like us to place this interpretation on his frequent and eloquent advocacy of peaceful coexistence.

Peaceful Coexistence: The Background

Khrushchev is not the first Communist leader to press for peaceful coexistence. Peaceful coexistence has been periodically a *strategy* of Soviet foreign policy. When Lenin saw that Communist revolutions were not going to sweep Europe at the end of World War I, he tried to "peacefully coexist" with the West. Even though the democracies opened diplomatic and commercial relations with the new Communist state, Lenin, and later Stalin, went on to construct the foundations of communism in one state, the Soviet Union. On the global stage, however, all states did "coexist" with the USSR, and peacefully so.

After 1934, when the Soviet Union entered the League of Nations and was recognized by the United States, the strategy of "peaceful coexistence" was again fashionable. "Popular fronts" between Communist parties and other parties in Western states, especially in France, stressed the "peaceful" nature of communism, and many people believed that communism had scrapped its proclaimed ambition to conquer the world. The West jumped off the peaceful coexistence bandwagon in a hurry when Stalin and Hitler joined forces in August, 1939. When Russia was subjected to Hitler's fury in June, 1941, however, the strategy of peaceful coexistence was quickly revived by Stalin. It was imperative for Russia's own survival for its government to cooperate with the West during World War II.

But Stalin hated the idea of peaceful coexistence, and viewed it only as a strategy necessitated by Russia's desperate need. As soon as the guns died down at the end of World War II, this strategy was junked and the cold war was resumed.

Khrushchev's Interpretation of "Peaceful Coexistence"

After 1955, Khrushchev pulled the old chestnut out of the fire, polished it off, and tossed it into the cauldron of world politics. For Khrushchev, however, peaceful coexistence is more than a strategy. It is an integral part of all aspects of his policy. It consists of the application of various tactics and instruments of Soviet policy which will advance world communism *without using actual armed force*. The "peaceful" signifies the use of non-military means for the goal of world domination. The "coexistence" means that the USSR intends to permit non-Communist states to exist side by side with the Communist states until communism wins out.

There is no reason whatever to believe that the USSR's concept of peaceful coexistence is anything more than a smoke screen erected by Khrushchev to dull the vigilance of the non-Communist world. Should communism win, there would be no "existence" whatever of non-Communist governments or democratic societies. A Communist "peace" would then prevail. This would be, of course, domination.

Khrushchev wrote to Americans in 1959 that the USSR and the United States must *"keep to the positions of the ideological struggle, without resorting to arms in order to prove that one is right.*"[1] Naturally he would like us to follow this policy until the Soviet Union can gain the upper hand. In reality, of course, any genuine or lasting compromise with democracy is absolutely rejected by the Communist states. According to Communist ideology, peaceful coexistence is impossible because communists are convinced of the inevitable triumph of their doctrine. The following statement issued in 1960 by eighty-one Communist parties meeting in Moscow makes the Soviet view of peaceful coexistence quite clear.

> Peaceful coexistence of states with different social systems does not mean reconciliation between the Socialist (Communist) and bourgeois ideologies. On the contrary, it implies an intensification of the struggle of the working class and of all Communist parties for the triumph of Socialist (Communist) ideas. But ideological and political disputes between states must not be settled through war.[2]

Khrushchev's Reasons for Peaceful Coexistence

What is behind Khrushchev's brand of "peaceful coexistence"? Three factors appear to be important. Khrushchev fears that a World War III would destroy all Communist efforts to build their "new world" and thus he seeks other means to attain the communist objective of world domination. Secondly, Khrushchev apparently is convinced that the Communist approach to economic policy is really superior to that of capitalism, and thus he prefers economic competition to military adventurism. In the third place, Khrushchev feels that the idea of peaceful coexistence provides the right climate in world affairs for undermining legitimate governments in various non-military ways. Peaceful coexistence has great propaganda value, and while the non-Communist world focuses on the "peaceful" nature of Soviet foreign policy, that policy is hard at work in other ways, striving toward the international Communist empire.

Fear of nuclear war. In all probability, Khrushchev is just as

[1] Nikita Khrushchev, "On Peaceful Coexistence." *Foreign Affairs,* October, 1959, p. 5. (Italics are Khrushchev's.)

[2] *The New York Times,* December 7, 1960.

anxious as anyone else to avoid World War III. It takes no genius to realize that a nuclear war would destroy civilization as we know it on this earth. Khrushchev must certainly be impressed with what American nuclear might could do to the Soviet Union. He is prepared for war, and probably very well prepared indeed. On the other hand, this statement of the Communist dictator probably reflects the truth.

> We want to eliminate war. We are members of governments and are responsible not only for our own lives but for the lives of our people. We are living in a world in which war can be made and therefore we must be prepared for war. But we want peace.[1]

Khrushchev is reasonable on this score. He realizes and has said many times that World War III could destroy the very foundations of communism. He added that the USSR would survive a nuclear war while the democratic states would be ruined, but one doubts whether he really believes this. It may be assumed, however, that Khrushchev genuinely wants to prevent the outbreak of World War III, and thus he seeks other means to advance the goals of communism.

The nineteenth century Prussian authority on military strategy, General Karl von Clausewitz, once noted that "war is a continuation of politics by other means." Khrushchev can well say that other means are more politic than war in continuing the contest with the non-Communist world. These "other means," however, present a serious ideological dilemma to Khrushchev, as we have seen. The Chinese Communists, led by Mao Tse-tung, accuse Khrushchev of a massive heresy in departing from the necessity of violent conflict in proceeding toward communism. They charge that Khrushchev's idea of peaceful coexistence undermines the revolutionary spirit of Marxist-Leninism.

Khrushchev's reliance on tactics and instruments other than nuclear war only highlights the importance of the ideological battle in our era. The accent is on a war for the minds and hearts of men, and in this war, ideas and ideologies come to the fore as they never have before in the history of mankind.

Desire to prove Soviet economic superiority. Khrushchev has a

[1] *The New York Times,* June 22, 1962.

strong desire to prove that the Communist economic system is superior to capitalism or to any other economic structure. Economics provided the foundation for Marxist theory, and thus it is only natural that communists stress their intention to achieve superiority in the production and distribution of goods and services.

Russia had a long way to go after the revolution of 1917 and after World War II ravaged much of the USSR. Today, however, Khrushchev is going all out to propagandize the "superiority" of the Communist approach to national economic problems. He wants to prove that communism can defeat the West in a peaceful manner through economic competition. The whole world, in his view, will come to accept communism as the means by which the needs of all people can be met and their national well-being can be furthered. (See diagram, page 129.)

Khrushchev boasts that the Soviet economy has surpassed that of Great Britain and France, and that it will overtake the United States within fifteen years. The USSR's gross national product (total output of goods and services measured in dollars) in 1962 was about 270 billion as compared with the 554 billion of the United States. Assuming continual growth of the American economy, it is extremely doubtful that the Soviet Union will come anywhere near its goal by 1980. The Soviet economy is expanding rapidly, but this rate of growth will slacken off as time goes by.

Desire to lull suspicion. Khrushchev uses peaceful coexistence as a device to lull us to sleep. Peaceful coexistence "creates favorable conditions" in which the forces of communism can aid "liberation movements" in non-Communist countries to overthrow the legitimate governments and seize power under the Communist banner. The Soviet Premier wrote the following words in the fall of 1959 for an American audience:

> It is often said in the West that peaceful coexistence is nothing else than a tactical method of the socialist states. There is not a grain of truth in such allegations. Our desire for peace and peaceful coexistence is not conditioned by any time serving or tactical considerations. It springs from the very nature of the socialist society in which there are no classes or social groups interested in profiting by war or seizing and enslaving other

THE PLANNED ECONOMY IN THE USSR[1]

The planned economy of the Soviet Union is, in theory, supposed to proceed toward the Communist goal along the following lines:

1. The construction of the foundations of socialism, 1928-1932 (First Five-Year Plan).

2. The creation of a Socialist society and the completion, in the main, of the construction of socialism (1933-1938).

3. The beginning of the gradual transition to communism (1939-1958).

4. The period of expanded construction of communism as expressed in the goals of the Seven-Year Plan (1959-1965) and the Fifteen-Year Targets (1957-1972).

5. The tasks of the Twenty-Year Plans, divided into two decades, during which the "construction" of the material-technical base of communism is to be begun (1960-1970) and then finished (1970-1980).

6. The complete construction of a Communist society on this material and technical base "in the subsequent period."

(Points 4, 5, and 6 were set forth in the Party Program of 1961.)

peoples' territories. The Soviet Union and the other socialist countries, thanks to their socialist system, have an unlimited home market and for this reason they have no need to pursue an expansionist policy of conquest and an effort to subordinate other countries to their influence.

Peaceful coexistence does not mean merely living side by side in the absence of war but with the constantly remaining threat of its breaking out in the future. *Peaceful coexistence can and should develop into peaceful competition for the purpose of satisfying man's needs in the best possible way.*[2]

[1] Ritvo, *op. cit.*, p. 114.
[2] Khrushchev, *op. cit.*, pp. 3, 4.

Americans like competition, but clean competition, and this is hardly what Khrushchev has in mind.

2. What Problems Does the Soviet Economy Face in Its Struggle with the West?

One of Khrushchev's aims, as we have seen, is to develop the Soviet economy to the point where it can surpass the free economy of the West. He has two good reasons for this.

He knows that, in the long run, a strong government cannot exist unless it is upheld by a healthy economy. He only has to look at the Russian revolution to see what can happen to a government which neglects the well-being of its people.

Secondly, communism, as originally developed by Marx, had strong economic foundations. Thus Khrushchev feels that it is of utmost importance to prove that the Communist economic system really is superior to all others.

But in his desire to promote a thriving economy in the USSR, Khrushchev has run into various problems.

Inconsistency with Marx's Ideals

Because it is almost totally dominated by the government, the economy of the USSR is a direct instrument of state policy. Nearly all the basic decisions in the economic realm are geared to political and ideological requirements, at home and abroad.

Western economies, on the other hand, are largely shaped by market conditions. Basic decisions are made by owners, managers, executives, trade-union officials, and consumers. Government regulation of economics in the democratic world varies from state to state. But the general economic goal of the West is the well-being of the people. The general economic goal of the Soviet Union is the advancement of the power of the state.

The Soviet economy is not really communism as Marx would interpret the economics of his doctrine. In the USSR, the *state* makes the profits and retains the "surplus value." It would be interesting to have Marx's views of state capitalism in the Soviet Union where the government itself is the sole agent of exploitation.

The economic system found in Russia today is certainly not in line with the Marxian definition of communism. "From each according to his ability, to each according to his work" is still an unrealized ideal.

The Consumer Comes Last

"Peaceful economic competition" with the West is not benefiting the Communist cause. The limits of the Soviet economy make it difficult to meet the rising demands by the Russian people for higher standards of living, and to advance the power of the Soviet Union at the same time. This dilemma, for dictators, is often reduced to the slogan: "guns or butter?" For the present, the answer is guns.

The Soviet economy in the Five-Year Plans has always emphasized heavy industry and the broadening of the military and economic power of the state. Production and distribution designed to give the people a genuine rise in living standards have always taken a back seat. This continues to be the case. In June, 1962, the price of butter shot up 25 percent while meat prices rose 30 percent. An income-tax cut in the USSR was suspended in September of the same year "to help pay for further economic development and increased defense preparedness." The Soviet newspaper *Izvestia* said these denials of increased income to Russians were "dictated by the interests of all working people and the interests of the security of our country." Khrushchev promised his people a fantastic future of abundance in his 1961 Program of the Communist Party. But it will be a long time before the genuine well-being of the people will be placed ahead of the power goals of the Soviet state.

Failure of Soviet Agriculture

One of the most glaring failures of communism is in agriculture. Communist ideology has little to offer to the farmer, traditionally a person of great independence. Lenin promised all "land to the people" but the Soviet government has always kept tight reins on all facets of agricultural production and distribution. Stalin was responsible for the death of millions of independent farmers when they refused to accept his collective farms and state farms. Communist agricultural regimentation resulted in a horrible famine in the Ukraine in the 1930's. The farmer tends to resent dictation, and one has the feeling that the millions of Russian farmers have never become reconciled to their Communist government. In any event, agriculture has not kept pace with Soviet industry, and repeated agricultural failures in the Soviet Union each year, as well as in all other Communist states, testify to the dismal failure of this sector of communism to meet the goals set.

Soviet crop failures in 1963 forced Khrushchev to buy wheat from the West. Although Russia usually exports grain, it negotiated with Australia to purchase $200,000,000 worth of wheat in the summer of 1963 and paid $500,000,000 for Canadian wheat in October, 1963. In that same month, President Kennedy gave permission for American wheat producers to sell some $250,000,000 worth of wheat to the USSR. With Soviet grain production in 1963 down 18 percent from 1962, the Communist approach to agriculture is hardly winning blue ribbons, especially when capitalist states are called upon to supply food for the Soviet peoples. In October, 1963, Czechoslovakia, Bulgaria, and Hungary also asked the United States to sell wheat to them.

Difficulty in Competing with Capitalism

When Khrushchev seeks to prove the superiority of his economic system over capitalism, the results are embarrassing to communists. Capitalism and democracy, marching hand in hand, have come a long way since Marx's time. The "welfare capitalism" we have today shows increasing vigor with each passing year. Capitalism has defied Communist predictions that it would decay and die.

Capitalism, or the free market economy, in which the well-being of the consumer is the key goal, has many problems. But it has proved to be the most robust response to man's continual quest for well-being. This has been particularly true in the West. Khrushchev's attacks on the European Common Market, a bastion of capitalism, testify to his real fear of the effectiveness of the democratic approach to economic problems. The tremendous accomplishments of capitalism in Germany since World War II disprove the Communist charges that capitalism can't rise from the ashes to provide abundance for a nation.

Japan was down and out at the end of World War II, with vast areas of total destruction scarring a nation of more than 80 million people. Today, some 95 million Japanese look back on what a capitalistic system and extensive aid from capitalistic United States has done for them during the past fifteen years. Most would laugh at Khrushchev's claims for the superiority of the Communist economic system. Between 1950 and 1960 in Japan, the gross national product more than doubled, as did the per-capita income of the Japanese people. Agricultural output zoomed upwards. Industrial production rose from five billion dollars in 1950 to fourteen billion, four hundred million in 1960. This is the record of democratic capitalism, not state capitalism!

Khrushchev continues to push the great merits of the Communist economy and claims that in this manner the USSR and its allies can outclass the West in this era of peaceful coexistence. But the victories of capitalism can blast Communist boasts of economic supremacy to bits.

3. What Part Do Russian Communists Play in the Western World?

Communist Parties in Western Nations

In the world of diplomacy, relations between two states as carried out by diplomats have a veneer of politeness and a desire to avoid friction. The Soviet Union attempts to have its diplomats in any state conform to ways of life of that state in order to get its policies across in the smoothest manner. But underneath the gloss of diplomacy, the Soviet ambassadors and official Soviet representatives often work closely with the legal Communist party in the state or with the underground, subversive apparatus (*or with both*), in the continuous attempt to bring that particular state into the Communist camp.

Legal parties. Some Western states, such as France or Italy, have sizeable Communist parties.

In these Western states and others, Communist parties, operating in the open, make their voices constantly heard and continually seek to use the platform of democracy to kill democracy itself. Communism has not risen to power through direct democratic means in any nation, but Communist party activity in Italy and France has taken a new lease on life in recent years.

Is the Communist party of Italy, for instance, really an instrument of Soviet policy, or is it a left-wing but basically Italian party? The leader of the Italian Communist party, Palmiro Togliatti, would naturally prefer you to believe that his organization is strictly Italian. He would scoff at the idea that his group is a tool of Premier Khrushchev. And yet, the facts are that his party and all other Western Communist parties follow the Party line, direct from the Kremlin.

In Italy. In May, 1963, the Communist party of Italy received 25 percent of the 33 million votes in the national elections. Togliatti's party, therefore, is the second largest in the Italian Chamber of Deputies. Togliatti is a strong supporter of Khrushchev and the idea of peaceful coexistence, and is as determined as the Soviet leader to bring Italy into the Communist bloc. If he is successful in doing this, Italy would fall behind the iron curtain, drop out of the North Atlantic Treaty Organization, and fall under a full dictatorship once more.

Why did so many Italians vote for the hammer and sickle? Actually, the vast majority of Italians voting for the Communist party in May, 1963, were not *members* of the party. For the most part, they were people in lower-income brackets who fell for the Communist propaganda that a Togliatti victory would give them a better future. They voted the Communist ticket largely out of protest, rather than out of conviction. They accepted Communist idealism and ignored the harsh realities of Soviet communism. This only demonstrates how a legal party supporting a totalitarian ideology can use democratic instruments to seek power. Once its goal is reached, democracy is shoved aside.

The other parties would not permit the communists to be represented in the new Italian government as far as the ministry or executive branch is concerned. But the Italian parliament must play along with the communists to some extent because of the sheer power and size of the party. As a matter of fact, Togliatti has warned that, unless the new ministry cooperates with the Communist party in official governmental policy, "agitations, riots and possible bloodshed" would be the result. Thus he is blackmailing the Italian government with all kinds of reprisals unless the views of the Communist party are incorporated to some extent in future Italian national policies.

In France. One might think that the legal Communist party is dormant, but it most certainly is not. In April, 1963, French and Soviet Communist leaders met in the Soviet Union to chart a course for the future, when General de Gaulle is no longer at the helm of the French government. The French communists are presently cooperating closely with French Socialists in a united front against the De Gaulle government, hoping that the day will arrive soon when they can increase their power in the French National Assembly.

Western Communist parties in France and Italy and elsewhere follow the Khruschev lead rather than Mao Tse-tung. Through their legal political activity, propaganda, and cooperation with the Russian diplomatic delegations in their nations, they serve as Khrushchev's leg men in advancing the fortunes of international communism.

Illegal parties. The activities of illegal Communist parties are many and varied, as we have seen. Some party members work underground. They will not shout communism from the rooftops but will constantly sell the Communist line to all with whom they come in contact. The party might be quite small. The Communist Party of the United States has only about 10,000 members. But it is not the size that counts. It is what the party is able to do that really matters. Let us not forget that Bolshevism in Russia rose to power from a very small nucleus of fanatic supporters.

Communist party members in states where the party is illegal maintain close contacts with the official delegation of diplomats from the Soviet Union. Usually, it is the Soviet Union itself which directs the espionage or sabotage activity. There have been many revelations of this pattern of events. The Soviet Union relied heavily on American and British Communist agents during and after World War II to obtain secrets about the atomic bomb. The trial of the Rosenbergs and Harry Gold in the United States, and of Klaus Fuchs and others in England revealed one of the most massive espionage efforts in all history.

In Canada. On the night of September 5, 1945, Igor Gouzenko, a clerk for the Soviet Embassy in Ottawa, fled from his headquarters, carrying with him a mass of official documents. When he was caught and the documents examined, a vast espionage effort conducted by communists in Canada and directed by a Soviet Embassy official, Colonel Zabotin, was revealed. The Royal Commission, investigating the documents Gouzenko brought to the Canadian Government, declared that:

> Zabotin's organization was particularly anxious to obtain technical information regarding devices which would be used in the postwar defences of Canada, the United Kingdom, and United States; secret information regarding political plans and policies of these countries; economic information which would be useful in assessing the economic and military potential of Canada; details regarding the location of Canadian defense industries; information on certain telephone land-lines and tapping devices; and documents which could be used by Russian agents "planted" in Canada or elsewhere, plus information whereby such agents could enter Canada and acquire a base of operations here.[1]

All of this demonstrates that Soviet agents, working with Communist party members in Western states, can do a great deal to undermine the political and strategic security of other nations.

In the United States. The Communist party has not, on the surface, been particularly successful in the United States. Communist groupings, splintering off from the American Socialist Party in 1919, finally united in May, 1920. The Party went under various names in the 1920's (generally, the Workers' Party of America) and became the Communist Party of the USA (CPUSA) in March, 1929. The CPUSA remains intact in the United States, although the scope of its activities has been substantially curtailed as a result of enforcement of the Smith Act of 1940, the Internal Security Act of 1950, and subsequent Supreme Court decisions concerning its operations. The Smith Act provides for certain legal restrictions on groups or parties

[1] Hook, *op. cit.*, pp. 245-246.

in the United States which seek to overthrow the American government, and this is exactly what the United States Subversives Activities Control Board found was true with respect to the CPUSA. The Board declared in 1953 that:

> It is so innate in the Respondent's (CPUSA) nature that it seek and accept Soviet Union direction and control that, in actuality, it does not function as the purely domestic political party whose role it would, *de jure,* assume. Rather, nurtured by the Soviet Union, it labors unstintingly to advance the world Communist movement.[1]

One may be quite certain, therefore, that the CPUSA continues to work underground with agents from the Soviet Union, and that it aspires toward the overthrow of the United States government. This must be by illegal means because the party has no recourse to advancing communism in America by direct, open, and legal activity. Federal Bureau of Investigation Director, J. Edgar Hoover, has written extensively on the nature of Communist subversive activity in America.

Soviet Anti-Western Policies in World Politics

On the world stage, the Soviet Union concentrates on promoting *disunity* among the democratic Western states, and on distorting the *image of the West* in all areas outside the democracies. In a few instances, the USSR directly confronts the West in an out-and-out power struggle, such as in Berlin, but Khrushchev would far prefer to use devious means to strengthen communism and weaken democracy in world affairs.

Soviet efforts to promote Western disunity. Lenin and Stalin in particular called for policies which would divide the Western states and prevent them from standing united against a Communist offensive. In his book, *Imperialism,* Lenin wrote that the Western states would become weak in continuous struggles for power among themselves, thus paving the way for communism to march in and pick up the pieces. In 1920, however, Lenin realized that a Communist revolution was not going to sweep the world and that the new Soviet Republic was much too weak

[1] *Ibid.,* p. 176.

to take direct action against the West. But he clung to his idea
that the West would fall apart.

> If we are unable to defeat (the capitalist states) we must know
> how to dispose our forces in such a way that they fall out among
> themselves; because, as is always the case, when thieves fall out,
> honest men come into their own. But as soon as we are strong
> enough to defeat capitalism as a whole, we shall immediately take
> it by the scruff of the neck.[1]

Thus the Soviet Union has always concentrated on "disposing
its forces" in such a way as to divide and conquer the West.

At the 19th Party Congress in October, 1952, Stalin again discussed the possibility that disunity among the democratic states
would open the doors wide for the Communist take-over. But
Stalin's many thrusts directed at the West only tightened Western cooperation. The United States "Truman Doctrine" of
March, 1947, was a sharp rejoinder to Stalin's efforts to take
over Greece and Turkey. The Marshall Plan in Europe in 1948
and the high degree of Western cooperation in making the Plan
work was a firm answer to communism's exploitation of the economic and social chaos in Europe following World War II. The
Western European states united in the Brussels Pact in 1948 following Stalin's seizure of Czechoslovakia, and the North Atlantic
Treaty Organization of April, 1949, was an effective allied answer
to increased Soviet pressures in Europe, especially in Berlin. The
United Nations Security Council, strongly backed by members
of NATO, responded quickly and powerfully upon the occasion
of Communist North Korea's aggression against the Republic of
Korea in June, 1950. Stalin's jabs against the West served only
to strengthen Western unity, and perhaps Stalin realized by October, 1952, that less direct action on his part would result in
less unified measures among the democratic nations.

Khrushchev has picked up where Stalin left off. For the most
part, he has avoided a direct confrontation with the West,
realizing that such overt thrusts only increase Western unity.
Khrushchev vowed in November, 1958, to throw the West out
of Berlin, but he has not been able to keep this promise because
threats of such direct moves against the democracies only bring

[1] Hook, *op. cit.*, p. 74.

the Western states closer together. There was a near direct confrontation with United States armed force in Cuba in October, 1962. However, the prompt counteraction by the United States called Khrushchev's bluff, forcing him to withdraw his missiles from Cuba. Realizing that allied unity is the product of direct Soviet threats and military action, Khrushchev stresses more indirect routes in seeking to divide the Western states.

If the Kremlin leader can convey the impression among Western states that he really wants peace and coexistence for all states, then some elements within the democracies may press for a substantial reduction in military preparedness. They would also call upon their governments to rely less and less upon NATO as an instrument of allied unity in responding to the Communist threat in Europe. In this design for allied disunity, the USSR sees little prospect for persuading the United States to abandon its position of Western leadership. America is the central core of allied unity against the international Communist threat. But Khrushchev hopes that if the Soviets can peel off other democratic states from this core of strength, the total "bourgeois" bloc will fall apart. Then the USSR would pick up the remains.

Khrushchev employs all kinds of tactics to inject fear into the Western European states. For instance, he uses nuclear blackmail. He warns the democracies that if they persist in remaining in a tight alliance with the United States in NATO, they must suffer dire consequences. He has threatened Greece with the bombing of the Acropolis, Italy with the destruction of Rome, and the English with the extermination of their homeland.

The Soviet Union, through threats and propaganda, wants the people in Western Europe to think along these lines: "Why should we Western Europeans put so much money and effort into military strength against the Soviet Union? After all, isn't the cold war really a conflict between the USSR and the United States? Let *them* fight it out! If there is a war, we'll be the first ones to feel Soviet military might. Why don't we take a neutral stand between Russia and America?"

The Communist parties in the Western democracies push these ideas all the time. Similarly, Khrushchev has expressed strong approval for groups in the West that advocate withdrawal of the democracies from the arms race, unilateral disarmament, and defenseless neutralism. Khrushchev corresponded approvingly with Bertrand Russell and other Western supporters of one-sided disarmament. He, of course, would never tolerate the expression of similar views within the Soviet Union. But he hopes that in fostering Western disunity through threats and pacifist action within the Western states, he can break up the Western alliance and proceed with picking up these states one by one.

Soviet distortion of the Western image. The Soviet Union wildly distorts the image of the West, reduces the appeal of democracy to the rest of the world, and endeavors to present communism as the wave of the future for all mankind. Most of us in the West simply do not realize the lengths to which the communists will go to vilify the democracies and their leaders, and to foster hatred of the West.

In the Communist world. Vanya Ivanovich, a typical high school student in Moscow, has been taught since childhood to believe in the Communist ideology and in the inevitable triumph of worldwide communism. He has learned in school and at home that capitalism and democracy enslave people, and that high school students in the United States are held in virtual bondage by American "ruling circles." He has read Steinbeck's *The Grapes of Wrath* and has been taught that this novel of the American depression gives an authentic picture of conditions within the United States today. He has no first-hand knowledge whatever of the United States or the other democracies; he knows only what Russian censors permit him to know. He has access to no American magazines or books other than what the government admits for circulation.

Vanya reads such papers as *Pravda* and *Izvestia.* In June, 1962, he opened up the pages of *Pravda* and read that "the pretenders to world supremacy (the United States and its allies) have surpassed Hitler in their savageness, shamelessness and hypocrisy and are openly threatening to unleash a nuclear war." Tass, the official Soviet news agency, shapes all the news to the ideological mold of communism. Vanya will be exposed only to news which is advantageous to the Communist cause, and he and his fellow countrymen will never read about world events which would be damaging to the reputation of the USSR.

Vanya's knowledge of the Russian withdrawal of missiles from

Cuba, for instance, was completely distorted. Khrushchev was made to appear as a true man of peace, as one who saved the world from war. President Kennedy, on the other hand, was a "warmonger" and a savage instigator of belligerent action against "peaceloving" Russians and Cubans. *Pravda,* on October 24, 1962, had a long editorial entitled: "Defeat the Criminal Plots of the Enemies of Peace," when, in fact, it was the Soviet Union which placed the offensive missiles in Cuba, within easy striking force of the United States. But Vanya came to the conclusion that Khrushchev had saved the world from war and that the world was hailing the Premier as the savior of peace.

When Vanya turns on the radio or television, he hears and sees largely what the Soviet government wants him to hear and see. For the most part, Vanya is exposed only to music, poetry, theatre, movies, and writings which support the Communist doctrine and which castigate the West.

Vanya, therefore, enters adult life with a mind that simply has not been opened to ways of thought other than those drilled into him by Communist indoctrination. He doesn't *hate* the American people as such, but he does have a profound hatred for the capitalist system and for Western democracy. He has never had the opportunity to learn the truth, although he probably would like to know much more about the West. The picture in his mind of the West and democracy is distorted to the extreme. He views capitalism much in the way Marx described it in the middle of the nineteenth century.

In the Afro-Asian World. In the Afro-Asian world, the USSR goes to town with propaganda designed to undermine the West on the one hand, and play up the attributes of the Soviet Union and communism on the other. This massive propaganda offensive is part and parcel of the total Communist effort to win over the non-Communist world, which can only be done if the power and unity of the Western democracies can be subverted. The USSR uses many tactics and instruments of policy to chip away at the West, but this approach has met with little success. Therefore, the Soviet Union turns to the Afro-Asian countries in its efforts to distort the image of the democracies and to advance the theory and practice of communism.

Soviet use of the United Nations. The Soviet Union finds the

United Nations an important forum for attacking the West. In the early days of the international organization, Soviet delegates, especially Vyshinsky, sought to use the United Nations to divide the democracies. After the founding of the North Atlantic Treaty Organization in 1949, this approach met with little success. But the propaganda barrage was continually on, with all Communist-bloc delegates doing their utmost at the United Nations to undermine the image of the West in the eyes of Asian and African states. Charges of United States "germ warfare" in Korea, capitalist "oppression" over the territories which were still colonies, and "warlike" intentions of the United Nations were repeated over and over.

After a while, the Soviet Union became its own worst enemy at the General Assembly. The delegates from other nations could see for themselves in the United States that these charges were patently false. United States delegates answered accusation by the Soviets with effective countercharges. Khrushchev's incredible shoe-pounding behavior at the Assembly in 1961 lost friends and alienated fence-sitters at the UN. The attacks still continue, but their value to the Soviet propaganda effort is highly doubtful. Today, the Soviet bloc seeks to attack the West primarily through the uncommitted nations in Asia and Africa, hoping to win over the new states to the Communist cause, and then pick off the West.

Communist Ideology and the Afro-Asian World

Afro-Asian states share some common characteristics. Most received or recovered their independence after World War II. Some of the Arab Middle Eastern states had sovereignty or at least a distinct national identity before 1945. A good many of the new nations, such as India and Egypt, have deep roots in the past, and thus should be considered "new" only in the sense that they have gained full independence from Western control only in recent years. Most of the Afro-Asian states have authoritarian, one-party governments. Their various authoritarian ideologies, which lie between democracy and totalitarianism, may veer in one direction or the other, or may well remain fixed on this middle ground for some time to come. The forces of communism are working intensely to steer Afro-Asian authoritarianism toward the hammer and sickle.

Most of the Afro-Asian states are afflicted with serious economic and social handicaps which lend support to authoritarianism as a way of life and way of governing. But the leaders and most of the people in these nations have a great desire to participate actively in the life of the twentieth century. They are seriously searching for the best route to high levels of national security and well-being. Most, however, do not want to align themselves with either the Western or the Communist bloc in their effort to jump over the centuries and land in the twentieth. They want security, but not big-brother protection. They want help from all quarters, but help without strings.

1. How Have Soviet Leaders Differed in Their Approach to Afro-Asia?

Many years ago, Lenin is reported to have said: "the road to Paris is through Peking." Substitute "control of the West" for Paris, and "conquest of the Afro-Asian world" for Peking, and you have the Communist road map for world domination.

In recent years, the third grouping of states in world affairs — those in Africa and Asia, or "Afro-Asia" — has come to play an important role in the war for the minds of men. More than fifty new states have been carved out of old colonial empires since World War II. Competition for their friendship is keen between the Western and the Communist nations.

There are, of course, some Afro-Asian states which belong to one of the two major blocs. Pakistan, Thailand, and the Philippines are members of the Southeast Asia Treaty Organization, along with the United States, Britain, France, New Zealand, and Australia. Iran is in the Central Treaty Organization with Britain, Turkey, and Pakistan. The United States has defense commitments with Japan, Nationalist China, and the Republic of Korea. On the other side of the coin, Communist China, North Vietnam, and North Korea belong in the Communist bloc. This demonstrates how difficult it is to categorize states in world affairs, in terms of alliances and geographical terms. But the generalization still stands with respect to the threefold division of states in world affairs — the Western, Communist, and Afro-Asian groupings.

Communist leaders today are putting far greater emphasis on controlling the Afro-Asian world than ever before. The Soviet Union is, however, confronted by Communist Chinese ambitions in the same direction. The stakes in the Afro-Asian world are high for both Communist giants and for the West as well. What happens to and within these new nations during the next few decades may well determine the outcome of the worldwide ideological struggle of the twentieth century.

Lenin's Views

After the Communist take-over in Russia, Lenin gave serious thought to the future of communism in the Afro-Asian world. At that time, and until 1945, Africa and Asia were largely under the domination of the Western European colonial powers, and the Middle Eastern states, except Turkey, were independent in name only. Lenin viewed the situation in the Afro-Asian world in 1921 as follows:

> It is perfectly clear that in the impending decisive battles in the world revolution (of communism), the movement of the majority of the population of the globe, which at first is directed toward national liberation, will turn against capitalism and imperialism and will, perhaps, play a more revolutionary part than we expect. . . . In spite of the fact that the masses of the toilers, of the peasants, in the colonial countries are still backward, they will play a very important part in the coming phases of world revolution.[1]

Lenin was excited about the idea of a massive uprising of the Afro-Asian proletariat against the bourgeois West. (The "proletariat" part of the Marxian dialect has come to mean all "toilers" and "peasants.") Marx and some communists have felt that a state must go through a capitalistic stage before the Communist revolution can take place. Lenin, however, in words and action revised this key principle of the founder of modern Communism.

Lenin was also hopeful that the sheer numbers of people in the Afro-Asian countries, along with the people of the USSR, would outweigh the much smaller number of people in the democracies, and that this was important for the future of communism. In 1923, he declared that:

> In the last analysis, the outcome of the struggle (between the Communist and non-Communist world) will be determined by the fact that Russia, India, China, etc., account for the overwhelming majority of the population of the globe.[2]

[1] Mager and Katel, *op. cit.*, pp. 111, 112.
[2] Hook, *op. cit.*, p. 186.

Although Lenin opposed nationalism in "bourgeois" Western states, he called on all Communists to support nationalist movements in African and Asian colonies. Obviously he expected communists to ride these waves of nationalism and to seize the reins of governmental power in succession to the nationalistic revolutions.

Stalin's Approach

Stalin, who quickened the pace of Communist party development throughout the world, laid down some guidelines for the Communist seizure of the Afro-Asian world, which was still under Western control.

> The immediate tasks confronting the revolutionary movement in the capitalistically developed colonial and dependent countries are as follows: (1) to win over the best elements of the working class to the side of communism and to form independent communist parties; (2) to set up a national revolutionary *bloc* of workers, peasants and revolutionary intelligentsia as against the *bloc* of compromising national bourgeoisie and the imperialists; (3) to guarantee the hegemony of the proletariat in this *bloc;* (4) to fight for the liberation of the urban and rural petty bourgeoisie from the influence of the compromising national bourgeoisie; (5) to secure the linking of the national liberation movement with the proletarian movement of the advanced countries.[1]

Stalin felt that if communism could be identified with the rising independence movements in the colonies in the Afro-Asian world, these states would fall eventually into the Communist bloc. Some years later, Stalin elaborated on Lenin's idea that the route to "Paris" should go through "Peking."

> If Europe and America may be called the front (or the key target of the Communist drive toward world domination), the scene of the main engagements between socialism (communism) and imperialism, the non-sovereign nations and colonies, with their raw materials, fuel, food, and vast store of human material should be regarded as the rear, the reserve of imperialism. In order to

[1] Joseph Stalin, *Leninism.* New York: International Publishers, 1933, vol. 1, p. 194. By permission of International Publishers Co., Inc.

win a war, one must not only triumph at the front but also revolutionize the enemy's rear, his reserves.[1]

When the Western states more or less peacefully abdicated their control over Africa and Asia after World War II, it appeared that the Soviet Union might step right in and dominate the Afro-Asian world. But Stalin believed much too strongly in the two-bloc theory of the ideological struggle to apply the declarations he had made about the Afro-Asian world. He therefore concentrated on the "front" or the West and gave little attention to the "reserves" — the Afro-Asian states. He condemned the independence of Burma, India, and Pakistan in 1946 and 1947 as a capitalist trick, and viewed Nehru as a lackey of the West.

Stalin's efforts to crush the West with the resumption of the cold war in 1945 and 1946 failed. He did take Eastern Europe, but thanks to Western unity and United States economic and military aid, he could advance no farther.

What explains Stalin's reluctance to seize the independence movements and ride the tide of nationalism to Communist control? Stalin had a fixation on the brute force of power, especially military power and violent conflict. After all, did not Marx say that the victories of communism could come about only by a violent conflict? The Red Army did a very thorough job of implanting Communist regimes in Eastern Europe. Stalin believed that without tangible pressure from Soviet armed forces, communism would stand little chance of gaining ground. He believed strongly that Communist parties abroad could be useful allies but that the decisive factor would be the power of the Soviet Union itself.

The Aims of Khrushchev

In the 1961 Program adopted by the 22nd Congress of the Communist Party of the Soviet Union, the Khrushchev policy toward the Afro-Asian states was outlined in clear and precise terms:

> The world is experiencing a period of stormy national-liberation revolutions. Imperialism suppressed the national independ-

---

[1] Mager and Katel, *op. cit., p.* 112.

ence and freedom of the majority of the peoples and put the fetters of brutal colonial slavery on them, but *the rise of socialism marks the advent of the era of emancipation of the oppressed peoples.* A powerful wave of national-liberation revolutions is sweeping away the colonial system and undermining the foundations of imperialism. Young sovereign states have arisen, or are arising, in one-time colonies or semi-colonies. Their peoples have entered a new period of development. They have emerged as makers of a new life and as active participants in world politics, as a revolutionary force destroying imperialism.[1]

The Kremlin leader notes that "the young sovereign states do not belong either to the system of imperialist states (the Western bloc) or to the system of the socialist states (the Communist alliance)." He clearly recognizes the third grouping of states which had been snubbed by Stalin. This third system blurs the neat structure of the Marxian dialectic. Where do you put the "middle force" in a dialectic which has room for only two competing sides? This doesn't seem to bother Khrushchev much, especially since he has high hopes of closely identifying the interests of the third group with those of the Communist camp.

In his speech to the Supreme Soviet of the USSR in December, 1962, Khrushchev stressed Soviet support for Afro-Asia.

One of the fundamental trends of the Soviet Government's foreign policy has been and remains to render all-out support to peoples waging a sacred struggle for their freedom, for the consolidation of national independence.

A new Asia is emerging and the last debris of former colonial empires is tumbling down. The victorious procession of the national liberation movement continues in Africa. Latin America, where foreign monopolies have held undivided sway in the recent past, has entered another stage in its history — the stage of the struggle for genuine national independence.[2]

The Soviet Union thus has great aspirations for guiding these new states into the Communist orbit.

[1] Ritvo, *op. cit.,* p. 84.
[2] *Present International Situation, op. cit.,* p. 37.

Desperate people, surrounded by misery, often are easy targets for the myth and promise of totalitariansim. In the 1930's Mussolini hypnotized millions, promising to deliver them from poverty. Today, Duvalier (right) has woven a similar myth to win the support of the impoverished Haitians.

Although Hitler's Germany was defeated in 1945, the ideology of nazism continues to poison men's minds. In 1960 an outbreak of neo-nazism in West Germany, with Nazi propaganda openly displayed in bookstores, served as a grim reminder of the continuing threat of right-wing totalitarianism.

In recent years Franco (left) and Salazar have ruled less strictly. But because they continue to limit the freedom of their people, Spain and Portugal still have far to go to achieve democracy.

Since its erection, the Berlin Wall has become a symbol of communism. It is a barrier to freedom, separating relatives and friends. Its grim concrete and barbed wire indicate the Communist lack of regard for individuality and human values. The men who guard the Wall, ready to shoot anyone attempting to escape, display the contempt for human life which is characteristic of totalitarianism.

Communism permits no opposition to official policy. For resisting land reform, this Chinese peasant was brought before a People's Tribunal. The type of trial shown symbolizes "justice" under the totalitarian state. It cannot be too strongly condemned by those who believe in the democratic ideals of equal justice for all and trial by jury.

2. What May Facilitate Soviet Penetration of Afro-Asia?

Khrushchev feels that the Soviet Union has two distinct advantages for making substantial headway in the Afro-Asian world. He believes that he can exploit the past and present role of the West in the new states, and that he can sell the Communist ideology as a way of life and way of governing to the Afro-Asian states.

The Image Left by Western Colonialism

Khrushchev directs great effort toward emphasizing the harsh aspects of Western colonialism, while the positive contributions of the West to the Afro-Asian states are naturally never mentioned.

In his *Imperialism: the Highest Stage of Capitalism*, Lenin declared that Western competition for control over Africa and Asia brought about misery and exploitation for the peoples of the non-Western world. He and other communists declared that "capitalistic imperialism" had small regard for human beings everywhere, whether in the colonies or in the Western states themselves.

And so, as Khrushchev notes, the peoples in the Afro-Asian states have risen up, overthrown their "exploiters," and achieved independence. He continually seeks to identify this new-found freedom of the Afro-Asian states with the rise of world communism. Both are supposed to represent the overthrow of the bourgeoisie by the proletariat. In 1955, in one of his first statements on the subject, Khrushchev pointed out that:

> A historic victory has been achieved by the peoples of great China, our mutual friends and brothers. Great India has achieved political independence. Other peoples of Asia (and Africa) are freeing themselves from hateful colonial oppression. They are choosing the path of development and non-interference in this great cause.[1]

[1] Mager and Katel, *op. cit.,* p. 113.

But Khrushchev warns the Afro-Asian states that the era of "western imperialism" did not end when these states gained independence. He points out in the Party Program of 1961 that:

> . . . the overwhelming majority (of the new states) have not yet broken free from the world capitalist economy even though they occupy a special place in it. They constitute that part of the world which is still being exploited by the capitalist monopolies. . . .[1]

The Program adds: *U.S. imperialism is the chief bulwark of modern colonialism.*[2]

Nothing is said about how much the democracies did to usher in independence for the Afro-Asian countries after World War II. And nothing is said about the extent to which the West, especially the United States, has lent assistance to the new states so that they may leap over centuries of backwardness and into the twentieth century.

The Appeal of Communism

Khrushchev implores the new states to reject the West and embrace communism. Again we turn to the Party Program of 1961.

> *Capitalism* (democracy, Western style) *is the road of suffering for the people.* It will not ensure rapid economic progress nor eliminate poverty; social inequality will increase. The capitalist development of the countryside will ruin the peasantry still more. The workers will be fated either to engaging in backbreaking labor to enrich the capitalists, or to swelling the ranks of the disinherited army of the unemployed. The petty bourgeoisie will be crushed in competition with big capital. The benefits of culture and education will remain out of reach of the people. The intelligentsia will be compelled to sell its talent.[3]

Khrushchev realizes that communism will not swell up immediately in the Afro-Asian world. He accepts the views inspired

[1] Ritvo, *op. cit.*, pp. 84-85.
[2] *Ibid.*, p. 86.
[3] *Ibid.*, p. 89.

by Lenin on this matter and expressed by the Second Congress of the Third Communist International (Comintern) in 1920: "the revolution in the colonies is not going to be a Communist revolution in its first stages."[1] Therefore, the Communist idea must be carefully sold and exported to the Afro-Asian world.

Communism as the "solution" for economic and social problems in Afro-Asia. The 1961 Program, after condemning the capitalist way for the Afro-Asian states, proceeds to outline the "merits" of the socialist (communist) approach in lifting the lives of the people in that part of the world.

> *Socialism is the road to freedom and happiness for the peoples* (in the Afro-Asian countries). It ensures rapid economic and cultural progress. It transforms a backward country into an industrial country within the lifetime of one generation and not in the course of centuries. Planned socialist economy is an economy of progress and prosperity by its very nature. Abolition of the exploitation of man by man does away with social inequality. Unemployment disappears completely. Socialism provides all peasants with land . . . (it) provides a high material and cultural standard of living for the working class . . . (it) lifts the people out of darkness and ignorance.[2]

Khrushchev thus holds out the promise that the Communist ideology can give the Afro-Asian world "instant twentieth century." The Soviet Union points out that Russia itself made tremendous strides from backwardness in 1917 to become the second most powerful state within four decades. The capitalistic-democratic world took a much longer time to develop, so goes the Communist argument.

Communism as the "solution" for problems of governing in the Afro-Asian world. The Soviet Union has a natural asset in its attempt to export communism as a way of governing in the Afro-Asian world. Most of the Afro-Asian states have authoritarian regimes and do not base their governments on the consent of the governed. One Western analyst reports:

> . . . a quiet and persistent effort (by the Soviet Union) to export the political techniques of communism. To new nationalist lead-

---

[1] Hook, *op. cit.,* p. 189.
[2] Ritvo, *op. cit.,* pp. 89, 90.

ers, eager to strengthen their power, Moscow offers its methods of one-party control, one-party propaganda and cruel but effective methods of repressing dissent, actual and potential.[1]

The way of governing under the Communist ideology in some respects parallels the way of governing in the Afro-Asian world. The leaders of the new states do not want to share their newly found power with competing political forces. Thus they may well find the totalitarian way of governing closer to their tastes than the democratic way of governing and all that it implies.

In his Party Program, Khrushchev hails the governments of the new states, which he calls "national democracies:"

> The establishment and development of national democracies opens vast prospects for the peoples of the economically under-developed countries. The political basis of a national democracy is a bloc of all the progressive, patriotic forces fighting to win complete national independence and broad democracy, and to consummate the anti-imperialist, anti-feudal, democratic revolution.[2]

What a play on words! Everyone wants democracy, presumably, so Khrushchev identifies the interests of communism with democracy; but he certainly doesn't mean Western democracy. He advocates a bloc of authoritarian power in the new states, wants to sell the idea of one-party, one-man rule, and follow this up with Communist principles and ideology. Then the "national democracies" would become "peoples' republics" along the Eastern European order, and thus under the control of the USSR.

3. What May Hinder Soviet Penetration of Afro-Asia?

On the surface, it would appear that the Soviet Union might have clear sailing in winning over the non-Communist world. In fact, however, its efforts have met with considerable failure. The United States Ambassador to India, Chester Bowles, points out that:

---

[1] Philip E. Mosely, "Is It 'Peaceful' or 'Co-existence?'" *The New York Times Magazine*, May 7, 1961.

[2] Ritvo, *op. cit.*, pp. 90-91.

Communist parties have been suppressed by either decree or statute in some 45 nations (in the Afro-Asian world). This does not count the many new nations in Africa where the communist party has failed even to get a start. Even where communists are tolerated in one of their many guises, their effectiveness is often limited. Where they have merged into the local political system, they have lost their identity; where they have failed to merge, they have often found themselves in jail.[1]

Let us examine one case in point. In 1958, Guinea, on the West coast of Africa, won its independence from France and refused to be associated in any way with De Gaulle's French Community. It was a small and weak nation, with very few friends in the world and badly in need of assistance of all kinds. Its independence leader and new president, Sékou Touré, was a dedicated Marxist and naturally turned to the Soviet Union for help. Soviet aid and technicians poured in. The USSR sent over $125,000,000 worth of aid to Guinea from 1958 to 1961.

Within three years, however, Touré ordered the Soviet ambassador to leave the country, and turned to the West for support. Private investment from the West helped to bail out his chaotic national economy. This was a profound failure for the Soviet Union. Why?

There are at least three reasons to explain the over-all failure of the Soviet Union to win over the Afro-Asian nations. The nationalism of the new states has no room for foreign domination, the Communist ideology in practice has been proven irrelevant, and the Soviet-Chinese split blunts the entire offensive thrust of international communism.

The Nationalism of the Afro-Asian States

International communism in the end means international domination, which is quite the opposite of the nationalism of states. Stalin recognized the threat that nationalism posed to international communism when he wrote in 1934 that:

> The lack of an international revolutionary outlook threatens us with nationalism and dissolution. That is why the fight against

[1] Chester Bowles, "Is Communist Ideology Becoming Irrelevant?" *Foreign Affairs,* July, 1962, p. 562.

the danger of nationalism is a matter of such urgency for the party.[1]

The communists hope that those falling in with their ideology would get the "international" spirit of the thing and forget about the national interests of their home nations.

Khrushchev boasts that communism backs nationalism in the Afro-Asian states to the point where this sentiment of the people can surge forth in gaining independence for their nation. But this is where Communist support for nationalism comes to an end. The Party Program points out that nationalism *after* independence is a monopoly of "bourgeois" elements within the state, and therefore it must be crushed.

> . . . the nationalism of the oppressed nation has yet another aspect, one expressing the ideology and interests of the reactionary exploiting top stratum.[2]

Therefore, eliminate this "top stratum" or bourgeois element and let communism of the international variety take over; join the Soviet Union, and march forward with the classless society!

Clearly Lenin, Stalin, and Khrushchev feared the continuation of nationalism in a state which had secured its independence, and they had every right to be afraid of this phenomenon. The new states have become aware of the fact that Communist support for their nationalism was only a device to bring them under Communist control.

In Guinea, the people realized that the Soviet Union did not support them in 1958 just to guarantee their free status in world affairs. They became aware of the fact, in 1958, 1959, and 1960, that the real intent of Soviet communism was to impose a *new imperialism* upon them rather than to back their *new independence*. This they could not accept. They found Soviet aid geared toward the USSR's control of their economy. The material sent was shoddy and in many cases useless. Guinea wanted some military equipment, and got caissons that had to be drawn by horses. Unfortunately, the Guineans had no horses. Deliveries of economic aid were extremely slow, although promises

---

[1] *Strategy and Tactics, op. cit.,* p. 18.

[2] Ritvo, *op. cit.,* p. 88.

were fabulous. Soviet technicians were haughty and pompous. The subversive intent of the aid became crystal clear. The local Communist party tried to take over Touré's one-party, one-man rule rather than subordinate itself to Touré's government. The Communist party was banned and the Soviet Ambassador was told to depart for Moscow.

The leaders and the people of the Afro-Asian states are not fools. They can recognize attempts by foreign nations to dominate their national lives. They have had considerable experience with foreign rule, and did not struggle over long years for independence only to succumb to a new imperialism which would make the old era of colonialism look like a Sunday school picnic. The nationalism of the new Afro-Asian states has no room for the imperialism of Communist internationalism. This is the major reason why Russia's attempts to penetrate the Afro-Asian world have, on the whole, failed.

Clash of Communist Ideology with Afro-Asian Interests

Many of the nationalist leaders who now head the governments of the new Afro-Asian countries embraced Marxism at one time or another. Marx seemed to offer them hope during those long years when they bickered with the West for their freedom from colonial rule. Touré himself has written:

> The Marxism which served to mobilize the African populations, and in particular the working class, and to lead that class to success, has been amputated of those of its characteristics which did not correspond to the African realities.[1]

He and others accepted some aspects of Marxism, but not those elements which could not explain African realities. They rejected what Lenin, Stalin, and Khrushchev did to Marxism. They spurned the doctrines of international communism in particular.

At least four aspects of modern Communist ideology do not jibe with the realities of the new states.

Value of capitalism. Most of the new states have socialist economies, but they also recognize that capitalism and an open

---

[1] Colin Legum, *Pan-Africanism.* New York: Praeger, 1962, p. 105.

market economy have much to offer as well. They see that the welfare capitalism of the twentieth century is something quite different from the capitalism which Marx described in the middle of the nineteenth century. Private investment and free markets are found to be necessary in the new states. Capitalism offers many advantages to the Afro-Asian states. Its vigorous condition in the twentieth century is present for all to see. Most of the states reject the deep hostility which Communist ideology holds against capitalism.

Importance of trade unions. The trade-union movement in the Soviet Union is an instrument of the state, and unions in Russia have no bargaining power whatever. The leaders of the new states recognize the real value of unions and find that Communist ideology is, in fact, alien to the labor movement. They want to control their own unions and not let them be manipulated from outside.

Importance of unregimented agriculture. The economies of the new states, for the most part, are agrarian. But Communist theory and practice has failed dismally in this area and the Afro-Asian states know it. No matter how hard communists try, they cannot avoid the fact that Marxist-Leninism is keyed largely to states which already have some basic industry, and that Communist dogma does not fit in with the needs of agrarian nations. The farmer must be free. He cannot be collectivized. The failure of collectivized agriculture in Russia and China is testimony to the inability of communism to address itself to the massive problems of growing crops and raising livestock, of distributing produce, and of providing continuous levels of well-being for farmers. Here again, Communist ideology does not fit the needs of the Afro-Asian states.

Need for religion. The Communist ideology has no room for any other god than the founders and leaders of the Communist movement. The Moslem, the Hindu, the Buddhist, the religious believer in Africa of a native faith, the Christian — among the many devout people in the Afro-Asian world — cannot really accept the full Communist creed and their own religious convictions as well. Communist ideology simply cannot replace age-old convictions about the Deity, life after death, prayer, and sacred rites. Communism is alien to the religious need of mankind.

The Split Between Communist Russia and Communist China

Finally, the intense duel between Russia and China for leadership of the Communist movement has done much to undermine the appeal of communism in the Afro-Asian states. Soviet communism tends to appeal to the more industrialized states, while Mao Tse-tung declares that his communism fits in more closely with the background and interests of the Afro-Asian world. Both Mao and Khrushchev are competing intensely for commanding positions in Africa and Asia, and many Communist parties are debating as to which side to support.

All of this has retarded the Communist movement. If the ideology is to have one voice, one explanation of Marxist "truth," and one program for bringing about the classless society, which side should one follow? Does it not make more sense to follow neither and work things out independently? If the proletarian camp cannot settle its own ideological problems, can it offer the Afro-Asian world anything but continuous feuds and eventual domination?

On the whole, therefore, Soviet communism is making little headway in Afro-Asia. Indonesia has a sizeable Communist Party but is by no means a Soviet satellite. Many states, such as Nasser's UAR, accept Soviet assistance but put local communists behind bars. If Khrushchev were really elected by the Soviet people and truly responsible to them and to the Russian parliament, the Supreme Soviet, he might be tossed out of office for his massive policy failures in the Afro-Asian world.

On the other hand, the West cannot disregard by any means Communist hopes for penetrating, subverting, and finally controlling the Afro-Asian world. As Lenin pointed out, the Afro-Asian world contains the majority of people in the world, and the masses "will play a very important part in the coming phases of the world revolution." The forces of communism will continue to seek united fronts with left-wing groups to unseat neutralist or pro-Western leaders in the Afro-Asian states and gradually to bring communists into power. Continuous broad appeals to the masses, accompanied by the vast array of Communist tools of subversion, will be employed in pursuit of this goal. Experience has shown that when the above-ground activities of communism have died down or ceased, people seem to think that the threat itself has "withered away." But when Communism goes underground, the threat to peace and freedom becomes all the greater.

4. How Is Communism Promoted in Afro-Asia?

Flexibility is the key to Communist instruments of policy and tactics in the Afro-Asian world. Each nation in Africa and Asia is characterized by a different heritage, different economic and social conditions, and different kinds of leaders with different personalities. Religious, cultural, and political variations in each state must be taken into consideration. Communist pressures are intense in some states, as in Laos, and gentle in others, as in Pakistan. Communist parties are illegal in some countries, as in South Vietnam, and both legal and powerful in others, as in Indonesia.

As always, beneath the surface of official Soviet policy and Communist party tactics, communists make constant attempts to subvert each nation. The Communist effort in all non-Communist states is like an iceberg. Much is above the surface, and can be seen and analyzed. But beneath the surface is a large bulk of activity that attempts to eat into the fiber of the state, pit man against man, corrode the economic and social foundations of the nation, and drive the state toward instability and chaos in order to overthrow the legitimate government of the nation.

Instruments of Official Soviet Policy

Diplomacy, aid, and propaganda have a special significance for the USSR as instruments of policy toward the Afro-Asian world. Mao Tse-tung stresses other instruments, such as guerrilla warfare and belligerent action, but Khrushchev prefers the milder approach.

Diplomacy. On the whole, Soviet diplomats stationed in Afro-Asian states receive extensive training in the language, history, culture, social structure, religious beliefs, and politics of the countries to which they are sent. This is the "soft-sell." The objective is to weave more and more of the tenets of communism into the fabric of the national societies of the Afro-Asian states.

Soviet diplomats tend to be effective agents, and they also know full well the theory and practice of subversion and espionage, which are coordinated with Communist party elements in the countries in which they are stationed.

Economic and military aid. The Soviet aid program, launched by Khrushchev in 1955, clearly demonstrates how the present Kremlin ruler varies from Stalin's approach to the Afro-Asian countries. The late dictator used only a little aid as an instrument of policy designed to further the Communist cause. He did extend aid to China, but only after the communists gained power in 1949.

Khrushchev prefers a wide variety of means other than brute force to further communism; and economic and military aid has been very much in the picture since 1955. During this period, the Soviet bloc has promised $7,100,000,000 worth of economic and military assistance to the Afro-Asian world. This excludes the vast amounts of aid which go to Cuba. Of this figure, 4.6 billion dollars has been allocated in the economic sphere, while 2.5 billion has gone toward military assistance. The Soviet Union is responsible for about 70 percent of this assistance, while the Eastern European states extend about 22 percent, and Communist China 8 percent.

This aid has gone to almost thirty states, including Bolivia, Brazil, and Argentina in Latin America, and fence-sitting Yugoslavia. The nation receiving the most economic assistance has been India ($982,000,000) with the United Arab Republic second ($716,000,000), and Indonesia third ($638,000,000). Soviet economic and military assistance, however, has been tapering off. Bloc aid amounted to about $900,000,000 in 1961 but went down to around $450,000,000 in 1962. This drop may be attributable to economic problems within the Communist bloc, Soviet doubts as to the effectiveness of the program, and doubts among the recipient nations as to the desirability of receiving this brand of assistance. Almost 70 percent of the economic aid has yet to be distributed by the Communist states. Big and flashy commitments are made, but deliveries have been slow. All of the military aid, however, is distributed immediately.

Most of the Communist aid is in the form of long term credits. The economic assistance usually is geared to specific projects, such as the recently completed Bhilai steel mill in India, oil exploration in Afghanistan, India, and Pakistan, and the Aswan Dam project in the UAR. Only a small part of the aid (about 3 percent) goes toward "showpiece" projects, such as a hotel in Burma and a stadium in Indonesia. More than 10,000 technicians from the Communist bloc are at work on the aid projects in the Afro-Asian nations, and they spend considerable time in training people on technical projects. Many thousands of Afro-Asians are also brought to Moscow to receive special training.

The assistance program, interwoven with the efforts of diplomats and party agitators, is a key weapon in penetrating the Afro-Asian states. The state of Indonesia, for instance, is in third place as far as receiving economic aid is concerned, but first when military aid is added in, for a total of more than $1,700,-000,000 worth of assistance since 1955. Russian military assistance, in particular, gave Sukarno the support he needed to assume control over West New Guinea. In this action against the Dutch, Sukarno gained such ill feelings from the West that he has been persuaded to rely more strongly than ever on USSR support. An additional Soviet goal lies in the background in this extensive aid to Indonesia.

> Once the Soviet military assistance program has been completed, it will have destroyed the fabric of Indonesian society by fomenting runaway inflation comparable to that of Germany in the 1920's. The chaos and despair created may well bring the Communist Party (of Indonesia, which has more than two million members) to power.[1]

[1] Guy Pauker, "The Soviet Challenge in Indonesia." *Foreign Affairs,* July, 1962, p. 617.

Inflation, which eats at a nation like cancer, has hit Indonesia hard, and the communists yell that only a Communist government can cure it. Soviet aid and Communist party activity in Indonesia, *acting together,* are proceeding rapidly to undermine the entire Indonesia nation.

Propaganda. Official Soviet propaganda in the Afro-Asian countries has two aspects. A positive side seeks to highlight the attractiveness of communism, and the negative side castigates the role of the West, especially the United States. The aim of the USSR is to condition the mind of the Afro-Asian to believe that the communists are dedicated to furthering his goals of independence, progress, and peace. The West is held up as the chief enemy of these important objectives of Afro-Asian life. All the tools of propaganda — official statements, radio, the press, books, and other communications media — have this pro-Communist, anti-Western bias.

Pro-Communist Propaganda. The Party Program of 1961, widely circulated throughout the Afro-Asian countries, declares that *"the Communists' aims are in keeping with the supreme interests of the* (Afro-Asian) *nation."*[1] In expanding this point, the Program notes that:

> The (new) national states become ever more active as an independent force on the world scene; objectively this force is in the main a *progressive, revolutionary, and anti-imperialist force.*[2]

Thus the new states represent a "force" which has characteristics the communists claim for the Communist ideology itself. The idea of "peace" is put across in the attempt to link up the new states with the "peaceful" Communist bloc.

> *The joining of the efforts of the newly-free peoples and of the peoples of the socialist countries in the struggle against the war danger is a cardinal factor of world peace.* This mighty front, which expresses the will and strength of two-thirds of mankind, can force the imperialist aggressors to retreat.[3]

Khrushchev uses the slogan of peaceful coexistence as an um-

---

[1] Ritvo, *op. cit.,* p. 92.
[2] *Ibid.*
[3] *Ibid.,* pp. 92-93.

brella for the support of "national liberation movements," or
efforts within a country to overthrow a legitimate government,
especially in Afro-Asia.

> Marxist-Leninists proceed from the assumption that the only
> reasonable principle of relations between countries with different
> social systems is peaceful coexistence. Our party has always held
> that peaceful coexistence creates favorable conditions for the
> development of the class struggle by the working people of cap-
> italist countries, for a steady development of the national libera-
> tion movement. The Soviet Union and all the Socialist countries
> regard it as their internationalist duty to give every support and
> all-round assistance to the national liberation movement.

> Marxist-Leninists make no secret of the fact that they want
> to win all the people on the earth for Socialism. This we regard
> as our most important aim on the world arena. We are advanc-
> ing toward this goal, not by imposing our system on other
> peoples. It is by creative labor, by the great constructive force
> of the liberated peoples, by the revolutionary energy of the
> working people that we raise the authority of Socialism, steadily
> change the balance of forces in the world.[1]

The peaceful-coexistence slogan appeals to many in the newly-
independent countries who have no desire whatever to get involved in a major world war. The slogan has great propaganda
value for Khrushchev, especially when he continues to throw
all the blame for militarism in world affairs directly into the
laps of the democratic states.

And so the "peaceful coexistence" idea is brought home to the
Afro-Asian states in full propaganda dress. It is the Soviet
camp which seeks peace, not the "imperialistic" West. Khrushchev
wants a Communist world, but declares that this can come about
peacefully. This could happen, unless we make it quite clear
that peaceful coexistence is a clever disguise for the real aims
of Communist ideology.

Finally, the Communist Party Program goes all out in identifying the aims of communism with those of the Afro-Asian
world:

[1] *The New York Times,* May 24, 1963.

The Communist Party of the Soviet Union considers fraternal alliance with the people who have thrown off the colonial yoke to be a corner-stone of its international policy. This alliance is based on the common vital interests of world socialism and the world national-liberation movement.[1]

Soviet policy, in attempting to line up the aspirations of the Afro-Asian peoples with those of communism, is carried on in many ways: policy statements, the broadcasts of Radio Moscow, cultural offensives, statements of Soviet diplomats in exchanges with officials in the Afro-Asian states, and by many other carriers of Soviet propaganda. Tremendous stress is laid on reading materials, especially cheap pamphlets and books, in advertising the virtues of Communist ideology, accomplishments, and the Soviet Union itself. The Afro-Asian is learning to read, and literacy rates are climbing. The avid readers in Asia and Africa grab up every book they can, especially when they are free or inexpensive, as is the case with Communist literature. The Soviet Union circulates billions of books or pamphlets each year, while the United States tally is only in the low millions. If we measure ammunition in terms of reading materials, the Communist effort is far ahead of the West in the war for the minds of men.

Anti-Western propaganda. According to this material, the USSR and the Afro-Asian states support progress, independence, and prosperity, while the West's role in Africa and Asia aspires toward war, reaction, a new colonialism, and exploitation. It is hard to realize how deceitful and treacherous the Communist propaganda can be unless one actually sees this propaganda at work in the Afro-Asian world.

Look at the Western aid program. The United States has extended about 29 billion dollars' worth of aid to all the countries which the Communist bloc has assisted since 1955. Approximately four times as much aid has come from the West to these states in the same period of time! And yet, the Soviets say that the American aid is a "new imperialism." Khrushchev has charged that:

[1] Ritvo, *op. cit.,* p. 93.

The colonizers (the West) give a dollar in "aid" to receive ten dollars later in return by exploiting the peoples who have accepted such "aid." After this, they enslave the peoples politically. Such are the "new" forms of colonial domination.[1]

The United States, with absolute legitimacy, could turn around and apply this statement to the Soviet aid programs.

The West should be quite clear about one thing in viewing Soviet anti-Western propaganda in the Afro-Asian world. Much of it is blatantly false, most of it is misleading, and all of it is calculated to damage the image of the West in Afro-Asian eyes. On the other hand, Soviet propaganda experts pick up some rough spots in Western societies and play them up in the Afro-Asian countries. Special efforts are made to stress American racial problems. A race riot in Chicago or the anti-Negro views of some Southern governors receive headlines in Afro-Asian newspapers. Khrushchev has made this point many times.

Capitalism has given birth to the man-hating theory about the inferiority of the so-called colored peoples. Who doesn't know the attitude in the United States toward the Negroes? Or remember the notorious "theories" of the German fascists about the necessity of establishing the rule of the Aryans over all other nations?[2]

Soviet propaganda on this score conveniently forgets strong elements of racial prejudice within the Soviet Union. It also hushes up the outbursts against African students which took place in Romania and Czechoslovakia and in Soviet universities.

This official two-edged sword of propaganda works day and night in the Afro-Asian world. The word *official* must be stressed because, while the USSR is determined to distort the Afro-Asian view of the West, it officially calls for peaceful coexistence in dealings with the West. The propaganda attack in the Afro-Asian world is only another attempt to weaken the West by an indirect manner, or to go through Peking to reach Paris.

[1] Mager and Katel, *op. cit.,* p. 123.
[2] *Ibid.,* pp. 146-147.

Communist Party Tactics in the Afro-Asian World

Status of the party. The status of the Communist party in each country is an important clue to the way in which the party operates. We have already noted that the party is either *in control of the state* (as in North Vietnam or North Korea), *a legal entity* which can operate in the open (as in Indonesia and India), or *an illegal force* which can only function underground (as in South Vietnam or the UAR). Where it is the sole party, it dominates the state. Where it is legal, it can carry on its affairs in the open as well as beneath the surface. Where it is illegal, it must rely on subversion, espionage, and front activities to further communism.

With the exception of those Communist parties which hover close to Chinese communism, the party generally works closely with the official Soviet delegation to the Afro-Asian state and harmonizes its activities with official USSR policy. Khrushchev gave Communist parties in the Afro-Asian world a plug in his 1961 Party Program when he said that:

> The communist parties are steadfastly carrying on an active struggle to consummate the anti-imperialist, anti-feudal, democratic revolution, to establish a state of national democracy and achieve social progress.[1]

But the Party, whether legal or not, must make it appear that it is a "national" party and not an instrument of political revolution.

Variation of tactics. Thus Communist party tactics must be many and varied, according to the status of the party in any one country. The contrast, for instance, is amazing when one views the party's activity in Indonesia as compared to its role in South Vietnam. In Indonesia, the Communist party is the largest of any outside the Communist bloc, with over two million members. Its open propaganda plays an important role in the government of President Sukarno. The Communist press in the capital of Djakarta and in other cities is strong, and parrots the Communist line continuously. It claims to be the most nationalistic,

[1] Ritvo, *op. cit.*, p. 92.

most anti-imperialist, most anti-Western. In South Vietnam, however, Vietnamese soldiers, aided by United States military advisers, shoot at Communist insurgent troops whenever they can. Communists in India are seen everywhere, but are in jail in the UAR. Thus the picture of the Communist parties in the Afro-Asian world is scrambled.

Indonesia affords the best example of legal above-board activity. In *most* of the Afro-Asian states, however, the party is illegal. In such states, party members inject their ideology wherever and whenever they can into all kinds of organizations, especially in trade-union movements. They sell communism but do not openly identify their affiliation with their ideology.

Nevertheless, continual harrassments in order to make the most of instability is a firm Communist party tactic. The communists had a field day — or year and a half — in the Congo. Much of the turmoil in that new state had other roots, to be sure. But Congolese communists, supported by Soviet agents, did everything they could to exploit and prolong the crisis and to keep the United Nations' work in the Congo off balance. In the end, however, their efforts failed.

The key problem of Communist party activity in the Afro-Asian states is that of handling the differences between the two Communist giants, Communist Russia and Communist China. Many of the parties in the Afro-Asian world go along with the policies of Khrushchev, but an increasing number are taking up the views and tactics of Mao Tse-tung. Khrushchev seeks to have Communist parties in the Afro-Asian states work up to a point where they can participate in governments through front movements, and take over control in a fairly peaceful manner. Mao Tse-tung, an old Stalinist, stresses militant approaches to a Communist take-over, with guerrilla warfare as the principal tactic in subverting the legitimate government of a state. This is the important thing to watch in the unfolding struggle of communism to seize the Afro-Asian countries.

Whether in the open or underground, whether legal or illegal, whether through the "front" movement or through guerrilla warfare, communists everywhere seek to dominate the Afro-Asian states and, if successful, to link up the new Communist regime with the worldwide Communist movement.

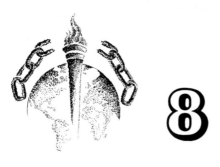

Variations in the Theory and Practice of Communism

Karl Marx might be a bit shocked if he were to show up today and scan the uses to which his ideas have been put during the past sixty years!

First, the founder of modern communism would probe Lenin's activities in Russia, a nation which, on the whole, Marx and Engels strongly disliked. Undoubtedly, he would seriously question Lenin's Bolshevik or Communist Party as *the* instrument of revolution, when Marx preached that the dialectic or clashing of classes would move of its own accord. And how would Marx react to the knowledge that communism first gained control of a state which was backward in many ways and not highly industrialized?

What would Marx think of Stalin's thirty years of tyranny and the exploitation of the masses by the communists themselves? Would Marx approve of Stalin's personality cult and the Soviet Union's claim to leadership of the worldwide Communist movement?

So much for the past! Today, would Marx clink glasses with Khrushchev on the subject of peaceful coexistence, a nuclear test-ban agreement with the "capitalist" nations, and the soft sell of communism in world affairs? Or, would he support the hard line of Communist China's Mao Tse-tung, who clings to the stern principle that the road to communism must be through revolution, warfare, and red-hot hostility toward the democracies? Would Marx be at home in Tito's Yugoslavia, where many evidences of private enterprise blur the original ideas of communism's founding fathers? What would Marx say about all the variations in the theory and practice of communism to be found in world affairs today?

The House of Communism is indeed divided. As a matter of fact, it always has been. Revisionists of Marxism were much in evidence even before Marx died. On the matter of party organization and tactics, Lenin split the ranks of Russian Marxists in 1903. Leon Trotsky differed with both Lenin and Stalin on advancing communism in world affairs, and this deviation cost him his life in August, 1940. Stalin rubbed out all who were at variance with his own interpretation of the teachings of Marx and Lenin. In view of the checkered career of Communist ideology, the many claims to orthodoxy in the Communist camp today should not be too surprising.

We have taken a good look at Khrushchev's brand of international communism. Let us now focus some attention on Tito's national communism in Yugoslavia and the militant Communist ideology which boils over in Mao Tse-tung's China.

1.   What Is Tito's "National Communism"?

Once a black sheep in the family of communism, Tito of Yugoslavia is now warmly embraced by Khrushchev. On the other hand, China's Mao, as did Stalin, sees Tito as the arch traitor to the cause of communism. Tito declares that his "communism in one country" is, after all, exactly what Lenin came up with in Russia after the Revolution. In fact, Tito has wandered far from international communism.

Tito's Rise to Power

Josip Brozovich, or Broz, was born in 1892, the son of a Croatian blacksmith. His early years were marked with poverty, but he moved out in the world as a soldier in the Austro-

Hungarian Army in World War I. Fighting in Russia, he fell into the hands of the enemy, and this was to change the course of his life. After the Russian Revolution, he volunteered in the Red Army and fought in a number of battles for the new Communist government. He became a convert to Marxist-Leninism and, as an agent for the Communist cause, returned to his native Croatia, now a part of Yugoslavia. An active unionist, Broz sought to bring the doctrines of communism directly to the workingman, but he was arrested and spent the period of 1929 to 1934 behind bars. He spent the rest of the 1930's in typical Communist subversive activities. After Yugoslavia was overrun by Germany in 1941, Broz, now Tito, emerged as an important leader of internal rebellion against the Nazis.

Another Yugoslav resistance movement, headed by Draža Mihajlović, had the support of the exiled Yugoslav government and some Western nations. Tito's movement, however, liberally sprinkled with communists, eventually assumed the commanding position in the fight for national freedom. Tito's followers used guerrilla warfare, which has become such an important tool of Communist rebellion. Although he had no support from Stalin's Red Army in flushing the Nazis out of Yugoslavia, Tito was in full control of his nation at the end of the war. The important point to note here is that Tito, unlike other Communist leaders who rode to power on the coattails of the Russian Army, marched to the top through his own independent efforts. This independent establishment of his regime, as well as geographical remoteness from Russia, placed Tito in a unique position in the Communist camp.

Tito, nevertheless, joined the revived Communist international organization, the Cominform, and was pleased to have its headquarters located in his capital at Belgrade. In his efforts to manipulate all Communist parties and tie them directly to the Communist Party of the Soviet Union, Stalin encountered resistance in the independent-minded Tito. The Yugoslav President did not approve of Stalin's demands for economic control. In June, 1948, an abrupt break took place between Tito and Stalin. The Kremlin dictator tossed Yugoslavia out of the Cominform, moved the organization's headquarters to Bucharest, and labelled

Tito as a traitor and a fascist. Until the day he died, Stalin worked toward Tito's downfall. Today, however, Tito's position in Yugoslavia is stronger than ever.

The Nature of Tito's National Communism

Tito and his Communist-dominated government of Yugoslavia stood alone in the world in 1948. The United States, quick to realize the importance of this rupture in the wall of communism, began to extend economic aid to Tito in 1950. It has been a strong force in maintaining Yugoslavia's independence since that time. In breaking with Stalin and accepting American assistance, however, Tito by no means considered himself a traitor to the whole House of Communism. "I am a communist and nothing but a communist," he repeatedly declares.

But to Tito, being a "communist" has come to mean something quite different from Stalin's version of a "communist." Tito's break with Stalin forced the Yugoslav ruler to come up with a definition of his version of communism. His answer was "national communism," or communism for one country. Tito insists he is a loyal Marxist and a good Leninist. He is convinced of the inevitable triumph of communism but believes that capitalism will wither away as new forms of socialism sweep over the non-Communist states. Tito de-emphasizes the use of armed force, violent conflict, or revolution as instruments of a Communist take-over. He even feels that communism need not be imperialistic because of his strong convictions about the natural and peaceful evolution of the Communist ideology.

In reality, Tito was forced into "national communism" by the circumstances of his nationalistic split with Stalin's international imperialism.

Domestic aspects. Tito has been quite active in world affairs since his split with Stalin in 1948. He appears, however, to be more concerned with the building up of communism inside Yugoslavia, hoping that this will serve as a model for expanding communism elsewhere.

The Yugoslav Federal Parliament unanimously adopted a new constitution in April, 1963, which provides for the basic structure of government for Tito's national communism. The constitution declares that Tito is President for life and confers on him full governing powers. The Yugoslav League of Communists, with one million members, is the only legal party. It dominates the Socialist Alliance of Working People, a broader political organization which has more than seven million members. This is a totalitarian government. All power stems from one man, criticism of the political system is not permitted, and the nineteen million Yugoslav people know full well who is boss. Restrictions on freedom of religion are another hallmark of totalitarianism in Yugoslavia.

Despite these facts, the internal policy of the Communist Yugoslav government has some interesting aspects. A flourishing market economy exists, and industry is decentralized — both contrary to the doctrine that concentrated economic planning is the essence of Communist production. Workers' councils in the many plants and factories in Yugoslavia make most of the basic economic decisions, in line, of course, with national directives and targets. This has resulted in increasing rates of production during the past fifteen years as well as progressively higher living standards for the Yugoslav people. On a visit to Yugoslavia in late August of 1963, Khrushchev hailed the workers' councils and indicated that he might try them out in Russia.

In the area of agriculture, "national communism" hardly resembles communism at all. About 90 percent of the land is privately owned. The largely unregimented Yugoslav agricultural system has been quite successful and is ample repudiation of the collectivized approach one finds in most Communist states.

In an economic sense, there is little communism to be found in Yugoslavia. Governmental ownership of most productive facilities does exist, but local initiative and decision-making certainly counter the Communist doctrine that only the few must make decisions for all. The rate of economic growth has see-sawed in recent years, and Yugoslav agriculture has suffered considerably from unfavorable weather conditions. Nevertheless, the over-all economic expansion under the decentralized economic system and the high degree of private enterprise on the farms have given Yugoslavia a standard of living unparalleled among the Communist states in Eastern Europe. This has proven embarrassing to collectivist Communist doctrines and flattering to the proposition that people can best provide for themselves with a minimum of governmental direction.

In national life in Yugoslavia, one also finds considerably more freedom than anywhere else in the Communist world. Areas of freedom exist in research, science, the press, and culture. Western periodicals are widely sold at public newsstands, and overt evidences of a police state are rare. There is no jamming of foreign radio broadcasts, and tourist doors to and from Yugoslavia are wide open. Tito is indeed an odd member of the Communist family, but he is convinced that his pattern of domestic life and economic policy will further the Communist cause, by example if by nothing else.

Foreign aspects. Tito is a fence-sitter in world affairs. He receives aid from the United States and the Soviet Union and places himself in the neutralist bloc of nations. He is a communist but not a militant imperialist. He is violently condemned by the Chinese communists, and some Westerners are equally critical of Yugoslav "national communism," which they rank with communism in general.

Policy toward the Communist bloc. With respect to the Soviet Union, Tito has had many ups and downs. Between 1948 and 1955, Yugoslavia was strictly an outcast as far as the USSR and the other Communist states were concerned. On June 2, 1955, however, Khrushchev signed a pact with Tito which declared that both leaders respected "different forms of Socialist development." This, in a sense, was the formal beginning of Khrushchev's recognition that the route to Communist goals could be achieved by means other than war.

Independence movements within Communist ranks expanded in 1956, resulting in the Polish and Hungarian uprisings. Khrushchev's efforts to put down the Budapest revolution with armed force in November, 1956, was condemned by Tito, and once again a breach between Yugoslavia and the Soviet Union appeared. Since that time, the two Communist nations have blown hot or cold toward each other. The warmth of Tito's reception of Khrushchev on the latter's "vacation" trip to Yugoslavia in August, 1963, gave one the impression that the two are closer than ever before.

Actually, Khrushchev has come to accept many of Tito's convictions about the means to Communist ends. Since Communist China strongly rejects this ideological proposition, Khrushchev needs the support of Tito as a bulwark against the pressures of Communist China. The Soviet Union, in the May Day Proclamation of 1963, included Yugoslavia in the Communist bloc of nations — proof that Khrushchev considers Tito on "his side." In the fall of 1963, Yugoslavia gained observer status in the Soviet bloc's Council for Mutual Economic Assistance. It also seeks observer status in the European Economic Community.

Tito accepts closer relations with the Soviet Union but maintains his neutral status in world affairs. Tito's independent stand in the House of Communism has gained favor in Eastern Europe. Khrushchev has been forced to permit more freedom among the Eastern European satellites because he realizes how much he needs the backing of these states.

Communist China, of course, cannot think of enough unkind things to say about Tito. He is a fascist, traitor, renegade, agent of imperialism, and just plain crooked. Mao Tse-tung hints strongly that good relations between China and Russia will be impossible until Khrushchev severs all ties with Tito — something which Khrushchev cannot afford to do. Mao Tse-tung finds it impossible to believe that a communist who rose to power through warfare, as did Tito, could reject the use of armed force as the only route to Communist victory.

Policy toward the Western bloc. Since 1948, the United States has extended almost 2½ billion dollars' worth of aid to Yugoslavia. Three fourths of this assistance has been for economic purposes, while the rest has gone toward military programs. Without this aid, Yugoslavia would long ago have been gobbled up by the Soviet Union. The United States and its allies have felt that an independent Yugoslavia is in the interest of the democracies because its national brand of communism has substantially jarred the principle and power of the international Communist movement. Tito's disengagement from the once monolithic Communist bloc has helped greatly to undermine the unity of the Communist world.

Yugoslavia maintains close relations with some Western nations, and about 53 percent of its exports go to the democracies. About 24 percent of its trade is with the Soviet bloc, while the rest is with the neutralist states.

Western backing of Tito has been criticized by those who feel that assistance to any Communist state is automatically a bad thing. Aid, of course, does not necessarily imply that the giver approves of everything the receiver does. Tito has made it quite clear that he is a communist and that he expects communism to dominate the world. But Western intervention and influence may well be the instruments whereby Tito's belief in the ultimate Communist triumph could be altered in time. The switch in Communist thinking away from violent revolution would be a welcome change to the world. Undoubtedly the power of the West would be a significant factor in bringing Tito and Khrushchev to this conclusion. Further Western power and policy might possibly change the focus on the *goals* of communism as well as the *means*. If economic and military aid can possibly advance this objective, then the security and well-being of the West would be furthered as well.

Policy toward the neutral nations. Tito feels very much at home with the Afro-Asian nations. He embraces Nasser, hugs Nehru, and is wild about Nkrumah. Since Tito has ideological problems with both the Soviet and Western blocs, he is much more comfortable with the neutralist states. The Afro-Asian states, in return, find much to like in Tito's Yugoslavia. They find its independent position in world affairs and its moderate successes in agriculture and industrialization appealing.

One of Tito's old colleagues, Milovan Djilas, became disenchanted with the entire theory and practice of communism and set forth his views at some length in a book entitled *The New Class.* He not only condemned communism itself but leveled an attack against Tito's national communism.

> National communism *per se* is contradictory. Its nature is the same as that of Soviet communism but it aspires to detach itself into something of its own, nationally. In reality, national communism is communism in decline.[1]

[1] Milovan Djilas, *The New Class.* New York: Frederick A. Praeger, Inc., 1957, p. 190.

Unable to stomach this strong denunciation of his own movement, Tito expelled Djilas from his post as Vice President of Yugoslavia in 1954. Djilas was imprisoned, released, and then jailed again in 1962 for another book indicting communism (*Conversations with Stalin*). Djilas serves as ample testimony that Tito will not permit political dissent, but the former Yugoslav official perhaps hit the nail on the head in his analysis of national communism.

How long Tito can retain his unique position of defying both friend and foe is difficult to say. He maintains a thirty-division army, the largest single military force in Europe next to the Soviet Union's. He therefore is well prepared to defend his independence. Whatever one may say about Tito's national communism, this ideology may lend itself to new possibilities for removing armed imperialism from the House of Communism itself.

2. How Did Communism Become Dominant in China?

Sun Yat-sen's 1911 Revolution

The history of China during modern times is crowded with imperialism, revolution, famine, and absolute chaos. After the middle of the nineteenth century, China fell under the domination of the Western powers. The decadent Manchu dynasty succumbed to imperialism and paid little attention to the hundreds of millions of Chinese people. An American-educated Chinese, Sun Yat-sen (1866-1925), founded a revolutionary society in Honolulu in 1894. Its aim was the complete overthrow of the Manchu dynasty and the termination of foreign domination of China. Sun's movement, later known as the Kuomintang, continually gained strength and launched a revolution against the Manchus in 1911. This historic uprising brought the old dynasty to an end. Although many warlords and large-scale landowners stood firm against Sun's movement, the uprising gave China a new lease on life.

Sun Yat-sen, named the first President of the Provisional Chi-

nese Republic, hoped to combine some of the ancient and traditional concepts of Chinese society, especially Confucianism, with
the elements of modern democracy. He knew that it would take
decades to graft the new onto the old. But he had three key
principles — nationalism, democracy, and human well-being.
He believed that they would progressively be eagerly accepted
by his people, and in a peaceful manner. He felt that military
rule would have to come first, followed by education for democratic obligations, and finally, constitutional government.

His greatest disappointment was his failure to receive American or British support for his genuine attempts to bring democracy to China. He admired Lincoln deeply and could not
understand why the West continued to aid the northern Chinese
warlords who opposed his democratic revolution. In 1917, therefore, he began to turn to Lenin's new regime in Russia for guidance and support.

Turn to Marxism

That same year a strong supporter of Sun Yat-sen, Mao Tse-
tung (1893-   ), was forming a "New People's Study Society"
to discuss political matters. Young Mao was a peasant's son who
had struggled as a boy for every scrap of education and knowledge he could get. He worked hard to get an education and
later became a librarian and teacher. In 1918, he and some members of his "study group" organized a society at the University
of Peking for the study of Marxism. In 1921, after reading Marx's
Communist Manifesto carefully, Mao became a full-scale Marxist
and participated in the founding of the Chinese Communist
Party in that same year.

World events brought Sun Yat-sen's movement closer to the
new Communist government in Russia and to the new Communist Party in China. After the Bolshevik Revolution in 1917,
Lenin renounced all rights Russia once had in China. On the
other hand, at the Treaty of Versailles in 1919 the Western powers gave Japan, which made strong demands on China in 1915,
former German holdings on the important Chinese peninsula
of Shantung. Thus the West continued to take a heavy hand in
Chinese affairs, while the new Russian government saw distinct

possibilities for advancing communism in China. The West ignored Sun Yat-sen and refused to accept his delegates to the Washington Disarmament Conference of 1921-1922. Late in 1922 and early in 1923, therefore, Sun Yat-sen brought the Communist Party into the Kuomintang with the blessing of Russian agents who were advising the Chinese leader. Sun even sent one of his top aides, General Chiang Kai-shek (1886-   ), to Moscow to examine the Soviet system and to seek additional assistance from Lenin.

Sun Yat-sen, embittered by the failure of the Western democracies to back him, declared shortly before he died that communism was distinctly in line with his three principles of nationalism, democracy, and human welfare. In the meantime, the Communist Party organization was rapidly growing in power. A split in its ranks had developed, however, between those who thought the Party should concentrate on the urban proletariat and those, led by Mao Tse-tung, who wanted to stress revolution among the peasants in China. The "urban" communists tried uprisings in Canton and Changsha and failed miserably, but Mao was still too weak politically to advance his peasant approach.

Chiang Kai-shek's Nationalists Combat Mao Tse-tung's Communists

With the death of Sun Yat-sen, Chiang Kai-shek took over control of the Kuomintang. Unable to accept the growing Communist influence within his movement, Chiang moved against the communists. In July, 1927, the united front between the communists and the Kuomintang formally ended. Mao had about 100,000 supporters who moved north with him, among them Chu Teh, who later became Supreme Commander of the Chinese Army. In 1931 Mao formed a Chinese Soviet Republic in the Kiangsi region of China, with an army of some 60,000 men. One of the main attractions to Mao's movement was his decent treatment of the Chinese peasant. Mao's communism became identified with a "new deal" for millions of destitute Chinese peasants. This is the most important single reason why the communists eventually seized control of China.

Chiang Kai-shek found Mao his bitterest enemy and attacked

the Communist leader with large forces in 1930, 1931, and 1933. By October, 1934, it was clear to Mao and his followers that they had to travel further north, and so the famous Communist "Long March" began. During the course of a year, over 100,000 followers of Mao trekked more than six thousand miles under extremely arduous conditions to the province of Shensi. Only 20,000 survived this tortuous trek. The Long March, however, won hundreds of thousands of Chinese peasants over to Mao's side because of his good treatment of them and his policies of land reform. It was a massive propaganda migration and brought Mao's idea of communism for the peasants home to countless Chinese.

The War Against Japan and the Communists

Chiang became the undisputed leader of the Kuomintang and the Chinese government. Although he never controlled all of China, he was viewed by most of the Chinese, as well as other nations, as the legitimate head of state. But Chiang was confronted with the Japanese invasion of Manchuria in 1932 and with full-scale war with Japan in 1937. From that point on, Chiang fought the Japanese and the communists, and Mao fought both in return. Mao's armies in northern China occupied many areas after tough guerrilla warfare and brought Communist ideas and land reform to Shantung, Shansi, and other key provinces. Mao called for a coalition between the communists and the Kuomintang, but Chiang would have none of it.

The complexities of fighting multiple enemies continued into World War II, but Mao extended his control far and wide in the north. By the war's end, Mao had an army of almost one million men and controlled an area encompassing about ninety million Chinese.

Mao's rise to power was largely based on his good treatment of the Chinese peasant, eviction of the hated landlord, land reforms, and a disciplined army. He had very little support from Russian communists during the period between 1927 and 1945. Stalin viewed Mao as an artificial communist because of the rural foundations of Mao's communism. Some Westerners who visited Mao during these years called him an "agrarian reformer" and not an orthodox communist. Mao was indeed a dedicated communist, but felt that the route to communism in an under-developed agrarian country such as China must be peasant-oriented rather than based on the city proletariat.

With Chiang's support, the United States took the initiative in attempting to bring the communists and the legitimate govern-ment of Chiang Kai-shek together after the end of World War II. These efforts, directed by United States General George Marshall, met with failure. Mao then launched a massive offensive against Chiang early in 1947. Mao's great experience with guer-rilla warfare, with winning the peasants over to his side, and with a large, disciplined army brought him victory over Chiang by the fall of 1949. The Soviet acquisition of important parts of Manchuria in 1945 aided Mao's cause, but the Chinese Com-munist leader, on the whole, directed his own victory parade.

Communism Victorious in China

Chiang's army was exhausted after long years of internal strife and warfare. Inflation was rampant in Chiang's part of China, and his allegiance with the old warlords and the landowning classes lost him the support of the masses. On October 1, 1949, Mao proclaimed the establishment of the new People's Republic of China, and Chiang Kai-shek fled to the island of Taiwan (Formosa).

3. What Is the Nature of Mao Tse-tung's Stalinist Communism?

The official title of Mao's government is "The Central People's Government of the People's Republic of China." Its basic con-stitutional structure was completed by 1954. The *structure* of government is much like that of the Soviet Union, with a demo-cratic front but a totalitarian core. The Chairman of the People's Republic is Liu Shao-ch'i, and the Premier is another veteran Chinese communist, Chou En-lai. The Communist Party, headed by Mao Tse-tung, dominates the government and directs all of its activities.

Domestic Policies

Mao controls a nation of over 700 million people, with 1700 children being born each hour. When he gained control, he was faced with famine, illiteracy, and staggering poverty. How did he tackle the problem of lifting up the nation and unifying it for the first time in over 100 years?

Mao's answer, of course, was framed in the totalitarian mold. He set out on a massive program of land reform, industrialization, and over-all restoration of the nation's economy. Although he has made important strides in raising production, constructing dams, building railroads, and unifying the nation under a central authority, the price has been tremendous in terms of human toil and suffering. The *commune* has been the main organizational device for "progress" in China, with more than 550 million Chinese organized in some 26,000 collective beehives for agricultural and industrial purposes. Life is strictly regimented in the commune, each one of which has some sixty to seventy thousand people. These units function in line with Communist Party-Government directives. While they have enabled Mao's nation to forge ahead in some areas, the individual is totally submerged in a choking collectivity of human beings.

In the area of urban development, Mao has made considerable strides in comparison to pre-Communist China. In 1958, Mao called for a "Great Leap Forward" for industry and agriculture, but this leap has never even approached all the expectations that propaganda promised for it. Thousands of refugees have tried to escape from Communist China through Hong Kong and elsewhere. They have told of the fantastic oppression to be found within the communes and the industrial centers and about the stark failure of the Communist regime. They have described the tragic famine which has swept over China and the staggering Communist indoctrination of the Chinese mind and spirit.

Mao's regime imposes a straitjacket on the minds of all Chinese. Propaganda hails the "great forward movement" of the Chinese people. For millions, perhaps, life *is* better under Mao's rule. Absence of warfare and decreased internal strife, along with some aspects of modernization, have helped to promote the myth and promise of communism.

America is depicted as the absolute devil in China. Young Chinese are taught to memorize hate slogans about the United States and its leaders. Confucianism has been tossed out the window, and Mao's brand of Communist ideology has become the sole doctrine of the state.

The regime concentrates on making certain that Chinese youth become fully devoted to the Communist cause. In the communes, children are educated by professional communists and not by their parents. They are taught to copy the bee as the perfect model of collective behavior. Communist leaders point out that:

> Bees are not only remarkable workers but also fight bravely to safeguard the collective achievements. They are courageous in struggling firmly against those who damage the collective interests and will not hesitate to sacrifice their own lives when necessary.[1]

The beehive of China is an ominous threat to world peace.

Foreign Policies

Mao is on the militant path toward world domination. He views himself as the true leader of the Marxist-Leninist-Stalinist movement, labels Khrushchev a revisionist and tool of the West, and insists that the Chinese brand of communism is the authentic and exclusive approach to the world Communist empire.

Mao revels in the use of armed might, or "violent conflict," to step up the pace of Communist domination. He cascaded his blue-ant army into North Korea against the United Nations' forces in November, 1950, and through his control of Communist North Korea, keeps the United Nations' armistice line in constant turmoil. Mao's army swept into Tibet in 1959, dislodged the Dalai Lama, and virtually annexed Tibet to China.

That same year the Communist Chinese provoked border skirmishes with India over territory nestled high in the Himalayas. In 1962, Mao's troops launched a major invasion with a view to occupying this territory, over which India claims sovereignty. Although this border dispute has quieted down somewhat, China continues to pose a massive threat to Nehru's

[1] *The New York Times,* October 13, 1962.

domains. Elsewhere, Mao extends moral and material support to insurgent guerrilla movements in such nations as Laos and South Vietnam.

In the mid-1950's, Mao Tse-tung did flirt with a more peaceful approach to advancing communism in Asia. In 1954, China and India reached agreement on five principles which were supposed to improve relations between the two most heavily populated states in the world. These points included respect for each other's territory, vows of non-aggression, policies of noninterference in each other's internal affairs, equality for all, and peaceful co-existence. In 1955, at the conference of Afro-Asian neutralist nations in Indonesia, Communist Premier Chou En-lai spoke softly and sweetly about Communist China's intentions in world affairs. He tried to win friends and influence leaders among the uncommitted states and to identify their interests with those of Communist China. On February 27, 1957, Mao delivered a most uncharacteristic speech in which he said that various schools of thought on Marxism should stand up and express their views. "Let a hundred flowers blossom," he declared.

Well, some flowers did rise up and try to blossom, and were immediately cut down. And then, in short order, the five points designed to govern relations between China and India were buried under the snowdrifts in the Himalayas. Chinese military action against India poisoned relations between Mao's government and many of the neutralist states, and the Chinese thereafter reverted to the militant approach toward the Communist millennium. Apparently Mao came to feel that peaceful coexistence would do little to advance the Communist cause, either at home or abroad. Today, he pushes for internal subversion and guerrilla warfare to spread communism rather than for any united front between the Communist Party and the governments in the Afro-Asian world. He now views the leaders of the new states as front men for the Western nations.

Outside of Asia, Communist China has played a minor role in world affairs. Mao's government has repeatedly been denied membership in the United Nations, with most of the world's states continuing to recognize Chiang Kai-shek as the head of the legal government of China. Mao's People's Republic maintains very few relations with Western states and is particularly violent when making any reference to the United States. On the other hand, the Chinese Communists are seeking stronger trade relations with Britain. Perhaps their poor relations with the Soviet Union will lead to further attempts to do business with the West.

4. What Are China's Relations with Russia?

What about China's relations with Khrushchev's Russia? On February 14, 1950, Mao's People's Republic of China and Stalin's Soviet Union were united in a thirty-year treaty of peace, friendship, and aid. On the surface, relations between the two Communist giants appeared to be smooth during the subsequent years. In 1957, for instance, Mao Tse-tung declared that:

> In the course of the struggle for national liberation, the Chinese people enjoyed the fraternal sympathy and support of the Soviet people. After the victory of the Chinese Revolution (1949), the Soviet Union is also rendering tremendous all-round assistance to the cause of the construction of Socialism in China. The Chinese people will never forget this.[1]

Chinese and Soviet Ideological Differences

By 1959, however, it became apparent to the outside world that a "cold war" was taking shape between the Soviet Union and the People's Republic of China. Russian aid was being withdrawn. "Friendship" was taking flight as well, and "peace" was simply going to pieces. Today, a state of intense antagonism exists between the Communist Parties of Russia and China, the heads of which both claim leadership for the international Communist movement.

At its roots, the Soviet-Chinese cold war is ideological in nature. Mao is the self-styled heir to the leadership of the Communist world. He rests this claim on his more than four decades of pre-eminence in the Chinese Communist Party, on his position of power at the time of Stalin's death in 1953, and on his insist-

[1] *The New York Times,* July 15, 1963.

ence that his views fit firmly within the box of Marxist-Leninist orthodoxy. He therefore does not hesitate to shout "heretic!" at Khrushchev and deride the Soviet Premier's peaceful co-existence policy. He considers Khrushchev an ideological "revisionist," one of the nastiest words in the Communist lexicon. Mao roundly condemns all facets of the Russian Communist Party and its approach to advancing the mission of communism in world affairs.

Khrushchev and his Communist associates in the Kremlin are aghast at such charges:

> How can they say such a thing about the party of the great Lenin, about the motherland of Socialism, about the people that, first in the world, accomplished a Socialist revolution, upheld its great gains in violent battles against international imperialism and domestic counterrevolution and displays miracles of heroism and dedication in the struggle for the building of Communism, honestly fulfilling its internationalist duty to the working people of the world?[1]

In this brief paragraph, Khrushchev's Party lays out its claim to the leadership position of the international Communist movement. The Communist Party of the Soviet Union goes on to declare that Mao's Stalinist line, so very much in disrepute in Russia, will lead the world directly toward a nuclear war. Khrushchev labels Mao a "left-wing deviationist," one who has veered off in a radical, senseless direction.

Khrushchev has refused to support Mao's belligerent attitude in world affairs. The Soviet Premier has declined to lend material assistance to the Chinese Communists in their strong desire to attack the Nationalist Chinese stronghold of Taiwan, 100 miles off the Chinese mainland. Russia has worked hard to keep China out of the exclusive club of states possessing nuclear weapons. Khrushchev has condemned the Communist Chinese approach to collectivity through the beehive communes. Khrushchev's visit to the United States in 1959 and the emergence of the Russian peaceful coexistence policies have infuriated Mao. Khrushchev's neutral stand on the Chinese invasion of Indian territory in 1960

[1] Open letter from the Central Committee of the Soviet Communist Party to all Party organizations, reprinted in *The New York Times*, July 15, 1963.

also added fuel to the fire. Russia has withdrawn its technical-assistance experts from China and has demanded that Mao repay the more than $300,000,000 of Chinese indebtedness to the Soviet Union.

By 1960, the deep split between China and Russia could no longer be concealed. Some students of history have declared that this was to be expected in view of the fact that over the ages the relations between the two nations have been marked with hostility. The oriental Mongol hordes invaded and occupied Russia for two centuries between 1250 and 1450. Russia, in turn, bit off large chunks of Manchuria in the late nineteenth and early twentieth century, treating the Chinese in a high-handed manner. The new Communist government of Lenin renounced imperialist rights in China after the 1917 revolution, but border controversies between the two Asian nations have risen on many occasions. The two states have played a long game of tug-of-war over Outer Mongolia as well.

This break between China and the Soviet Union has had a profound impact on the substance of Communist ideology, the loyalties of Communist parties throughout the world, and on the totality of relations between the West and the Communist bloc. Ideologists of China and the Soviet Union met in Moscow in July, 1963, presumably to iron out differences. During these discussions, however, both sides stuck to their basic positions and departed in an atmosphere of even greater hostility. Since that time, both have sought to further their respective views within the worldwide Communist movement.

For all practical purposes, the Communist world has a cold war of its own. All indications point to the dropping of any pretense of unity between Russia and China and to the possibility that the Chinese communists might construct a worldwide organization of their own.

The many areas in which there are profound disagreements between the Russian and Chinese Communist Parties are set forth in the excerpts which follow on pages 186-188. Probably the only point on which both sides would agree would be the ultimate goal of communism — world domination. As the following excerpts indicate, the central issue of the Chinese-Soviet cold war revolves around the *means* to this end.

Summary of Major Points in Soviet-Chinese Dispute

Following is a summary of the Chinese charges on the main issues of the Peking-Moscow dispute and of the Soviet replies as outlined in the open letter in PRAVDA:

War

Chinese Charge — The Soviet leaders have forsaken the Marxist-Leninist approach to the question of war, encourage illusions that war can be abolished while imperialism exists, and take a bourgeois pacifist attitude on the question of war.

Soviet Reply — The Chinese Communists do not believe in the possibility of preventing a world war and encourage illusions that mankind could build a bright future upon the ruins of what would remain in the world after a thermonuclear war.

Nuclear Weapons

Chinese — The Soviet leaders exaggerate the impact of nuclear weapons on the world situation and are trying to justify revisionist retreats from revolutionary Marxism-Leninism by frightening people with stories about what nuclear war would do.

Soviet — The Chinese Communists "obviously underestimate all the danger of thermonuclear war" and some Chinese leaders are willing to sacrifice hundreds of millions of lives in a nuclear struggle.

Revolution

Chinese — The Soviet leaders and their allies are seeking to weaken the world revolutionary movement by excessive emphasis upon legal and parliamentary means of overthrowing capitalism, though there is no precedent for such a change.

Soviet — The Chinese Communists are being adventurous and endangering the victory of world Communism by encouraging armed revolutions prematurely, before there exist proper revolutionary situations.

Cuba

Chinese — The Soviet Union was adventurous in putting missiles in Cuba and then capitulated to United States power when it withdrew the missiles under the threat of President Kennedy's ultimatum.

Soviet — The Soviet Union put missiles in Cuba because it had "trustworthy information that an armed aggression of United States imperialism against Cuba was about to start." The Soviet Union withdrew the missiles to prevent the outbreak of thermonuclear world war and only after the United States Government had given a commitment not to invade Cuba.

Soviet Development

Chinese — The Soviet leaders have encouraged baseless illusions among the Soviet people that full Communism and complete abundance can be achieved in the Soviet Union during this generation. The Soviet leaders are helping to restore capitalism in Russia by trying to abandon the dictatorship of the proletariat and changing the proletarian character of the Soviet Communist Party.

Soviet — The Chinese are wrong and they understand neither correct Marxism-Leninism nor the actual situation in the Soviet Union, where no hostile classes exist that must be kept down by a dictatorship of the proletariat.

Stalin

Chinese — The Soviet leaders injured the world Communist movement by their exaggerated and unwise attacks on Stalin.

Soviet — The Chinese leaders have betrayed Leninism by coming out as supporters of the "cult of personality" of Stalin. Moreover, the Soviet Union and world Communism are stronger because of the exposure of Stalin's crimes.

Economic Relations

Chinese — The Soviet Union inflicted great damage on China by unilaterally reducing its trade and violating hundreds of agreements. Moreover, the Soviet Union tries to exploit other Socialist countries under the pretext of encouraging national specialization of production and international economic division of labor.

Soviet — It is the Chinese who are responsible for the sharp drop in Soviet-Chinese trade, and the Chinese inflicted serious damage on other smaller Socialist countries by unilaterally cutting their trade with them by half in the past three years. Moreover, the Chinese are now trying to discredit the significance of the vast economic and military aid the Soviet Union has given to China since 1949.

Racism

Chinese — The Soviet leaders are really supporting colonialism and the rule of "superior" nations over "inferior" nations by refusing to give top priority in world revolutionary activity to the national liberation struggle in Asia, Africa and Latin America.

Soviet — The Chinese are actually following a racist, anti-white policy having nothing in common with Marxism-Leninism, and they are harming the national liberation movement by seeking to divorce it from the working-class revolutionary movement.

(*continued on next page*)

Albania

Chinese — The Soviet leaders are responsible for the break with Albania, which they exacerbated grievously when Premier Khrushchev, in defiance of correct Marxist-Leninist policy, made the dispute with Albania public in October, 1961.

Soviet — The Chinese incited the Albanians to adopt an incorrect line and they have used the Albanians as mouthpieces against the Soviet Union.

Yugoslavia

Chinese — Yugoslavia is not a Socialist country and the Yugoslav leaders are capitalist agents. The Soviet leaders are damaging the cause of Communism by praising Yugoslavia and courting its leaders.

Soviet — Yugoslavia is a Socialist country though its leaders do have some incorrect ideas with which the Soviet Union does not agree. The Chinese effort to excommunicate the Yugoslavs and separate them from the Socialist camp is precisely what the imperialists want.

Communist Parties

Chinese — The Soviet leaders are trying to rule the world Communist movement and force all Communist parties to accept Moscow's unilateral decisions as binding doctrine. The Soviet leaders are using their temporary majority among world Communist party leaderships to try to impose their will upon the Chinese.

Soviet — The Chinese Communists are deliberately trying to split the world Communists by encouraging pro-Chinese and anti-Communist party groups in many parts of the world. It is the Chinese who are really trying to impose their will upon all other Communist parties.[1]

Reasons for Chinese-Soviet Split

Four factors do much to explain the roots of Mao's ideological differences with Khrushchev. They include the independent nature of Mao's rise to power, his tactics and instruments of attaining power, the agrarian aspect of his brand of communism, and the durability of Mao and other Chinese Communist leaders.

Mao's independent rise to power. Mao gained control of China with exceedingly little assistance from Communist Russia. Like

[1] © 1963 by *The New York Times* Company. Reprinted by permission.

Tito, he feels no real obligation to the Soviet Union. Stalin continually snubbed Mao while the Chinese leader was virtually isolated from the rest of the world during the 1930's and early 1940's and badly in need of assistance. Stalin, indeed, backed Chiang Kai-shek for many years. He even told Mao in 1945 that the time was not ripe for revolution in China. Mao blazed ahead, and after Stalin saw what success he was having, invited Mao to climb on the international Communist band wagon. Mao was happy to do this because he needed all the backing he could get. But the fact remains that Mao refuses to accept Soviet leadership of the international Communist movement, largely because he attained power in China through his own drive and initiative.

Mao's tactics in attaining power. Mao fought his way to control. He is a revolutionary. To his mind, armed conflict is the principal route to Communist power. He expanded his control of North China in the 1930's and early 1940's through guerrilla warfare. His armies marched southward between 1947 and 1949, using basically the same tactics.

Mao's guerrilla warfare is characterized by well-trained military cadres spreading out like cancer from small centers over a rural area and seizing control of small towns and villages. Clandestine communications, organized intelligence and counterintelligence activity, clever propaganda, and good relations with the local populace are all integral parts of well-organized guerrilla warfare. It is a cruel but effective method of undermining a national society. It is particularly useful to Communist activity in the Afro-Asian world, where populations and terrains lend themselves better to guerrilla action than to organized warfare.

Mao has used this approach to power over a larger area and for a longer period of time more effectively than any other Communist leader. He has become an acknowledged expert on the subject. His book, *Mao Tse-tung on Guerrilla Warfare,* has been the basic guide to communists everywhere who seek power through insurgent action.

Mao feels that the Afro-Asian world can be captured by his special tactics of guerrilla warfare. Because of his experience in this tactic, he believes that he, not Khrushchev, holds the keys to the future of communism. The success of the F.L.N. (National Liberation Front) movement in Algeria and the guerrilla warfare of Castro and Guevara in Cuba are largely attributable to guidance provided by Mao Tse-tung.

Agrarian background of Mao's communism. Mao always supported the idea that the peasant, not the urban proletariat, was the stepping-stone to power. Mao struggled for many years with other Chinese Communists who tried to bring the Chinese city workers into line. They failed, and Mao's peasant approach succeeded. When he took over power in China in 1949, he established a dictatorship of the proletariat, but 90 percent of the "proletariat" were peasants.

Mao points out that most of the people in Afro-Asia and in Latin America are "peasants." He feels that his peasant foundation of Chinese communism is another reason why he should command the destinies of communism in world affairs. Mao does not see much opportunity, naturally, for peasant communism and guerrilla warfare to conquer the Western world. But he does foresee his peasant communism as the means by which the rest of the world can be seized.

Mao points out that Russia is a "have" nation. He notes that the revolution is settling down there, standards of living are rising, and the country is becoming rich. Mao adds that China is poor like the rest of the Afro-Asian world. He claims to be the spokesman for communism among these poorer nations. He also declares that the industrialized nations will be communized only by conflict and war, which Khrushchev wants to avoid.

In the peasant-crowded Afro-Asian world, Mao feels that the time is ripe for wars of national liberation. He feels that communists should jump in wherever the opportunity presents itself, and use *his* approach to power. Mao advises communists to tell the West that its intervention in wars of liberation sparked by communists will result in nuclear war. Khrushchev's failure to maintain a nuclear threat against the United States in Cuba defied this view. Mao feels that Khrushchev thereby let down the entire Communist offensive.

The durability of the Chinese Communist leaders. Mao was one of the founders of the Chinese Communist Party, and he still heads it today. He and others, such as Chou En-lai, Liu Shao-ch'i, and Chu Teh, fought for decades for their victory in 1949.

The revolutionary leaders of yesterday are the governmental leaders of today, and their revolution has never "settled down." Khrushchev did not fight at the barricades during the Bolshevik Revolution of 1917, nor did any of his colleagues in Russia today. He is more bent on conserving the revolutionary work of others. But Mao still feels the heat of the revolutionary fires with which he has lived for so many years.

Effects of Soviet-Chinese Struggle for Power

Who speaks for communism?   A totalitarian ideology calls for one doctrine, one myth, and one voice. As head of the Communist Party of the Soviet Union, Khrushchev considers himself supreme in the ranks of world communism. Because the first successful revolution for the Marxist cause took place in Russia, the Soviet Union has naturally exercised leadership over the international Communist movement.

On the other hand, the Central Committee of the Chinese Communist Party declared in September, 1960, that Mao Tse-tung was the "greatest contemporary theoretician of Marxism and Leninism." Thus the personal struggle between Khrushchev and Mao for leadership of international communism is a key aspect of the present cold war between the Soviet Union and Communist China.

Divisions in the Communist world.   The cold war in the ranks of communism has produced many conflicts within Communist parties everywhere. Most of the parties in the West and in Eastern Europe are sticking with Khrushchev, although minority groups in some parties, such as in the Italian party, back Mao. Many Communist parties in Latin America are split down the middle on the Khrushchev-Mao issue. Castro (page 239) is indulging in some fancy fence-sitting. The Communist party of Indonesia, the largest outside the Communist bloc, gives strong evidence of backing Mao Tse-tung.

Communist North Korea sides with Mao, and North Vietnam is closer to China than to Russia, although the veteran North Vietnamese leader, Ho Chih-minh, is Moscow-trained. Many Communist parties are becoming neutralist and find Tito's national communism interesting and useful. Both the Soviet and Chinese centers are vying intensely for influence within all Communist parties throughout the world.

Albania is an interesting symbol of the Russian-Chinese split. The defection of Tito from the Communist camp gave the Albanian leader, Hoxha, the idea that he might pick up some Yugoslav territory in the event Stalin successfully dislodged Tito. After Khrushchev embraced Tito in 1955, the entire anti-Stalin campaign inspired by Khrushchev thwarted Hoxha's ambitions, alienated him from the Soviet Union, and increased his support for the hard-line doctrines of the late Stalin.

These factors united Mao and Hoxha in a unique ideological marriage and isolated Albania from the other Eastern European Communist states. Khrushchev has continually accused Hoxha and his Albanian party of a long series of ideological heresies. In the Party Program of October, 1961, Khrushchev blasted away at Albania, and in so doing, he really leveled a violent attack at Mao's China. At the same Party Congress, Chinese Premier Chou En-lai praised Hoxha's leadership and tore into "those" who deviated away from the Stalinist line. He was really lunging at Khrushchev. Poor Albania has become a pawn in the massive feud. How long it can cling to the Mao-Stalin line remains to be seen.

Impact on Khrushchev. The force of Mao's thrusts against the Soviet Union has only driven Khrushchev deeper into the theory and practice of peaceful coexistence with the West. The test-ban treaty of August, 1963, with the United States and Great Britain, might never have been achieved without the cold war in the camp of communism. Khrushchev has been forced to apply his doctrines of flexibility in the theory and practice of communism to the Eastern European satellites. They, in turn, have demanded far greater measures of freedom from Soviet control than ever before — their price for backing Khrushchev in the world arena. This whole loosening up of the western Communist network may well offer opportunities for the West to blunt the imperialistic nature of the Communist ideology as practiced by Khrushchev. On the other hand, some officials at the Kremlin may compel Khrushchev to reverse his stand. Mao has indicated that the price of peace in the Communist cold war is the retirement of Khrushchev and the ostracism of Yugoslavia from the Communist fold. Will other Kremlin leaders, ambitious for power, pay this price?

Impact on Mao Tse-tung. Mao's seeming disregard for the effects of World War III on mankind has cost his nation a great deal. Soviet economic support is gone, and without Russian engineers, technical know-how, and financial assistance, economic progress in China is exceedingly difficult. Mao's economy would grind to a halt if Khrushchev struck the final economic blow and cut off his exports of oil to China. No longer can China offer itself as a "model" to other Communist societies aspiring toward industrialization. The "great leap forward" has become a great leap backward. It is possible, however, that with the French recognition of Communist China early in 1964, new patterns of economic support for Mao's nation will develop.

Nevertheless, in recent years Mao has taken an increasingly militant line in world affairs, as evidenced by the seizure of Tibet, the invasion of India, and the support of guerrilla warfare in Laos and South Vietnam. The cold war, while bringing Khrushchev closer to the West, has thus hardened the Chinese Communist approach to the rest of the world. Mao is forcing Communist parties in Africa, Asia, and Latin America to choose between peaceful or militant approaches as means to Communist ends.

In recent years the Chinese have taken the position that their brand of communism champions all nonwhite people on the face of the earth. The politics of pigmentation has been introduced by Mao to impair Khrushchev's standing with the Negroes of Africa, the peoples of the Mongoloid races of Asia, and other nonwhite people anywhere on the face of the earth. On his extensive swing through Africa in January, 1964, the Premier of Communist China, Chou En-lai, continually harped on the theme that Chinese communism was the true champion of the African people.

During recent years, the Chinese have stepped up their claim that Russia, along with the Western powers, only wants to serve the interests of the white race.

Peking is contentedly aware that the earth's colored population is far greater than its white population. If China can ever plant the idea that it alone is the power leading downtrodden colored peoples against the white masters, it could achieve a massive psychological advantage. By linking Communist Russia and the anti-Communist West as imperialists, China hopes to convince simple-minded folk in underdeveloped Asia and Africa that there is only one true champion of anti-colonialism and communism: China.[1]

Communist China is also aiming its racial propaganda toward American Negroes, with the hope that sizeable support for Mao may arise in the United States. The irony of this new racial emphasis which the Chinese are giving to the ideological warfares of communism is that Marx himself had strong racial prejudices, especially against the Slavs and the Russians!

Possibility of World War III.   Will the Communist cold war result in Mao's forcing World War III on all nations? Mao clearly does not fear this possibility:

> A struggle to the death, an armed conflict between communism and imperialism, remains the essence of Maoist thought as still expressed in the editorials (in the Chinese press) couched in the unmistakable style of the Party Chairman (Mao). "Imperialism," as embodied by the United States, cannot fail to unleash a war in order to escape the inevitable destruction, even though war is bound to hasten its doom.[2]

Mao sees the United States as an "imperialist tiger," as a state that really will not go to war. "What are you afraid of, anyway?" he challenges Khrushchev. The Soviet leader feels that wars of national liberation, in particular, can trigger World War III and thus does not want to let any kind of conflict proceed so far as to permit the possible use of nuclear weapons. Khrushchev has declared that the United States and the Soviet Union have the most to lose should World War III break out, and the United States shares this view. But Mao does not seem to care.

In a way, Mao Tse-tung is desperate. Many feel that he, not

[1] C. L. Sulzberger, "The New Chinese Skin Game," *The New York Times,* August 21, 1963.

[2] Bernard Ullmann, "The Long Shadow of Mao Tse-tung," *The New York Times Magazine,* April 16, 1961.

the Soviet Union, is the real danger to world peace today. Mao has failed to advance the well-being of his people through economic means, and he may go to war in a futile attempt to prove his ideological case. The threat of Communist China will not recede if Mao sticks to his guns. It is expected that China will have a population of more than two billion people by the year 2000, and this massive nation may well pursue violent means as a way out of its dark problems. If Mao's theory and practice of communism are exported effectively to Communist parties throughout Afro-Asia and Latin America, the security and well-being of all other nations will be in graver peril than ever.

The present conflict within the Communist world contains the possibility of a new era in international relations. The gigantic conspiracy of communism is no less powerful and determined than before. But its monolithic might has been shaken. We are faced now with two distinct kinds of communism — both out to conquer the world, but in different ways.

The ideas of a man thinking and writing in obscurity in the British Museum in 1848 are carried on by two powerful and antagonistic leaders who, in the twentieth century, are changing the course of world affairs. Mao Tse-tung is now ranged against Khrushchev, and the heirs of Jefferson stand facing them both.

The task of the democracies may become simpler or more difficult, depending on the moves in this complicated chess game.

But there is no doubt that ideological battle lines are drawn, and the fate of the world may well hang in the balance.

The Background of Right - Wing Totalitarianism

Hitler's dream of the "Thousand Year Reich" went up in flames after twelve years of tyranny and bloodshed. Mussolini, the Italian dictator, was strung up by the heels in a square in Milan by his own people. The grass has grown over the graves of the infamous Nazi concentration camps of Auschwitz and Buchenwald.

Is right-wing totalitarianism an ideology of the past? Although men and governments die, are ideas ever completely buried?

The vital battles for freedom today are being fought between the forces of freedom and communism in the jungles of Southeast Asia, in diplomatic clashes at the United Nations, over the conference tables at Geneva, and at the Wall in Berlin.

So why should we concern ourselves with right-wing totalitarianism? Isn't this kind of terror and brutality stamped out forever?

Communism is only one form of the creed that claims total control over the lives and governing of people. It is the most powerful form today but there are some good reasons for taking a close look at the other side of the totalitarian coin.

First, what is the *appeal* of extreme right-wing creeds? How can civilized men fall so deeply into the trap of tyranny? Tracing the development of fascism in Italy and nazism in Germany between 1920 and 1933 yields some vital information on this point. We can see how broken nations, broken economies, and broken men may find supernationalism a force which explains their plight and provides a promise to guide them out of the abyss of hopelessness. We must understand how right-wing totalitarianism was accepted by the majority of people in Italy and Germany after World War I if we are to prevent the rise of such ideologies again.

Secondly, we simply must not forget what incredible damage these right-wing ideologies inflicted on civilization. During the quarter of a century of their domination, fascism and nazism led to a fantastic loss of life and property. Social institutions were bent to the will of power-hungry rulers, and human values were crushed in the machinery of the octopus state. We will never be able to estimate the cost to humanity of these doctrines of destruction. If we toss the memory of these events into the trash can of history, right-wing totalitarianism will continue to rob civilization of lives and human values.

In the third place, remnants of fascism and nazism rear their ugly heads in some states today. Some of the cancerous ideas of Mussolini and Hitler live on. As old wine in new bottles, they continue to plague and harrass the progress of the democratic doctrine in many states. It would be rash indeed to consider right-wing totalitarianism dead and departed.

1. How Does Right-Wing Totalitarianism Differ from Communism?

Left-wing and right-wing totalitarianism have many similar characteristics. Both are alien to the dignity and freedom of the individual. Both consider the power and authority of the state supreme over the rights and interests of its people.

There are, however, several important distinctions between Communist totalitarianism and its right-wing counterpart. Fascism and nazism are supercharged forms of *nationalism*. The state, with its myth and promise, is supreme. Communism, on the other hand, emphasizes class warfare applicable to all nations, and thus stresses *internationalism*. Right-wing theorists view their state as "organic," as a living, breathing idol which has a glorious past and an even greater mission for the future. The state, for Communist theorists, is a device controlled by the few to exploit the many. But when the dictatorship of the proletariat seizes the power of the state, it "guides" all people toward the classless society. Hitler declared:

> Anyone who speaks of a mission of the German people on Earth must know that it can exist only in the formation of a State which sees its highest task in the preservation and promotion of the most noble elements of our nationality, indeed of all mankind, which still remain intact.[1]

Engels, on the other hand, relates the state to social classes which dominate at any one time.

> . . . in ancient times, the state of slave-owning citizens; in the Middle Ages, the feudal lords; in our own time, the bourgeoisie. When at last it becomes the real representative of the whole society, it renders itself unnecessary. As soon as there is no longer any social class to be held in subjection . . . a state is no longer necessary.[2]

Furthermore, those on the right believe that there should be one perfect, all-powerful voice for the living state. He is the leader, *Il Duce* or *Der Führer*. Marxist theory holds that the dialectic moves of its own accord. While communism has had many dictators, such as Stalin or Mao Tse-tung, they usually are not as supreme as is the right-wing leader.

The *supremacy of the state*, its *organic nature*, and *its infallible leader* are three aspects of right-wing totalitarianism which distinguish it from international communism.

2. What Are the Roots of Right-Wing Totalitarianism?

One can find many varieties of totalitarianism throughout history. Most were of the right-wing variety, glorifying the rulers

---

[1] Adolf Hitler, *Mein Kampf*. Boston: Houghton Mifflin Company, 1943, pp. 397-398.

[2] Friedrich Engels, "Socialism: Utopian and Scientific," in *The Essential Left*. New York: Barnes & Noble, Inc., 1961, p. 141.

and the special authority they magically possessed for their supreme control of whatever political entity happened to be in vogue at the time. The Pharaohs of Egypt and the kings of other ancient empires, the rulers of such totalitarian Greek city-states as Sparta, and the emperors of the Roman Empire were all in the common category of firm right-wing rule.

Of course, the degree to which such rulers applied their policies and doctrines varied considerably. Such is the case today. Some right-wing totalitarian dictators rule with a stronger hand than do others. But most claim some particular keys to a myth which gives them the exclusive authority to lead their people to the promise.

As states began to crystalize in Europe during the Middle Ages, the myth of the divine right to rule was claimed by kings and princes. During the past three centuries, other excuses for a special right to rule have been advanced by dictators, with all kinds of promises accompanying them.

Machiavelli and Hobbes

Writers who justified totalitarian ideology were plentiful. Plato left little room for liberty and freedom in his famous work, *The Republic*, written early in the fourth century B.C. For the next two thousand years, totalitarianism of one variety or another abounded in Europe and Asia, with very few voices raised in opposition. Early in the sixteenth century, the Florentine Niccolo Machiavelli wrote that, "in the actions of men, and especially of princes, from which there is no appeal, the end justifies the means.[1] Machiavelli had one important goal, or "end," that of the unity of Italy. But his declaration that the end justifies the means, set forth in *The Prince*, has been a constant slogan for dictators from that time forward.

At the same time, in England, Thomas Hobbes tried to make a case for dictatorship or the all-powerful state in his book, *The Leviathan*. Hobbes felt that men would war with each other unless they were held down by firm rule. As with so many other

---

[1] Niccolo Machiavelli, *The Prince*. New York: Mentor Books, 1952, p. 103.

political theorists, his principles on how men should be governed were based on observations as to how men live. Most ideologies of totalitarianism call for dictatorial methods of governing because the theorists feel that the nature of man requires the discipline of a strong ruler.

Rousseau

In the eighteenth century, the Geneva-born philosopher Jean Jacques Rousseau (1712-1778) wrote extensively on the organic or "living" nature of the state. Because the political community has a life, interest, and destiny of its own, it must have a "general will" of its own as well. All citizens must subordinate themselves and follow the course charted by the general will, which expresses the "true" will of each person. If one doesn't want to "go along," he must be subjected to force. "It may be necessary to compel a man to be free." Is freedom really the same thing as uniting and following the one and only "general will" of the state?

Of course not! Only a myth! But during the grim, bloodsplashed days of the French Revolution's "Reign of Terror," the dictator Robespierre claimed that *he* exercised the "general will" or inner voice of the French nation. He took Rousseau's myth and translated it into a declaration of principle which dominated France for over a year. Napoleon went on to implement the "general will" of France for almost two decades. In the myth of total identity of the people with the mystical state we find nationalism rising to the fore and giving birth to supernationalism, or modern right-wing totalitarianism.

Colonialism and Anti-Semitism

Discussions of modern totalitarianism tend to focus upon such states as Germany, Italy, Japan, and some Latin American nations. We forget that some democratic states have practiced certain brands of totalitarianism in their foreign policies and are not totally free from a totalitarian stain within their own boundaries.

The real reason behind colonialism was the quest for political, military, and economic power, but the myth of the "white man's burden" (as Kipling put it), glossed over the West's control of Asia and Africa. The argument went: In order to give non-Western peoples a better way of life and the benefits of democracy and Western civilization, it was necessary to subject them to rigid controls since the non-Western peoples did not know what was best for them.

The United States' record of imperialism is short, although this nation exercised strong measures of economic control over Central and South America for many years. At the end of the nineteenth century, President McKinley declared that the United States should take over the Philippines in order "to civilize and Christianize" those island peoples. Theodore Roosevelt wasn't too fussy about gaining land for the Panama Canal early in the twentieth century. The history of Western imperialism, it should be added, has many credits along with its liabilities, and with only a few exceptions, this brand of imperialism and totalitarianism is a matter of the past. But the fact remains that most Western states eulogized democracy at home but in many instances did not practice it abroad.

The Western states also have some traces of totalitarianism within their own borders. Anti-semitism in any form is a shade of totalitarianism because it holds that Jewish people are inferior. The Jewish ghetto, which used to be found in many major cities, glaringly revealed this outlook. Government-imposed discrimination toward anyone is a totalitarian idea. It would be unrealistic to say that the democracies have been unsoiled by totalitarian beliefs and practices. But it is of great significance to note that traces of totalitarianism are rapidly disappearing within democracies today.

Hegel's Theories

The dialectic. Early in the nineteenth century, students flocked to the University of Berlin to hear a renowned teacher expound his nationalistic philosophy. George F. W. Hegel (1770-1831) laid the foundations, in theory at least, for much of modern right-wing totalitarianism. For Hegel, the state (especially Germany) is a living, supreme ideal. It has a throbbing mainspring, a "folk-spirit," which drives it forward. All of history is the unfolding of a world spirit which ignites the folk-spirit of each state at different times and places, resulting in the rise and fall of states over the course of time. Hegel used the dialectic or the old idea of thesis, antithesis, and synthesis, to explain this flow of history. People within the state must identify themselves with this folk-spirit, which moves them on to unity and greatness. "Individuals vanish" before the folk-spirit, which "forms for itself the individuals which it requires for its own purposes." The folk-spirit is thus the creative force, the mover of history, and the myth which propels the people of the nation to Olympian heights.

This is certainly a myth, an irrational explanation of things. But people believe myths because they want to. An important philosopher, Georges Sorel (1847-1922), once said that "myths are not descriptions of things but determinations to act."

Hegel spoke and wrote at a time when Germany was divided into many parts. He and many like him looked forward to the unity and power of the German nation. He probably honestly felt that there was a driving force which would lead to this goal, a force which was shaped by the folk-spirit of the German people. His powerful book, *The Philosophy of History*, relates the dialectic to the general will or spirit of the state. The "folk" or the racial idea is also mixed in with this recipe for nationalism. For Hegel, Germany had an unalterable "manifest destiny" which the people must believe in and identify themselves with.

Influence of Hegel's ideas. The German, Karl Marx, converted Hegel's dialectic of state clashes into the idea of class warfare as an explanation of history (page 66). Thus Hegel unwittingly contributed toward the ideology of international communism, something quite different from supernationalism.

In Germany, meanwhile, the belief in the folk-spirit goaded the people and leaders alike. Under the guidance of the "Iron Chancellor" Otto von Bismarck (1815-1898), the unity of Germany was forged in the crucible of the war with France in 1870 and 1871. Some giants of German culture, such as Goethe and Beethoven, were not of the extreme nationalistic and racially oriented frame of mind and purpose. But the over-all tenor of German philosophy, springing forth from Hegelianism, pointed toward the ideological foundations of nazism and fascism in the twentieth century.

Some ideas of Hegel fascinated other Westerners as well. The American historian George Bancroft studied in Germany during Hegel's time. In his epic history of the United States, written during the middle of the nineteenth cenutry, Bancroft evolved the concept of America's "manifest destiny," which influenced millions of his fellow countrymen during the latter part of the century. Others in the West glued Hegel's ideas onto the "natural right" of white men to control the non-Western world.

Some of the biological theories of the naturalist, Charles Darwin, were merged with Hegelian ideas to produce the slogan, "the survival of the fittest." This was to justify the power and authority of the Western states in world affairs during the era of imperialism. The older Western nations, however, had spent the fervor of their nationalism in years gone by. Germany and Italy did not achieve complete unity until 1871. It was within these two states, therefore, that the latent force of nationalism exploded into supernationalism.

3.   What Was the Nature of Mussolini's Fascism in Italy?

Mussolini's Rise to Power

Italy at the end of World War I. Although on the Allied side in World War I, Italy suffered greatly as a result of the four-year conflict. Adverse economic and social conditions plagued the nation after 1918, providing fertile soil for totalitarianism. Italian statesmen were distinctly displeased with Italy's failure to get more territory in the World War I peace settlements. The ideology of communism was boring into the fabric of Italian society. On the other hand, the nation was engulfed by the rampant nationalism preached by the Italian poet D'Annunzio. Democracy, standing in the center between left-wing and right-wing totalitarian appeals, lost ground daily.

Fascism to the fore. The essence of German nationalistic doctrines and philosophies, especially Hegelianism, interested many Italian thinkers and statesmen early in the twentieth century. Right-wing ideological convictions began to crystallize during the tumultuous months after the end of the war. They took the form of the Fascist Party, founded by a former socialist, Benito Mussolini (1883-1945). A journalist from Milan, Mussolini borrowed the firebrand nationalism of D'Annunzio, along with the symbol of the poet's followers, the black shirt, for his fascists.

Mussolini's young party attracted the war veterans who shared their leader's distaste for democracy. Unemployed and disillusioned, they sought an explanation for their sorry plight and a promise of better days to come. The Fascist movement grew in proportion to national unrest and to the intensity of the internal Communist menace. By 1922, King Victor Emmanuel III was no longer able to cope with the surrounding political, economic, and social chaos. Following a massive march on Rome by the black-shirted fascists on October 28th, the King asked Mussolini to form a government, and on October 30th the new Premier took over the reins of power. Twentieth-century right-wing totalitarianism had become a reality.

Fascism rode to power on the waves of nationalism, with the dual claim that it possessed the keys to solving Italy's problems and that it alone could save Italy from the hammer and sickle of communism. But what *was* the creed of this new ideology? How would Mussolini define the goals of Italian national policy and what would he do to achieve them?

The Theory and Practice of Fascism

The organic state. Actually, it was only after the fascists attained power that they began to devise and articulate their ideology. Italian philosophers, such as Gentile and Rocco, provided fascism with some ideological foundations, but the most authoritative expression of Fascist thery is to be found in Mussolini's speeches and writings, especially his *Doctrine of Fascism.* Other documents, such as the Charter of Labor of 1927, also spell out the Fascist myth and promise. The ideas of Hegel burst forth to justify right-wing totalitarianism.

The Italian nation is an organic whole having life, purposes and means of action superior in power and duration to those of the individuals, single or associated, of which it is composed. It is a moral, political and economic unity, which is realized integrally in the Fascist State.[1]

The myth continues:

Fascism is a religious conception in which man is seen in his imminent relationship with a superior law and with an objective Will that transcends the particular individual and raises him to conscious membership of a spiritual society . . . Against individualism, the Fascist conception is for the State; and it is for the individual in so far as he coincides with the State, which is the conscience and universal will of man in his historical existence. . . .[2]

Italy, therefore, is the superstate, the reincarnation of the Roman Empire. The mythical idealism of the state brings forth a will to which all must bow. There is no room for liberty or freedom as they are known in the West. The Fascist philosopher Gentile declared that liberty is identified with the state. "The maximum of liberty coincides with the maximum strength of the State," he added. The organic, living state, however, needs a voice, a leader. Mussolini supplied this requirement, and as "Il Duce," became the first of the twentieth century's right-wing dictators. He, and he alone, could understand the will of the state and thus lead the people toward the promise, or the authority, power, and domination of the "New Empire" as the guiding force in world affairs. Mussolini held out the plum to his people.

The Fascist state is a will to power and to government. In it the tradition of Rome is an idea which has force. In the doctrine of Fascism, Empire is not only a territorial, military, or mercantile expression, but spiritual or moral. For Fascism, the tendency to Empire, the expansion of nations, is a manifestation of vitality; its opposite, staying at home, is a sign of decadence. Fascism is the doctrine that is most fitted to represent

---

[1] Article 1 of the Charter of Labor. *The Social and Political Doctrines of Contemporary Europe,* Michael Oakeshott (ed). Cambridge, England: The University Press, 1939, p. 184.

[2] Mussolini, *The Doctrine of Fascism.* Oakeshott, pp. 165, 166.

the aims, the states of mind, of a people, like the Italian people, rising again after many centuries of abandonment or slavery to foreigners.[1]

The myth of the state and the promise of a great future brought waves of support for Mussolini cascading into Rome. An average Italian might have put it this way: "Here is a nation that is going to lift me, an Italian, to new heights. Here is a doctrine proclaiming the Italian nationality, *my* nationality, as the greatest on earth because it represents the revival of the power and strength of Rome. My leader, Il Duce, gives me and millions like me a new faith. His brilliant speeches, his exciting promises for the future, his drawing no distinction between me and the state — this fascism is the thing for me!" The capacity of the totalitarian myth and its promise to lift the masses from the abyss of national hurt should never be underestimated.

Il Duce. Mussolini quickly acted to consolidate his power after he became Premier in 1922. In the rigged parliamentary elections of 1924, the Fascist Party won a clear majority in the Chamber of Deputies. The latter declined in power, and in 1938 was replaced with a Chamber of Fasces and Corporations which handled the bulk of duties of Mussolini's new "corporate" state. The Party organization was naturally headed by Mussolini and in most cases the real power in the state represented a combination of Grand Council rule and Party activity.

The corporate state. Mussolini was particularly proud of the idea of the "corporate state," which symbolized the economic aspects of his totalitarian rule. In a democracy, the economy seeks to promote human welfare. Competition in the free marketplace and the right to private property enables varied interests, peoples, and groups in the democracy to harmonize their economic interests in an atmosphere of freedom. The economy of the totalitarian state, on the other hand, is invariably harnessed to the power goals of that state. One finds not a competitive economy but an economy of governmental control and coercion. The 1927 Fascist Charter of Labor makes this point clear:

> Work in all its forms — intellectual, technical, or manual — whether organization or execution — is a social duty. And for

[1] *Ibid.*, p. 178.

this reason only it is regulated by the State. The process of production, from the national point of view, is a single whole; its aims are united and identified with the well-being of the producers and the promotion of national power.[1]

Mussolini set up twenty-two corporations representing agriculture, industry, and public service (such as banking, transportation, and communication). The heads of these corporations served in the Chamber of Fasces and Corporations and thus ran the economy at Mussolini's will and direction. Laborers were called upon to follow the dictates of the corporation executives in this government-manipulated economy structure. All wages and profits were controlled by the state. Priorities of production were harmonized with the demands of national and foreign policies. Mussolini's determination to expand Italy's territory slowly but surely necessitated placing the economy on a war footing.

And yet, at first the results of the government-controlled economy were surprising. The economy itself rose to unprecedented heights in the 1920's, and Mussolini's prestige shot up with it. The desolate Pontine Marshes were drained, providing new farmland. New roads were constructed. A vast improvement in transportation systems and erection of countless buildings and monuments proclaimed the glories of fascism. By the end of the 1920's, most Italians were convinced that Mussolini was on the right track, and many foreign observers saw great merit in some of the improvements Il Duce brought to his nation.

Mussolini's Conduct of Foreign Affairs

Mussolini could not get away from the idea that Italy had a profound mission in world affairs. Perhaps he even believed that he could revive the power and glory of the Roman Empire. In any event, in the mid-1920's he launched a vigorous foreign-policy program which was to lead to his doom by the spring of 1945. First of all, he sought to expand his power across the Adriatic. In 1924, he gained control of the city of Fiume, the object of D'Annunzio's furor only a few short years before. His influence spread rapidly in Albania, over which he established a

[1] Oakeshott, *op. cit.,* p. 184.

protectorate in 1927. He tightened his authority over the Italian colonies in Africa. He called upon his people to "Believe, Obey, Fight!" But not until a new dictator rose to prominence in Germany was Mussolini really willing to flex his Fascist muscles.

"Victory" over Ethiopia. Hitler became Chancellor of Germany in January, 1933, and was initially viewed by Mussolini with some disdain. Who was this funny little German upstart who was copying his ideas and style? It didn't take many months, however, for Mussolini to realize that Hitler meant business. It might be a good idea, therefore, to show "Der Führer" that Italy was the big frog in the pond of world politics. And so, off to imperialistic grandeur. The target of Mussolini's armies was weak, feudalistic Ethiopia in East Africa. Emperor Haile Selassie's kingdom was attacked by Il Duce's "brave" troops in December, 1934. The League of Nations was shocked, and statesmen throughout the world wondered what was the goal of this military foray. The halls of diplomacy buzzed with suggestions for concerted action against Mussolini during 1935. In the end, however, Britain and France appeased the dictator, and Hitler stood by, smiling at this fascinating display of weakness against aggression. Ethiopia was absorbed into the Italian Empire by 1936. Mussolini thus proved to Hitler that aggression paid off.

World War II. From this point on, the unfolding of the Italian Fascist drama took a back seat to the onrush of Hitler's moves toward World War II. Mussolini and Hitler drew close together in the Axis Alliance of 1936, and both supported Franco in the Civil War in Spain. Mussolini was only Hitler's shadow in the diplomatic moves that led to World War II, but after the outbreak of hostilities in September, 1939, he waited to see how the tides of war would go before jumping in. Convinced that Hitler would seize Europe with ease, Mussolini decided to get into the act as well. He launched an infamous attack on gravely weakened France on June 10, 1940, to become a full partner to Hitler in the fight against the democracies.

Mussolini's hopes for conquests and stirring victories in World War II were short-lived indeed. His armies attacked Albania and Greece, only to suffer many defeats before being bailed out by the Nazi armed forces. The Italians suffered countless setbacks in North African fighting in 1941 and 1942 and finally succumbed by the thousands to the Allied forces on the hot sands of Libya. The will to fight among the Italian soldiers was gone. The belief in Il Duce dissolved in a few short years of defeat and disaster.

The End of Mussolini

In Italy, the handwriting on the wall was quite clear; the leadership of Mussolini could no longer be tolerated. The Fascist Grand Council discarded Mussolini in July, 1943, and two months later Italy surrendered to the Allies. With assistance from Hitler, Mussolini escaped from Italy on September 12, 1943, and tried to cast his old Fascist ideas in a new form. His new Republican Fascist Party, with headquarters in Vienna, attracted very few adherents to the falling star. Mussolini returned to Italy but was captured by Italian partisans in late April, 1945, and executed. His body was taken to his home town of Milan, and, before the hoots and jeers of thousands of disillusioned Italians, strung up for all to see and to condemn. Pompous Il Duce never dreamed of an ending like this.

4. How Did Hitler's Nazism Cause World War II?

Germany After World War I

The growth of the Fascist ideology in Italy was closely watched by those in Germany who were looking for new approaches to ancient problems of political, economic, and social disorder. As in Italy, conditions in postwar Germany were hardly favorable for democratic ways of life and governing. The Treaty of Versailles placed the blame for the origins of the War squarely on German shoulders. The penalty for starting the War and being the loser was represented by enormous payments of money, goods, and services to the victorious allies. The Germans lost their Kaiser, the symbol of national unity, and were called upon to accept a new "republic," a form of government which had very shallow roots in German national and political history.

Search for answers to national chaos. Germans in 1919 felt humiliated. World War I had not been fought on German soil, and many Germans were convinced they really had not been defeated in the great conflict. Their national spirit lay buried in the depths of despair. Many began to ask: "Why must we suffer this degradation, this international stigma? Who is really to blame for selling us out to France, Britain, and the United States? Why is it that we must suffer and pay off those who were as much to blame as ourselves?" Many young veterans of the war, in particular, raised questions about the German present and future. They did not necessarily seek rational answers. They leafed through the pages of German nationalism, reading about the spirit of the "folk" and the promise of Germany's true "place in the sun." What might explain the chaos of 1919? Wasn't some gigantic but shadowy conspiracy operating against them? What might provide a guide to the true destiny of Germany? Out of the heritage of German nationalism and the probing about the crisis of the present and the prospects of the future rose the totalitarian ideology of nazism.

Emergence of the racial myth. An irrational myth soon developed to provide an explanation of the present and a promise for the future. The idea of the German folk and the presumed "superiority" of the German or "Aryan" race led some to believe that the Jews were responsible for the plight Germany found itself in. Anti-Semitism had deep roots in Germany, and in 1919 some saw in the Jews a convenient scapegoat and basis for shaping a new ideology which would revive power and glory for Germany. A small group in Munich pounced upon this theory, and from this group sprang the Nazi Party which was to lead the world to war exactly twenty years later.

Alfred Rosenberg's theories. Alfred Rosenberg (1893-1946) was a native of Estonia and a student in Moscow when he was first attracted to the idea that Jews were responsible for all the evils of the world. He read a book entitled *Protocols of the Wise Men of Zion,* which claimed that there was an active Zionist plot to undermine all governments and dominate the world. Rosenberg escaped to Germany in 1918 with the *Protocols* tucked under his arm and ended his journey in Munich in 1919. There he found a group of young German veterans of World War I, who met in the back rooms of beer halls to discuss the reasons

for Germany's downfall and what they might do about it.
Rosenberg's poisonous ideas about anti-Semitism fitted in well
with the thinking of this crowd, the "German Workers' Party."
Were not the Socialist Jews the ones who had negotiated the
armistice and peace with the Allies? Weren't the Jews the ones
who manipulated German finance while the "true" Germans were
fighting the war? Weren't the Jews responsible for all the grief
Germany was suffering in 1919?

Men who are down and out will seize at almost anything to
explain their plight. This small Munich group combined the
hideous doctrine of anti-Semitism with the strong undercurrent
of German nationalism and the old "folk" idea to come up
with a new ideology which was to alter the course of history
incredibly. Some years later, Rosenberg's major work on the
racial basis of the "new Germany," *The Myth of the Twentieth
Century*, defined the mission of maintaining the supremacy of
the Nordic "Aryan" race and eliminating all other strains, especially the Jews, who might rob the "pure" German people of
their "natural" supremacy. This concept, wrote Rosenberg:

> . . . puts folk and race higher than the state and its forms. It
> declares protection of the folk more important than protection of
> a religious denomination, a class, the monarchy, or the republic;
> it sees in treason against the folk a greater crime than high
> treason against the state.[1]

Rosenberg was one of the principal authors of the Nazi racist
doctrine. It was Adolf Hitler, however, who fused the ideas
of Aryan supremacy, violent anti-Semitism, German supernationalism, and world domination into an ideology.

Adolf Hitler Develops Nazism

Hitler's early years. Born in Austria in 1889, Hitler wandered
through a maze of poverty and failure for the first 25 years of
his life. He marched to war for Germany in 1914, however, thoroughly identifying himself with the German cause. Corporal Hitler fought bravely, was awarded the coveted Iron Cross, and was

---

[1] *National Socialism.* Washington: United States Government Printing
Office, 1943, p. 32.

gassed toward the end of the war. Associated with the skeleton German army as a civilian employee after the cessation of hostilities in 1918, he was stationed in Munich and found time dragging slowly by. In September, 1919, Hitler wandered into a beer hall and happened to overhear some fellow veterans of the German Workers' Party blaming the Jews for the German defeat, the high level of unemployment, and for just about everything else. He heard these men express a loathing for the newly formed German Republic. Hitler nodded his head in agreement as these few men asked each other what should be done to fill the void of national life.

> The void was open, and into that void after a pause there strode a maniac of ferocious genius, the repository and expression of the most virulent hatreds that have ever corroded the human breast — Corporal Hitler.[1]

Hitler, who had long been attracted to anti-Semitic views, joined the tiny Party on September 16, 1919.

Policy for German Workers' Party set. Hitler at last had found himself. He became deeply involved in Party discussions. Within a few months Hitler was shaping up Party policies and recruiting new members from among the vast numbers of unemployed, angry veterans in the Munich area. At the Party's first mass meeting in the Hofbrauhaus in Munich on February 24, 1920, Hitler rose to speak and articulated for the first time 25 planks of the German Workers' Party. The first four principles were of particular importance:

1. We demand the union of all Germans to form a Great Germany on the basis of the right of self-determination enjoyed by nations.
2. We demand equality of rights for the German people in dealing with other nations, and the abolition of the Peace Treaties of Versailles and St. Germain.
3. We demand land and territory (*Lebensraum* or "living room") for the nourishment of our people and for settling our superfluous population.
4. None but members of the nation (or folk) may be citizens

---

[1] Winston Churchill, *The Gathering Storm*. Boston: Houghton Mifflin Company, 1948, p. 11.

of the State. None but those of German blood, whatever their creed, may be members of the nation. No Jew, therefore, may be a member of the nation.[1]

Hitler was not the sole author of this platform, but the manner in which he set forth these principles persuaded his audience that here was the new leader of a movement destined to bring greatness and glory back to Germany. Of this occasion, Hitler said that:

> When I finally closed the meeting, we were not alone in feeling that a wolf had been born which was destined to break into the herd of swindlers and misleaders of the people.[2]

The German Workers' Party now became the National Socialist Party, and its ranks swelled with all kinds of disillusioned men. The "Socialist" in the National Socialist Party had no relation, of course, to Marxism or democratic socialism, but it did attract workers who saw in this nationalist movement a promise for better laboring conditions in the future. Veterans, both former officers and enlisted men, flocked to the National Socialist, or "Nazi," banner, which took the form of a swastika. Hitler rose to supreme leadership because of his oratorical skills and organizational ability and soon became known as "Der Führer." Day and night he pounded home the racist idea. Germany, to be united, great, and powerful must also be pure. The Jew must go! Many believed that Hitler had found the key to Germany's distress and that his new nationalist doctrine would restore Germany to its true "place in the sun."

The Nazis attempt revolution. The heart of Nazi power was in Munich, the capital of nationalistic Bavaria. Here and elsewhere in Germany, conditions grew progressively worse as the new German Republic tried to maintain the vital center while warding off threats from right and left. Inflation was rampant in Germany by 1923 — a loaf of bread cost over a million marks! French troops entered the industrialized Ruhr area to collect reparations or debts owed by the Germans to the French as a

---

[1] *National Socialism, op. cit.,* p. 52.

[2] Konrad Heiden, *Der Fuehrer.* Boston: Houghton Mifflin Company, 1944, p. 92.

result of the Treaty of Versailles. Everything looked black to the Germans. Hitler felt the time was ripe for seizing the powers of government in Bavaria. He and his fellow nazis, aided by a German World War I leader of great renown, General Ludendorff, organized a *putsch*, or attempted overthrow of the government, on November 8 and 9, 1923. This grasp for power failed, and Hitler was sentenced to four years' imprisonment. His loyal followers and many others, however, considered him a martyr for the cause of German nationalism. Hitler's term was reduced to thirteen months, but during this brief span of time he wrote the major treatise of nazism, *Mein Kampf* ("My Struggle"). In this book he laid before the world his entire philosophy of government and life. He presented his ideology and the policies he would pursue to achieve the "Thousand Year Reich."

Mein Kampf. What was the message of *Mein Kampf* for Germany and the world? Let us turn to Winston Churchill's lucid condensation of Hitler's morbid doctrines.

> Man is a fighting animal; therefore the nation, being a community of fighters, is a fighting unit. Any living organism which ceases to fight for its existence is doomed to extinction. A country or race which ceases to fight is equally doomed. The fighting capacity of a race depends upon its purity. Hence the need for ridding it of its defilements. The Jewish race, owing to its universality, is of necessity pacifist and internationalist. Pacifism is the deadliest sin; for it means the surrender of the race in the fight for existence. The first duty of every country is therefore to nationalize the masses; intelligence in the case of the individual is not of first importance; will and determination are the prime qualities. The individual who is born to command is more valuable than countless thousands of subordinate natures. Only brute force can ensure the survival of the race; hence the necessity for military forms. The race must fight; a race that rests must rust and and perish. Had the German race been united in good time, it would have been already master of the globe. The new Reich must gather within its fold all the scattered elements in Europe . . . The world is now moving towards (a great upheaval) and the new German State must see to it that the race is ready for the last and greatest decisions on this earth.[1]

[1] Churchill, *The Gathering Storm, op. cit.,* pp. 55, 56.

Here are all the elements of right-wing totalitarianism, including supernationalism, the organic state, and the infallible leader. Here is the myth of racism and the promise that the "New Reich" will be the "master of the globe." Many of these ideas would be expanded upon in theory and practice during the next twenty years, but the core of nazism was laid out for all to see and inspect in 1924. Millions of Germans read *Mein Kampf*, believed in its myths and promises, and later permitted its ideological convictions to guide the course of German national policy. Why didn't people outside of Germany see in the program of *Mein Kampf* a totalitarian challenge of massive proportions?

Allen W. Dulles, former chief of the United States Central Intelligence Agency, asked this question as well:

> I have always been impressed at our seeming reluctance to give credence to official statements which are made by political leaders in other countries when we disagree fervently with what they say or when their statements seem at times to be bombastic or unrealistic.

> For example, Hitler's *Mein Kampf*, written in 1924, had a wide circulation in Germany and left a deep impression on the German people. Over here (in the United States), it received comparatively little attention until after the outbreak of World War II. Yet this book was the blueprint for Hitlerian policy of superiority of the *Herrenvolk* (folk), of the manifest destiny of the German Reich, of the anti-semitic campaigns, and of the whole trend of Hitlerism.[1]

Winston Churchill was one of the very few prominent people in the West who absorbed the message of *Mein Kampf*. He did not consider it a foolish or rambling document, but a policy statement of a creed that could cause untold horror if it were unleashed on the world. He constantly warned his nation and the Western states of Hitler's aims and called the shots with fantastic accuracy when Hitler came to power in 1933. And yet few listened to him until Hitler's invasion of the Lowlands in 1940 convinced Great Britain that Churchill was not a "war-

[1] Allen W. Dulles, "The Communist Attack upon Parliamentary Government" in *Soviet Total War* (U.S. House of Representatives, Committee on Un-American Activities). Washington: U.S. Government Printing Office, p. 423.

monger" but one who had understood the goals of the Nazi ideology.

Temporary decline of nazism. When Hitler emerged from the Lansberg Prison at the beginning of 1925 with fellow nazi Rudolf Hess, he had practically been forgotten. The Western states had helped Germany get back on its feet during 1924, and the new German democracy was slowly taking root. Economic stability was rapidly returning, and Germany had been accepted in the League of Nations. The German Foreign Minister, Gustav Stresemann, was the architect of a new era of good will with France and Britain. This broad upswing in the destinies of Germany bolstered the democratic ideology and substantially reduced the appeal of totalitarianism. The vital center was restored, and Communist appeals on the left, along with those of nazism on the right, fell on deaf ears.

Nazism Marches to Power

Depression strikes. In 1929, however, the depression struck, and struck hard. Germany's economy took a sharp plunge, and the psychological shock reverberated throughout the nation. Stresemann died in the same year, and Germany's position in the international community began to slide. These disastrous events were accompanied by the swelling appeals of the reduced Nazi ranks: "We have the solution to our national problems! Our program is the answer to all German troubles! Democracy is weak, the National Socialist program is strong! Here! Read our leader's book *Mein Kampf!* Let Hitler and the nazis lead Germany out of this pit of national distress! *Heil Hitler!*"

The myth and the promise rose again. The racist doctrine — irrational? Yes! But the irrational myth — Rosenberg's *Myth of the Twentieth Century* — offered hope, honor, and glory. The myth can sink in and be believed when democracy fails to do the job. In the Reichstag elections of 1930, the German people voted strongly for the Nazi Party, making it the second largest grouping in the German legislature. The next two years were marked with further failures of the democratic center to ward off totalitarian challenges from both the German communists and the nazis. The latter did their utmost to jam the democratic machinery of governing. In the Reichstag elections of 1932, the nazis gained a plurality in the legislature. They did a magnificent job of making the public believe that some gigantic internal and external conspiracy was poised against Germany, and only the nazis could cope with it.

In the same year, Hitler ran for the Presidency of Germany. He lost, and the aged General von Hindenburg was re-elected, but the national campaign gave Hitler and his fellow National Socialists the opportunity to spread their insidious doctrines throughout Germany.

Hitler becomes Chancellor. By January, 1933, the political scene in Germany was pure chaos. On January 31st, President von Hindenburg was compelled, with disgust, to elevate Hitler to the rank of Chancellor (Prime Minister) of Germany. Playing up the German fear of communism, Hitler conducted elections on March 5, 1933. Although the nazis intimidated other political parties, and Hitler's brown-shirted elite guard used strong-arm tactics, the nazis won only 44 percent of the total votes. Then Hitler outlawed the Communist Party, which gave him a clear majority. The Reichstag, now under his control, voted him dictatorial powers on March 23rd, and Der Führer at last reached the pinnacle of power.

Lessons from Hitler's "legal revolution." The main lesson of these events is the fact that this was a "legal revolution." Hitler and the nazis marched to power by using democratic processes and machinery. It must never be forgotten that National Socialists put across to millions of Germans the myth and promise of the Nazi creed, and the people in turn responded by *electing* the nazis to public office. Does not this clearly prove the triumph of ideas over force? Does not this prove that a literate and basically economically sound nation can permit the democratic process to be used by those who would destroy it, once in power? Let us turn to Hitler's propaganda expert, Dr. Paul Goebbels, for a candid confession on this crucial matter.

> National Socialism is now engaged in gradually stabilizing in Germany the new legal situation which has been brought about by the revolution. This is basically different from the old legality and dispenses with the possibility of criticism which it made use of under the old system (of the German Republic, 1919-1933). If

democracy permitted us to use democratic methods in the time of our opposition, it was because this was necessary under a democratic system. We National Socialists have never maintained that we were representatives of a democratic viewpoint, but we have openly declared that we only made use of democratic means in order to gain power, and that after the seizure of power, we would ruthlessly deny to our opponents all those means which they had granted to us during the time of our opposition.[1]

Hitler in Power

Once in power, Hitler converted the ideas of *Mein Kampf* into national policy. The Constitution of the German Republic was cast aside. It was made quite clear that all governmental power and authority were to stem from Hitler and no one else. The nazis imposed strict controls over all newspapers and radio, with Dr. Goebbels holding a complete monopoly on the flow of news and propaganda. President von Hindenburg died in 1934, and Hitler took over the Presidency, in addition to the Chancellorship. Der Führer exterminated Ernst Röhm in the "blood purge" of June, 1934. Röhm had joined the German Workers' Party before Hitler in 1919 and had been an invaluable aide in Hitler's rise to power. But Hitler could tolerate no contender to supreme power, and with this internal show of force, Hitler gave clear notice that he was the sole leader of the new totalitarian regime.

Der Führer. The idea of "Der Führer" was one of the central elements of the "Third Reich" of the nazis. One of the most prominent of Hitler's philosophers of National Socialism, Ernest Huber, explains the "Führer" principle:

The Fuehrer Reich of the (German) people is founded on the recognition that the true will of the people cannot be disclosed through parliamentary votes and plebiscites but that the will of the people in its pure and uncorrupted form can only be expressed through the Fuehrer. Thus a distinction must be drawn between the supposed will of the people in a parliamentary democracy, which merely reflects the conflict of the various social interests, and the true will of the people in the Fuehrer-state, in

---

[1] *National Socialism, op. cit.,* pp. 3, 4.

which the collective will of the real political unit is manifested. The Fuehrer is the bearer of the people's will. He shapes the collective will of the people within himself and he embodies the political unity and entirety of the people in opposition to individual interests.[1]

Here is a distorted application of Rousseau's "general will!" Here is the idea of the "superman," who cannot be an ordinary human being. The sacrifice of ordinary human beings to the machine of the superman, to the embodiment of the "general will," and to the "purity" of the "super-race" was the incredible tragedy of nazism.

Nazi government. What can one say about the "government" of this totalitarian regime? There is little value in describing the governmental structure of Hitler's Third Reich, because all authority was vested in one man. Hitler was the supreme, infallible leader, both in domestic and foreign policies. His was one of the most complete dictatorships in history. Education was geared toward drilling Nazi principles into the minds of people at all levels. The Gestapo (the secret police) employed vicious tactics to keep the populace in line. If one opposed the regime, the only recourse was the privacy of one's mind.

Economic policy. Nazi economic policy was another matter of state control. Many economic titans had supported Hitler's rise to power in the early 1930's, believing that the National Socialists would be the best bet against a Communist Germany. Once in power, Hitler forced the leaders of industry and finance to conform strictly to his own interpretation of national security and well-being. Two "four-year" plans were hatched to direct the resources and production of the economy toward military goals. All trade with other states had a distinct political purpose. The "well-being" of the average consumer was sacrificed to the domination of the regime, Hitler's version of true security. In the spring of 1933, trade unions were led to believe that Hitler was more socialistic than nationalistic. But after the massive May Day rally of 1933, the unions were crushed, and the workingman became only one more unit in the machinery of totalitarianism.

---

[1] *National Socialism, op. cit.,* pp. 34-35.

Action against Jewish people. The unfortunate Jews were the prime target of the Nazi march toward domination. True to his word, Hitler moved rapidly against these people who, in his opinion, diluted the purity of the racial state of Nordic-Aryans. Never was there a more corrupt myth than that which Hitler, Rosenberg Goebbels, and others concocted about the Jews. Never was there a more harsh policy against a specific category of people. On April 1, 1933, Hitler declared that all Jewish enterprises, economic and social, should be boycotted by the German non-Jewish populace. The Gestapo moved quickly to drive the Jews from their homes, their stores, their social organizations, and their places of worship. Propaganda was studded with anti-Jewish invectives. Citations from the speeches of Hitler on this score would add nothing to the unbelievable story of persecution, terror, and torture of these scapegoats of the "new Germany."

Shortly before World War II, a "final solution" to the "Jewish problem" was formulated. This was a policy of human extermination. At the end of World War II, it was estimated that more than 6,000,000 Jews had met their death in concentration camps as a result of an ideology which was based upon the superiority of the Aryan race. There is no "Aryan race," and no category of human beings is superior to any other. But this "myth of the twentieth century" swept millions off the face of the earth.

The Foreign Policy of Nazism

With a firm grasp on internal affairs by 1935, Hitler was prepared to project his ideology into the arena of world politics.

> The foreign policy of the folkish (folk) state must safeguard the existence on this planet of the race which is embodied in the state, by creating a healthy, viable, natural relation between the nation's population and growth (of the folk) on the one hand and the quantity and quality of its soil and territory on the other hand.[1]

Hitler called for *lebensraum* (living space) to the East and a

---

[1] Hitler, *op. cit.*, pp. 642-643.

unity of all Nordic peoples for the control of the rest of the world. At the same time he promised that Germany really did not seek conquest. In September, 1935, he declared that:

> National Socialism has no aggressive intentions against any European nation. On the contrary, we are convinced that the nations of Europe must continue their characteristic national existence as created by tradition, history, and economy; if not, Europe as a whole will be destroyed.[1]

Are not these two declarations inconsistent with each other? Absolutely. But the leaders of the other European states chose to believe the latter and ignore the former. Except for statesmen like Churchill, Western leaders felt they could "ride the tiger," just as many today feel they can ride the "Communist tiger."

Defiance of Treaty of Versailles. In 1935, Hitler proceeded to make a shambles out of the Treaty of Versailles. Against the specific provisions of the World War I peace treaty, he introduced military draft in 1935 and occupied the demilitarized area of the Rhineland in March, 1936. He quickly built up his air force, the Luftwaffe, in 1936 and 1937, and Churchill's warnings on this score went unheeded. In March, 1938, Hitler annexed Austria to the German Reich, and although some authorities in Britain and France expressed great anxiety about this move, Hitler assured them over and over again that he would seek no more territorial gains.

Czechoslovakia and Munich. Shortly after the Austrian annexation, however, Hitler indicated that the Sudetenland area of neighboring Czechoslovakia should come within the confines of the German Reich because the German people in the Sudetenland desired to be reunited with their homeland. Actually, the Sudeten German Party in this area engaged in Nazi propaganda to "prove" to the world that the Czechoslovakian Government was discriminating against Germans. As in the case of Austria, Hitler used the local pro-Nazi movement to produce conditions which would give Der Führer a pretext for moving in to "protect" his fellow Germans. Hitler told the world that if he could bring Sudetenland into the Reich, he would make no further territorial

---

[1] *National Socialism, op. cit.,* p. 55.

demands on any state. Again, many Western leaders tended to take Hitler at his word.

Great Britain's Prime Minister Chamberlain negotiated with Hitler on the Sudeten crisis, which everyone hoped would not erupt into a major war. Finally, Chamberlain and Premier Daladier of France met with Hitler and Mussolini in Munich on September 29th and 30th, 1938. Daladier, and especially Chamberlain, thought that by permitting Hitler to absorb the Sudeten area, war could be avoided, Hitler would be satisfied, and his promise that he would seek no further territory would be honored. Hitler continually took advantage of Western disunity, lack of decision, and absence of backbone.

In March, 1939, Hitler established a protectorate over all of Czechoslovakia and began to prepare aggressive designs against Poland. Britain and France at last realized that the totalitarian Nazi ideology and Hitler were preparing for new conquests, and that it was time to take firm action. Churchill, of course, had been pushing for strong collective measures against Hitler for years. Only in the spring of 1939 did his fellow countrymen realize that he had been right all along.

War and the end of Hitler. In the early hours of September 1, 1939, Hitler launched his attack on Poland. Thus the ideology of nazism took the world into the abyss of the most destructive war in history. Hitler was convinced of the righteousness of his ideological doctrines and adhered to this cause down to his death in a Reichstag bunker on April 30, 1945, with Russian troops on the threshold of his "invincible" chancellery.

He sought "security and well-being" for his national interests, defined by the racial myth. Security was world domination, and well-being was the elimination of all the non-Nordic elements in his society. He hated the Slavs and the French but actually hoped that the Scandinavian peoples and even Britain might cooperate with him because of the "Nordic" complexion of peoples in these nations. Many of the policies Hitler formed to achieve his goals were confusing, and his direction of policy was incredibly bad. But his conviction that he alone could translate the racial "myth of the twentieth century" into effective policy, thereby achieving the "Thousand Year Reich" drove him on and finally buried him and millions of others as well.

The catacysmic results of the Nazi ideology will continue to be felt for decades. If the majority of Germans had refused to be persuaded by the completely false and irrational myth of "Aryan" supremacy, perhaps they would not have backed the National Socialists in the latter's rise to power. If people had realized how totalitarianism thrives on economic and social chaos, efforts might have been taken in the 1920's to root out these carriers of the seeds of tyranny. If more people outside Germany had read *Mein Kampf* and realized that it was no idle program hatched by a warped mind, perhaps the impact of ideology on world affairs would have been understood at an earlier date. If the leaders of the democracies had possessed the fortitude to stand up for their ideology, perhaps the war would never have taken place. These things did not happen, but the lessons of history can now be understood and applied to the present and future. George Santayana once said, "unless we remember the mistakes of the past, we are condemned to repeat them in the future." The past, indeed, is prologue.

5. What Was the Militarism of the Japanese Empire?

While Mussolini and Hitler were driving toward domination in Europe, the Japanese had their own ideas about reducing Asia to a massive Japanese province. Germany, Italy, and Japan were on the same side during World War II and the events that led to it in the 1930's, but the totalitarian militarism found in Japan had ideological roots which differed considerably from its right-wing counterparts in Europe.

Japan Enters the Modern World

On July 8, 1853, a strange sight appeared in Tokyo Bay in Japan. Four ships with the American stars and stripes appeared off the city of Tokyo, an area definitely "out of bounds" for foreigners. Japan had been a feudalistic nation for centuries. From the twelfth century, it had been ruled by powerful warriors who preached the virtues of militarism and the supremacy of armed might. Foreigners of all kinds were ordered away from the shores of this isolated, totalitarian state. The port of Nagasaki was opened up in the sixteenth century for some limited trade relations with a few nations, but this was the extent of Japan's exposure to the outside world. Commodore Matthew Perry, in charge of the 1853 United States' expedition to Tokyo, was ordered to go to Nagasaki if he wished to have any communication with the Japanese government. Perry and his ships departed but returned in greater numbers in February, 1854. The head of the Japanese state, the Shogun, concerned with this display of force, signed a treaty on March 31, 1854, with the Americans, permitting trade and diplomatic relations.

This Western intrusion into the domains of the Mikado split Japan wide open. Some of the old Japanese aristocracy wanted to perpetuate the feudalistic system, while others wanted change and participation in the modern world. Finally, in 1867, a revolution cast out the old Shogun dynasty, and the Emperor was placed on the throne. Commodore Perry had blazed the way for modernizing Japan.

During the next twenty years, the Japanese jumped from the Middle Ages to the world of the late nineteenth century with amazing facility for change. The nation was industrialized, and the Japanese launched a vast network of trade relations with other states. The economic and governmental styles of the West were studied. The Prussian governing system and military organization were copied. A parliamentary government was organized in 1889, in which power was vested in military and business leaders. The old folklore and myths of the divinity of rulers and the mission of militarism were resurrected and grafted onto the texture of modern Japan. Hail the noble warrior! Bow down before the holy Emperor! Glorify the flag of the Rising Sun!

This mixture of the old and the new led Japan to imperialism. A war with China in 1894 and 1895 took Japanese legions into Manchuria, but the wary Western powers ordered them to retreat. Nevertheless, Japan seized the island of Formosa, or Taiwan, and held on to it tightly until 1945. To the world's surprise, the Japanese defeated Russia in the war of 1904 and 1905 and gained important commercial and territorial rights in Manchuria. Japan's status in world affairs shot upward. In 1910 Korea was occupied. Additional Asian real estate, formerly belonging to Germany, was obtained after World War I, largely because Japan was identified with the Allied cause.

Emergence of Japanese Imperialism

This pageant of militaristic success fortified the belief held by many in Japan that their divinely inspired nation was the wave of the future. Business interests backed the militarists, whose momentum elevated them to the highest ranks of the Emperor's government. Japanese totalitarianism was therefore a mixture of convictions about the divinity of the Emperor, the worship of militarism, and the mission of Japan to dominate Asia. The Japanese, for the most part, profited from the powerful role the nation was playing in Asian affairs.

Japanese conquests in Asia. A neatly concocted military foray in Manchuria in September, 1931, gave the Japanese "cause" to seize this most industrialized part of China. Japan detached Manchuria from China, called it Manchukuo, and installed a puppet emperor. The League of Nations denounced Japan's imperialism in China but took no firm measures against this breach of international peace and security. Japan angrily left the League of Nations and moved closer to the Nazi-Fascist alliance. The Emperor's government concluded the Anti-Comintern (Anti-Communist) Pact with Hitler in November, 1936. It declared that it would establish a Greater East Asia Co-Prosperity Sphere in Asia, in which Japan would be the predominant nation. Hopes were directed toward linking this scheme with Hitler's ambitions to control Europe. The proposal almost worked.

Another Japanese-engineered conflict with the Chinese in Peking in July, 1937, brought the two Asian nations to war, although there never was any formal declaration of hostilities. Japanese armies swooped down on many Chinese cities, bringing terror, atrocities, and a crushing iron-fisted control to the key industrial and political centers of China. The alliance with Germany was tightened in 1940, and in October, 1941, the civilian Prime Minister was replaced by General Hideki Tojo.

Further Japanese advances in Asia indicated Japan's plans for domination of the Pacific. But Japanese conquests centered around Southeast Asia did not seem to pose an immediate threat to United States' possessions. Deceitful diplomacy with the United States late in 1941 further disguised the fact that Japan had long planned to attack American territory at Pearl Harbor in the Hawaiian Islands. The vicious, unprovoked bombing on December 7, 1941, brought the United States into World War II.

World War II. Inspired by the creed of militarism and the myth of Asian supremacy, the Japanese had many successes in 1941 and 1942. But Allied forces, especially those of the United States, delivered a number of staggering blows in late 1942, and the tide reversed in 1943. The long march toward Tokyo, led by General Douglas MacArthur, provided some of the bloodiest and most heroic episodes of World War II. The "Greater East Asia Co-Prosperity Sphere" was finally shattered with the dropping of the atomic bombs on Hiroshima and Nagasaki early in August, 1945. Following these epic bombardments, Emperor Hirohito told his people, in a classic understatement, that the war had not necessarily gone in favor of the Japanese.

The Japanese surrender was accepted on August 14th. The formal surrender was signed on the United States battleship *Missouri* in Tokyo Bay, September 2, 1945, 92 years after Perry first steamed into the forbidden ports of Japan.

The Japanese style of right-wing totalitarianism was rooted in Japan's unusual history. Its ideology was shallow, and the Japanese democracy of today gives little evidence that this brand of mystical militarism and glorification of the warrior will be revived in that nation. Nevertheless, right-wing totalitarian ideologies based upon militarism and accompanying myths of security and well-being by domination are by no means confined to the Japanese experience and can certainly rise again.

The forms of right-wing totalitarianism that brought such untold horror to the world over two decades ago are now a matter of history. But the *conditions* which permitted them to be born and thrive can be repeated. The manner in which nazism rose is of particular importance; it is a classic example of how totalitarianism can use democratic processes to destroy democracy. The havoc brought to the world by these right-wing ideologies must never be forgotten, for some aspects of right-wing totalitarianism endure today, continuing to threaten the democratic ideology.

Right - Wing Totalitarianism in Recent Times

In 1945, the military might of the Allies crushed three of the most intense right-wing dictatorships ever witnessed by history. Did the victory of World War II wipe out fascism, nazism, and Japanese militarism? Can they rise again? The *exact form* of the ideologies concocted by Hitler, Mussolini, and the glorifiers of Japanese imperialism probably will not be seen again.

But the threat to democracy from the right continues to thrive. The seeds of the rightist style of dictatorship still find fertile soil in the economic and social conditions of many countries.

The underlying conditions and the ways of life in any state do much to shape its government. Communism and right-wing totalitarianism both seem to rejoice in depressed standards of living, people who are down and out, and international crisis, which produces instability and chaos. Both are wrapped around myths and promises which have little basis in fact but which have a magnetic emotional appeal. Dictators come and go, but their corrosive creeds often remain. Unless the democracies try to correct the conditions which undermine the security and well-being of men, totalitarianism may emerge.

Supernationalism, militarism, the proclaimed "infallibility" of the dictator, doctrines of racial superiority, and residues of fascism and nazism all contribute to the prolonging of the rightist dictatorship. A swastika scratched on a synagogue door in Newton, Massachusetts, or Nürnberg, Germany, dictatorship in Paraguay, and the "infallible" Dr. Duvalier in Haiti — all are visible evidences of right-wing totalitarianism. Extreme racism in the Republic of South Africa and the manifestations of the racial myth in some other states smack of Hitler's "superiority of the Aryan race." On the global stage, the challenge from the right has by no means vanished.

Within the democracies themselves, seeds of right-wing totalitarianism occasionally spring forth as poisonous weeds. Patterns of racial discrimination, religious prejudice, appeals to supernationalism, declared infallibility of some political leaders, and irrational myths which "explain" difficult conditions all represent a profound lack of confidence in democracy itself as a way of life and governing. The soil in which right-wing totalitarianism takes root lies within the state itself, although international crises can do much to promote dictatorships.

Democracy is in the middle, with communism on the left and right-wing totalitarianism on the right, both always ready to rise up and move toward the center. Sometimes, of course, the lines are hard to draw. Left-wing socialism in Italy and Japan, for instance, occasionally makes common cause with communism. On the other side of the spectrum, the line between Salazar's control of the Portuguese and outright dictatorship of the right is not too clear. All of this is somewhat like treading on egg shells without breaking them. But if we are to have a better understanding of the vital role ideologies play in world affairs, we must establish some guidelines for analyzing the ideologies.

1. What Is the Nature of Right-Wing Totalitarianism in Latin America?

Latin American Politics

Most of the Latin American states received their independence early in the nineteenth century when the overlords of Spain and Portugal were preoccupied with Napoleon's control of Europe. The nations to the south of the United States became republics because they wanted to repudiate the monarchial form of government. "Republic" is a chameleon-like word. A republic can be a democracy, such as the United States republic, or a totalitarian state, such as the Union of Soviet Socialistic Republics. A republic generally has a democratic structure of government, including a parliament, elections, and political parties. A *totalitarian* republic has these visible evidences of democracy, but the parliament is controlled by one or a few men, elections are usually rigged, and there is only one political party — that of the dictator.

Over the long span of their history, the Latin American states have, with a few exceptions, been republics of the right-wing variety. Twenty years ago, right-wing totalitarianism flourished as never before in Latin America. The regimes of Getúlio Vargas in Brazil, Marcos Pérez Jiménez in Venezuela, Gustavo Rojas Pinilla in Colombia, and Rafael Trujillo in the Dominican Republic were oblivious to the basic rights and well-being of their peoples. Today, only a few dictatorships remain, among them Stroessner's Paraguay and Duvalier's Haiti. The history of Peronism in Argentina gives us a good example of the growth of right-wing totalitarianism in Latin America.

The Argentina of Juan Perón

Rise of Perón. Before the defeat of the Axis in 1945, many Fascist and Nazi doctrines made their way across the Atlantic to South America, especially to Argentina. A group of young Army officers, deeply influenced by Fascist ideas in particular, overthrew the semi-democratic government of Argentina in 1943. The central figure of this coup was Juan Perón (1895-   ), who had served his government in Italy. As an attaché of the Argentine Embassy in Rome, Perón was thrilled by the speeches and views of Mussolini and found the idea of the organic state, the infallible leader, and supernationalism music to his ears. Perón particularly admired the way Mussolini could appeal to the poverty-stricken Italian masses. These poor people, who had nothing in their pockets, seemed hypnotized by Il Duce's orations and promises of a great future for all Italians.

Perón packed up the Fascist principles in his briefcase and

toted them off to Buenos Aires. His colleagues in the Argentine Army were impressed with Perón the man and Perón's parroting of Mussolini's ideas. During World War II, fascists and nazis circulated freely in Argentina, which was the one Latin American state which delayed declaring war on the Axis until the spring of 1945, when hostilities were practically over in Europe. Slowly but surely, Perón spun his web of Fascist ideas around his fellow officers who headed the Argentine government, and thus rose to leadership of the group. He was elected President of Argentina in February, 1946, and at last had the opportunity to impose his fascism upon the Argentine people.

"Peronism." Perón articulated the principle of the living, organic state and the need for infallible leadership — his own! Supernationalism rose to the fore, accompanied by governmental controls on radio, press, and speech. Perón accused the United States of enslaving Latin America and made Uncle Sam the scapegoat for Argentina's problems. The army was expanded as the guardian of the new Argentine dictatorship. Perón continually declared that he was the champion of the masses, the *descamisados* ("shirtless ones"). The people fell in line and were thrilled with their new leader. They swallowed the myth of the state, the promise of high standards of living, and the growing power of Argentina in Latin American and world affairs. Perón really gave them very little, but the *descamisados* looked on him as their great leader.

With his wife Eva as a powerful political asset, Perón labeled his Fascist carbon copy "Peronism," and his followers "Peronistas." The Peróns catered to the masses with expanded governmental services and benefits. At the same time, Perón's manipulation of the Argentine economy led it toward gradual bankruptcy, although this fact was cleverly concealed. He stifled all political opposition and thus won handily in the Presidential elections of 1951. He even had Eva Perón installed as Vice President of the regime. Perón's army gave him strong support as long as he could convey the impression that the masses of the Argentines were behind him.

Downfall. A dictator can permit no other powerful organization to deviate from his controls. He must exercise complete power and be the sole voice of authority. The Roman Catholic

Church in Argentina could not accept Perón's absolute dictatorship. In schools, for instance, Perón insisted on the teaching of the vague doctrines of Peronism and the pre-eminence of Perón himself. The Church, a powerful force in Latin American education, could not tolerate Perón's monopoly of the minds of the Argentine youth, and therefore began to oppose him. Unable to bring the Church into his ideological edifice, Perón began to take punitive action against clerics who had the courage to disagree with his ideas and policies. Clashes between Peronism and the Church mushroomed in 1954 and early 1955, and finally, in June, 1955, the Church excommunicated the dictator.

The army and other key people in Argentina began to lose their enthusiasm for Perón. In September, 1955, a group of army officers led a revolt against him, forcing him into exile. He fled from Argentina to Franco's Spain.

Conditions Which May Lead to Totalitarianism

Adverse economic, social, and political conditions characterize many of the Latin American states. This does not give democracy much of a chance as a way of life and governing. Low standards of living in Latin America and an inequitable distribution of the national wealth prevent the rise of a strong middle class, so essential for democracy. A tight class structure, low levels of literacy, and limited social services simply do not add up to high expectations for life on this earth. Widespread ignorance of public affairs and a historical absence of political democracy do not lend themselves to a vigorous multi-party democratic system or an effective democratic style of governing. Look at Bolivia!

Bolivia: a case study. Until reforms in the 1950's, a few people — usually either of European extraction or foreign investors — owned most of the land. These few, in turn, received most of the national income and had the major say in the government. The average per-capita income was very low — under $100 a year. There was no opportunity for the advent of a large middle class. The cities grew too fast for adequate housing and sanitation, and the traditional farmland was nearly exhausted by centuries of cultivation. About 75 percent of the people were crowded into the western two fifths of the country. Educational standards were low; the majority of Indians — over half the population — were unable to speak Spanish, much less read or write it, and there was a low level of literacy even among the rest of the population.

The political situation was no better. Since its independence in 1825, Bolivia has had one disastrous war after another. Civil wars have undermined the economy and prevented normal growth, while wars with neighboring countries have resulted in losses of valuable territory. Dictators, most of whom rose out of the army to overthrow the existing government, ruled for long periods. There has been little to encourage or promote an effective democratic style of governing.

This is a black picture indeed. But Bolivia's problems are those of Latin America in general. Everywhere, however, dictatorial leaders are becoming concerned with the unrest manifested by the people. They are being forced to loosen their grip — to raise the standard of living, to provide for more equal distribution of land and wealth, and to give their people more say in the government. No Latin American leader — dictatorial or otherwise — wants his country to travel the same road as Cuba.

Importance of the military. The military has always played a prominent role in Latin American politics. Between 1810 and 1914, over one hundred successful military revolts took place within Central and South American states. The power of the army in Latin American politics continues down to the present. The armies in Latin American nations tend to conserve the existing state of affairs rather than to advance the economic and social welfare of the people. The army has often joined forces with the wealthy and the landowners to form right-wing governments with no concern for the rights and well-being of the people. These armies are used much more for internal security than for guarding the state against the possibility of attacks from without.

A dictator can often gloss over economic, social, and political shortcomings of his regime, provided he can do several things at the same time. If he can infuse the people with a feeling of supernationalism, they might well identify themselves with the "greatness of the state." If he can provide stimulating and emotional leadership and at the same time give the masses a few lumps of sugar in the way of reforms and scattered public services, they might praise the leader, as the *decamisados* did Perón. If the supernationalist leader can put his myth across through a monopoly of the radio, press, and other forms of public expression and if he can dangle all kinds of promises for a bright new future, his control over the people may well be assured.

Most important, if the army, the main bulwark of physical force in most Latin American states, feels that the national leader (usually selected by them) is keeping the people in line and not disturbing the well-being of the army itself, it will support the *status quo*. As far as the national economy is concerned, the relative few who manage the main industries are permitted to conduct business as usual. Economic progress is valued highly, but only as far as those in power are concerned. The majority of wealthy Latin American businessmen and landowners generally have little interest in sharing their income and favorable living conditions with the masses. In some states the strong-arm role of national armies has retarded the advance of democracy. On the other hand, some contend that the role of the army in keeping internal peace and order may help to restore the democratic center.

Paraguay. In 1954 General Alfredo Stroessner became just the latest in a long line of totalitarian rulers in the land-locked South American state of Paraguay. With the army firmly behind him, Stroessner and his National Republic (*Colorado*) Party firmly controlled the 1,700,000 Paraguayans.

Stroessner gave his people little myth or promise. Supernationalism was replaced by a virtual police state when Stroessner dissolved the Chamber of Deputies. The role of the army was particularly important. It received well over one third of the national budget and reciprocated by making certain that no one upset the Stroessner applecart. The General permitted elections in Paraguay in both 1958 and 1963, and won easily by making certain that most of the members of the opposition were either in jail or exiled. Those who stayed around to offer some fight to the National Republic Party were only puppets to give a semblance of opposition.

It is interesting to note that General Stroessner became slightly more liberal as he plodded into his second "term." Anxious to improve his public image, he introduced a number of public-works' programs. Like many Latin American leaders, Stroessner has been forced to give his people a freer life in order to save his own skin.

Haiti. French-speaking Haiti, with more than three and a half million people, has been tightly controlled by Dr. François Duvalier, a man who considers himself the very incarnation of the nation. His regime has both the army and a brutal secret police behind it. Duvalier has given his people a strong myth and promise and has appeared to have their support. He has identified himself, in their minds, with the future of Haiti. His public declaration of May 1, 1963, reminds us of remarks certain dictators have made before.

> I am the personification of the Haitian Fatherland. Those who wish to destroy Duvalier wish to destroy the Haitian Fatherland.
> I don't take orders or dictates from anybody, no matter where they come from, even if the anti-nationalists think they have the power to tell me what I ought to do.[1]

Attempts made on Duvalier's life by people desperate for a better way of life have all met with severe reprisals. But the continuing unrest in the state shows that Duvalier's regime is far from secure.

Peru and Argentina. Unstable conditions, characterized by a series of military dictatorships, prevailed in Peru from the 1930's until 1956. At that time free elections took place and President Manuel Prado y Ugarteche came to power. Prado introduced some democratic reforms, but many people considered the APRA party, which had supported him in the elections, too radical. The APRA began in the 1920's as a pro-Indian, Marxist movement. Several times it was declared illegal, but it continued to gain strength. While retaining its leftist leanings, it has become strongly anticommunist. The army, which has generally leaned to the right, has always opposed APRA.

The 1962 elections gave the APRA candidate for the Presidency, Víctor Raúl Haya de la Torre, more votes than the other

[1] *The New York Times,* May 2, 1963.

candidates, but he did not have the necessary one third of the votes cast. The army, suspicious of APRA's aims, stepped in, arrested President Prado, and nullified the elections on the alleged grounds that they were fraudulent. An army *junta*, or ruling group, declared that elections would be held in 1963, and kept their promise in June of that year.

The winner was Fernando Belaúnde Terry, a candidate of the Popular Democrat Party, supported by all those who opposed APRA's power. This time, Dr. Haya de la Torre accused the army of conducting fraudulent elections, but did not succeed in overthrowing Belaúnde Terry. The democratic governing process was thus restored to this important Latin American nation, temporarily at least.

The army performed in the same manner in Argentina. A constitutional government was established in 1958, three years after the murky cobwebs of the Perón era were swept away. President Frondizi tried hard to restore the democratic center, but Perón's *descamisados* still retained much loyalty for the exiled dictator. Frondizi, the person, and his policies simply didn't appeal to the people. In the March, 1962, elections, the Peronistas demonstrated unusual strength at the polls.

The army, terrified at the prospect of Peronism returning to power, tossed Frondizi out of office and placed him under house arrest. All activity of the Peronistas was banned, and the army took over control of the state. Thus the army thwarted the voice of the people by nullifying the elections. The irony is clear. A military rule was imposed on the Argentine people because of the army's fear that the democratic process would elevate some people to power who would, in turn, usher democracy out the back door.

Elections were promised by the army for 1963, and they took place in early July. Everyone held their breath. Would the Peronistas win? Backed strongly by communists and Castrotypes, and heavily endorsed by Perón himself (vacationing permanently in Spain), the Peronistas, operating under various party labels, had high hopes of taking over governmental power. But they suffered a smashing defeat, receiving only 16 percent of the nation's vote. A constitutional government was restored, and Dr. Arturo Illia was elected President.

In both Peru and Argentina, therefore, the army played a role of holding off threats to the democratic center. The army seized power in both states, presided over governmental affairs during a long cooling-off period, and then permitted elections to take place. Had these elections gone to radical groups, the army probably would have stepped in in a high-handed manner once more. On the other hand, perhaps the army saved democracy for Peru and Argentina. In other words, should force be used to save democracy when there is a possibility that democracy itself will be crushed by those who get elected to office? Military seizures of power in the Dominican Republic and Honduras in the fall of 1963 point up the continuing powerful role of the army in Latin American politics. The dilemma of right-wing militarism in Latin America will probably be with us for a long time to come.

Importance of the Church. The Latin American dictator can never completely control all facets of the society because of the importance of the Roman Catholic Church. Catholicism prevails throughout most of Latin America, and frequently it is the Church rather than the government which provides for education, social reforms, and progress. When a Latin American dictator becomes too oppressive in his exercise of power, the Church may well be a strong influence in bringing his dictatorship to an end. For example, Trujillo, who ruled the Dominican Republic for 30 years, came to believe that his strength exceeded that of the Church. In so doing, he helped bring about his own downfall. The Church casts an increasingly critical eye on other dictators. It can serve as an important force in bringing about the downfall of totalitarianism in Latin America.

One could well ask why the plight of the people in Latin America is not favorable to the growth of Communist totalitarianism rather than to the right-wing totalitarian ideology. Communism *is* a distinct threat in Latin America, especially since Castro's seizure of the government of Cuba in January, 1959. On the other hand, communism and Catholicism are bitter enemies.

But if communism promises that it can correct the economic and social ills of the more than 200 million Latin Americans, will it not sweep over the continent? The material aspects of life cannot be brushed aside in any discussion of ideologies and world affairs. Religions or ideologies cannot put food into stomachs, make people read and write, cure all kinds of diseases, and raise living standards.

The conditions which permit right-wing totalitarianism to flourish can, in turn, open the doors to Communist totalitarianism. No better proof of this statement could be found than in the Cuban case. But, in the last analysis, ideologies are a matter of faith and conviction, and Christianity in Latin America remains a powerful barrier to the atheistic ideology of communism.

The Case of Cuba

When a right-wing dictator has real concern for the well-being and rights of his people, his rule may gradually change into a benevolent authoritarianism. This is more or less what seems to be happening in Latin America today.

On the other hand, when a right-wing dictator refuses to heed the protests and desires of the majority of his people, making his rule increasingly strict and intolerable, he can cause such hatred and disgust with his regime that the people turn to the ideology which seems to promise them an end to all government control — namely, communism. This is what happened in Cuba.

Totalitarianism of one brand or another has long been the tragic fate of Cuba. On the whole, totalitarian governments have dominated Cuba from the date of its independence in 1902 to the regime of Fulgencio Batista of the late 1950's. Batista, as a right-wing dictator, supported by the army and thwarting all political opposition, used police-state tactics to perpetuate himself in power. Conditions in Cuba favored a few wealthy landowners and industrial elites, but the majority of people had little opportunity to improve their lot.

During the 1950's, a rebellious movement in Oriente, the eastern province, began to attract the attention of Cubans and the hostility of the Batista government. The leader of this movement, Fidel Castro, proclaimed democratic aims and called for all Cubans to join him in restoring freedom and economic opportunity to the beleaguered nation. Castro's guerrilla warfare tactics and clever propaganda brought much support to his side and some admiration from abroad as well. After an extended civil war, Castro's forces finally reached Havana by late 1958. Following Batista's New Year's Eve flight from the country, Castro took over the government on January 1, 1959.

Castro continued to promise a democracy for Cuba. He vowed that elections would be held fifteen months after he took office. He assured the people that the democratic constitution of 1940 would be fully restored. But none of these things happened.

Instead, Castro imposed a new brand of totalitarianism on the estimated 6,700,000 Cuban people — that of communism. Apparently Castro and his associates had been devoted to the Communist cause all along, and during his first months in office, the red core of Castro's movement became increasingly apparent. He took over American economic properties in Cuba without fair compensation, and increasingly applied measures which made it obvious where his true loyalties lay. The United States finally severed relations with Cuba in January, 1961. Many of the Latin American states followed suit, and the Organization of American States voted to expel Cuba as long as it was dominated by Castro or the communists. In December of the same year, Castro admitted that he was fully in line with Marxist-Leninist thought. Cuba, allied with the USSR, became the first "peoples' republic" in the Western hemisphere. Castro is now working hard to push communism in Latin America by exporting terrorism and subversion. Communist tactics in creating chaos in Venezuela's democratic elections of early December, 1963, although unsuccessful, were a clear example of Cuba-directed efforts to advance the Communist cause in Latin America.

Castro's police state controls the Cuban people to an intense degree. Church officials have been exiled. Education has been thoroughly nationalized and cast in the Communist mold. The army supports the totalitarian government, and the Soviet Union maintains thousands of soldiers in Cuba, making it difficult for the Cubans to revolt. Had Castro been true to his original promises, he could have raised the low standards of living and prepared the way for genuine democracy. Instead, he chose to replace one style of dictatorship with another. His totalitarianism has taken advantage of the low levels of economic and social ways of life in Cuba. The Castro case demonstrates that the swing from the far right to the far left can take place without permitting the ideological pendulum to stop at the democratic center.

2. Is Right-Wing Ideology in Spain and Portugal Dangerous?

One could probably muster a heated discussion on whether the governments of Spain and Portugal should or should not be placed in the camp of right-wing totalitarianism. The strong rule of Generalísimo Francisco Franco in Spain and the firm control of António de Oliveira Salazar over his fellow Portuguese hardly fit within the democratic fold, and yet they differ in many ways from the patterns of authoritarianism found in the Afro-Asian world. Franco and Salazar are not Mussolinis or Hitlers. Spain and Portugal represent the gray area in the spectrum of dictatorships.

Franco's Spain

Francisco Franco (1892-   ) led a militant movement of rebellion against a shaky Spanish government in July, 1936, thus starting three years of fierce civil strife in Spain. In this bitter war, Franco had the help of Hitler and Mussolini, who used the civil conflict as a proving ground for their own military forces. Franco's movement won out in March, 1939, and the Generalísimo installed himself as the supreme ruler of Spain — a position he has held since that time. He extended token military assistance to Hitler's ill-fated offensive against Russia in 1941, but never formally allied himself with the Nazi regime. Because of his relations with Hitler and Mussolini, Franco was generally ostracized from the leading tables of international diplomacy after World War II.

A Basic Law of 1942, supplemented by a Franco decree of 1946, set up a "parliament," the Cortes. Franco was named absolute Chief of State and possessor of supreme governing power. As Premier of the Spanish government, Franco was head of the only legal party, his own Falange organization, also called "The National Movement."

A Law of Succession of July, 1947, labeled Spain a "monarchy" with Franco as Chief of State, but provided that a person of royal descent might one day head the nation. The man who would be King of Spain today, if it were a monarchy, is Don Juan de Bourbon y Battenberg, who is in exile in Portugal. He hopes that his son, Juan Carlos, might possess the throne when Franco is no longer on the scene. Events of the future may well permit a constitutional monarchy to be revived in Spain.

During recent years, Franco has gained a toehold in the active game of world politics. The United States now has bases in Spain and extends military assistance to Franco's government. Spain is represented in the United Nations as well. Its doors are increasingly open to tourists, and the Spanish economy is slowly being transformed into a more modern structure. A Falange leader, José Solis Ruiz, declared in May, 1963, that Spain needed a peaceful social revolution to give the nation structural reforms and "social justice." He endorsed workers' demands for better pay and improved industrial conditions. A four-year, multi-billion dollar economic development plan, laying heavy stress on private enterprise, was launched by the Spanish Government in 1963.

Thus the winds of change are altering economic and social conditions in Spain, possibly bringing with them the foundations of modern democracy.

Salazar's Portugal

António de Oliveira Salazar (1889-   ) took over control of Portugal in 1932 and gave a constitution to his people in March, 1933. This organ of government provides for a series of state-controlled corporations similar to Mussolini's government, which Salazar admired.

The National Union Party runs Portugal and has outlawed all other political organizations. Salazar is the President of the Central Committee of the National Union Party and has also served continuously as Premier of the government, permitting other close associates to hold the honorary office of President. Here is another state with democratic structures serving as a

front for dictatorship. Opposing political groups have attempted
to unseat Salazar in recent years, but with little success.

In foreign affairs, Portugal is a member of the North Atlantic
Treaty Organization and the United Nations. Membership in
NATO is largely based on the fact that the Portuguese Azores
Islands have military value to the Western Alliance, but Portugal
is hardly in accord with the democratic ideals of the other members of NATO. Portugal is the only remaining colonial power in
Europe of the old nineteenth-century style. Its African colonies
of Mozambique and Angola are considered by Salazar to be
"provinces" of Portugal. A swelling of nationalistic spirit in these
possessions, however, threatens to loosen Portugal's grasp on
these remnants of the imperialistic era.

The "Gray Area" of Iberian Totalitarianism

Exactly how can we classify Spain and Portugal in our analysis
of modern right-wing totalitarianism? On one side of the coin,
Franco's and Salazar's governments do not seek to extend their
dictatorships to other states. With the exception of Portugal's
hold on Mozambique and Angola, the Iberian states are not imperialistic. Neither Franco nor Salazar has formulated a myth
to justify his rule, and neither puts forward a fantastic promise
of great things to come. Ideologically, their regimes are devoid
of the usual right-wing trappings. It is true that force is often
applied against those who oppose the regimes politically, but
terror and concentration camps do not exist to bolster the dictatorships of Franco and Salazar.

Let us take a look at the other side of the coin. Spain and
Portugal have a combined population of about 40 million people.
Low economic standards afflict the way of life in both states. The
freedoms of religion, speech, press, assembly, and opportunity
are limited. Franco and Salazar impose strong censorship in
many areas of life and permit only one channel of political expression — that which favors their own parties. Can these
national practices and policies be ignored by those who seek to
extend democracy in world affairs?

We can argue that these two states deserve the support of

the democracies because Franco and Salazar take a vigorous stand against communism. For this reason, the United States' military bases in Spain serve as part of the armed network of defense against possible Soviet aggression in Europe. Portugal, as a member of NATO, is taking its stand in the defensive effort against communism. Doesn't any anti-Communist state merit strong backing from the democracies?

On the other hand, does the democracies' support of Spain and Portugal merely on the basis of their stand against communism damage democracy's image in the minds of the people of the African and Asian states? After all, Hitler and Mussolini were against communism too, and under the "anti-Communist" banner, brought their own brand of totalitarianism to millions. Many people argue that the burning issue in world affairs is the threat of communism. Do they realize that other brands of totalitarianism can also crush the democratic spirit? Enlisting Spain and Portugal in the fight against international communism is important. But the doctrines of Salazar and Franco, as they have been practiced in these two countries, are hardly an asset to democracy in world affairs.

In all probability, both Franco and Salazar realize that their right-wing totalitarianism is something of the past. Their regimes are largely personal creations. With the passing of these two dictators, Spain and Portugal may well enact liberalizing programs and doctrines. Successors to Franco and Salazar might promote democratic ways of life and governing in the Iberian Peninsula. On the other hand, totalitarianism might be extended into the future by other dictators.

The lesson from Cuba tells us how communism could seize Spain and Portugal. What Franco and Salazar do now can do much to prevent this from happening. The foreign policies of the democratic states can also play a role in directing change in Spain and Portugal toward democratic goals.

3. The Continuing Menace of Racism

Hitler was not the first of the racial supremacists. Ideas concerning the presumed "superiority" of one race over another have deep roots in history. Nevertheless, the manner in which Hitler and his associates wove the doctrines of Aryan racial supremacy into a totalitarian ideology gave a tremendous boost to the combination of racism and totalitarian governmental policy. Although this fusion of the idea of racial superiority with national policy was weakened considerably by the revelation of the horrors of the Nazi years, it continues to plague the democratic ideal in our times.

The Republic of South Africa

In the Republic of South Africa, a totalitarian national policy of extreme racism has been imposed upon some thirteen million people. Security and national well-being for the white government of the Republic's Prime Minister H. F. Verwoerd means security for the white against the nonwhite — progress for the white and vast restrictions for the nonwhite.

The background. The southern part of the African continent was originally a sparsely populated area of Negroid men. Then the Dutch arrived in the sixteenth century. In 1814 the British took over the Cape area. Soon the old Dutch settlers had had enough of the enlightened British view toward the dark man. In 1836 the Dutch, or Afrikaners, moved northward to seek their own white-controlled settlements, only to be followed a few decades later by the British seeking gold and diamonds. The many conflicts between the British and Dutch in the nineteenth century culminated in the Boer War of 1899-1902. Although the British won, the British and Dutch territories were joined in 1910 to form the Union (now, Republic) of South Africa, a new member state of the British Commonwealth. All went well for the most part until 1948, when the Afrikaner Nationalist Party took over the reins of government. At this point, the fireworks started, but the lid did not blow off right away.

"Separate development" of races. The Afrikaners and their National Party hold tightly to the view that only the white man deserves to enjoy the full fruits of society, while the nonwhite is naturally an inferior person. Segregation of races had always existed in South Africa. But from 1948 on, the Nationalist government has imposed a policy of extreme racial segregation between the whites on the one hand and nonwhites on the other. This policy is called *apartheid*.[1] South African legislation carries out this ideological conviction in the most rigorous manner.

The nonwhite people in the Republic are divided into several categories. About one and a half million are of mixed European and nonwhite descent. The lighter color skins of these "Coloreds" confer on them greater privileges than the much darker "Blacks" receive. There are also about 500,000 people of Asian descent, especially Indians, who are classified as nonwhites. The harsh measures of apartheid are leveled against the nearly eleven million "Blacks" who are almost considered non-persons.

There are slightly more than three million whites in the Republic, of which the Afrikaners number about 1,700,000, and people of British origin make up the rest. The Afrikaners of the Nationalist Party trace their doctrine of apartheid to the Book of Genesis. A plank in the platform of the Nationalist Party declares that:

> As a basic principle of its attitudes towards natives and coloureds, the Party recognizes that both are permanent parts of the country's population, under the Christian trusteeship of the European races.[2]

The United Party, made up largely of whites of British descent, loudly protests the increasingly severe segregation measures. The Nationalists, firmly convinced that the white man is far superior to the nonwhite, pursue a policy of a "separate and segregated development" for the whites and nonwhites. The Afrikaners hold that, biologically, the nonwhites are totally unable to attain a level of civilization even approaching that of the white man. Thus these unfortunate thirteen million people, whose body chemistry produces a dark skin, are forced to lead a life vastly different from the relatively affluent existence of the whites.

[1] In late July, 1963, the government of the Republic of South Africa dropped the use of the word "apartheid" in favor of *separate development* to describe the rigid policy of racial segregation.

[2] Herbert Spiro, *Politics in Africa: Prospects South of the Sahara.* Englewood Cliffs, New Jersey: Prentice-Hall, 1962, p. 43.

If one reduces this "religious" and "biological" doctrine to its inner core, a more basic explanation of apartheid blazes forth. Most of the South African whites lead a comfortable life. The chores of the society are performed by the nonwhites, especially the tough, hot work of mining. All political, social, and economic power is a white monopoly. Any white concession to nonwhite, anywhere along the line, is viewed by the whites, especially the Afrikaners, as something which would start a chain reaction toward white oblivion. As usual, if we remove the myth, the real purpose of an ideology stands out like a sore thumb.

The grim irony in the Republic of South Africa is that the whites enjoy their version of democracy, while totalitarianism is imposed upon the vast majority of about 13 million nonwhites. The national policy of apartheid applies to all public facilities (park benches, post-office windows, beaches, elevators, and toilets), housing, working conditions, forms of transportation, and all social relationships. The nonwhites are not permitted to worship in white churches. Apparently the Afrikaners assume that God distinguishes among men on the basis of color. Once a Negro was apprehended in a white church. "What are you doing here?" growled the policeman. "Scrubbing the floor," was the Negro's answer. "Go ahead," said the white man, "but make certain you don't pray in here!"

Nonwhites may not remain in any urban area for a period longer than seventy-two hours without special permission. They are cast in jail if they do not have their identification papers on them. They are brought before "special" courts and most have no voting rights. A new Nationalist policy of February, 1963, seeks to transport the nonwhites to back country areas so they will not constitute a threat to the whites in the major cities. Segregation policies and practices pile up on each other day after day and year after year.

This intense racial policy is clearly reminiscent of the Nazi approach toward the Jews although the South African whites have not resorted to mass extermination in the Hitler style. Because of condemnation of apartheid, the Republic left the British Commonwealth in May, 1961. Prime Minister Verwoerd's government has been strongly criticized by most other nations of the world and has been the subject of many recriminations at the United Nations. In October, 1963, the United States banned further sale of American arms to the Republic of South Africa as clear evidence of its opposition to Verwoerd's policies. Apartheid in its South African form is not likely to be exported, although white supremacists everywhere support the national policies of the Republic. This form of totalitarianism for the majority of the people of the Republic, however, is a strong barrier to advancing the democratic idea in world affairs. This is particularly true in Africa where the hope is that whites and nonwhites can live together peacefully in the new nations, which have a majority of nonwhite citizens.

The Middle East

Racism is also a problem in the Middle East. Hostility between Jews and Arabs in the Middle East and North Africa greatly complicates international relations. As a dimension of right-wing totalitarianism, racism is ingrained in the national policies of many Arab states.

There is no inherent hostility between Arabs of the Moslem faith and Jews. Jews and Moslems lived peacefully side by side in medieval Spain. And it should not be forgotten that both Jews and Arabs belong to the same general ethnic category — that of Semites.

In modern times, the Jewish belief in Zionism, or the quest for a national homeland in the Biblical land of Palestine, has caused feelings of anti-Jewish sentiment in the Arab countries. In 1948 Jews in Palestine, backed by fellow Jews in other parts of the world, furthered the goal of Zionism with the declaration of independence of the state of Israel. The Arab states immediately resorted to armed force in order to destroy the new state, but with no success. Hostility has continued to mark Arab-Israeli relations since that time.

The opposition of the Arab states to the existence of Israel has spilled over into a strong sentiment against Jews as such. Arab leaders tend to fear the progressive and democratic qualities of the Jewish state. Israel's outstanding accomplishments in land reform, irrigation of arid lands, development of a broad industrial structure, and genuine concern for the well-being of its citizens all seem to threaten the general complacency of life in the Arab states. Arab leaders, while in broad disagreement with each other on most issues, unite in calling for the annihilation of Israel. They teach their youth to hate the new Jewish state. Arab maps designate the area of Israel as "Jewish-occupied Arab territory." "Push Israel into the sea" is a common declaration in the Arab Middle East.

Arab leaders fear the impact of Israel's democratic institutions on their own authoritarian regimes. They violently oppose continued Jewish immigration to Israel and the substantial material support extended to the new state by Jewish people from all over the world. The Jewish doctrine of Zionism, which is deeply imbedded in Jewish history and religion, is identified in the Arab mind with a racial threat to the security and well-being of the Arab states. This is hardly advantageous to the growth and development of democracy among the Arab people.

The Arab states take harsh measures against Jews within their own territories. But military action against Israel has been a bitter experience. A full-scale attempt by the Arabs to "push Israel into the sea" would undoubtedly bring about a major war in that part of the world.

Other Evidences of Racism

In surveying the world scene today, we can find other evidences of racism in a number of nations. It would appear that a small number of the "lunatic fringe" in both Italy and Germany still adhere to the myths of fascism and nazism, more so in Germany than in Italy.

Allied efforts to eradicate fascism in Italy and nazism in Germany after World War II were, on the whole, successful. The trials of former Nazi officials, particularly those at Nürnberg in 1945 and 1946, did much to bring home to Germans the hideous effects of nazism on mankind. Most Germans today find it difficult to believe that some of their fellow countrymen could have engaged in such inhumane behavior. Politically, nazism and fascism attract only a very few adherents in national elections. One distinct note of criticism can be raised, however. Very little is done in Italian and especially in German schools to make certain that the young people of today understand the full impact of right-wing totalitarianism.

The racism of Hitler's Nazi Germany, as we have seen, by no means ended in 1945. Racism has reared its ugly head in many nations. Besides the Republic of South Africa and the Arab Middle East, anti-Semitism exists in the Soviet Union, in a few Latin American states, and to a limited extent, even in some Western democracies. The USSR has been severe with its Jewish populace, denying them freedom on their holy days and applying continual policies of persecution. In the West, warped personalities still scratch the Nazi swastika, symbol of Hitler's anti-Semitism, on the walls of synagogues. Most authorities feel that such evidences of racial hatred are products of sick minds. Even so, democracies have no place for them. Racial hatred of any kind is totally alien to the meaning of democracy.

It should always be remembered that certain national and international conditions can give rise to the climate for a revival of right-wing totalitarianism. In all probability, totalitarianism in the economically poor and socially unstable states, such as those in Africa and Asia, will be of the Communist variety. Totalitarianism tends to be of the right-wing variety in the more industrialized states of the West. Both communism and fascism can emerge, however, if the vital center of democracy is not nourished.

Authoritarianism
in the
Contemporary World

Growing up is a difficult process, both for people and for countries. We all go through a period of walking before we run, of leaning upon some authority before we assume command of our own affairs. The father in the family has authority, as does the teacher in the classroom, the minister in the pulpit, the captain in the army. Authority can be good or bad, stern or lenient, oppressive or helpful. An authoritarian person is generally one who exercises strong leadership, maybe for the good of others or perhaps just for the delight of being the "boss."

Today, some fifty countries, especially in the Afro-Asian world, are struggling to grow up and take their place in the modern world. The ideologies of these countries are complex. Their ways of living are varied. Their ways of governing do not fit neatly into democratic or totalitarian camps. They are, for the most part, states with *authoritarian* ideologies.

1. What Is the Nature of Authoritarianism?

Authoritarianism is halfway between freedom and tyranny. Strong new leaders have suddenly come on the world scene, leaders who cannot be pigeonholed as either totalitarian or democratic. These authoritarian leaders will come and go, rise to power or be toppled in revolution. Their names will change, but their role in the Afro-Asian world will remain.

Some of these men are genuinely trying to create the conditions which will lead their nations toward democracy. Others increasingly seek personal power and seem to be pushing toward totalitarianism. Still other leaders give every indication of remaining on the authoritarian fence. Which way will they lead their countries, or will they go anywhere at all?

Some Views of Afro-Asian Leaders

"Capitalism is too complicated a system for a newly independent nation," says Kwame Nkrumah of Ghana, who in the 1930's was an impoverished student at Lincoln University in Oxford, Pennsylvania. "Hence the need for a socialistic society. But even a system based upon social justice and a democratic constitution may need backing up, during the period following independence, by emergency measures of a totalitarian kind. Without discipline, true freedom cannot survive."[1]

"Let us find a democracy which is suitable for our own identity, and use sources and material which are to be found in our own country,"[2] says Sukarno of Indonesia, the man who led his country to independence from the Netherlands.

". . . it is necessary that Islam be taken out of the recesses of the past and presented to the world in a way and a language that are absolutely modern . . . not as an ideology but as a true plan of political, civic, and spiritual action, because this is the fundamental meaning of Islam,"[3] says President Ayub Khan of Pakistan, the man who has cultivated the democratic spirit at the grass roots in Pakistan.

President Sékou Touré of Guinea defines democracy in terms of the whole society of his nation. "We have chosen the freedom, the right, the power, the sovereignty of the people, and not of the individual. Before this people, you should have no individual personality. Our personality becomes part of the personality of the nation."[4]

[1] Paul E. Sigmund, Jr. (ed.), *The Ideologies of the Developing Nations.* New York: Frederick A. Praeger, 1963, p. 186.

[2] *Ibid.,* p. 62.

[3] *Ibid.,* p. 110.

[4] *Ibid.,* p. 5

Dr. Julius Nyerere of Tanganyika, a leader in the independence movement of his West African nation, stresses the functioning of democratic processes *within* the one dominant party of the new state. He thus does not consider a two-party political system essential for a democracy. He points out that:

> Where there is *one* party — provided it is identified with the nation as a whole — the foundations of democracy can be firmer, and the people can have more opportunity to exercise a real choice, than where you have two or more parties.[1]

He adds that "true democracy depends far more on the attitude of mind that respects and defends the individual than on the form it takes."[2]

Tom Mboya, a prominent national leader in Kenya, strongly agrees. "The party system is not a necessary part of democracy." He goes on to say that "what is necessary is the freedom to form parties. It is not necessary that more than one should in fact exist and function effectively."[3]

National Goals of Afro-Asian Leaders

Most of the authoritarian rulers in the Afro-Asian states, such as Sukarno in Indonesia, Bourgiba in Tunisia, and Nkrumah in Ghana, were key figures in the independence movements of their nations. Because they fought hard for independence, they take an equally strong stand in attempting to preserve the full security of their new states.

Security and well-being are goals of national policy for authoritarian rulers, just as in all states. Most of the authoritarian states gained their full independence after World War II, and the governing officials in these nations are particularly anxious to keep their nations independent of outside control. Most authoritarian leaders, moreover, face stiff competition within their countries from those who aspire to national power. Thus many of them, such as Algeria's Ben Bella, treat all opposition in a rough manner in the cause of "national security."

[1] Tom Mboya, "The Party System in Africa." *Foreign Affairs,* July, 1963, p. 655.
[2] Sigmund, *op. cit.,* p. 199.
[3] Mboya, *op. cit.,* p. 653.

The authoritarian leaders are apt to feel that they and they alone can maintain security, and for this reason they maintain strong governmental controls. Authoritarian leaders tend to view elections and political parties as luxuries of democratic governing which they cannot afford.

But most of these leaders sincerely seek to advance the well-being of their people. Well-being for these authoritarian leaders usually means trying to reduce hunger, poverty, disease, and illiteracy. Leaders such as the Shah of Iran or President Ayub Khan of Pakistan feel that this hard work of slowly raising the standards of living for the people in their states must be a concentrated drive. If progress can be made in this direction, then perhaps the fundamentals of democracy also can be introduced.

Not all authoritarian leaders are equally dedicated to opposing the threat of totalitarianism. President Sukarno in Indonesia flirts with communism, as does Nkrumah of Ghana. Both feel they can "ride the Communist tiger." This is a difficult and dangerous stunt. In the meantime, progress is short-circuited. Former President Diem in South Vietnam was intolerant of democratic rights, irrespective of the tough guerrilla warfare going on with the communists in his Oklahoma-size nation. President Nasser is spending more time in expanding the power of his United Arab Republic in the Middle East and bellowing about Israel than in doing a solid job for his people within Egypt.

Authoritarianism Is Not Totalitarianism

The picture is uneven. Some leaders seem to be headed toward eventual democracy, while others show dangerous signs of moving toward one brand or another of totalitarianism. Some will be content with perpetuating authoritarianism. Almost all of the authoritarian leaders feel that democratic governing is not practical at this time. But they are not totalitarian. On the whole, they permit their people a fairly wide latitude of freedom of thought, speech, assembly, publication, and job opportunities as long as such action does not threaten the stability of the regime. They do not have concentration or labor camps. They do not *force* their people to believe in only one approach to human behavior.

Only a few peddle a phony myth. They do not hold out fantastic promises. Authoritarian states, with only a very few exceptions, are not police states. Some possess several earmarks of totalitarianism, but they do not pose a threat to existing democracies, as do many totalitarian regimes.

2. What Is the Background of Authoritarianism?

If you examine any democracy today, you will note that it emerged from some previous non-democratic form of government and society. Democracies do not just spring forth in full bloom. They arise because some people at some time or another refused to accept the patterns of authoritarianism or totalitarianism thrust upon them. Through peaceful change or revolution, they helped to bring about a way of life and governing which greatly expanded their access to freedom.

History gives us many examples of democracy flowing out of authoritarianism. Political philosophers have been intrigued with the relation between stern rule and the introduction of more liberal patterns of governing. Perhaps we can gain some knowledge for today if we make use of the lessons of the past.

Plato and Aristotle

In the fourth century B.C. Plato and Aristotle devoted much thought to the changing nature of governing systems. Plato discussed the matter in detail with his students, emphasizing how certain brands of totalitarianism lead into various kinds of authoritarian systems, and then into democracy. But Plato simply did not like democracy.

In *The Republic* Plato declared that democracy always produces rulers who cater to the popular sentiment of the voters. Therefore, the rulers cannot make decisions which advance the security and well-being of the city-state. Plato preferred an authoritarian government, headed by "philosopher-kings" who, because of their knowledge and education, would make the right decisions for all. Obviously, Plato wanted the ideological elevator to stop on the authoritarian floor without going on up to democracy. Nevertheless, later in his life, Plato veered more toward a government of laws than one of educated aristocrats.

Aristotle also studied the evolution of democracy from previous totalitarian and authoritarian ideologies of the Greek city-states. But he was more sympathetic than Plato toward democracy. He felt that a limited democracy was the best of all governments but added that democracy required obligations of the citizenry if they were to enjoy its benefits.

Machiavelli

During the Renaissance, some of the city-states of Italy, such as Florence, developed patterns of democratic liberties. In fifteenth-century Florence, a fairly firm kind of republic was shored up by the strong hand of the Medici family. The greatest of the Medici, Lorenzo the Magnificent (1449-1492), sat behind the scenes and pulled the political and economic strings of Florence during this great period of its history. Lorenzo was somewhat like a twentieth-century big-city boss. Florence and many other Italian city-states emerged from the medieval era of totalitarianism as states which were partly authoritarian and partly democratic.

One of the most prominent Florentines was Machiavelli (1469-1527), whose famous work *The Prince* still causes controversy. *The Prince* is usually viewed as a handbook for dictators, largely because Machiavelli coined the often-used phrase: "The end justifies the means." Many totalitarian leaders, such as Napoleon and Mussolini, relied on Machiavelli's political prescriptions in their own rise to power. But Machiavelli's goal or "end" was solely Italian unification. His "means" to this end would not receive our approval today, but they were in vogue in Machiavelli's time.

Machiavelli's name has become a synonym for political power and deceit. But in another book, *The Discourses,* he charts a course of national unification for the Prince. Then he calls upon the Prince (the ruler) to develop more liberal ways of governing. *The Prince* and *The Discourses,* taken together, give us some important ideas on authoritarianism and how rulers can use it as a stepping-stone toward eventual republican ends.

The Emergence of Modern Democracy

In England. Patterns of democratic governing and ways of life have evolved from strong rulers. The homeland of modern democracy, England, had powerful monarchs who, with some exceptions, gradually gave way to limitations on their rule after the Magna Carta of 1215. Yet the Kings and Queens of England dominated the scene until the Glorious Revolution of 1688, when Parliament assumed a commanding position in England. The Stuart monarchs of the seventeenth century, in particular, based their authority to govern on special powers received directly from God. Until the nineteenth century, the *authority* of the wealthy and the titled few monopolized English society and government. Until the majority of British adults received the right to vote and to hold public office during the past 100 years, an aristocratic authoritarianism tended to prevail. During this era, the people had many freedoms, but the style of governing was not one of democratic participation for all.

In Great Britain today, Queen Elizabeth reigns but does not rule. Nevertheless, she reigns "by the grace of God," a symbolic reference to the theory of Divine origin of government in English history. This symbol of monarchial states is the indispensable core around which the British democracy is constructed. It reminds us that the great democratic nation of Great Britain has deep roots in monarchial authoritarianism.

In the United States. In the United States, the early colonialists of the seventeenth century borrowed heavily from English and other European philosophers to draw up their initial organs of government, such as the Mayflower Compact of 1620. There were strong strains of authoritarianism in the colonies before democracy really got under way. In Massachusetts, the religious doctrines of Calvin held sway for many decades after 1630, and tolerance for people of other religious persuasion was not particularly generous. Access to voting and political office was confined to those of authority, based upon status and wealth. True, the Declaration of Independence and the Constitution are landmarks in the evolution of democracy. But the control of the new nation was to be vested in those few whose wealth, education, and status qualified them to rule.

The administration of George Washington stressed national unity, strong federal government, and neutrality. The first President faced the tough problem of bringing together thirteen independent-minded colonies into one national framework, much as contemporary authoritarian leaders seek unity for their countries. Washington always referred to his administration as the "national government" and did not hesitate to impress upon state leaders that the unity of the new United States must come ahead of states' rights.

As the first Secretary of the Treasury, Alexander Hamilton pressed strongly for centralized economic powers to be placed in the hands of the federal government. The Bank of the United States and Hamilton's tariff policies are examples of this desire of the national government to stabilize the economy. Washington did not want to get his new nation involved in the great power politics of Europe, so he formally declared America neutral in world affairs in 1793. One can see many similarities between the United States during its early years and the new states of the Afro-Asian world.

The Constitution itself did not provide for political parties, because the authors assumed that the new United States government would be controlled by the authority of the privileged few. The men who wrote the *Federalist Papers* to defend the new Constitution and to support its adoption in 1788 argued for centralized authority and warned against factions and political groupings. In *Federalist Paper Number Ten,* James Madison said that factions, even those representative of the majority of the people, should be controlled. It was the government's role, he pointed out, to preside over factions and arbitrate their varied interests when and where they might clash.

At the very end of the eighteenth century, Thomas Jefferson, who supported states' rights rather than the authoritative centralized form of government, began to organize a new political party. In the Presidential elections of 1800, Jefferson's Democratic Republican Party defeated the Federalists, and from that time on, the United States has generally had a two-party political system. But the majority of male American citizens did not receive the vote and right to compete for public office until early in the nineteenth century. It was not until the twentieth century, of course, that these political rights were extended to women.

Before the advent of mass democracy in Great Britain, the United States, and other Western democracies, the authoritative few who ran the governments honestly believed that their wealth, education, and high status in society entitled them to be the stewards for their peoples. They took their governing seriously. They deeply believed that their guidance of the government required them to exercise many responsibilities and restraints in handling the powers of governing. Jefferson believed that this style of governing carried with it the obligation to lead people toward ultimate democracy, and that this could best be done through education. Thus these examples of "democratic authoritarianism" show how democracy as a way of life and of governing emerges from patterns of government that were not at first fully democratic as we understand this term today.

The Case of Kemal Atatürk

Kemal Atatürk (1880-1938) was a great national hero and the authoritarian leader of Turkey after World War I. To borrow a slogan from Rousseau, Kemal Atatürk "forced his people to be free." Assuming power in feudalistic Turkey in 1922, he brought unity to his nation and assured its external and internal security. Then he launched a wide program of internal reform, designed to "westernize" his nation and to bring it into the twentieth century. He was Machiavellian in the sense that he sought national unity, security, human well-being, and ultimate republican governing for Turkey. And he was not too sensitive about how he accomplished these objectives. His rule was authoritarian, but he permitted a wide range of human freedom. He was effective in introducing literacy, economic and social progress, and political liberalism in Turkey. He encouraged his people to place an increasingly high value on life on this earth rather than to sit around quietly awaiting the trip to paradise after death.

Atatürk imposed no ironclad "ism" on his people. He tried to cultivate the total culture of his nation and to lead it into an open rather than a closed society. One could hardly say that Turkey is totally democratic today. It is a nation with many problems, but progress toward freedom continues. It is also probable that without the authoritarian rule of Kemal Atatürk betwen 1922 and 1938, Turkey would not be in the Western democratic camp and a member of NATO today.

The Case of Japan

The militaristic, right-wing ideology which dominated Japan for so long was crushed at the end of World War II. The occupation forces of the United States stepped in with a policy of "forcing the Japanese to be free." Under the leadership of General MacArthur, the United States military government exercised authoritarian rule and brought Japan within the framework of the democratic ideology. A new democratic constitution for Japan was introduced in 1947, accompanied by educational, economic, and social policies designed to bring about Japanese acceptance of a democratic way of living.

The policy worked well. Today Japan has a vigorous democracy and is a staunch ally of the United States. The multi-party system has been most effective. This is a rare example of a democracy (the United States) using authoritarian rule (United States military government) to convert a totalitarian state into a democracy. While democracies, ideologically speaking, cannot impose policies on a state except by military occupation following a war, the Japanese case does prove that democracy can emerge from authoritarianism in a short period of time. Conceivably, shorn of American military and economic support, Japan might revert to totalitarianism. The risk can be substantially reduced by effective United States foreign policies designed to help maintain the democratic center in Japan.

There is another interesting feature of Japan's new democracy. At the end of World War II, American policymakers had the wisdom to retain the Japanese Emperor, Hirohito, as the central symbol of the Japanese nation and the new constitutional democracy. The United States could have tried the Emperor for war crimes. But he was recognized as a vital symbol to the Japanese. While his former position as a virtual god was eliminated, he was

Tom Mboya of Kenya, noted for his brilliant oratory and capacity for hard work, was relatively unknown a few years ago. First prominent as a spokesman for labor, his rise in power was little short of spectacular. With the independence of Kenya in 1963, he was named Minister of Justice.

Benevolent authoritarianism characterizes the Shah of Iran's reign. He has a genuine concern for the well-being and rights of his people. His approval of opposing political parties shows a desire for more democracy in government. Programs of land reform and projects designed to improve health conditions and educational facilities figure strongly in the Shah's plans for raising the standard of living in Iran.

Independence leader and a favorite of his people, Sukarno is virtually unchallenged as Indonesia's President. His authoritarian government loudly proclaims its neutrality in world affairs, but over the years Sukarno has leaned increasingly toward the Communist world.

Egypt's Nasser (right) teeters on the brink of totalitarianism. Like Hitler, he feels he has a destiny. Nasser's goal — to unite the Arab states. He accepts aid from the USSR, but if he turned to the left, his hatred of foreign control might well keep him as independent of Moscow as Tito is.

In 1962 Ahmed Ben Bella became Premier of an Algeria staggering from seven years of a bloody and violent civil war. Opposition to his government, general lack of technical knowledge, a high illiteracy rate, and generally miserable living conditions were among the many problems Ben Bella faced in the difficult task of giving Algerians lasting security and well-being.

Son of Moslem peasants and grandson of Samori, who fought France long after it had conquered the rest of Guinea in the 19th century, Sékou Touré rose to power through the trade unions. A staunch neutralist seeking a union of African states, Touré has long demonstrated his leftist beliefs. His nationalist sentiments, however, take strong precedence over his African version of Marxism.

retained as a powerful link between the past and the new democracy of Japan.

Why Did Wilson's Hopes for Democracy in Europe Fail?

We were not as wise in Germany after World War I. Woodrow Wilson was determined to see democratic regimes installed in all the defeated or new nations in Europe. Germany drew up the democratic Weimar Constitution in 1919. Practically all of the other new or defeated states likewise became "democracies." With the exception of Czechoslovakia, all of these new democracies failed because of inadequate foundations to sustain them.

The German Weimar Constitution of 1919 was almost technically perfect. The organization of the new democratic government was neat, coherent, and precise. But many historical, cultural, economic, and social factors in Germany were not favorable to the support of the democratic government. With most of the links to the past gone, the new government floundered. It had no meaningful myth for the German people, who had always strongly identified themselves with those who ruled them. It is true that national and international conditions permitted the German democracy to thrive between 1924 and 1929. But when crisis struck, totalitarianism swept constitutional democracy out the window.

The democratic constitutions in other states such as Poland, Hungary, Yugoslavia, Romania, and Bulgaria also gave way. None of these states in Eastern Europe had a solid foundation to support a democratic style of governing. The transition from monarchies to democracies in 1919 was too swift and too shallow. Some states, such as Yugoslavia, Romania, and Bulgaria, had governments which combined kings with parliaments and thus were rooted in the past. Their peoples, however, were not trained in the obligations which democratic governments demand of citizens in order to function effectively.

Democracy survived in Czechoslovakia largely because it had strong and wise leaders in Thomas Masaryk (1850-1937) and Eduard Beneš (1887-1948). The Czech economy could support relatively high standards of living, and President Masaryk's land-reform policies did much to strengthen the cause of economic democracy. The educational system in Czechoslovakia backed up political democracy. However, as we have seen, the Western powers sacrificed Czechoslovakia to Nazi Germany. Today, Czechoslovakia is again under totalitarianism.

History is the greatest of teachers. It tells us that a democratic governing system, in all probability, will not survive unless it is preceded and supported by a democratic way of life. Frequently, authoritarian rule is required to construct the foundations of democracy.

3. What Are Some Patterns of Contemporary Authoritarianism?

This is the era of transition for the non-Western world. More than one billion people in Afro-Asia and Latin America are moving rapidly into the twentieth century. The quick pace of the modern world has not touched many of these people. But the impact of competing ideologies most certainly will affect the security and well-being of all of them.

The variety of authoritarianism found in Afro-Asia and Latin America makes it difficult to generalize. But the states embracing this "third force" among the ideologies of our time have certain common aspects.

Some Common Factors

With a few exceptions, the authoritarian states have achieved independence from colonial rule and are strongly nationalistic. They are proud of their new status and are determined to maintain their sovereign position in world affairs. Security is a cardinal aim of their respective national policies. These states also want to bring their peoples into the twentieth century as quickly and safely as possible.

Most of the leaders of the new states feel that they are not yet ready for Western-style democracy. Most of them also reject totalitarianism.

Most of these states are guided by one man, often a leader of the independence movement. These men tend to be strong rulers, jealous of other men and parties competing for power. They may permit parliaments, as long as they can control them. They generally support socialism, or state control of the economy. They feel that conditions within their nations do not permit a free-market economy. Their socialism may have a Marxist foundation, but they usually reject all the ideological trappings of communism. Capitalism has a negative meaning to many of them because they associate it with the way they were controlled during the colonial period. It remains to be proved to these leaders that an economy without governmental restraints will do the job they desire in raising the standards of living for their peoples.

In world affairs, the new states tend to be neutral, standing between the blocs led by the United States and the Soviet Union. Neutralism is less of a "third bloc" and more of a "third force" in world politics. These states may often vote the same way in the United Nations, but they are not organized into any major alliance.

Most new states are neutral also in that they seek material assistance from both the Western and Soviet camps. They are, as we have seen, opposed to the attempt of international communism to dominate them, but many authoritarian leaders feel that they can prevent communism from subverting their political, economic, and social institutions.

If we look more closely at the authoritarian nature of some of these states in various parts of the world, we may be able to see in what direction they are moving.

Authoritarianism in Asia

Indonesia. President Sukarno has presided over the destinies of Indonesia ever since it gained its sovereignty in 1949. Although the influence of communism is strong in this Asian nation, both in terms of extensive Soviet assistance and in the size of the Indonesian Communist Party, Sukarno labels his authoritarian ideology "guided democracy." He poses as a neutralist in world affairs, an intense nationalist in Indonesia, and a leader who will tolerate no internal opposition to his rule.

What, then, is "democratic" about Sukarno's style of authoritarianism?

Sukarno stresses "democracy with leadership." He points out that in the many Indonesian villages, various issues are discussed by all, and then unanimous agreement is reached. This process is guided by the village elders, who channel discussion toward decisions which advance the security and well-being of all. Sukarno is carrying on this traditional approach to governing at the local level and at the national level. However, Sukarno's "guided democracy" dissolved Parliament in March, 1960, and within a few weeks organized a new Parliament which consisted of people appointed by Sukarno. This 281-man body is divided into representatives of nine political parties and representatives of various labor, agricultural, and military groups. It follows the President's leadership and thus is not really a deliberative and policy-making organ of government.

Sukarno is a forceful leader. He maintains a large army and plays a strong role in his area of the world. Sukarno lays heavy stress on the distinctly Indonesian nature of his style of democracy. But this brand of authoritarianism reveals little evidence of guiding people toward democratic ways of life and governing along Western lines.

Military authoritarianism. Military leaders have assumed control of a number of Asian states, claiming that they are "protecting" their nations against external and internal threats to national security. In Southeast Asian nations such as Burma and Thailand, for instance, military rulers thoroughly control the governing apparatus but stress the fact that their particular authoritarianism will ultimately recede when external and internal dangers to national independence are removed.

Thailand. Thailand's Field Marshal, Sarit Thanarat, took over the reins of power in his country suddenly but peacefully in October, 1958, and ruled in an authoritarian manner until his death in December, 1963. Actually, Thailand is a monarchy under King Phumibol Adulyadej, but Field Marshal Thanarat, as the Premier, dominated the nation of more than 26 million people. Thanarat viewed Thailand's position in Southeast Asia as one gravely threatened by the forces of communism. Thailand is allied with the United States in the Southeast Asia Treaty Organization and is concerned about Communist guerrilla warfare in neighboring Laos.

Thailand has a provisional constitution. A 240-man National Assembly, appointed by Premier Thanarat and dominated by members of the armed forces, is presently drafting a new constitution. A wide range of economic and social freedoms exists in Thailand, but on the governmental level firm authoritarian control is being continued by Thanarat's successors.

Burma. To the west of Thailand lies Burma, another state dominated by military authoritarianism. The President is General Ne Win, who has been the leading governmental authority since 1958. Elections were held in Burma in February, 1960, returning independence leader U Nu and his Union Party to office, but General Ne Win assumed power in a bloodless coup in March, 1962. He and his Revolutionary Council dissolved the nation's parliament in the same month and also gave notice to the Supreme Court that it was out of business. Shortly thereafter, however, Ne Win introduced a program of broad economic and social reforms.

The President is anti-communist and neutralist in foreign relations. He seeks military security against his giant neighbor, Communist China, and considers that Burma's well-being will best be advanced through socialism. His Revolutionary Council established the Burma Socialist Program Party, the only party with any real political power.

Although he no longer is in power, the influential U Nu points out that the Burmese believe in democracy, socialism, and neutralism. As a strong Buddhist, like most of his fellow countrymen, U Nu cannot tolerate atheist communism. He accepts some economic aspects of Marx's writings but rejects class warfare, violent revolution, and the withering away of the state. U Nu calls for a "Burmese" style of socialism, which means a rejection of external forces in shaping the socialism of the state. "We must rely on our own ideology, our own policy and program, our own ability and our own integrity."[1]

---

[1] Sigmund, *op. cit.*, p. 74.

Authoritarianism in the Islamic World

The Moslem world extends from Morocco on the Atlantic to Indonesia in the Pacific. The religion of Islam emerged from the teachings of Mohammed (570-632 A.D.), who is considered the true prophet of Allah by millions of Moslems. This great religion plays a vital role in the ideological struggle of our times. A Moslem ("true believer") rejects the atheism of Communist ideology. Islam itself means "submission" or subjecting oneself totally to the will of Allah.

The Moslem states prefer a position of neutrality between imperialistic communism and the freedom of action which plays such a large part in the democratic ideology. Some Islamic states, such as Pakistan, are allied with the West and seek to advance the democratic ideology for their peoples. Others, such as Egypt, flirt with communism and also give strong evidence of right-wing totalitarian practices.

We have placed Indonesia in the category of Asian nations, although the vast majority of people under Sukarno's rule are Moslems. Our examination of the Islamic world in Western Asia, the Middle East, and North Africa thus begins with Pakistan and ends with Morocco.

Pakistan. This Islamic nation has had a turbulent political history since gaining its independence from Great Britain in 1947. A military seizure of power took place in October, 1958, when President Iskander Mirza cast aside the 1956 Constitution and also the parliament. Later that month, full government powers were turned over to Field Marshal Mohammed Ayub Khan, who assumed the office of President. During the years following, President Ayub ruled with a firm hand, but he also took a number of steps to guide his nation toward democracy.

In March, 1962, President Ayub gave his nation a new constitution. He devised a democratic structure from the bottom up, which led to a new National Assembly. At the opening of the Assembly in June, 1962, the President said that martial law was at an end. He pointed out, however, that the military security of the state came first. This means, in effect, that he will continue to dominate the national scene.

This authoritarian leader eagerly wants to prove that democracy can be cultivated in a nation that has little experience of the democratic tradition or practice. President Ayub relates the Islamic religion to democracy, pointing out that both Moslems and true democrats believe in equality and fraternity. On the other hand, Ayub has noted that the "otherworld" outlook of Islam — the belief that earthly life is just a preparation for a life to come — may hold his people down and prevent them from participating in a vigorous life which places a high value on human well-being on earth.

President Ayub constantly stresses the necessity to modernize and democratize Pakistan, although he admits this must come slowly. He declares that: "Democracy provides the only healthy and dignified way for arousing the willful co-operation of people and harnessing it to a sustained national endeavor."[1]

Ayub Khan's support for the principles of freedom is bolstered by Pakistan's participation in the Southeast Asia Treaty Organization. On the other hand, he has entered into some border agreements with Communist China, and Pakistan and India continue to duel over the State of Kashmir, which is divided between them. President Ayub's deep concern for the security of his state detracts somewhat from the extension of more political freedoms in Pakistan and also from the effort to advance his people's well-being. On the other hand, he sincerely desires to convert his authoritarian control into an increasingly democratic regime during the years to come.

Afghanistan. Afghanistan's King Mohammed Zahir today is striving to bring economic and social progress to the estimated thirteen million people who live in his remote, landlocked nation. Monarch since 1933, King Zahir receives support from both the United States and the Soviet Union for his ambitious program of modernization.

With the USSR next door, Afghanistan feels that it is necessary to steer a neutral course in world affairs. On the other hand, this Moslem nation rejects communism. King Zahir appears to be dedicating himself toward introducing political, economic, and social reforms in Afghanistan, although he realizes that the backwardness of his nation puts many obstacles in the way of such

[1] Mohammed Ayub Khan, "Pakistan Perspective." *Foreign Affairs,* July, 1960, p. 551.

programs. He is moving ahead on constitutional reform, however, by placing commoners in key governmental positions which had previously been occupied by members of his family.

Iran. Mohammed Reza Pahlavi, the Shah or ruler of Iran, has led his nation since 1941. His long rule has had many ups and downs. Today, he still faces opposition within Iran, and the threat of communism from neighboring Russia is always present. Although the Shah permits some political party activity, he and his group of ministers possess full governing authority. His is a benevolent authoritarian government.

During his reign, the Shah has expanded the economic and social horizons of his people. His land-reform program has given 50,000 peasants title to at least two million acres of land that once was privately held. Much of this land had belonged to the Shah himself. He has made certain that those from whom the land was taken received proper compensation.

Many conservative and wealthy Iranian landowners oppose this liberalizing move by the Shah, while Iranian student groups have declared that the Shah is not sufficiently liberal for their tastes. In 1963 some rebellious religious leaders caused extensive riots in Iran's capital, Teheran, because of their opposition to the Shah's liberalizing policies. They condemned the government's land reform and political emancipation of women. Quite frequently, a national leader who is neither totalitarian nor fully democratic finds himself between the devil and the deep blue sea.

The Shah himself states clearly the difficulties he is encountering in the changeover from authoritarianism to democracy:

> Almost from the first day of my reign, I started to warn the nation's leaders to prepare for an evolution from the top before there was a revolution from below. As long ago as 1952 I proposed a program of reform based on five principles of social justice: housing, food, clothing, education and hygiene for all. I endeavored to implement these measures and improvements through the parliaments that succeeded one another, and by encouraging the formation of political parties.
>
> Unfortunately, progress was not achieved in the manner I expected. . . . More and more I came to realize that it was going to fall to me alone to safeguard the welfare of my people and prevent this ancient country from becoming the mere toy of events. I resolved, using my prestige as monarch and my power

as commander-in-chief of the armed forces, to take the issue of reform directly to the people. . . . Last year, using my constitutional power to initiate laws, I decreed a nationwide referendum which has been described as a 'revolution from the throne.'[1]

This "revolution from the throne" points definitely in a democratic direction. The Shah totally rejects communism, believing that the religion of his people is incompatible with Communist ideology. On the other hand, like many other Islamic leaders, he would prefer that his people value a strong and active life along with upholding the tenets of Islam. The Shah's reforms were strongly endorsed in Iran's national elections of September, 1963. Ninety percent of the members of the new parliament supported the Shah's policies and programs for a modern Iran.

United Arab Republic. Today, President Gamal Abdel Nasser's Egypt is the only state remaining in the United Arab Republic. Egypt joined forces with Syria in 1958 to form the UAR, but this merger was dissolved by Syria in 1961. Plans are afoot to bring Syria back into the Republic, along with Iraq and possibly some other Moslem states. In any event, President Nasser is the kingpin in this part of the world. He and a group of young army officers forced pudgy, dissolute King Farouk into exile in 1952, and Nasser emerged as the supreme power in Egypt in 1954. Since that time, he has dabbled in all kinds of ideological experiments. It is difficult to describe Nasser's definitely authoritarian rule, because he has borrowed from many political and economic doctrines to produce what he calls "Arab Socialism."

Nasser states that he has "established the basis for a democratic, socialist, cooperative society." His National Union, says Nasser, "is based upon the liberation of the individual from economic, political, and social exploitation" — a theme he repeats over and over. On the other hand, the National Union is now being changed into the Arab Socialist Union. Nasser's government has assumed wide controls over the economy and has tossed all remnants of free enterprise aside. The government has taken over the press, the Suez Canal (which it is running

[1] Mohammed Reza Shah Pahlavi, "A Future to Outshine Ancient Glories." *Life,* May 31, 1963.

very efficiently), and most other productive or money-making enterprises. Almost 90 percent of industry and business is now in the hands of the Egyptian government. This national form of socialism may possibly reduce the human exploitation about which Nasser talks so much, but on the other hand, his brand of authoritarianism shows certain danger signals.

President Nasser, like most other leaders in the Afro-Asian states, is very security conscious. He harps on the military threat of Israel and Zionism and, on this ground, channels a considerable amount of his national income into his military forces. This large expenditure could better be allocated toward economic and social programs designed to elevate the low standard of living in Egypt.

In world affairs, Nasser speaks of expanding his influence over an area covered by three circles. Egyptian radio broadcasts in the "three-circle" area add up to about 700 hours of pro-Nasser propaganda each week. Nasser sees Egypt at the center of an Arab circle in the Middle East and desires to enlarge the United Arab Republic with himself as chief of state. Then there is the larger circle covered by Africa, which Nasser would also like to control. (In August, 1963, Egypt pledged $30,000,000 to help finance the new African Development Bank.) Finally, there is the circle of the whole Islamic world. In his dreams, Nasser sees himself as the guiding force of this circle, too. Nasser's ideas in foreign affairs would seem to add up to imperialism. Should he proceed with his circle theory, he would pose a distinct threat to other nations in his part of the world.

The racism implicit in Nasser's speeches and policies concerning Israel suggests right-wing totalitarianism. This is balanced on the left by the extensive aid given to Egypt by the Soviet Union in the construction of the Aswan Dam on the Nile River. Nasser has moved strongly against Egyptian communists and is convinced he can control communism in his country. Adding up all these varied domestic and foreign policies of the authoritarian regime of President Nasser, one easily sees the difficulty of labeling his real ideological designs.

Nasser probably does want to improve the lot of his people. And yet, he cannot resist intense activity in world affairs, actions which verge precariously on the brink of totalitarianism. Nasser is conscious of the role that Islam plays among some 26 million Egyptians, and he sees in Islam the possibilities for advancing his wordly ambitions. He said that those who go to Islam's holy city of Mecca each year to pray should be "devout, but mighty; unambitious of power, but active and full of energy; submissive to divine will, but immutable in difficulties and implacable with their enemies."[1] Nasser thus wants to bring about some changes in the Moslem outlook as well as to gain strong influence in the Islamic world.

Jordan and Saudi Arabia. In Jordan and Saudi Arabia, King Hussein and King Ibn Saud maintain the *status quo* as authoritarian monarchs, but the economic and social changes sweeping the Middle East are already affecting their regimes. Late in 1962, demands for a more liberal government caused King Saud to bring back Crown Prince Faisal, ousted for his liberal tendencies in 1960, as Prime Minister. Attempts on Hussein's life and the collapse of the monarchy in Yemen led to a Jordan-Saudi Arabia alliance, aimed at mutual defense against Nasser's growing power.

The Ba'ath movement. In several of the Moslem states, a fairly new movement with a progressive ideological base seems to be making a marked advance among young people. The Ba'ath or Arab Socialist Renaissance is led by young, well-educated Arabs who feel that democratic socialism will do much to raise the living standards of the millions of poverty-stricken Arabs. Members of this movement support modernization of Islam as well. The Ba'athists are strong nationalists and neutralists in world affairs, often opposing Western intrusion in the Middle East and taking an even stronger stand against communism in any form. The Ba'athists support Arab unity but are opposed to Nasser, whose imperialist tendencies they feel will undermine their ideas of democratic socialism.

> The Ba'ath has shown that its ideology of socialism and Arab unity qualify it for the role of alternative to Mr. Nasser in the Arab Middle East and that a growing number of Arabs are ready

[1] Sigmund, *op. cit.*, p. 127.

to follow an ideology rather than a personality. Among Arabs, this is something new.[1]

Islamic North Africa. In *Tunisia,* President Habib Bourguiba is another revolutionary leader who continued as the authoritarian ruler after his country won full independence from France in 1956. President Bourguiba is the guiding force of the government, although the 90-man National Assembly does have some deliberative and policy-making powers. Tunisia has only slightly over four million people, and it is poor. But Bourguiba, like many other authoritarian rulers, has a genuine desire to build economic and social foundations for democracy. In so doing, he finds, like other leaders in Islamic states, that the Moslem faith drags heavily on the lives of his people.

Bourguiba has much to say about bringing some aspects of Islam up to date in order to put life and incentive into the minds and hearts of the Tunisians. In particular, he implores his fellow citizens not to follow too closely the ritual of fasting during the Holy Month of Ramadan, which Moslems observe toward the end of the winter months. Bourguiba feels that this continuous fasting saps the strength of the nation and retards its progress. He told his people that:

> I can be more useful to my country if I am not sitting in a corner yawning and hungry because of Ramadan. . . . For those who want to deny themselves, I suggest an extra hour of work rather than fasting.[2]

In *Algeria,* which gained its sovereignty from France in 1962 after a long and bloody struggle, President Ahmed Ben Bella is the authoritarian leader of the new but struggling state. Ben Bella has declared that leading an independence movement is easier in some ways than exercising the powers of government, especially when the climb toward economic stability is so rough. His National Liberation Front Party is the only legal political grouping in Algeria, and he rules it with an iron hand. He says that socialism is necessary for the present. "We want an Algerian socialism, which is based on our own experience and, at the same

[1] *The New York Times,* December 8, 1963.
[2] *Ibid.,* March 11, 1962.

time, also draws on that of the socialist countries." The Ba'ath movement holds some interest for well-educated Algerians, but the authoritarian leadership of Ben Bella reacts strongly against any threat to his power as he tries to bring Algeria into the twentieth century in his own manner.

Morocco won its independence from France along with Tunisia in 1956. King Hassan II, the son of Sultan Mohammed V, the Moroccan nationalist leader, is in complete control of Morocco under the constitution which he gave his people in December, 1962. The first parliamentary elections were held on May 17, 1963, and the King's royalist party failed to win a majority of the seats. Although the King may appoint a cabinet without any concern for the wishes of the parliament, there are many political groups in that legislative body which challenge the King's supreme power. The parliament also has some important powers in the economic area of national policy. Thus, the authoritarianism of the King may have to give way.

Authoritarianism in Africa

Some aspects of authoritarianism in Africa. Six years after World War II, there were only five independent African states (Ethiopia, Union of South Africa, Liberia, Egypt, and Libya). Take a look at the map of Africa today! Count the number of independent states!

The majority of these new states are authoritarian, with one-party governments, for the most part socialist economies, and a policy of neutralism in world affairs.

The complexity of cultures among the more than 236 million African peoples makes any accurate description of ideologies on that continent rather hazardous. The history of the African people runs deep. Most of us have the impression that Africa was a sleeping giant until Europeans began to take an interest in the central and southern part of the continent after the fifteenth century. Such an impression is quite wrong. In Africa below the Sahara Desert there were several thriving independent nations, with well-developed patterns of government, education, and social life. Although these nations were long under colonial control, most of them are again independent. Most of their leaders want to bring the various elements of their states, especially tribes, together into one nation.

Tribal life is widespread in Africa. The old tribal chief, backed up by the witch doctor and other elders, dominated the lives of many. The European overlords in the nineteenth and the early twentieth century did not infringe upon tribal life as long as the tribes, in turn, did not intervene in the colonial government. Now the tribal chiefs must look to the new national leaders as the sources of authority. The heads of government must exercise strong powers to prevent the tribes from making war on one another. Tribal hostilities which ran rampant in the Congo, for instance, vastly complicated the organization of centralized governmental power in Léopoldville.

The authoritarian leaders have many problems in constructing the economies of their states. The European powers performed this task in days gone by and harnessed the economy of the African colonies to the needs of the European states. While the great majority of Africans still pursue their traditional life in thousands of villages, the governments of the new states must organize patterns of production and distribution along new and unknown lines. It is probably safe to say that millions of Africans have not confronted the life of the twentieth century in terms of many goods and services of modern economies. Yet the pace of the modern world is setting in very quickly. Little marketplaces are expanding rapidly, and transistor radios are found everywhere. Nasser has said:

> The transistor radio has created a revolution. Many of the peasants carry them in their pockets. Now all the workers are asking for television sets too. We have 160,000 of them in Egypt, with long waiting lists, and we are increasing our production of 40,000 a year. We are assembling the sets through an agreement with R.C.A., and we are building a big electronics factory with the Czechs to produce more transistors.[1]

These radios pick up Nasser's frequent propaganda broadcasts in addition to those from Moscow and the United States. The

---

[1] Robert Sherrod, "The Violent and Vital World of Nasser." *Saturday Evening Post*, May 25, 1963.

"Voice of Ghana" is also on the air with news and views from Kwame Nkrumah.

Awareness of the outside world is increasing each day. The idea that a man can make money and spend it on new things is beginning to touch each tribal village. But the channeling of all of these forces into a coherent pattern of national life and interdependence within the state calls for strong direction by the new authoritarian leaders.

The collective, family nature of tribal life had little to do with private property as we have known it in the West. Thus the African brand of socialism is rooted in this tendency toward patterns of group sharing. President Leopold Senghor of Senegal, in defining African socialism, declared that "We have developed cooperation, not *collectivist,* but *communal.* For cooperation — of family, village, tribe — has always been honored in Black Africa."[1]

On the other hand, since many small marketplaces have sprung up throughout Africa, there is every possibility that exchanges of goods and services in an atmosphere of freedom at a fairly elementary level can evolve toward larger patterns of economic free enterprise. But in the major areas of the new nations' economies, such as transportation and the production of most commodities, government ownership will continue for some time.

Most of the African states do not want to be identified with either major bloc in world affairs. They are jealous of their new independence and are particularly anxious that Africa not be "balkanized" or divided up into competing states controlled by larger, non-African nations.

Despite the tremendous varieties of authoritarianism in Africa, let us look briefly at two important regimes: Nkrumah's Ghana and Touré's Guinea.

Authoritarianism in Ghana. The first Negro state to achieve independence after World War II was Ghana, once the Gold Coast. Its national leader, Dr. Kwame Nkrumah, blazed the trail to freedom in 1957, but Britain contributed greatly in preparing its former colony for an independent status in world

[1] Colin Legum, *Pan-Africanism.* New York: Praeger, 1962, p. 128.

affairs. President Nkrumah and his Convention People's Party rule with a very strong hand indeed, and some suspect Nkrumah of moving toward totalitarianism.

Civil liberties are greatly restricted in Ghana. Nkrumah presents himself as a virtual god, and any criticism of him or his government results in a jail sentence. Within Ghana, Nkrumah is referred to as "Osagyefo" or the redeemer, and Nkrumahism is virtually a new "ism." Somewhat like Nasser, Nkrumah combines tendencies toward an intense right-wing rule with a distinct leaning toward socialism.

Some years ago Nkrumah voiced the hope that socialism and democracy could be combined. He said that the aims of his party:

> . . . embrace the creation of a welfare state based upon African socialist principles, adapted to suit Ghanian conditions, in which all citizens, regardless of class, tribe, color, or creed, shall have equal opportunity . . . our party also seeks to promote popular democracy based upon universal suffrage — on "one man one vote."[1]

Today, however, Nkrumah runs a police state and leans heavily toward the left.

Some years ago, Nkrumah fancied himself as the dominant figure in the march toward independence among the African states. His own successful voyage toward national freedom inspired many other independence movements in Africa after 1957, but other African leaders did not want anyone, even a fellow African, to control them. Thus Nkrumah has played a less forceful role in African affairs in recent years.

Authoritarianism in Guinea. President Sékou Touré of Guinea led his people to independence from France in 1958. After a flirtation with communism, Touré has reverted to an intense but independent authoritarian rule and has the solid backing of the three million citizens of his new state. He points out that he is working toward democracy but defines this term as follows:

> We are in favor of democracy as real and as complete as possible and based solely on the interests of the people. This is the

[1] Legum, *op. cit.,* p. 128.

only form of democracy we recognize, the only interpretation we give to the word "democracy." . . .[1]

Most of the other authoritarian leaders, like Touré, claim that they are giving democracy to their people in their one-party states. One can debate this matter for hours on end. The fact remains that the symbol of democracy is exceedingly important to these leaders, although their style of democracy appears authoritarian to us in the West.

Authoritarianism in Latin America

Totalitarianism and authoritarianism had the upper hand in the Latin American republics until a few decades ago, when the forces of democracy began to pick up steam and tossed the dictators from power. Authoritarianism still exists in states such as Nicaragua and in military regimes such as that which took control of Honduras in 1963. On the whole, however, the few dictators and authoritarian leaders who remain seem to be moving steadily toward more democratic ways of governing.

4. Is Contemporary Authoritarianism Benevolent or Malevolent?

Since authoritarianism is an ideology midway between democracy and totalitarianism, it obviously can move either toward freedom or dictatorship. An authoritarian regime can also stay in dead center and not move at all. Authoritarianism is a risky business, both for the leader and his people and for those outside the authoritarian state who seek to pull it in one direction or another.

Naturally, we would like to take effective measures to halt further Communist penetration of Africa, Asia, the Middle East, and Latin America. But how can we tell whether contemporary authoritarianism is headed in the Communist direction? What about authoritarianism which shows danger signs of right-wing totalitarianism? How can we have some assurance that an

---

[1] Sigmund, *op. cit.*, p. 162.

authoritarian leader is really guiding his people toward ultimate democracy?

Here are several tests which we can apply to states embracing authoritarian ideologies. They can give us some guidelines for appraising the direction in which these states are moving. First, there are some general questions we might ask about authoritarian rulers. Then, we must examine earmarks of communism in authoritarian states, and finally, clues on the right-wing side. Take any authoritarian state you please, and ask these questions.

Some Tests for Trends Toward Totalitarianism or Democracy

1. Is the authoritarian ruler genuinely trying to advance the security and well-being of his state and people, or does he erect a myth and a promise which have little to do with real security and well-being?

2. Is the authoritarian ruler more concerned with concentrating on internal policies of advancing the economic and social well-being of his people, or does he spend more time seeking glory for his state in the foreign policy field?

3. Does the authoritarian ruler permit a fairly wide range of freedom of speech, assembly, press, and religion, or does he clamp down on these basic freedoms for "security" reasons?

4. Does the authoritarian leader genuinely try to find real causes for national problems, or does he seek convenient scapegoats on whom he can place the blame?

5. Is the ruler taking any steps toward constructing some elementary democratic political practices, or does he exercise complete governmental power throughout his state?

6. Does the authoritarian leader share power with other officials of prominent stature, or does he absolutely dominate his government?

7. Does the authoritarian leader take steps to permit the minds of his people to search objectively for the truth, or does he engage in constant propaganda, especially in education, to support his rule?

8. Does a close feeling exist between the ruler and the people which generates a genuine identity of national purpose and progress, or is there dissension and hostility?

If the answer is "Yes" to the first part of each of these questions, then the authoritarian ruler is headed toward democracy. But if the answer is "Yes" to the second half, then it would appear that the authoritarian ruler is leaning toward totalitarianism. What do *you* think?

Moving Toward Communism?

If contemporary authoritarian rulers are engaged in the following practices, it would appear that they are moving toward the Communist camp.

1. Do they permit the national Communist party in their state to operate in the open as a legal entity? Can the Communist party engage in propaganda in public, seek new members, and participate in "united front" activities?

2. Do the authoritarian leaders and other important people in the state have close connections with the local Communist party and with Russian and/or Chinese Communist leaders?

3. Do the authoritarian leaders accept and use generous grants of money and technical assistance from the Soviet Union?

4. Does the authoritarian state generally support the Communist cause in the United Nations and at other tables of international diplomacy?

5. Do the authoritarian leaders strongly and persistently condemn the Western world?

Moving Toward Right-Wing Totalitarianism?

If the authoritarian leaders make statements which include the following ideas, then it would seem that they are attracted to the right-wing side of totalitarianism.

1. Do they view their state as organic — living and breathing, with a "soul" and a distinct personality? Do they require all their peoples to be identified with this almost human state?

2. Is the authoritarian ruler deified? Is he practically a god, or is he made to appear to his people as a rather sacred person?

3. Does the authoritarian leader talk about supernationalism? Does he seek to thrust his nationalistic sentiment on other states?

4. Does the authoritarian leader stress one form of racial

superiority or another, and does he likewise feel that some races are "naturally" inferior?

5. Does the authoritarian ruler always rely on the internal and external danger of communism as an excuse to rule in a dictatorial manner?

6. Does the authoritarian leader have a large and strong army to bolster personal rule?

None of these "tests" is conclusive, but they do help in searching for the answer to the all-important question: How do we know whether the authoritarian ruler in any one state is moving toward ultimate democracy or toward totalitarianism? There are more than fifty states which have some variety of authoritarian ideology. Each of these states is different and has political, economic, social, and cultural conditions by no means absolutely identical with other states. Each was conceived in its own crucible of history, and each must be appraised as a separate entity. But we can still apply some general observations and tests to all.

Even the Western states have some tinges of authoritarianism within their confines. The rule of President de Gaulle in France has some heavy-handed aspects. De Gaulle's Fifth Republic pays only lip service to some aspects of democratic governing, such as the effective and unhampered functioning of the legislature, the National Assembly. On the other hand, De Gaulle's government provides an interesting example of how a mild authoritarianism can be called in to quell the excesses of democracy which afflicted France before De Gaulle took over in 1958. The Federal Republic of Germany, the Philippines, and India also have some authoritarian overtones.

We may find that we cannot separate either ideologies or men into neat compartments of good or bad, democratic or totalitarian. It is extremely important at this time in the world's history to distrust the label and to look closely at the realities. The world does not just consist of two hostile camps. It consists also of millions of people living under authoritarian leaders, struggling to enter the twentieth century, striving toward means to a better life, hoping for both bread and freedom, and depending often upon the wisdom of one man or a handful of men to lead them.

We still call George Washington the "father of our country."

We know that we had to have a strong leader to further our experiment in democratic living. In many ways, we have traveled the same road that newly independent states of the world today are traveling. We are still traveling because our democracy is by no means a perfect model.

Even democracy has different shades and hues. So has totalitarianism. And so has authoritarianism. The less dogmatic and the more flexible our view of all the ideologies, the closer we can come to the truth about world affairs.

Democracy's Role in Afro-Asia and Latin America

1. How Can Democracy Take the Initiative?

Algeria Presents Some Common Problems

Ahmed Ben Bella, the President of Algeria, is one of the many national leaders who has suddenly become prominent on the world scene. What kind of man is he, and what are his problems? The more we get to know about men like Ben Bella and a country like Algeria, the more we are likely to understand what the Afro-Asian states are struggling to do and what we in the democracies can do to help.

Ben Bella spent five and a half years in French jails. He is a socialist. His independence movement, which fought for seven grim years to get rid of French rule, had the strong backing of Communist China. On July 3, 1962, his country was declared independent of France. But a declaration of independence is one thing. Achieving security, well-being, and a democratic government is quite another.

Ninety percent of the 11 million Algerians are illiterate. The economic training and knowledge and the talent of the country were largely concentrated in the 1,300,000 Frenchmen who fled to their homeland when Algeria became independent. It will probably take at least two billion dollars to get Algeria on its feet. These are immediate, practical matters with which Ben Bella has to deal. Algeria lacks money, time, talent, knowledge — everything, it seems, except people. And this pattern is repeated in many of the other newly emerging states of the world.

What does *freedom* mean to the Algerian who does not know if he can feed himself and his family tomorrow? What do *democracy* and the obligation to be well-informed and to vote mean to an Algerian who can neither read nor write? What does *liberty* mean to the Algerian whose festering sores and aching limbs imprison him in abject misery? What does a *free-market economy* mean to a man who cannot find work anywhere and whose annual income is less than $100 a year? How can capitalism as an economic system get across in a country where the farmer can at best plow his lands for survival, where the businessman is hindered by the flight of capital and economic knowledge from his country, and where the government cannot provide the stability and enlightened support required by capitalism?

What should we in the prosperous democracies do about it — if anything? Can we do anything? Should we extend assistance to Ben Bella, who has dismissed from his government all critics of his handling of domestic and foreign policy? Should we give help to a man who has had the support of Communist China? And if we help, should we do it to keep Algeria from becoming a Communist country? Or should we do it because we want to advance the cause of democracy in world affairs? Does democracy have a mission, or is its only obligation to improve its own way of life and governing? Should it be hands off, or hands across the sea?

We cannot dodge these questions. The winds of change are blowing throughout the world as well as in our own country. We live in revolutionary times and can neither ignore them nor isolate ourselves from them.

Authoritarianism, as we have seen, can be a stage toward totalitarianism or democracy. What we think and do can tip the balance. It is a breathtaking moment in history — a time of world-wide revolution — in which people everywhere are demanding entrance to the good life. If *evolutionary* change without help and guidance from the democracies becomes impossible, *revolutionary* change directed by the forces of totalitarianism becomes inevitable. This is where we are "eyeball to eyeball" with communism. We cannot blink or turn away.

A Positive Approach

The Afro-Asian world will not accept democracy if our only aim is to prevent the spread of communism. But the positive approach and the defensive approach can be one and the same. We push back communism as we advance democracy. The best defense is still a good offense. And the best approach to any problem is the positive one.

But we must understand that the democracy we seek to advance need not be exactly like our own democratic ideology in the United States. There are variations within all three major ideologies; democracy is no exception.

What we might seek as democratic goals for Afro-Asia and for Latin America are nations in which the rising economic and social standards permit an increasingly democratic way of life. We might support national leaders who govern in such a manner that the personal and legal freedoms of their peoples will be guaranteed. We might welcome different points of view through contending political parties and variations in national life. But we might also promote *e pluribus unum,* the democratic idea that — although diversity and opposing points of view may well exist — there is still agreement on the unity of the whole society and state.

Democracy is possible without many of the conveniences we enjoy in the United States. India is a democracy, and yet life in that nation is not the abundant one we have in the United States. Democracy is possible in Kenya where the tribes may continue to have their magic fetishes. Democracy can have many political, economic, and social variations. But a democratic governing system must strive toward equal justice for all and guarantee the rights of all. These are the aspects of democracy which we must work toward in world affairs. They can flourish in any nation.

Dr. Rafael Caldera of Venezuela reveals that Latin Americans also hold this point of view. In speaking of human rights throughout the Americas, he states:

America has an inescapable obligation to offer man the guarantee of his rights. And these rights must be removed from the level of abstract claims and be translated into tangible realities. . . . But the liberty, the democracy, and the hope of the American people must lead to something. And this "something" means the recognition of the right to live, the right to work, the right to the free expression of ideas, but it also means the right to food, the right to housing, the right to education, and the right to health.[1]

A Timetable for Advancing Democracy

Timing is important in advancing democracy. *National freedom* is the first step, one which most nations have already taken. *National unity* of the state must be furthered next. Then comes the third step — *the building of a democratic way of life* by reducing the obstacles to democracy and constructing the foundations for democratic living. The fourth step is the adoption of a *democratic way of governing*. This timetable may vary from state to state, and these steps may come in a different order. (India, for instance, had much internal democratic governing before it became a sovereign state in 1947.) But this timetable will apply to most new states.

Authoritarian leaders have already blazed the trail toward step one — national freedom. They are now concerned, for the most part, with step two — national unity. In guiding their people toward the democratic way of life, or step three, they need our assistance. In bringing about step four — the democratic way of governing — the authoritarian leaders will find our moral support most useful. But democratic governing within a state can come about only when people *want* to govern themselves. If the first three steps go well, however, democratic governing may also evolve.

Sun Yat-sen had a similar program for China in 1911: overthrow the totalitarian Manchu dynasty, establish authoritarian military rule, guide the people toward democracy, and then set up a constitutional government. He accomplished the first two

[1] From "Today's Revolution," printed in *Americas,* October, 1961, pp. 21-22.

objectives but got no assistance from the West in making democracy safe for China. He then turned to the Soviet Union for help. Communism became a fact in China partly because the democracies did not respond to Sun's original belief in a government of, by, and for the people. We cannot let this happen again.

Totalitarianism is much easier than democracy. The great South American liberator, Simón Bolívar, noted that "it is a terrible truth that it costs more strength to maintain freedom than to endure the weight of tyranny."[1] It is much simpler to let someone else run your life than to do it yourself — providing, of course, that you care little about human freedom. Democracy is a demanding ideology, exceedingly tough to get across to the world in which we live. Some say that to try to advance democracy in the Afro-Asian world is sheer and stupid idealism. But we have seen the power of idealism in our own nation. If those who declared, fought for, and won American independence many years ago had not been inspired by the idealism of human freedom, where would the reality of democracy in the United States be today?

2. What Are Some Obstacles to Advancing the Democratic Ideology?

If democracy is to take root, it must recognize those factors which make its planting and growth hazardous. Most of the states in Africa and Asia know well the meaning of colonialism. Most are characterized by an authoritarian ideology, which sinks deep into their history and culture. Most, including Latin America, have serious economic and social problems. Communist penetration in each of these states is a severe challenge to the forward march of democracy.

The Western Colonial Heritage

The long era of Western colonialism is generally viewed in the Afro-Asian world as one in which the following facets of Western rule predominated.

[1] C. Northcote Parkinson, *Evolution of Political Thought*. Boston: Houghton Mifflin Company, 1958, p. 253.

1. Most Western colonial powers exploited their colonies for the benefit of the Western rulers and economic titans.

2. Western rule was generally characterized by the power of the white man over the nonwhite. Kipling's idea of the "white man's burden" was the order of the day.

3. Most Western colonial rulers cared little for the history, culture, or basic human sentiments of those whom they governed.

4. Many Western colonial rulers did little to encourage these peoples to learn how to govern themselves or how to develop a vigorous, market economy.

5. Generally speaking, Western rule was a giant lid imposed over parts of the world where change was not supposed to take place, where people were not supposed to aspire toward anything but meager subsistence, and where fundamental human values were considered by many to be "primitive and strange."

Obviously, all these things did not apply to all forms of colonial rule. But *today*, to most of the people in Africa and Asia, this is the memory of the colonial period. While the Western states were developing along the democratic path and building the foundations of capitalism, they were imposing what amounts to a totalitarian rule on the Afro-Asian world. Many people in Africa and Asia today identify democracy and capitalism with the colonial era. This colonial heritage is a great obstacle to advancing democracy and the idea of free enterprise in Africa and Asia.

The Authoritarian and Cultural Environment

The people of the Afro-Asian world are not oriented by history and culture toward assuming the responsibilities of self-rule. The rulers, as we have seen, tend to be authoritarian. Most of them are not in tune with democracy, although many of them, in the long run, seek to bring it to their peoples.

Most of the social *structures* found in the Afro-Asian states are generally authoritarian as well. They tend to be rigid and often closed, somewhat like the feudal structure of society found in the Middle Ages in Europe. People born into a certain station in life often expect to remain there. It is true that many of the traditional structures are changing, permitting people to move around and upward. The elimination of the caste system in India, for instance, is becoming a *fact* as well as a *law*. But many old holdovers of rigid social stratification remain.

The authoritarian *substance* of many of these societies is also a hindrance to democracy as a way of life. The liberalizing trends which swept over the West did not penetrate most other areas of the world.

Many of the great faiths of Africa and Asia, as we have seen, are only now facing the modern world. Men such as Bourguiba in Tunisia, the Shah of Iran, and Ayub Khan in Pakistan are calling on their peoples to consider that life on this earth may be as desirable as the great rewards which lie beyond. But countless millions in Africa and Asia still cling to the old ways. Religious fanatics in Iran fight against the unveiling of women. Many Hindus feel that outlawing the caste system will deny reincarnation to them. Many Moslems insist on a total fast during the Holy Month of Ramadan, a fast which saps their strength and vitality.

Millions accept the traditional fatalistic, complacent outlook and willingly submit to the closed society. They tend to find decisions made by the majority contrary to the "one way" dedicated by their ancient faiths and ironclad traditions. Little value is placed on the capacity of the human being to plot his future. Human "rights," so important to democracy, are basically contrary to much of the culture found in Africa, Asia, and Latin America.

In Africa, for instance, the collective entity of the tribe leaves little room for the basic principles of individual liberty. In Latin America, the tradition-bound societies have been closed to much of the progress taking place in the Western world. Some of the leaders or "elites" in these states are democratic in every sense, and their examples are causing changes to percolate through all levels of society. But, in general, the over-all environment in Asia, Africa, and Latin America has tended to encase many of the people in a traditional society which often is pointed exclusively toward worlds other than our own. This is not to be critical of any religion or culture. But it is a fact that millions of people in Afro-Asia and Latin America possess an outlook on man and society which has no vision of social progress and human well-being.

The Prison of Economic and Social Misery

Statistics can be terribly cold, and yet we must keep a few facts and figures in mind when we try to understand the plight of most of the people in Afro-Asia and Latin America.

Most of these people have a daily diet averaging 1500 calories. Nutrition experts declare that the human body requires at least 2000. (The American daily average, incidentally, is 3200.) The abundance of food in the Western world makes it difficult for us to realize that half the people on earth live in conditions of near-starvation.

The annual per-capita income of people in the Afro-Asian world and most of Latin America is between $80 and $150, while the figure for the United States stands at around $2600. The total yearly income for the more than one billion people in Afro-Asia is around 130 billion dollars, while 190 million United States citizens have an annual income of over 430 billion dollars.

Outside of the Western and Soviet blocs, diseases of all kinds afflict millions. The average life expectancy is around 30 to 35 years. In Indonesia, for instance, there is an average of one physician per 70,000 people, while the average in the United States is one for each thousand citizens.

Illiteracy is high as well. About 80 percent of the people in Africa, Asia, and Latin America cannot read or write. Education, even of the most basic sort, is available only to the minority.

All of these conditions are alien to democracy as a way of life and a way of governing. Barbara Ward, a brilliant scholar of world affairs, notes that:

> When we talk so confidently of liberty, we are unaware of the awful servitudes that are created by the ancient enemies of mankind: the servitude of poverty when means are so small that there is literally no choice at all; the servitude of ignorance when there are no perspectives to which the mind can open because there is no education on which the mind can begin to work; the servitude of ill-health which means that the expectation of life is almost too short to allow for any experiences of freedom, and

the years that *are* lived are dragged out without the health and
strength which themselves are a liberation.[1]

The Communist Offensive in Afro-Asia and Latin America

The forces of communism are working hard in all of these
states to promote the Communist ideology and to distort the
image of the West, especially the United States. On this score,
Barbara Ward tells us that we would be unwise:

> . . . to underestimate some of the immediate advantages which
> the communists enjoy in this tough tussle for influence in the
> newly independent nations. . . . This is a time of chaotic change
> and hence of chaotic ideas. It is dangerously attractive to many
> minds to be offered a political and economic panacea as complete
> and apparently self-explanatory as Marxism-Leninism. It seems to
> tie up all their problems in a single order of explanation and to
> make sense of a world which they feel they do not understand
> and fear they never may.[2]

Change, often called the *revolution of rising expectations,* is
enveloping Afro-Asia and Latin America in this era. Revolutionary Marxism does have an appeal, a myth, and a promise.
Revolutionary communism, a revolution harking back to totalitarianism rather than a revolution emancipating man from totalitarianism, is fighting hard to advance this ideological conspiracy.
Can anyone doubt the height of this hurdle to democracy in
Afro-Asia and Latin America?

3. What Are Some Steps for Promoting Democracy in Afro-Asia and Latin America?

Some Basic Understandings

Before we explore ways of advancing democracy in Afro-Asia
and Latin America, we should focus our sights on four basic
understandings about means to democratic goals.

[1] Barbara Ward, *The Rich Nations and the Poor Nations.* New York:
W. W. Norton & Co., 1962, p. 158.

[2] *Ibid.,* p. 130.

1. Our limitations. We should understand our limitations. The democracies cannot do everything. Even if we had endless resources, we could not *make* the Afro-Asian and the Latin American nations embrace the democratic ideology. We could not *impose* our ideology on the world because such an act would be contrary to the very nature of democracy. But by example, and then through advice, guidance, and wise national policies, we can *encourage* others to strive toward democracy.

2. Differences within and among nations. We should understand the many differences that exist within the nations in Africa, Asia, and Latin America, as well as the differences among these nations. In most Latin American states, the farmer and the city dweller, the rural peasant and the urban businessman are far apart in many ways. The Buddhist and the Roman Catholic in Vietnam, the Arab and the Kurd in Iraq, the Baluba and Luanoa tribes in the Congo, the Bedouin and the Palestinian in Jordan, and the Moslem and the Hindu in India all point up the many and frequently belligerent differences which exist within these nations.

We should understand the religious, social, economic, and political aspects of each nation. A knowledge of Islam is basic to any relationship we might have to President Ayub Khan's nation. The traditional social structure in Iran has much to do with the Shah's difficulties in introducing democracy. The varieties of socialism in such nations as Algeria, Egypt, and India must be understood with the clear recognition that many of these nations will probably have strong governmental control for years to come. Iran and India are now in their third series of Five-Year Plans. The idea is copied from the Soviet Union, but that alone does not make India or Iran a Communist state. While we might want to expand private or free enterprise in these nations and contract the public sector or state-controlled aspects, the fact remains that the foundations for capitalism are weak in this area of the world. Politically, we must understand the authoritarian leader — why he is authoritarian, and how his authoritarianism fits in with goals of national security and well-being.

3. Neutralism. We should understand why most of Afro-Asia is neutral in the cold war between the Western and Soviet blocs. These nations are new. They view the cold war as the old power struggle among great powers. They want aid from these powers but do not want to make military commitments. They feel that an alliance with a major power on either side of the cold war would impair their own security and well-being.

4. Relation of ideology to policy. We should understand the relation of ideology to policy. To sever the two is to get nowhere at all in giving democracy a forward thrust in world affairs. Democracy by the *example* you and I and our fellow Americans set in our everyday behavior is of tremendous importance in furthering the democratic ideology in world affairs. Nevertheless, our domestic and foreign policies must be infused with the principles of democracy as well, so that our nation may take an official stand in supporting the growth and strength of democracy in Afro-Asia and Latin America.

The United States Peace Corps is doing a splendid job in many nations of furthering the democratic creed by relating official policy to example. Here is a magnificent illustration of how American representatives abroad are demonstrating through official action what democracy really means.

The foreign policy of the Soviet Union is chock-full of Communist ideology. Relating policy to ideology has always been a key principle of Soviet behavior in world affairs; while we violently disagree with the Soviet brand of ideology, we might profit in many ways by understanding the vital relationship that exists between conviction and action in the conduct of foreign relations.

The official policy of a state cannot do everything. It is usually a connecting link between governments and often does not get down to the people of a state. Our policy toward Indonesia may aspire, for instance, to advance economic development in that state, but this policy can deal directly only with the government of President Sukarno. Many of our foreign-aid programs as instruments of American policy are beamed toward elevating standards of living in many nations. But official leaders of recipient states, in more than one instance, have used this aid for their own purposes and have been negligent in making certain that their people receive its full benefits.

Nevertheless, we have no alternative but to pursue policies

which will advance democracy in Asia and Africa and to strengthen the ideology of freedom in Latin America. There are four steps which our official foreign policies can take in trying to channel authoritarianism into the mainstream of democracy.

Supporting Independence

Nationalism, the force that brought independence to Afro-Asia, is a strong unifying factor in the Latin American states as well. Support of nationalism is the greatest weapon the West has, especially since communism seeks to bring all states into one international mold. National freedom must be won and preserved before human freedom within the state can be expanded.

It is true, of course, that most of the Afro-Asian states gained their freedom *from* Western control, and many leaders in these states find it somewhat inconsistent to see the West now backing their new independence. But while the era of colonialism did impose some harmful restraints on these peoples, some truly positive principles were conveyed to these nations as well. The idea of the nation-state is Western. Important strides in education, economic development, and experience in dealing with economic and social problems were Western offerings to Afro-Asia. The structure of democratic government, responsible civil service, respect for the law, and world organization (such as the League of Nations and the United Nations) are Western contributions to many of these nations.

Western policy, therefore, must do everything possible to preserve the newly found national freedom in Afro-Asia and must also strengthen independence in Latin America. American counter-guerrilla warfare in Southeast Asia is only one example of our seeking to sustain independence against armed Communist subversion which seeks to destroy it.

Supporting the Authoritarian Regime and National Unity

We cannot always find men like Ayub Khan, King Hassan, and the Shah of Iran who have the courage and determination to guide their peoples toward democracy. Often we must work with men like Nasser, Nkrumah, and Sukarno, even though we feel that they may be keeping authoritarianism on dead center or engaging in some totalitarian practices. But there is much we can do to persuade all of them to propel their nations toward democracy in the long run.

The authoritarian leaders and those who will succeed them are the real keys to the shape of things to come. Some of them consider themselves virtual gods and supreme national heroes, and some of them irritate us in countless ways. But we cannot ignore them because they appear to act contrary to our views.

Most of these leaders are desperately seeking to unify their nations. Unifying a country is not an easy task. The attitude of the rural or backwoods sections of any country is often one of independence and even antagonism to the central government. United States Secretary of State, Dean Rusk, once compared the villagers of his native Georgia to those of South Vietnam:

> Now I hope also we could keep a little perspective on what villagers are like in their political orientation. When I was four years old, we lived on a farm in Georgia where we were connected with about 15 other farms by a home-made telephone system which had no connection with the outside. Three long rings was a signal for everyone to come to the 'phone. We used it for three purposes: If a mad dog were coming across the area, we would follow it until someone killed it. If it were a fire, they needed the help of the neighbors to put out the fire; or if it were a Federal Officer coming into the area. . . .[1]

"A little perspective on what villagers are like," in Georgia or in Africa or in South Vietnam. And yet, the Afro-Asian leaders must achieve unity in order to expand the horizons of human freedom.

Dealing with governments. American official policy must deal with governments; the authoritarian rulers cannot be circumvented in an attempt to reach the people directly. Nor can they be subverted and toppled, unless extremely fortuitous circumstances permit such action. The United States did lend very limited support to Guatemalan exiles in 1954 when they attacked Guatemala in order to overthrow the pro-Communist President, Jacobo Arbenz Guzmán. But on the whole, there is no alternative

---

[1] Speech at Department of State, May 27, 1963. Quoted by permission.

in most instances but to work with official governments. Either we do business with these authoritarian governments and their leaders or else we retire completely to the sidelines. If we choose the latter, we may lose all chances of directing the authoritarian regime toward democracy, and we may also let the forces of Communist subversion surge ahead.

Of course, people in many Afro-Asian and Latin American states often take the initiative themselves in unseating dictatorial rulers. Trujillo in the Dominican Republic was hurled from power by inside forces. In the Congo Republic, the Chief of State, Youlou, was handed his walking papers in August, 1963, by his own countrymen. President Diem in South Vietnam is another example. Some political changes in these lands are violent; others quiet. But let us never underestimate the capacity of people in any state to cast from power those who violate fundamental human freedoms.

Using levers. When, in our judgment, the authoritarian regime is indeed veering toward the totalitarian camp in its attempt to bring about national unity or in its reluctance to permit a gradual introduction of democratic practices, certain things can be done. There are several levers that can be used. Economic aid is an example. The United States threatened to deny aid to the military government of Korea in the spring of 1963, when it appeared that that government was not going to permit free elections. As a result, the regime of General Park held the elections in October, 1963. General Park won by a narrow majority in the fairest and most peaceful elections the Republic of Korea has ever experienced. In December, 1963, civil rule was fully established in Korea. Earlier that same year the United States used aid as a lever to get Guatemala to promise that it would conduct elections within a two-year period.

In the Dominican Republic President Juan Bosch was elevated to office in May, 1963, in the first democratic elections in that country for over thirty years. After three decades of dictatorship under the firm hand of the late Rafael Trujillo, the Dominican people welcomed the new regime. Strong American support helped to make this transition from totalitarianism to democracy possible.

Unfortunately, a military coup drove Bosch from office in

September, 1963, erasing many of the new political reforms in one stroke. The United States reacted swiftly by withdrawing its economic and military aid programs as well as the American ambassador. It did the same thing when the military took over in Honduras in October, 1963.

Lending support to an authoritarian government in Africa and Asia in the necessary measures of national unification therefore has limits. If the ruler and his regime oppress the people and suppress religious rights in particular, all in the name of "national unity," support from the democracies would be inconsistent. Before he was overthrown by a military revolt in November, 1963, President Diem of South Vietnam was seeing American aid to his nation being slowly cut off.

In the process of unification, some governments may choose to take over United States property. They may "nationalize" American factories or plantations, for instance, without paying a fair amount to the owners. As an answer, the United States "Hickenlooper Amendment" forbids the American government to extend aid to any nation which expropriates United States property without proper compensation.

Each of these cases must be judged on its own merits. This does not mean that we must have a deep love for governments or leaders with whom we do not agree. Where democratic progress has been plowed under by military seizures — as is sometimes the case in Latin America — the withdrawal of aid and ambassadors may have the effect of ultimately restoring democratic processes. But where countries have not experienced genuine democratic governing, as in Indonesia, Egypt, or Ghana, the withdrawal of all aid and diplomatic recognition might mean letting a nation drift into the camp of totalitarianism. Through the influence we can mobilize with our aid program and with other kinds of support, however, we can perhaps prevent harsh measures from being taken by authoritarian rulers against their people, and we can also help to direct the government toward the theory and practice of the democratic ideology.

Helping change to take place. In helping an authoritarian regime to achieve national unity, we cannot, of course, force cultural change. We might hope that old traditional methods of doing things would give way to or be combined with more modern approaches. But this difficult job must be performed by the rulers and their governments. *We* cannot bring land reform to Iran. But through aid policies and strong moral support, we can support the Shah's program of modernization. *We* cannot voice any views about how fasting during the month of Ramadan affects the capacities of Moslems in Tunisia to build up their nation. But we can appreciate President Bourguiba's speeches on this matter and back his efforts to unite his people in a common cause. *We* cannot induce social change in India, radically alter class structures in Latin America, inform tribal leaders in Kenya what a national government for Kenya means to them, preach to religious leaders in Moslem Pakistan about the virtues of modern life, and make Nkrumah in Ghana be more tolerant of his political opponents. The advancement of unity through diversity and the introduction of cultural change must come from within. As necessary as national unity, stable government, and progressive social change are to the foundations of democracy, we cannot directly perform these functions.

Nevertheless, we can be a powerful backdrop to the process which guides a nation toward democracy as a way of life. We can emphasize to authoritarian rulers our strong belief in *e pluribus unum* — out of diversity, unity. We can back up their unifying policies with various kinds of assistance and guidance, given in such a way as to favor those who are doing a solid job. We can impress upon these governments the necessity of recognizing the rights of all in the move toward national unity.

Our economic assistance, furthermore, can do much to influence the process of social change. The launching of social programs, such as mass inoculation against cholera in Egypt, new methods of agriculture and irrigation in Tanganyika, improvements in sanitation in Pakistan, modernization of business practices in Guinea, or educational innovations in Nigeria, may at first offend the existing style of life in these nations. Many people may prefer the traditional patterns of life which they and their ancestors have followed. Not everyone in the Afro-Asian world seeks to participate in the so-called "revolution of rising expectations." But change is coming, and coming fast. And aid programs which help to usher the twentieth century into these nations can subtly bring about cultural change. This will help benevolent rulers to make long strides toward unifying their nations in a way which will promote democracy in the long run.

Tangible Assistance in Building the Democratic Way of Life

The British historian, Arnold Toynbee, has said that:

> . . . our age will be remembered chiefly neither for its crimes nor for its astonishing inventions, but for its having been the first age since the dawn of civilization, some five or six thousand years back, in which people dared to think it practicable to make the benefits of civilization available for the whole human race.[1]

We must make the "benefits of civilization" available to others if we are to advance the democratic doctrine. The question is, "How?" Since 1945, the United States has extended almost thirty billion dollars in economic and military aid to nations in Africa, Asia, and Latin America. It is sometimes difficult to see what this money has purchased in the way of democracy. So why stress aid of a tangible nature in trying to advance human freedom?

Aid programs require money. But so do wars. World War II cost over one trillion dollars, let alone the loss of life and human values. If we were to face a Communist Afro-Asia, the cost to the United States and the West of any attempt to roll back the frontiers of totalitarianism would be infinitely more than thirty billion dollars. We are not now confronted with the red flag in Afro-Asia and Latin America, and perhaps this thirty billion dollars had much to do with the fact that these independent states are flourishing today.

The third step in the time schedule of furthering our ideology is building the democratic way of life. Here are four key principles for relating aid policies to expanding the democratic way of life in Afro-Asia and Latin America.

1. The role of the authoritarian regime. Take another look at those tests in Chapter 11 which might give some indication as to whether an authoritarian leader is heading toward democracy or totalitarianism. Is he doing a genuine and compassionate job in unifying his nation? Is he offering an increasing latitude to his people to express their own views and cherish their own faiths

---

[1] *The New York Times Magazine*, October 21, 1951.

within the framework of national unison? Is he avoiding the scapegoat and honestly seeking the real roots of national problems? Is he surrounding himself with competent officials and taking steps toward eventual democratic governing? Is he striving toward national education rather than national propaganda? If the answer is "Yes," he deserves our strong assistance.

Aid cannot be a charity. It cannot be given in a paternal manner. But it can be channeled in such a way as to lend firm support to those governments which are dedicated to transforming present patterns of authoritarianism into foundations for democracy as a way of life.

There is, of course, risk in every step. There is no firm guarantee that substantially backing a democratically inclined authoritarian regime will create conditions favorable to the expansion of democracy. There is certainly reason to believe that in using aid as a lever for reforms in the new auhoritarian states, the ruler will actually change his ways. But sooner or later, most of the authoritarian rulers may come to realize that the fundamentals of democracy as a way of life and of governing are in the long-term interests of themselves and their nations. If they do, in all probability they then will join the West in the long and difficult process of making the democratic vision a reality.

2. The principle of reciprocity. Foreign aid as a means of advancing the democratic way of life is a two-way street. Aid should be geared in such a way that the receiving state views assistance in terms of partnership and therefore makes its own contribution as well. Secondly, foreign aid benefits the democratic states because trade with Afro-Asia and Latin America is vital to sustaining economic well-being within the democracies.

To receive assistance, a government should give evidence that it deserves this help. Land reform, effective use of the land, equitable tax laws, aid put to the use of all people in the state, and dedication to social progress are some of the things a government can do on its own to merit economic support. This is a fundamental point, for instance, in the aid program of the Latin American Alliance for Progress. This ten-year, twenty-nation *cooperative* project calls for the expenditure of some 100 billion dollars to advance the conditions which make democracy possible. Abut ten billion dollars will come from the United States and eighty billion from the Latin American republics. The rest, hopefully, will stem from some European nations and from private investors.

In the past few years, Brazil has set aside several million as its contribution toward this cooperative development program. Land reform has made rapid strides in Bolivia, and the Alliance is pushing hard for new school buildings in Peru. All of this makes aid a dual partnership rather than a charity. This kind of cooperation also gives assurance that the aid reaches the people and not the pockets of a few governmental leaders.

This assistance also makes it possible for the United States and other democracies to continue to receive the needed raw materials from Afro-Asia and Latin America. Without imports of certain valuable natural resources, American industry would be gravely weakened and our entire standard of living would be lowered.

Some statistics clarify this point. From Afro-Asia and Latin America, the United States imports 99 percent of its industrial diamonds, 96 percent of its chrome, 93 percent of its rubber, 77 percent of its hemp, 74 percent of its manganese, 69 percent of its cobalt, and 67 percent of its tin. These figures do not include such valuable imports as oil, coffee, bananas, sugar, and a wide variety of other items which we take for granted in our daily life.

Paul Hoffman, the Managing Director of the United Nations Special Fund (for assistance to developing nations), points to a very bright future for these nations and for our partnership with them. He declares that these lands are not poor in terms of natural resources and potential for future trade. He notes that if we can help them lift their annual per-capita income 2.5 percent during the 1960's, exports to them from the industrialized democratic nations would reach 350 billion dollars in the 1960's as compared to 164 billion in the 1950's. This would mean an additional 8½ billion dollars' worth of exports a year for the United States and an additional one million full-time jobs.[1]

Reciprocity in giving and reciprocity in terms of important benefits through trade to the United States and to these lands all make common sense in any alliance for progress.

[1] Adapted from "Paternalism: Foreign Aid Foe," by George H. Favre. The *Christian Science Monitor,* March 14, 1963.

3. The staging of aid. All nations are "developing" nations. Some are simply much more developed than others. Some states have "primitive" economies, and others, such as the United States, have highly industrialized economies. All, however, are evolving toward higher forms of economic production, distribution, and consumption. Therefore, aid from the more industrialized, wealthier states must be tailored to the particular phase of development found within the receiving states. Aid might well be "staged" to produce maximum economic and political effects.

Professor W. W. Rostow notes that there are five essential stages of economic growth for all states:

1. The traditional (fairly primitive) society.
2. The stage where "preconditions for economic take-off" prepare the way for advancement.
3. The actual "take-off" of the economy or strong movement forward.
4. The drive toward maturity.
5. The mature stage of mass production and consumption.[1]

As each state progresses up the trail of economic development, its government's capacity to give more self-rule to its people is enlarged. Progress in economic development must be accompanied by progress in democratic living and democratic governing. Authoritarian rule is probably necessary for Rostow's first two stages. By the time the state is ready for the third stage, the "take-off," the basic conditions for democratic living probably have been created. The way is open for wider participation in democratic governing; this door should be opened wider as economic development itself progresses toward the higher stages.

4. Stimulating private initiative. In the earlier stages of economic growth, at that point before the "take-off" toward economic maturity, private capital is generally not available in sufficient quantities for the necessary investment. Someone has to prime the economic pump during the initial stages of development, and this action usually comes from a government. In the opening stages of economic expansion in Western Europe and

[1] Adapted from W. W. Rostow, *The Stages of Economic Growth: A Non-Communist Manifesto.* Cambridge, England: The University Press, 1960, pp. 4-11.

the United States, government subsidies played a vital role in getting things started. The private investor will not be inclined to put much of his money into economic projects in Africa, Asia, or Latin America when many of these projects do not hold promise for profit. For the most part, conditions in these states are not yet ripe for the investment of large amounts of private capital. Thus governmental aid, which is really taxpayers' money, must take the initiative.

Nevertheless, it is capital or downright cash which must prop up any solid and enduring base for the advancement of democracy. Governments cannot create money. They tax those who have it and use the money received for desired purposes. But if those private individuals and corporations who possess capital do not or cannot create more money by making profits, then the money available for constructing the foundations of democracy will dry up and disappear.

For example, the President of X Tire Company will not invest money in a new tire plant in Brazil if he feels that the Brazilian government will seize his factory and fail to adequately reimburse him. If his plant is "nationalized" by Brazil, other foreign investors will not be anxious to build factories in that nation. The President of Y Canning Company cannot create capital if the United States government taxes his income to such an extent that selling cans brings practically no profits in return. Governments must rely upon private enterprise for making profits and for using these profits in a creative and useful manner. For the most part, the era is gone when the President of X Tire Company or Y Canning Company used much of the profit for his own fancy living.

Any United States aid program must stress the importance of private capital. There is no shortage of capital in the world, only a shortage of imagination and willingness to put it to work. Steps must be taken to encourage wealthy citizens in the poorer lands to put their money to productive use in their own lands, instead of keeping it in Swiss banks or investing it for pure profit in the industrialized nations. Any aid program, especially that of the United States, must do everything possible to call on states receiving assistance money to provide for an equitable tax structure which derives income from those most able to pay. African, Asian, and Latin American governments can do much to attract private capital for investment in the economic development of their lands. They can offer incentives for private investors. They can also remove barriers to investment of private capital, such as fear of expropriation, clumsy economic controls, and discrimination against foreign capital.

The whole problem of promoting free enterprise cannot be reduced to an easy formula. Small open markets are flourishing in Africa, and private capital has always been a powerful factor in Middle Eastern development. There is probaby far more private enterprise in Afro-Asia and Latin America than we realize.

Our aid is a partnership between the giver and the receiver in a mutual dedication to use this support to advance the democratic way of life. The democratic way of life involves the construction of economic and social foundations which will permit people to live in and breathe the air of freedom. Advances in health and living standards, adequate diets, enlightenment through education, and a positive outlook toward the good life on this earth will open up societies, bring vigor and initiative to people, and vastly increase their human expectations.

If progress toward national freedom, national unity, and patterns of democratic living is steady, then democratic processes of governing, hopefully, might follow. Such processes must come from within the state. The democracies can exert strong influence on the leaders of these states to build democratic governments in the long run, but such governments cannot be imposed upon any state.

Promoting Democratic Governing

Ideally, a democratic government would emerge from a nation's experience with democracy as a way of life and from the expansion of human freedoms. Furthermore, a democratic government at the national level might be helped to evolve if patterns of democratic governing were first launched at the local and regional levels. This is President Ayub's approach in Pakistan, and it was also the manner in which the Allies reconstructed democracy in West Germany after World War II. It would be out of order, as history has shown, to insist on a democratic strucure of government if there were no solid foundations on which such a structure might rest.

King Hassan in Morocco is making notable progress in devising a democratic government, and the Indian government is also doing much to lead the millions of Indians toward democratic horizons. India proves that the Western heritage of parliamentary government, a solid civil service, and a sound judicial system provide the necessary framework for democracy. Not all nations have been privileged, as has India, with these foundations of firm government, and thus need stronger brands of authoritarianism. But if the way is prepared for national freedom, national unity, and the democratic way of life, then this new-found freedom — freedom from the old and freedom for the new — will register itself in increasing patterns of democratic governing.

Finally, democratic governing must be genuine. As we have seen, a mere constitution or democratic structure of government is not enough. The Soviet Union has both. Elections are important, but they must have genuine meaning and must be open to all adult citizens. On a wall in Guayaquil, Ecuador, these words are scratched: *130 Años de Elecciones, 130 Años de Miseria* — "130 years of elections, 130 years of misery." Ecuador has had many elections since it received its independence in 1830. But the elections, as such, did not bring to power men who opened the vistas of democracy to this poor country. Pro-Castro agitators thus tell the people of Ecuador that elections and democracy are meaningless. Obviously, all facets of a democracy's governing process must have real meaning if the hard-won national freedom, national unity, and democratic patterns of life are to be guaranteed.

Propaganda in Afro-Asia and Latin America

Some positive approaches. The democracies must be much more positive about what they stand for and be much more effective in revealing the intentions of international communism. It is rather remarkable that Americans, who are such good salesmen within their society, have often been outsold abroad by the communists, who do not believe in commercial advertising and private profit. If we live in the midst of a war for the minds of men, the minds of men must be persuaded. It is impossible to believe that we can do so much in world affairs and still lose the crucial war of ideas.

We have seen how Communist propaganda simultaneously blows its own horn and undermines the West. We, too, should take a simultaneous propaganda and counterpropaganda approach. It is up to us to prove to the Afro-Asian and Latin American states that democracy and not communism will advance their goals of national freedom, national unity, and rapid economic and social progress.

It is interesting to note that the Afro-Asian nations, meeting in Bandung in Indonesia in 1955, opened their conference with a reading of the United States Declaration of Independence. This document of our heritage, which embodies the essence of the democratic ideology, should accompany all of our policies.

We might paraphrase the Preamble to our own Constitution in giving positive expression of our intent to further democracy in world affairs.

> We, the people of the United States, in the conduct of our national policy designed to broaden the horizons of democracy in the Afro-Asian and Latin American worlds, will:
>
> *Establish justice,* by promoting the substance of democratic ideology.
>
> *Insure domestic tranquility,* by assisting the governments of these states in uniting their nations within the framework of *e pluribus unum.*
>
> *Provide for the common defense,* by assisting these nations to defend themselves against internal enemies who seek to subvert and destroy their independence, and by defending them against external attacks as well.
>
> *Promote the general welfare,* by extending the necessary economic and social assistance necessary to construct the democratic way of life, and
>
> *Secure the blessings of liberty,* through partnerships and alliances for progress which will make certain that the fundamental blessings of human rights are guaranteed to all.

A positive thrust to our propaganda is as vital to us today as the physical thrust of our missiles. A sense of purpose and dedication must be conveyed to Afro-Asia and Latin America. We must speak in their language and speak up to them — not down. We must believe in the positive attributes of our authentic revolution — a revolution *from* totalitarianism and an evolution *toward* freedom.

Counterpropaganda. Nor should we be hesitant in demonstrating wherever and whenever possible that the intent of communism is to return totalitarianism as a way of life and way of governing to these peoples. Communism is alien to national freedom, national unity, and the kind of economic and social progress in which most men believe. We must persuade these people not to believe what the communists say communism is. We should show them what it has done to corrode the true promise of the human spirit.

Tell the Moslem, Buddhist, Hindu, or Catholic in Afro-Asia and Latin America what communism does to religion. Tell the unionist in the Middle East the truth about labor unions in the USSR. Tell the leftist politician in India about the total absence of political pluralism in the Soviet Union. Tell hungry people in Africa about famine in Communist China and the many failures of agriculture under communism. Tell the agitator against colonialism in Indonesia about the imperialism of the USSR over Eastern Europe. Tell the African about racism in the Soviet Union and about the striking discrimination by members of the Young Communist League against African students studying in Russia. Tell the anti-Nazi Polish people the full story of Soviet collaboration with Nazi Germany in the late summer of 1939, when these two totalitarian states dismembered the Polish nation. Tell leftists in all lands about Communist oppression, adverse working standards, stifling of creative work, and absolute governmental controls over speech and the press.

Demonstrate at all times the fantastic contradictions between Communist theory and practice, between Communist idealism and realism. Publicize the deceit of Soviet diplomacy and the guile of Russian and Chinese propaganda machinery. Do this in conjunction with the force of positive propaganda, and see what happens to the appeal of communism in Afro-Asia and Latin America.

Many Afro-Asian and Latin-American states recognize the threat of Soviet and Chinese communism. Let us not think that all non-Western leaders and people simply succumb to the blasts of Communist propaganda. In June of 1963, for instance, leaders of the Philippines, Malaya, and Indonesia gathered at Manila to take effective measures against forces of subversion operating within their nations. It took no genius to recognize that these measures were directed against Communist China. The truth about the theory and practice of communism is getting around these days, and we should do all we can to reveal the nature of the Communist conspiracy against independent nations.

The inner meaning of democracy — elevation of the freedom and dignity of man — has a universal appeal which we should not underestimate, for:

> Democracy takes into account the factor to which communism seems so invincibly obtuse: the unsearchable depths of the mind and spirit of man, who will forever thwart the attempts of dogma and ideology to predict him or hem him in.[1]

Conclusion

Consolidation of national freedom, the fostering of national unity, the building of foundations for the democratic way of life, and the introduction of democratic patterns of governing require time, patience, and partnership. Chances are that democracy in Africa, Asia, and Latin America will take many decades to grow and flourish. But it is far better to have this democratic goal before us than not to have any goal at all. As we advance toward democratic ways of life and ways of governing across the face of the earth, we also reduce those areas where totalitarianism, especially communism, can make its appeal.

[1] Adlai E. Stevenson, "What Is Their Purpose? and Ours?" *The New York Times Magazine,* November 4, 1962.

Democracy and the Western World

Power and responsibility go hand in hand. Because of its extensive resources and willingness to accept the responsibilities accompanying possession of power, the United States has served as leader of the democracies since World War II. For this reason, America has spearheaded the movement to broaden the horizons of the democratic ideology around the world.

But the democracies are engaged in a partnership, not only to defend themselves against the threat of Communist imperialism, but also to advance the democratic doctrine. Too often the positive thrust of the democracies in world affairs remains unseen. In any event, the job cannot be done by the United States alone, irrespective of its status and power in world affairs. The task of expanding the democratic ideology belongs to all democratic nations.

1. How Have Some Democratic Practices at the International Level Evolved?

The Idea of Collective Partnership of Nations

Down through history, most partnerships of states have been of a defensive nature. Thucydides' *History of the Peloponnesian War*, dealing with the Greek city-states during the tumultuous fifth century B.C., describes a multitude of defensive alliances.

It was not until the nineteenth century, however, that the broader foundations of international organization were laid.

The Western democracies have taken the initiative in the march toward modern world organization. The basic operating principles behind most world organizations are those of democracy. Many African, Asian, and Latin American states have also joined in to broaden the democratic scope of organizing for peace. But the Western democracies, individually and collectively, have had the bulk of power and the primary obligation to advance democracy in world affairs.

Early International Organizations

During the nineteenth century, the expanding roles of the Western nations in world affairs caused them to give serious consideration toward uniting their efforts. In 1865 a number of them organized the International Telecommunication Union to provide for mutual assistance and some standardization in electrical and, later, electronic communication among states. It was a small but important beginning in a partnership *for* rather than *against* something. The machinery of the I.T.U. was organized on a democratic basis, with decisions resting on the vote of the majority and representative consultation and election of officials.

From this little seed emerged a constantly widening pattern of international partnerships — *for* things — organized on a democratic basis. The Universal Postal Union was established in 1874. In 1899 and 1907 the leading states of the world gathered at The Hague in the Netherlands in peace conferences. These sessions were designed to further concepts of international laws of peace and war. Agreements emerging from the Hague Peace Conferences still provide the basis of much international law today. These organizations and conferences were conceived by the Western democracies and motivated by the desire to project some democratic concepts into international organization.

The League of Nations

The Fourteenth Point of Woodrow Wilson's democratic program for world organization called for: "a general association of nations" to be formed "for the purpose of affording mutual guarantees of political independence and territorial integrity to great and small states alike." The statement was defensive, but Wilson's idea was a partnership of nations which would put the ideology operating within the democracies themselves into effect on an *international plane.*

The Covenant of the League and its operation were based on democratic concepts such as resolving issues through open debate and through voting, providing a constitutional forum for resolving conflicts among nations, overseeing colonial areas through the League Mandate system, expressing concern for international economic and social problems through League economic and social organs, and applying some judicial principles to legal disputes through the Permanent Court of International Justice. The League was by no means an organization thoroughly based on democratic principles. But it was a step in the long process of trying to apply, to and *among* states, democratic concepts which had proven effective *within* the democracies.

The League floundered because of the inability of the democracies to use it as its authors intended. The United States, as you know, never joined the League, and the other great powers never fully accepted their League obligations. Winston Churchill, during the 1930's, advocated that at least *some* members of the League should use the organization to stand up to aggression by the dictators, but his was a voice in the wilderness. The League failed to preserve the peace because its members and other nations failed the League. But the years of experience which nations gained in working together *for* peace were essential to later experiments.

The United Nations

Like the world organizations which preceded it, the United Nations was largely a creation of the democracies. The Atlantic Charter of August, 1941, drawn up by President Roosevelt and Prime Minister Churchill, established some democratic principles which later were subscribed to by all states fighting the Axis powers. Even the Soviet Union hailed the Charter, although this was only a strategy called for by the times. Largely through the efforts of the United States, the ideas in the Atlantic Charter were broadened and translated into the provisional language of the Charter of the United Nations during World War II.

The 50 nations which convened in San Francisco during the spring of 1945 accepted most of the democratic principles of world organizaion which had been worked out largely by officials in the United States Department of State. Like the League Covenant, the United Nations Charter, in the Preamble and in Article One (purposes) and Article Two (principles), affirms many democratic approaches toward world peace. The provisions of the Charter call for democratic procedures to preserve international peace and security, resolve disputes among nations, and promote economic and social justice. The United Nations does not claim to be an organization of democratic states or to advance democracy in world affairs. But the United Nations does represent an approach, which includes many democratic principles, to world peace.

The Security Council. The United Nations has been faced with some of the same problems that the League of Nations encountered — the inability of its members, especially the great powers, to agree on basic issues of international peace and security. The Security Council of the United Nations has eleven members, five of which are the major powers (United States, Soviet Union, United Kingdom, France, and Nationalist China). The Council was designed as the policeman of international security. The five large powers must come to a unanimous agreement before the Council can take effective action against any aggressor. This is a fine assumption, but it falls apart when one or more of these states has different ideas about united action or whether or not aggression has been committed.

The principle of unanimity in the Security Council arose, of course, because the United States, Britain, and the Soviet Union declared during World War II that their close association should be continued after the war. The Western world hoped that the Soviet Union had changed its revolutionary ways and that it had dedicated itself to a partnership with other states to make certain war could not arise again. This assumption, fortified by assurances from Stalin and the disbanding of the Comintern in 1943, was never valid. As we now know, Soviet partnership with the Allies during World War II was only a strategy to further the security of the USSR.

A veto, or negative vote, on a specific issue prevents the Council from taking a unanimous stand and thus bars Council action on the issue. More than 100 Soviet vetoes following World War II have rendered the Council ineffective in furthering international peace and security. These vetoes show clearly that the USSR has its own ideas about world organization. It looks upon world organization as a vehicle for furthering communism and upon the United Nations not as a partner but as a competitor. The Soviet Union has tried to reorganize the UN Secretariat, induce financial crises, and do many other things to undermine the global organization.

United Nations action for peace. But the United Nations, while thwarted by the USSR in the performance of its main task — maintaining international peace and security — has done much since 1945 to encourage the peaceful settlement of disputes. It has assisted former colonies into the theater of statehood and has helped them to organize responsible governments. It has shown a genuine concern for human rights and well-being. The Economic and Social Council and the specialized agencies dealing with such areas as food, agriculture, health, education, and economic development, have made vital contributions in laying the foundations for democratic patterns of life. The United Nations emphasis on negotiation, arbitration, free and open discussion of international problems, and promotion of harmony among nations has projected the democratic way from the national to the international plane.

This has been most irritating to the Soviet Union. In the General Assembly session of 1961, Khrushchev did not get his way in the discussions. So he took off one of his shoes and banged it on his desk, like a little boy deprived of a piece of candy. Adlai Stevenson, the United States Ambassador to the United Nations, has noted that:

> If communism is a problem for the United Nations, so is the United Nations a problem for communism. The United Nations

is a community of tolerance, and a community of tolerance is a terrible frustration to the totalitarian mind.[1]

Collective self-defense. The very existence of the United Nations has hindered the goals of communism and advanced the democratic cause. And yet, the United Nations has been unable to carry out the intention of its Charter — defending the security and well-being of its members. States must have some assurance that their security and well-being are being defended before they can give full time and attention to the promotion of longer term objectives. Because of the inability of the Security Council to function effectively, many states have formed their own defensive organizations based upon Article 51 of the Charter, which recognizes the right of individual and collective self-defense.

Among these organizations are the Organization of American States (OAS), the North Atlantic Treaty Organization (NATO), the Southeast Asia Treaty Organization (SEATO), and the Central Treaty Organization (CENTO). These alliances have as their basic purpose the defense of the security and well-being of their members against the threat of international communism. The USSR also leads a collective-defense organization, with the Eastern European states, excluding Yugoslavia, as members.

The work of the United Nations continues. But the necessary work of defense is now undertaken by those organizations which lie outside the scope of the Security Council veto but still within the framework of the United Nations Charter.

2. How Does the North Atlantic Treaty Organization Protect and Advance Democracy?

The Development of NATO

The North Atlantic Treaty Organization — the strongest and most important of the collective-defense associations — was conceived as a clear Western response to Soviet designs of aggression. The North Atlantic Pact was signed in Washington, D.C., in 1949, by twelve Western nations (United States, Canada,

[1] *The New York Times,* June 20, 1962.

Iceland, Britain, France, Netherlands, Belgium, Luxembourg, Norway, Denmark, Italy, and Portugal). Greece, Turkey, and the Federal Republic of Germany have joined since that time, bringing the total membership to fifteen. NATO has effectively contained the spread of communism in Europe and has been a military bastion against communism in other areas as well.

NATO in Support of Democracy

On the positive side, the fact that NATO has provided support for democracy in the West is of prime importance. Its composition, its organizational procedures, and its military capacity in shoring up the democratic ideology represent firm democratic principles which should not be discounted merely because NATO seeks to *defend* democracy.

Variations of democracy among NATO members. NATO demonstrates that democracies can work together in spite of broad differences. It illustrates the fact that *e pluribus unum* can function on an international scale. Fourteen of NATO's fifteen members represent varied approaches to the democratic ideology. Portugal's long-standing alliance with Great Britain was a factor in bringing it into NATO, though Portugal clearly is outside the framework of the democratic ideology. It does, however, provide some military strength, such as the Azores Islands, to NATO.

In NATO we find these kinds of democracies: the separation-of-powers federal government of the United States; the constitutional monarchies of Britain, Belgium, the Netherlands, Norway, Denmark, and Greece; and the commonwealth, parliamentary democracy of Canada. There is the paternalistic democracy of De Gaulle's France, and the thriving West German democracy which arose out of the ashes of Nazi Germany. There is the parliamentarianism of Italy and Iceland, and the Grand Duchy of Luxembourg. There is the shaky democracy of Turkey, a nation where the conditions favoring a democratic way of life are meager. Democratic socialism is a strong characteristic in many of these states. Large, legal Communist parties are powerful forces in France and Italy.

The cooperation of these nations on basic issues and the manner in which they have held together through thick and thin in spite of some strong disputes among themselves indicate that NATO is an international testing ground for democracy. It demonstrates that the unity of democracies is more significant than the problems that tend to divide NATO members.

Decision-making in NATO. NATO functions largely in the open and is dominated by no one of its fifteen members. It reveals how states can wield common policies in many areas in a spirit of accommodation.

The United States is by far the most powerful member of NATO. Because of its power, it has the responsibility for bearing most of the cost of and military support for NATO. Nevertheless, the United States has only one vote and subscribes to the majority rule within the main decision-making organ of NATO, the Council. The fact that the United States had a difficult time during 1963 in pressing toward its desire to arm NATO with nuclear weapons without greatly expanding the spread of such weapons shows that this nation does not dominate NATO.

The independent positions taken by some NATO members indicate strong differences of opinion among the Western states. France has been by far the most reluctant and nationalistic member of the Alliance. Under De Gaulle, France has assumed an independent stand on nuclear arms and on contributions of naval forces to NATO. By vetoing Great Britain's application to participate in the Common Market, President de Gaulle refused to broaden the six-member European Economic Community (France, Italy, West Germany, Belgium, the Netherlands, and Luxembourg). This had an adverse effect both on Great Britain's economic position and on the United States. French recognition of the government of Communist China in January of 1964 further reveals General de Gaulle's desire to pursue a foreign policy independent of the Western democracies. But despite the gloomy outlook of some commentators, De Gaulle's actions and policies have not brought NATO to the brink of disaster.

Indeed, the public airing of differences on military and economic policy reveals democracy functioning in the open. No one has ever claimed unanimity in democratic processes. Unanimity is the basic principle of "democratic centralism" within

Soviet governing circles, where a decision is made by the few. Diversity of opinion, debate in policy-making, and disagreement in voting are all vital components of democratic governing machinery. Compromise is a vital principle of democracy and has enabled NATO members to forge ahead with their work.

The resolving of many kinds of issues, especially the tough ones of peace and war, is never easy. But the manner in which NATO has functioned has shown that democracy can work at the international level. NATO members have demonstrated that regard for national origin, language differences, cultural variations, or scars of past wars is not the most important factor of policy-making.

NATO military power. NATO has contained Soviet aggression in Europe, and the military power of its members serves as the main defensive shield for other nations throughout the world against the threat of Communist militarism.

Unity in NATO. Much attention has been focused in recent years on the disarray of NATO military forces. But there is far more military unity than division. Though the United States is the most powerful military partner in NATO, contributions of the other Alliance members have added greatly to NATO's power.

French insistence on its own nuclear force continues to impair military unity in NATO. Several years ago, General de Gaulle stressed the fact that France would strike out toward an independent nuclear force. He was motivated by his nationalism and by his dislike of the fact that the United States and Great Britain have worked closely together on nuclear matters for many years. With its successful development of supersonic bombers armed with plutonium atomic bombs in October, 1963, France became the fourth member of the exclusive nuclear-power club in world affairs.

The United States, on the other hand, does not want any more nations in the nuclear picture, and thus has sought to have an inter-allied nuclear force under NATO. Agreement was reached on this in May, 1963. Based upon the American nuclear-powered submarines and the Polaris missiles, this force also has fighter-bomber squadrons from eight NATO members, including France. Some members hope for NATO forces drawn from all the members' armed forces. What has been accomplished to date in the military defense of democracy is quite remarkable in view of the problems involved.

Containment of Communist imperialism. The military power of NATO has effectively deterred the Soviet Union. Communist military power, especially in ground forces and conventional weapons, exceeds that of NATO. But the Soviet Union realizes that the strength of NATO would deter aggression long enough for the sword of American nuclear power to be brought full force against the Soviet Union. Thus it would be safe to say that NATO has prevented a major military conflagration. Had NATO not existed, the USSR would, in all probability, have used threats and force to push its objectives in Europe. Shortly before NATO came into being, the communists, backed by the Red Army, took over Czechoslovakia. Soon after, Stalin imposed a blockade on Western access to Berlin. A month after NATO's formation, the blockade was lifted. Since that time, Communist military pressure against the non-Communist states has decreased. Khrushchev has continually threatened the Western military forces in Berlin, but the willingness of NATO's members to take a stand in Berlin has strongly influenced the Kremlin leader to proceed no further than the threat stage.

The protective shield of NATO has enabled its members and other states as well to continue their economic, social, and political progress. Since 1949, for example, the European states have united economically to an unprecedented degree. Today, the nearly 500 million people in the NATO states turn out more than 1,000 billion dollars in goods and services. More than fifty nations have received independence since 1949, countless international disputes which might have led to war have been resolved peacefully, and the volume of international trade among nations has broken all previous records. NATO itself did not do these things. But without NATO, it is doubtful whether so much progress of nations would have been possible.

Communism has always respected power. The West's capacity to restrain communism militarily has perhaps forced Kremlin leaders to seek alternative ways to further their totalitarian ideology. The West should take great pride in the fact that NATO has contained communism and has, at least, placed the emphasis of the cold war more on the ideological level than on the military.

NATO's role in Korea. The war in Korea, which erupted in June, 1950, was an act of Communist aggression which did take place after the creation of NATO. The Korean war is interesting on two counts with respect to the military deterrant nature of NATO. In the first place, this action occurred in Asia and not in Europe. The NATO Alliance probably caused militant communism to take its guns elsewhere. Secondly, although NATO had no military units of its own in 1950 and although the United Nations action in Korea was not a NATO operation, the bulk of the UN forces in Korea came from the NATO states. Thus, as far as the individual members of NATO are concerned, the obligation to defend the independence of states may extend far beyond the territory of the NATO nations.

NATO as a shield for non-members. It might be fair to say that NATO serves as a military shield for those non-Communist states which are not members of the Western alliance. NATO lies in the background, prepared to help states which do not have the military capacity to defend themselves. This point should be familiar to Americans. United States military power was weak in 1823 when President Monroe told the European powers to stay out of the Western Hemisphere. It was in Britain's interest to prevent the European monarchies from resuming their colonial power in Latin America in the 1820's, and thus British naval power was the bulwark of the Doctrine.

This idea of a military guarantee is equally important today. It is in the interest of the democracies to prevent military incursions by communists into any state, although, as far as democratic states are concerned, military assistance can never be given unless requested. In a sense, NATO is the military bastion of the entire non-Communist world. It is no idle speculation to add that the Soviet Union is fully aware of this. If strong counter-military action against Communist aggression were to be taken today, it probably would be within the framework of the United Nations. But the hard core of any defensive measures would undoubtedly be provided by the members of NATO, as was the case in Korea.

NATO's Positive Thrust

Many people view NATO only in terms of collective defense. The Preamble to the Pact and Article Two, however, indicate that NATO is *for* some important things as well as *against* communism. In the Preamble, the parties to NATO:

> . . . reaffirm their faith in the purposes and principles of the Charter of the United Nations and their desire to live in peace with all peoples and all governments. They are determined to safeguard the freedom, common heritage and civilization of their peoples, founded on the principles of democracy, individual liberty and the rule of law.

In Article Two:

> The parties will contribute toward the further development of peaceful and friendly international relations by strengthening their free institutions, by bringing about a better understanding of the principles upon which these institutions are founded, and by promoting conditions of stability and well-being.

Most of NATO's efforts to date have been to defend freedom, not to extend it. But, hopefully, it is not reading too much into these provisions in the Preamble and Article Two to say that they contain the idea of furthering democracy throughout the world.

Decolonization. Although decolonization is not a policy of NATO, the idea behind NATO is the national self-determination of people. This idea has been transmitted by the NATO states to their former colonies. The many contributions of the Western states to national and human freedom should not be forgotten.

Portugal still clings to its colonial possessions, although officially they are considered part of Portugal. Belgium performed most inadequately in preparing the Congo for independence, and France, in some cases, fought intensely to hold on to its colonial possessions. The principle of decolonization is nevertheless valid. The NATO states in general have greatly eased the birth pains of Afro-Asian states. There is little doubt that the anti-colonialism of NATO's strongest member, the United States, influenced other NATO members to grant their colonies independence.

Aid to developing nations. The members of NATO are placing increasing emphasis on "promoting conditions of stability and well-being," both within the alliance and in Afro-Asia and

Latin America, through policies and programs of economic co-operation and assistance. The European Common Market is only one evidence of the spectacular unity and economic growth achieved by six European members of NATO. Through the new Organization of Economic Cooperation and Development (which replaced the Organization of European Economic Cooperation of Marshall Plan vintage), programs for economic aid and technical assistance to Afro-Asian states are being developed. Britain's Department of Technical Cooperation extends British aid abroad, and France has done an excellent job in bolstering up the economies of former French colonies. The Colombo Plan of mutual assistance among 19 nations in the Asian area has been active since 1951. Much more remains to be done in this respect, and some have expressed the wish that NATO itself might be the organ to coordinate and extend more aid to Afro-Asia. Such an effort would clearly prove the desire of the democracies to give the growing democratic way of life in Afro-Asia strong foundations and tangible assistance in every respect.

Citizen support. Within the framework of NATO and within the context of semi-official and private organizations, considerable effort has been directed toward the unity of the alliance's members in the areas of political, economic, and social affairs. Such organizations include the North Atlantic Treaty Organization's Parliamentarians' Conference, made up of legislative members of the parliaments of the NATO states, and the Atlantic Treaty Association, comprised of "Atlantic Councils" in each NATO state. Furthermore, the Atlantic Institute in Paris is engaged in long-term studies affecting the unity of the alliance.

Within recent years, various organizations and groups have met frequently to take up the non-military issues affecting NATO and to report their findings and recommendations to their member governments and to official organs of NATO itself. Each member state has a national council which has the responsibility for channeling private and group opinion and interest about NATO into policy statements. These statements are given serious consideration both by the governments of the member states and by NATO headquarters in Paris.

Through this citizen action, NATO becomes responsive to the enlightened public opinion which supports it. This grass-roots' support and advice represents "strengthening the free institutions" of the NATO democracies and helps in "bringing about a better understanding of the principles upon which these institutions are founded." Naturally, within the NATO states, the "strengthening of free institutions" requires continual attention. But this evidence of a strong relationship between NATO and the "consent of the governed" in the democracies testifies that NATO does not exist solely to defend democracy.

Other Areas of Democratic Cooperation

The effective functioning of the democratic ideology in partnership with other nations is not confined to the NATO states. Australia, New Zealand, and the Philippines are active participants in the Southeast Asia Treaty Organization. The Organization of American States is likewise dedicated to broadening the horizons of human freedom and social justice. It has been an effective organ in the peaceful settlement of disputes among its members. Although Sweden, Austria, and Switzerland are neutral states in world affairs, as democracies they are fully committed to all for which the democratic ideology stands. It is interesting to note that Japan participates in the twenty-nation Organization for Economic Development and Cooperation and thus is also cooperating to extend economic assistance to the less privileged states. The democratic ideological drive is assuming an increasingly positive emphasis.

President Kennedy noted that in Europe, the nations:

. . . long divided by feuds far more bitter than any which existed among the thirteen colonies, are today joining together, seeking, as our forefathers sought, to find freedom in diversity and unity from strength.

. . . the Atlantic partnership of which I speak . . . would serve as a nucleus for the eventual union of all free men — those who are free now and those who are vowing that someday they will be free.[1]

An "eventual union of all free men" is both a shield against tyranny and war and a pathway to the future.

[1] *The New York Times,* July 5, 1962.

The Democratic Ideology: Problems and Promises

We may make every effort to advance democracy in world affairs. But what kind of progress will this be if we neglect democracy at home? Can we honestly preach what we do not always practice?

We tell the Africans that democracy means full citizenship, yet there are some American citizens who are denied the vote. We tell our South American neighbors that we believe in equality of opportunity, but we have slums and underprivileged children. We tell the Asians that democracy abolishes religious discrimination, and in certain places we have "exclusive" resorts. We undermine the official work of the United States Information Agency throughout the world when we neglect to practice democracy as a way of life in our home town. There are times when our friends abroad are embarrassed and our enemies gleeful. It is not enough to blame these lapses from democracy on the other fellow — on the South, on suburbia, on cities, on the rich or on the poor, on business or on labor, on the administration, on Congress or on the schools. As citizens, we are all involved in these national problems.

Adlai Stevenson has said:

In the long run, it will do us little good to demand the tearing down of the wall in Berlin unless we tear down the wall that separates us in our land.[1]

But some may say, "let the other democracies carry the ball in world affairs! Why should we Americans be so concerned about the future of the democratic ideology?" An answer may be found in these words of Secretary of State Rusk.

> . . . the United States is widely regarded as the home of democracy and the leader of the struggle for freedom, for human rights, for human dignity. We are expected to be the model — no higher compliment could be paid to us. So our failures to live up to our proclaimed ideals are noted — and magnified and distorted.[2]

1. What Are Some Problems and Promises of Democracy as a Way of Life?

Some Basic Attributes of Democracy

Democracy as a way of life means a dedication to equality of opportunity for all. It also means full acceptance of *e pluribus unum*, or a full and meaningful life for all people, regardless of their racial, religious, and national backgrounds.

The whole idea of fundamental human rights, especially those pertaining to justice and the law, is designed to guarantee that each individual has equality with the next person in political, economic, and social opportunity. Naturally, we do not all have equal assets. The strength of our bodies, the quality of our minds, our appearance, our personal wealth, our education, and our friends will certainly vary. These differences may be of tremendous importance in shaping our capacities to get good jobs, live in nice neighborhoods, and own material possessions. But in spite of the advantages we may or may not have, the democratic way of life means that we recognize the equal opportunity of all to use what capacities they have to strive toward those goals they con-

[1] *The New York Times,* June 26, 1963.
[2] *Ibid.,* July 11, 1963.

Organizations like the Peace Corps, the Alliance for Progress, and CARE have been widely hailed as truly democratic instruments for furthering the well-being of the developing nations. Here a CARE representative and a Colombian farmer discuss ways to improve crop yields.

Citizens eager to learn, such as these women in Ghana, are an important asset to any nation. Because there are often several languages spoken in the developing nations, a widely used language such as English or French is often chosen for use in the schools.

Millions of the world's people never have enough to eat. Outmoded farming methods, all too typical of the developing countries, result in poor crops. Rapidly increasing populations and the migration to cities further complicate the problem. Assistance from the democracies can help greatly to increase the world's food supply by teaching people better farming methods.

We are all too apt to take the right to vote for granted. But in the newly independent nations, it is a precious right indeed. Throughout Africa and Asia millions of people, like this woman in Guinea, are voting for the first time.

sider important in life. It means that all have an equal right to worship as they please, speak as they please, assemble with whom they desire, publish what they want — as long as, in so doing, they are not harming or depriving someone else of an opportunity to do these things. None of this refers to the process of governing. It is a way of life.

Democracy as a way of life means that the outward nature of an individual should not matter. The color of one's skin, one's religious beliefs, or one's national background makes no difference as long as all respect the rights and privileges of others. *E pluribus unum* means the national cooperation of a variety of people working toward national goals. What counts in a man is his individuality, his ability, and his personality. The differences which make us individuals are as valuable as the likenesses which make us all human beings. This is why any trend toward conformity is essentially undemocratic.

No society is perfect. History does not record any nation in which the ideal has ever been attained. But we can heal the scars found in America through our dedication to democracy. It isn't very difficult to catalogue the advantages of democracy. Many, however, are reluctant to talk openly and frankly about the obstacles within a democracy which impair equality of opportunity and *e pluribus unum*. Patterns of racial and religious prejudice and discrimination, the inclination to place a far greater value on the conspicuous, material, affluent way of life rather than upon the more meaningful aspects of democratic living, and an unwillingness to share with others set back the whole scheme of the democratic way of life.

Some Scars in the American Democracy

Racial inequality. Perhaps the ugliest scar in the American democracy is the failure of the majority of the American people to accord equality of opportunity to the American Negroes. Our Negro citizens make up more than 10 percent of our democratic society. The thirteenth, fourteenth, and fifteenth amendments to our Constitution, enacted almost 100 years ago, outlawed slavery, entitled the Negoes to citizenship, and gave them the equal protection of the laws and full voting rights. This is the law of the land. But in many instances we have not recognized this fact.

The Negro wants equality of *opportunity*. He wants the chance to prove himself. He does not ask for gifts, handouts, or pity. And yet some Americans have conspired to deny this equality of opportunity. Negroes who have the capacity to buy a house in a suburb of a big city are frequently denied this right because some homeowners and real estate agents fear that neighboring property may fall in value. Trade unions may discriminate against Negroes by making certain they are given menial jobs with poor pay, in spite of the ability of some Negroes to hold highly skilled positions. Some church doors may be closed to Negroes, and some educational institutions may have a private policy which keeps Negroes out. Voting rights in some areas are denied to Negroes. Threats of bodily harm are often used to intimidate the Negro who is merely trying to cast his vote.

Although publicity has focused on the American South as far as racial discrimination is concerned, the American North is hardly blameless. This national problem has disgraced democracy and has gravely impaired its appeal to people in the Afro-Asian world. If the patterns of racial discrimination found in the United States represent democracy, the Afro-Asians point out, then this is not the ideology for those of us who also do not have white skins! When a citizen of Ghana sees a Negro in Birmingham, Alabama, being attacked by a dog held by a white policeman, he is not moved to admire democracy. An Indonesian, reading in his papers about race riots in Chicago, is not apt to be favorably inclined toward the democratic ideology.

Other social problems. American democracy has further work cut out for it in the field of social problems. People in various minority groups, such as American Indians, Mexican migrants, and Puerto Ricans, are often subjected to patterns of discrimination in the United States. Conditions which permit juvenile delinquency to thrive and ripen into hardened criminality need more attention than ever before. The high levels of crime in th United States are black marks against democracy, as are increasing divorce rates and other disruptions of family life.

Neglect of the aged, school drop-outs, addiction to narcotics, and overconsumption of alcohol are all social maladies which contribute toward a weakening of the democratic way of life.

Economic problems. The American economy has been remarkably productive and has provided for the highest standard of living ever achieved by any society. And yet there are high levels of unemployment and conspicuous areas of poverty in the free-enterprise system. Any nation as large as the United States will have people who deviate from the over-all standards of the society. There will always be run-down conditions in many cities. On the other hand, the democratic society and government must lend a helping hand to those who genuinely seek to improve their lot.

Monopoly is another economic problem. The giant business enterprise which denies other business an equal opportunity is performing a distinct disservice both to capitalism and to democracy. Most of the national laws regulating American business strive to broaden equality of opportunity, not to restrict it. The Sherman Anti-Trust Act of 1890 and the Federal regulatory commissions, such as the Interstate Commerce Commission, the Federal Trade Commission, and the Securities and Exchange Commission, are set up to guarantee rights of business practice and democracy. There is no easy formula in this area, but it is not free enterprise when big business keeps the door closed to smaller business enterprises.

The same is true of labor organizations. The dictatorial labor leader who controls his union with an iron hand, who shuts off dissent with threats, and who uses union funds for personal benefit performs in a manner alien to the democratic spirit. Though national labor laws seek to broaden democracy in our trade unions, many violations of these laws adversely affect the rights of millions of union men.

Perfect democracy cannot exist in all American economic institutions. Authority and leadership are necessary if a company is to be operated efficiently and effectively and if a union is to advance the well-being of its members through collective bargaining with industrial leaders. But authority must always be accompanied by responsibility to others in the firm and the union

and to the consumer as well. Any barrier to equality of opportunity which is based on the motive of private gain is to be
condemned as harmful to the real meaning of democracy.

A Perspective on These Scars

These are some scars on the tissue of the American democracy.
Other democracies have some of the same problems as well as
others. Great Britain has some serious difficulties in race relations, and Belgium is plagued with language riots between the
French-speaking Walloons and the Dutch-speaking Flemish.
Italy is deeply divided between the poverty-stricken South and
the industrial North. And so on! It is no advantage to the
democracies to deny the existence of difficult problems. But
in trying to understand these scars and in attempting to outline
to people in other countries why these conditions exist, the
following points might be kept in mind.

The delicate balance of e pluribus unum. Providing for diversity within the framework of national unity demands more
of democratic peoples than of people living under any other
ideology. Democracy does not impose a rigid pattern of behavior.
There can be no absolute conformity in our democratic society.

The American democracy has always been characterized by
its rich diversity. Americans at some point trace their ancestry
to other lands. But despite the many races, religious creeds, and
backgrounds, the American people have developed a cooperative
and united society in many ways. The various sectional interests
in America provide for different modes of life. The federal
nature of the United States, which permits the governments of
our separate states to have considerable authority in many areas,
also contributes toward economic and social diversity.

The democratic ideal is practiced far more than it is violated.
The strife and disruptions of *e pluribus unum* gain the headlines.
The patient, behind-the-scenes cooperation of many people is not
so spectacular. But the over-all record of Americans cooperating
to further the true meaning of the democratic ideology is remarkable.

The open nature of democratic imperfections. Democracy
makes no attempt to conceal its shortcomings. The democratic

society is open to the world. It would be alien to the democratic creed to cover up all that goes wrong. Our space flights and our political conventions are thrown upon the television screen for millions to see, exactly as they happen.

The "open" aspect of our society may place us at a temporary disadvantage in advancing democracy abroad. The free press, radio, and television sometimes take advantage of a race riot or some demonstration of bigotry and give them ample play for the purpose of appealing to readers, listeners, or viewers. These scenes of imperfections in our democratic behavior are transmitted abroad, and, unfortunately, frequently viewed by non-Americans as true pictures of American life. What others may not understand is that these flashes of prejudice and discrimination characterize a minority of Americans and do not represent our daily mode of action.

We do not hide the fact, however, that strong differences of opinion and practice do exist and that parties representing all sides of inflammable issues can argue, debate, demonstrate, and propose reforms or defend themselves in the public forum. We are acutely aware of the difficulties Negroes have in finding suitable housing or getting a solid education. But we do not seek solutions to these and other problems behind closed doors.

It is the nature of totalitarian states to hide unfavorable trends within their own societies from the outside world. Totalitarian states rarely admit that conflicts exist within their societies. Juvenile delinquency has become a major problem in the Soviet Union, along with alcoholism and crime. The closed society may offer an image of perfection, but only the fool or the sheer idealist believes it. The open society cannot conceal its problems from the world. But at least it acknowledges that its difficulties exist and that the way to remedy them is to muster public opinion against social injustice and to bring about change through democratic processes.

The optimism of continual progress. Continual progress is taking place in America. The horizons of freedom are constantly widening. While the pace may be slow, the over-all picture is hopeful. No one can deny that our shortcomings exist. But neither can one deny that the lakes of bigotry and disregard for the rights of others are slowly drying up. Though we still have

far to go, we are well on the way toward the full enjoyment of
e pluribus unum without fear, persecution, or violence.

The Meaning of Altruism in the American Democracy

If democracy means that people have the capacity to rule
themselves, then the extent to which Americans volunteer their
time, money, and work for the well-being of others is of tremendous importance. This is altruism, the ideal of sacrifice and
cooperation for the good of all. It is a vital part of democracy.

The fruits of volunteer activity in medicine, education, charity,
commerce, and media (such as educational television) are truly
amazing. New and effective vaccines to prevent crippling diseases, the maintenance of private institutions for higher learning,
community improvements such as recreation centers and cultural programs, extending a helping hand to the needy such as
is found in the work of the Community Fund, the Salvation
Army, and many other groups would be impossible without
the desire of democratic peoples to help their fellow citizens.

Democratic altruism acts without the participation of government. If the volunteer organizations did not exist, the government would have to step in. Volunteer work thus reduces the
role of government.

The American pattern of voluntary sharing and giving is
also advanced through the many religious, educational, and char-
itable institutions which operate overseas. Efforts such as
CARE's can further the democratic spirit in Afro-Asia and Latin
America and can join with the Peace Corps in demonstrating the
principle of the brotherhood of man implicit in democracy.

The Continuous Compromise of Democracy

There is a continuous compromise between the benefits of
democracy and its obligations.

We know the rights and privileges of democratic living because we enjoy them each day. We have no massive government
breathing down our backs nor a police state which makes us
believe in some dubious myth or promise. We inhale the air of
freedom and enjoy the luxury of the open society.

But the benefits of democratic living come at a price. If that price is not paid, the benefits themselves will not long endure. It involves a sincere belief in and full practice of the brotherhood of man, the placing of no barriers to equality of opportunity for all, the full application of *e pluribus unum,* and effective participation in the processes of democratic governing.

> The country's strength is in the sum of the strengths of each American. Nations grow great as the integrity of their citizens rises. They fall when their people grow abnormally selfish and morally slack.[1]

The "strength of each American" is not an idle phrase but a reality. The practice of democracy in our everyday life helps to spread democracy throughout the world. The great appeal of our way of life lies in the power which it hands to each individual — saying, in effect: "You are free to develop your own unique power. You have a golden opportunity to use this power to help your fellow human beings achieve the same."

Men have struggled and worked and died for this dream throughout the pages of history. For us, it is no longer a dream. But this dream will fade unless we match the privileges of democracy with hard work and dedication to the principles of the democratic ideology. This compromise or balance may at times be difficult, but we must never think of democracy as a one-way street.

2. What Are Some Issues in Democracy as a Way of Governing?

Many people in a democratic society feel that they are remote from their governing processes. But a key element of the democratic ideology is that *we* are the foundation of government. We naturally must delegate authority to our elected officeholders to conduct the daily business of government. But if we "give consent" to these men and women in public office to make the decisions affecting all of us, we must participate in the governing

[1] *Challenge to Americans.* New York: The Advertising Council, 1963, p. 27.

process. Our responsibilities include being well-informed on basic national and international issues, entering into the political process at those stages where we can give consent, making certain that democratic governing is applied at all levels of government, and taking firm action against those who violate their public trust.

The Role of Enlightened Public Opinion

To give effective consent, especially in voting, democratic citizens must be well-informed. You and I cannot possibly keep up on all national and international issues. But we can enlighten ourselves about the major domestic and foreign policies in which our nation is engaged. We shall certainly have differences on these issues. Should our foreign aid be substantially raised or lowered? Should we blockade Cuba? Should we place a high priority on disarmament? Should we reduce subsidies to farmers? Should we have firmer civil rights' legislation? Should the government play a stronger role in collective bargaining between business and labor?

Before we can answer these questions in a reasonably objective manner, we must know the background and the facts pertaining to each major issue. We should try to answer these questions by asking this one — how does the resolving of each debatable issue, one way or another, affect the security and well-being of our national interests? There is no absolute yardstick. There cannot be in a democracy. But if we try to match our ideas on certain issues with what we honestly consider to be in the national interest, we will be living up to our responsibilities.

Public-opinion polls often reveal a sad story about our intelligence on governmental issues. Americans tend to get excited over "hot" problems and to neglect the less glamorous ones. People are usually well-informed on those matters which concern them personally. Farmers usually know a great deal about farm policies and many union members maintain an active interest in labor legislation. This is not enough. The farm problem, questions concerning labor, and issues in the area of civil rights are all *national* problems and have a profound effect on our national security and well-being.

The Role of Participating Citizens

Enlightenment on public issues has little significance, however, unless we do something about them. This "doing" or participation is the actual giving of our enlightened consent. Voting is giving consent, but too few of us vote. Any American, in all probability, would scream if his right to vote were taken away from him, but the fact remains that in all the opportunities Americans have to vote, less than half of our citizens bother to go to the polls. Of all democratic states, the American voting record is probably the worst in terms of percentages of those going to the polls.

The other ways by which a citizen can participate and give his consent on public affairs are many and varied. He can contribute toward or play an active role in the political party of his choice. He can be politically active in organizations to which he belongs and can influence the stand of those organizations. He can write letters to his Congressman and Senator on key issues. A citizen has the right to influence the political thinking of others. He can register his enlightened opinion in letters to newspapers and magazines. He can form his own political discussion groups. Most important of all, he can, when eligible, run for office at any level and give his consent in a direct manner. But to be well-informed without participation is futile; to participate without being well-informed is arrogant.

Over 200 years ago Jean Jacques Rousseau wrote that:

. . . good laws lead to the making of better ones; bad ones bring about worse. As soon as any man says of the affairs of the State, "What does it matter to me?" the State may be given up for lost.[1]

Democracy at All Levels of Government

The democratic governing processes in the city hall and the state house are just as important as those in Washington, D.C.

A New England Senator once came back to his state and made a long talk in a fishing town about many aspects of international

[1] Jean Jacques Rousseau, *The Social Contract.* New York: E. P. Dutton & Co., Inc. (Everyman's Library), 1950, p. 94.

relations. He waxed eloquent about our allies, our military superiority over the Russians, and the work of the United Nations, and tossed in a few criticisms of foreign aid to boot. He thought he wowed his audience with his great knowledge of world affairs and his brilliant grasp of all the key problems affecting the security of the United States. But an old sailor abruptly interrupted the speaker. "Senator," he said, "what we want to know is this — when do we get our new fishing pier?"

Many of the functions and obligations of state, county, and local government are closer to the people in states and cities, and tend to reflect their more immediate daily activities than do national and international issues. Public education and police protection, for instance, are local matters. State governments have broad responsibilities in such areas as highways, conservation, allocation of welfare support to the needy, care for the mentally disturbed, and state educational institutions. Many of the activities at the local and state level are undertaken in parnership with the Federal Government, and thus the whole array of democratic governments in America deserves equal attention. Of particular importance is the necessity of citizens to vote at the local and state levels. We have far to go to participate effectively in these important areas of democratic governing.

The Problem of Dishonoring the Public Trust

It is difficult for us to feel that democracy has a mission and a sincere purpose when we see that some of the officials making important decisions in our behalf are guided by graft, corruption, and bribery.

Those who dishonor their public trust by various kinds of unethical and even illegal practices impair the effectiveness of democratic government. They undermine the dignity of democracy and cause those in other lands to question government of, by, and for the people. Such practices deliver crushing blows to other dedicated, honest citizens who are performing vital tasks as public servants.

Haven't you heard this before? "Politics is a crooked business and I don't want to have anything to do with it!" Unfortunately, when the press or government officials reveal the dishonorable acts of a few, the idea gets around that every politician is greedy and dishonest. A few rotten apples frequently spoil the whole barrel. But in a democratic government, we should never reach this conclusion. The vast majority of government officials brush aside temptations to line their own pockets. But the few who do yield to this temptation tarnish the image of the rest.

Much of the malpractice in government takes place at the state level, where the watchful eye of public opinion and concern seems to be at its weakest. An apathetic public only breeds contempt for honesty and places a stain on the capacity of the democratic ideology to reflect the best that human beings have to offer.

Democracy — A Summary

Each generation can take justifiable pride in the long and difficult march toward freedom. This march has been the authentic revolution in releasing men from the bonds of tyranny. Each generation, however, must also make the sacrifices necessary for preserving freedom and for guaranteeing its future.

Democracy, at present, is more widely practiced than at any other time in history and is making encouraging progress. But this progress is dependent on our daily stressing of the *positive* side of democracy. David Lilienthal has said that: "I deeply believe in the capacity of democracy to surmount any trials that may lie ahead provided only we practice it in our daily lives."[1]

Democracy, in the future, holds out a stirring promise for all mankind. It will thrive at home and abroad, provided the peoples in the democracies make the promise of the democratic ideal come true, rather than leaning on the accomplishments of democracy in the past and the present.

Mankind is going through one of its most fateful moments. Throughout the world there are people who have never counted in the affairs of their society, whose powers have never been

[1] Hearings before the Senate Section of the Joint Committee on Atomic Energy, 80th Congress, 1st Session. Washington: United States Government Printing Office, 1947.

tested or given a full measure of respect. They are emerging from their ancient condition. Never before has mankind lived with the fear that it might totally destroy itself; but, on the other hand, never before have so many men and women had the chance to live in hope, and never before has there been the chance to release so much human intelligence, talent, and vitality. The democratic vision is the reason why this chance exists. To seize this chance and to act on it with faith and confidence is the great privilege of the Americans of this generation.[1]

Some may say that the "inevitable triumph of the democratic idea" is far too idealistic and impossible of achievement in the vastly complex world in which we live. But it is far better to have ideals and targets toward which all of us work, rather than to have no idealism at all. We must mix idealism with realism. Many minds must be brought to bear on establishing the goals toward which we work and a program through which to attain them. This task must continue into the unpredictable but exciting future which lies ahead of us all. It

> deserves the best efforts that can be given to it. For it may well be that our time will best be remembered for its painful and tenuous, yet immensely exhilarating, effort to allow men to be free.[2]

An ideology combines a way of life with a way of governing. By truly practicing democracy as a *way of life* at home, we can insure that our *example* will advance democracy abroad. By dedicated application of democracy as a *way of governing*, we can further democracy in world affairs through official *policy*. If democracy by example and policy *guides* our behavior within America and on the global stage, the *promise* of liberty and the dignity of man will be within the reach of all.

---

[1] From *The Power of the Democratic Idea.* Copyright 1960 by Rockefeller Brothers' Fund, Inc., p. 75. (As it appears in *Prospect for America,* copyright 1961.) Reprinted by permission of Doubleday and Company, Inc.

[2] Oscar and Mary Handlin, *The Dimensions of Liberty.* Cambridge: The Belknap Press, 1961, p. 162.

Ideology and World
Affairs: Pathways
and Prospects

Today, for the first time in history, we have an ideological conflict which could destroy civilization.

There is no more urgent problem before us than to give serious thought to pathways and prospects for resolving some of the key issues of the war for the minds of men. Can we resolve the ideological conflict of our times before it destroys all of us?

1. What Were the Lessons of the Nazi-Fascist Clash with Democracy?

The clash between right-wing totalitarianism and democracy a few decades ago provides some important lessons for dealing with the conflict between international communism and democracy today.

The Collision

The challenge to democracy from Mussolini's fascism and Hitler's nazism was not disguised. The speeches of the dictators and Hitler's *Mein Kampf* set forth their goals of domination and destruction of all vestiges of democracy as well as the means to be used in the pursuit of these goals. Nazism and fascism were filled with hatred for democracy, the freedom of the individual, and the rights of man.

The response of the democracies was extremely negative. The Western states themselves were divided on what measures to take; those who called for strong resolve and action were in the minority. Most people in the West wanted peace and had no desire to take firm collective measures against Hitler. Many of the leaders of the democratic states felt that Hitler could be "bought" by appeasement. Some in the West considered nazism to be the "wave of the future." The League of Nations was rejected as an instrument for even minor collective action. Some Western leaders, such as British Prime Minister Chamberlain, sought to deal with Hitler directly and individually. They did not unite with other democracies threatened by Nazi Germany.

This incredible display of weakness among the democratic states only goaded Hitler on toward conquest. The natural inclination for peace, particularly of the peoples in Britain and France, was viewed by Hitler as spineless behavior. He never understood, of course, that democratic peoples stand up and fight when they are really threatened with the loss of their freedom. In the force of his challenge and in the response of the democracies, Hitler saw an open road before him in his march toward the "Thousand Year Reich."

The Lessons

Five significant failures of the democratic states during this era should not be forgotten.

Failure to appreciate democracy. The Western states and peoples naturally valued their rights and freedoms, but they failed to appreciate the full meaning of democracy. They accepted its benefits but did not exercise its responsibilities. They were not well-informed on the challenge facing them. Indeed, many considered Hitler, Mussolini, and militaristic Japan as no challenge at all. Because they did not appreciate the full sweep of democracy, they did not participate effectively in the making of policy which would stand up against the totalitarian designs.

Failure to articulate democracy. Democracy as a way of life and a way of governing must be articulated in order to provide a guide to action in world affairs. The voice of democracy was muted in the 1930's. Its basic precepts were put on the defensive. Leaders sat back and followed public opinion, which wanted peace but not the price of peace. Leaders alert to the totalitarian challenge were unable to stir the sentiments of their people. The ideology of liberty in world affairs was quiet — without spirit, drive, or action.

Failure to unite. Despite the pleas of men like Winston Churchill for unity among the democracies, the Western states stood idly by while Hitler marched forward. Roosevelt, too, called for unity, but his voice also was lost in others' demands for no action at all. Hitler was thus able to snap up states, one after the other, while the democratic states failed to muster their collective forces to balance the power of totalitarianism.

Failure to contain totalitarianism. Individually, the democracies did very little to contain the spread of aggression. *Containment* means the use of power to meet and balance the threat of power. The democracies refused to arm as a measure of containment. Let us not forget that in America, military conscription, or the "draft," was renewed for one year in 1941 in the House of Representatives by the margin of only one vote. Without containment, there is a vacuum into which the poison of aggression inevitably flows.

Failure to take the offensive. Finally, throughout the world, the democracies refused to take any measures which would place democracy in the driver's seat. Democracy was viewed in world affairs as a doctrine which some states fortunately possessed, a doctrine which required no positive measures. Democracy on the defensive is weak. The collapse of democracy in Italy in 1922 and in Germany in 1933 was not countered by measures which might have revived the theory and practice of the democratic ideology. In Asia democracy was unassisted by action which might have warded off the Japanese. Effective support of the struggling Nationalist movement in China in the 1920's and 1930's might have provided a bulwark against Japanese aggression. But instead of acting against aggression, democracy was usually on the defensive, wholly devoid of any forward movement or initiative in world affairs.

These "lessons" of the inadequacy of the democratic response to the totalitarian challenge of the 1920's and 1930's are all negative. And yet, the Western states, along with totalitarian Russia, emerged victorious from World War II. Some might say: "We came out on the winning side after all. Democracy will win in the end!" But history does not necessarily repeat itself. Events don't always work out the way we would like. There is no assurance whatever that democracy will always defeat totalitarianism.

2. What Lessons Can Be Applied to the Communist Clash with Democracy?

The Collision

Fortunately, the nature and magnitude of the totalitarian threat to freedom today is much better understood than were those of nazism and fascism. The Communist determination to control the world is built right into Communist ideology. The democracies did not ask for this collision. It was thrust upon them.

In 1962 Khrushchev declared that "some day the red flag will fly over the United States and the American people themselves will raise it."[1]

The collision between communism and democracy need not be through war as far as the Kremlin leader is concerned. He fully anticipates that the ideology of communism will encompass the world because the masses of people will ultimately accept its doctrine. He see this collision as a war for the minds of men. But Mao Tse-tung, his adversary — as well as ours — prefers the path of war.

Khrushchev relies on the doctrine of "peaceful coexistence." He does not like to live side by side with the democratic world but feels that communism must endure this stage until it attains its "inevitable triumph." On this point, Khrushchev gives us some grim humor.

[1] *The New York Times,* June 20, 1962.

It just cannot be helped (living in the world with democracy). If you keep a goat in the house, you also get used to the smell and learn to live with it. So let's just suppose imperialism (democracy) is the goat, only the house would then be our whole planet. What the devil do we need war for? It is better to live with the goat and endure its unpleasant smell. But as the proverb goes, we cannot let the goat get into our kitchen garden, and for that we must strengthen our defenses and develop the national economy.[1]

Presumably, when the forces of communism are ready, the goat will be defumigated, forced into the Communist pen, and become completely subservient to the masters of the house. Or, if Mao Tse-tung were to have his way, the goat might be butchered.

Where do we go from here? In the first place, democracy must formulate an effective response to the Communist challenge, a response which will facilitate the advance of democracy in world affairs. This response can have the effect of blunting the Communist sword. It can lead to some accommodation with both Russia and China on the world stage. In order to proceed toward genuine peaceful coexistence in the future, this response should make use of the lessons of the past. To do otherwise might cause the collision between communism and democracy to erupt into a thermonuclear war, or witness democracy slowly but surely falling under the red flag. We have alternatives other than "dead or red."

The Democratic Response

Appreciation of democracy. One thing that has blurred our appreciation of democracy is that it seems to become invaluable only when it is in jeopardy or is lost.

Some of the most magnificent expressions of democracy have arisen when the ideology of freedom is under grave stress. The great Funeral Oration of Pericles at the end of the first year of the Peloponnesian War, the dramatic affirmation of liberty by Patrick Henry, the Declaration of Independence, the Gettysburg

[1] *The New York Times,* August 4, 1962.

Address, and the stirring speeches of Churchill and Roosevelt were all conceived in the crucible of democratic peril. The philosophy of John Locke and the American Constitution, which attempted to consolidate the gains of the democratic creed after national turmoil, were formulated in the wake of crisis. The strength of the unity of the democracies is generally in direct proportion to the threat they encounter. This is evidenced, for instance, by the conception and history of the North Atlantic Treaty Organization. The reverse of this observation is likewise true. In the absence of the totalitarian threat, democracy tends to revert to the enjoyment of the benefits of freedom without the realization of its obligations and responsibilities.

The appreciation of democracy must not be dulled by the frustrating trials through which all democratic processes must go. President Kennedy pointed out to Italian leaders that:

> Democracy, as both our nations know, is not without its problems. On the contrary, as Winston Churchill once remarked, it is probably the worst form of government on earth except for every other that has ever been tried. Democracy involves delays and debates and dissension. It requires men to think as well as believe, to look ahead as well as back, to give up narrow views or interests that retard their nations' progress. But given an opportunity to work, it completely contradicts and isolates the false appeals of the extremists who would destroy democracy.[1]

Articulation of the democratic ideology. Following an inner appreciation of democracy and an exercise of its obligations comes the full voicing of the democratic ideology. You and I have the obligation not only to practice democracy, but to encourage others to realize the full dimensions of its ideology, and to project it whenever we can.

We must articulate democracy in our behavior and attitude toward others. We must do this with pride, and with the assurance that the voice of freedom, if fully expressed, will become contagious throughout the world.

Unity of the democracies. Another response to the totalitarian challenge of today is the vital necessity for the democracies to

[1] *The New York Times,* July 2, 1963.

work more closely together. The North Atlantic Treaty Organization provides a solid mechanism for the unity of the Western democracies. Other American alliances with free nations also provide firm foundations for the tough work which lies ahead. President Kennedy declared that:

> The future of the West lies in Atlantic partnership — a system of cooperation, interdependence and harmony whose people can jointly meet their burdens and opportunities throughout the world. Some say this is a dream. I do not agree. A generation of achievement — the Marshall Plan, NATO, the Schuman Plan (for a European Coal and Steel Community), and the Common Market (in Europe) — urges us up the path of greater unity.[1]

The failure of democratic unity in the thirties points to the necessity of uniting the democracies more closely than ever before. Without this unity, the advances of communism are inevitable.

Containment of totalitarianism. The foreign policies of the democracies must both balance the power of the Communist nations and take firm measures to contain the spread of Communist ideology in world affairs. While effective measures of containment have been undertaken since 1947, continual emphasis must be placed on preventing the worldwide spread of communism. Power and responsibility must go hand in hand.

Containment is not a matter of mustering up sufficient military power to counter communism. It does not mean building a military bulwark and then standing still. The French Maginot Line could not stop Nazi psychological warfare or the German Air Force. Containment means a wide array of defensive instruments of policy to prevent the tools of Soviet and Chinese policy from undermining the independence of states. In the field of propaganda, in particular, the democracies should make known at all times the deceit of many Communist claims and the true imperialistic aims of communism itself.

The Democratic Offensive. Finally, the point should be repeated that the democracies would do well to seize the offensive in world affairs. Containment as a negative policy to hem in communism is vital, but it is not enough.

[1] *The New York Times,* June 26, 1963.

These five key responses to the Communist threat of our times provide no *guarantee* for retarding communism and advancing democracy. On the other hand, they do take into account the shortcomings of the past and can provide a solid basis for both defending and advancing democracy in the future.

Over the years these responses would make it quite clear to the Communist camp that its goal of world-wide communism has little or no chance of success. They would do much to persuade communists everywhere that the "inevitable triumph" of their ideology is an impossibility.

These responses can also have a powerful impact upon the people within Communist states. There is no doubt whatever that winds of change are starting to circulate among the Soviet people; in the long run, such currents will sweep over Communist China as well. Higher standards of living and imitation of the Western way of life are already making inroads in the Soviet Union. Economic and social advances and the pursuit of human happiness can cause millions of Soviet citizens to conserve what they have, build a happier life, and turn a deaf ear on propaganda which calls for hostility with the West.

3. What Are Some Possible Grounds for Accommodation?

Accommodation with the Communist bloc is not possible as long as imperialism and the goal of domination remain a part of Communist ideology. But if Communist drives toward global control can be blunted and if areas of cooperation between the democratic and Communist groups can be expanded, then an accommodation might be reached which could do much to guarantee peace on earth.

Some might argue that no accommodation is possible between Russia and China on the one hand and the West on the other. They might claim that either the democratic states must totally defeat Russia and China or else be conquered by these Communist giants. This view can be countered by the proposition that if China, Russia, and the other Communist states want to adhere to communism, that is their own business. But the brand of communism which they might continue to embrace must be shorn of its imperialistic goals. Furthermore, any totalitarian state which imposes a rigid dictatorship on its people deserves condemnation by the international community.

There are distinct possibilities for genuine coexistence between democratic and authoritarian states on the one hand and totalitarian nations on the other, as long as the latter are moderate in the controls they place upon their people and as long as they do not seek to dominate other states. We coexist with communism in Yugoslavia and with Franco's Spain. We may not like what takes place within these nations, but we get along with them nevertheless. The important point is that these totalitarian regimes do not seek to impose themselves upon others. Furthermore, there is every hope that they and all other totalitarian states, sooner or later, will evolve toward the democratic ideology. We should never forget that there are seeds of internal change for the better in all states cursed with a dictatorship.

The Blunting of Communist Imperialism

If the democracies diligently pursue the five responses we have discussed, the chances of communism advancing in the world will be greatly reduced. Strong patterns of democratic living and governing within the democracies, expansion of equality of opportunity, and a full measure of *e pluribus unum* would make Communist inroads in the free nations unlikely. The unity of the democracies, the balancing of Communist power, and the containment of possibilities of Communist aggression would do much to prevent the Communist camp from making war on any nation. The affirmative thrust of democracy in Afro-Asia and Latin America would greatly increase the chances of halting Communist penetration in these areas of the world.

The young people of today who will control the apparatus of the Soviet state tomorrow may well have ideas far different from those of present Soviet leaders about the future course of communism. One should not forget the changes which have taken place in the theory and practice of communism since Stalin's time. The revolution in Russia is settling down; conceivably the same process may take place in China. As each generation becomes further removed from the Marx-Lenin-Stalin concept of violent overthrow of the "bourgeois camp," the imperialistic aspects of communism may recede into the background. The international movement of communism gives evidence today of falling apart, as each Communist state proceeds to chart out its own national course.

The blunting of Communist imperialism will not happen overnight. It depends on what we do in world affairs and how the Communist world responds to our policies and initiative. Even without our offensive in world affairs, the forces for liberalization and the spark of human freedom are gaining momentum in the Communist world. But without our hard work, Communist imperialism will never recede.

Areas for Cooperation Between the Democratic and Communist Worlds

Expanding the areas of contact and cooperation between the democratic world and the Communist states is of prime importance in changing the tone of Communist ideology. Pursuing areas of contact and cooperation with the Communist world involves some rather important soul-searching on our side as well.

Widening the points of contact so that we may have access to the minds of people behind the Iron Curtain is not appeasement or weakness. Our own attitudes of hostility, if they exist, must be replaced with hope, initiative, and determination. We must remove the walls of misunderstanding and prejudice which exist on our own side of the Iron Curtain.

Some areas of contact and cooperation between the democracies and the Communist bloc include the following.

Mutual exchanges of people. The more Westerners who go to the Communist bloc nations and the more people who come from Communist lands to the democratic states, the greater the exposure of each side to the other. Such exchanges do much to break down false ideas and to bring the realities of the world home to all sides. People from the democracies — students, teachers, laborers, scientists, lawyers, doctors, farmers, and others — can do much to dispel the erroneous attitudes held about the West in Communist states. Conversely, such people from Communist states traveling and observing the ways of life, work, and play in the democratic states can have a profound effect in altering old patterns of thought.

Through propaganda and education, the image of the West is gravely distorted in Russia. It is of tremendous importance to encourage Russians, in particular, to see the realities of the world, to realize that American workers don't live in hovels and that the capitalistic system is just the opposite from oppression and exploitation. It is equally important that we know the Russian people better and rid our own minds of some of the harsh impressions we may have of peoples behind the Iron Curtain. Exchanges have been in effect for some years. However, much more can be done.

The average Russian should not be blamed for the Communist ideology of world domination constantly broadcast by Soviet leaders. After all, the average Russian is a human being like you and I. He, too, wants to live in a world in which he is guaranteed peace and human well-being. During the past 30 to 40 years his horizon has been greatly expanded. Generally speaking, he eats better, lives better, and has a greater amount of leisure time than ever before. The better you and I can get to know him and his fellow countrymen on a person-to-person basis, perhaps the more we can all strive toward a truly peaceful world.

Trade. Increase of trade between the Western and the Communist worlds would also increase contacts and facilitate cooperation in the economic sphere. It is of particular importance to help promote, through trade, an increase in the production of consumer goods and services in Communist states. Throughout history, trade among states has been an important vehicle for expanding knowledge of others, changing old patterns of life, and bringing about other devices for cooperation. We have much to offer the Communist world in this respect, and the Communist states have much to give in return. Western sale of wheat to Soviet bloc nations in 1964 opened up new possibilities for expanding trade relations.

Progress toward disarmament. Since 1945, negotiations on disarmament have generally been most frustrating. Nevertheless, the world was cheered by the nuclear test-ban treaty of 1963. Widely considered as an important step toward reducing the risk of thermonuclear war, this agreement has given hope to billions for progress toward peace rather than toward catastrophe. Although it is recognized that the nuclear test-ban treaty by itself will not avert war and that much remains to be done to further the cause of peace, the mere fact that an agreement was reached after eighteen years of trying is certainly of major importance. After all, the United States and the Soviet Union would be the main targets in a thermonuclear war. These two nations therefore have a greater obligation than any others to expand the network of agreements and understandings designed to curtail the use of force as an instrument of national policy.

The Soviet Union, of course, was motivated to draw closer to the West and to negotiate the test-ban agreement partly because of the hostility between it and Communist China. Furthermore, the USSR probably has been forced to cut down on arms production in view of the demands of the Soviet people for more consumer goods. But if these facts operate in favor of the West and world peace in general, contacts with the Soviet Union in other areas may further help to alter the imperialistic elements of communism.

Other Soviet-Western contacts. In 1963, a direct communication link between Moscow and Washington was set up to reduce the risk of accidental war. Conversations between the American President and the head of the Soviet Union on this "hot line" can take place at any time. American and Soviet scientists are working together in Antarctica, trying to learn more about the nature of cosmic rays. Some people hope that these and other areas of contact might bring the West and the Soviet Union closer together in a spirit of peace and cooperation.

On the other hand, others might agree with former Chancellor Adenauer of Germany, who has opposed warmer ties and trade relations between the democracies and the USSR. He has pointed out that:

> If the free peoples of the West, or certain circles among them, are ready now to help the Soviet Union, despite all the dangers that threaten us, then I must say, only the stupidest calves choose their own butcher.[1]

[1] *The New York Times,* October 6, 1963.

4. Can the United Nations Assist in Bringing About Accommodation?

The United Nations has been invaluable to the security and well-being of the United States. The members of the United Nations, with few exceptions, embrace the Western view of international peace and security. The economic and social agencies and functions of the United Nations, with strong American support, have done much to advance foundations for a democratic way of life throughout the world. The democratic processes of the global organization have furthered the principle of reaching decisions through negotiation, give-and-take, and respect for all points of view.

The very existence of the United Nations structure and headquarters has provided a center for the harmonizing of interests of states, and for revealing, in many instances, the deceit of international communism. The United Nations has helped all new nations since 1945 to become full-fledged members of the international community. Had the United Nations not been created in 1945, the United States would, in all probability, be in a much more difficult position today.

The great hope of the United Nations, however, is that it can serve as a house of accommodation among the diverse ideologies in world affairs. Its prospects for promoting shared security and progressive well-being for all nations are limitless, and it thus can serve as the principal agency for guaranteeing genuine peaceful coexistence on this earth.

The United Nations and International Security and Well-Being

The United Nations can truly be the global organization to further the aims of all states. Articles One and Two of the Charter can be accepted by all nations if the peoples and rulers of all nations realize that these planks provide the best guarantee and foundation for the goals of their foreign policies.

This depends on a willingness of states to use the global organization more than they have to date and to contribute their full share to its operations. It depends upon the Communist bloc, in particular, recognizing that the United Nations serves the interests of all states, including the Soviet Union. If the imperialism of communism were to recede with time, then the new leaders of Communist states might well use the United Nations in the manner intended by its authors.

As a universal organization, the United Nations can reconcile those ideological differences among states which today lead to suspicion, misunderstanding, and conflict. The United Nations is without an ideology itself. Indeed, it can be a framework for removing imperialism from all ideologies. It can extend aid to those states which do not want to be obligated to either of the two major blocs. It can, by effective functioning, provide the new nations of the world with stability and progress. The General Assembly can be strengthened in its service as the town meeting of the world. These possibilities, set forth in Pope John XXIII's great encyclical, *Pacem in Terris* ("Peace on Earth"), reflect the hopes of many other leaders.

There is no easy road to peace. It will take many years for the complex machinery of the United Nations to reach a high point of effectiveness. As President Johnson told the United Nations in December, 1963, "Peace is a journey of a thousand miles and it must be taken one step at a time."[1] It will take compromise among all nations and some loss of face as well. But there is no alternative. The United Nations is the best possible hope for peace. Its Charter contains all the provisions necessary for an effective accommodation of ideologies, providing its members, especially the big powers, show a willingness to progress toward peace rather than war.

Genuine Peaceful Coexistence

If the United Nations can evolve toward the point where Article Two, Paragraph Four, of the Charter — a banning of force or the threat of force to settle international disputes — is truly respected, peaceful coexistence can become a reality. Centuries ago, the religious differences among men and nations

[1] *The New York Times,* December 18, 1963.

were viewed as problems which could only be resolved through war. Some declared: "Either you are with us, or you are against us." But it was discovered that men could live side by side, hold different beliefs, and yet not go to war in order to exercise them freely.

Secretary General U Thant of the United Nations finds today's ideological conflict more dangerous than this earlier era of religious strife.

History is full of examples of religious intolerance, but the ideological fanaticism that we see today seems to me sometimes to be even more implacable, and certainly more deadly and dangerous to the human race, than the religious fanaticism which marked the history of the past centuries.[1]

U Thant adds that "the only alternative to coexistence is no existence."

Our goal, then, is to stand firm, improve the functioning of democracy at home, advance it abroad, respond to the Communist threat in a positive manner, strive to blunt imperialism and disprove "inevitability" in Communist ideology, strengthen the United Nations and recognize the fact that we must coexist peacefully with all states as long as they do not seek to dominate others. Such a goal will inevitably favor the cause of democracy if, by example and policy, we prove to the world that the beliefs of democracy provide the best route to the genuine pursuit of happiness for all people.

Our kind of peace will take time to achieve and certainly will not resolve all disputes among men and nations. But democracy gives each individual the power and the opportunity to work toward this goal. Within the framework of the United Nations and in relations among all nations, *e pluribus unum* may at last be fully realized on earth.

If men are divided by ideologies, they can also be united by them. The idea of a world of peace and freedom has always stirred men's minds. Democracy, if we can make it work more effectively, can strike a common human chord and fulfill the ancient dream of a world where — in progress, prosperity, equality, and freedom — every man shares peace.

[1] *The New York Times,* June 2, 1963.

For Greater
Understanding

CHAPTER 1

Review Questions

1. What are the three basic ingredients of an ideology?
2. What are the three principal ideologies?
3. What is the importance of studying ideologies today?
4. What factors shape the goals of any nation's foreign policies?
5. What is the relation of communism to the goals of the Soviet Union's foreign policies?

Discussion Questions

1. Why is it important to relate the way of life of a state to its way of governing in studying the ideology of that state?
2. Why is authoritarianism considered a "middle ground" ideology?
3. How would one compare "security and well-being" as goals of United States foreign policy with "security and well-being" as goals of the Soviet Union's foreign policy?
4. Why is communism as an ideology a threat to the security and well-being of non-Communist nations?
5. Do "wars begin in the minds of men?"

Further Readings

Ebenstein, William, *Today's Isms: Communism, Fascism, Socialism, Capitalism.* Englewood Cliffs, N.J.: Prentice Hall, 1962, 3rd ed.
Gyorgy, Andrew and Gibbs, Hubert (eds.), *Problems in International Relations.* Englewood Cliffs: Prentice-Hall, 1962, 2nd ed.
Heilbroner, Robert L., *The Worldly Philosophers.* New York: Simon and Schuster, 1961, 2nd edition.
Lee, Baldwin, *Capitalism and Other Economic Systems.* Washington: Council for Advancement of Secondary Education, 1959.
Ward, Barbara, *Five Ideas that Changed the World.* New York: Norton, 1960.

CHAPTER 2

Review Questions

1. What are some elements of democracy as a way of life?

2. What factors are vital to democracy as a way of governing?
3. What is the importance of Pericles "funeral oration"?
4. How did John Locke influence the development of democracy?
5. How is economic democracy related to political democracy?

Discussion Questions

1. Why is it difficult to define democracy?
2. Why is the strength of democracy so dependent upon a close relationship between democratic rights and democratic duties?
3. Why is government by contract fundamental to democracy?
4. How are the United States Declaration of Independence and John Locke's *Second Treatise on Civil Government* related?
5. Why isn't democracy more widespread in the world today?

Further Readings

Cohen, Carl (ed.), *Communism, Fascism and Democracy: Their Theoretical Foundations.* New York: Random, 1961, Part III.

Fein, Leonard J. (ed.), *American Democracy: Essays on Image and Realities.* New York: Holt, Rinehart & Winston, 1964.

Frankel, Charles, *The Democratic Prospect.* New York: Harper & Row, 1962.

Hand, Learned, *The Bill of Rights.* Cambridge: Harvard University Press, 1958.

Handlin, Oscar and Mary, *The Dimensions of Liberty.* Cambridge: Harvard University Press, 1962.

CHAPTER 3

Review Questions

1. What are some duties and functions of the President and Congress in making United States foreign policy?
2. Why are experts necessary in the policy-making process?
3. Why is Walter Lippmann so concerned about the role of public opinion in the making of foreign policy?
4. Why did the United States assume an isolationist position in world affairs during much of its history?
5. How did Franklin Delano Roosevelt differ from Woodrow Wilson in seeking to extend democracy in world affairs?

Discussion Questions

1. To what extent should the American public be informed about all the ingredients that go into the making of foreign policy?

2. What role does politics play in the policy-making process in Congress?
3. Can armed force or war further democracy in world affairs?
4. Was Woodrow Wilson a misguided idealist or an unfortunate victim of political warfare?
5. Throughout American history, has democracy been furthered in world affairs more by example or by official government policy?

Further Readings

Almond, Gabriel, *The American People and Foreign Policy.* New York: Harcourt, Brace, 1950.

Brockway, Thomas, *Basic Documents in U.S. Foreign Policy.* Princeton, New Jersey: Van Nostrand, 1957.

Kennan, George F., *American Diplomacy, 1900-1950.* New York: New American Library (Mentor Books), 1958.

Powell, Theodore (ed.), *Democracy in Action.* New York: The Macmillan Company, 1962.

CHAPTER 4

Review Questions

1. What were the aims of the "Utopian Socialists?"
2. What do "dialectical materialism" and "surplus value" mean?
3. What is the importance of Lenin's book, *What Is to Be Done?*
4. What were the foundations of Stalin's power?
5. What was the course of Khrushchev's rise to power in the USSR?

Discussion Questions

1. Why were such men as Fourier and Owen called "Utopian Socialists"?
2. Can the dialectic adequately explain the course of history?
3. Can socialism of any variety be "democratic"?
4. What explains Lenin's ultimate success in bringing about a Communist Russia?
5. What was the significance of Khrushchev's reconciliation with Tito in 1955 and the years thereafter?

Further Readings

Note: There are many good books available which explain the evolution of Communist ideology. Among them are the following:

Cohen, Carl (ed.), *Communism, Fascism and Democracy: Their Theoretical Foundations.* New York: Random, 1961, Part I.

Curtiss, John S., *The Russian Revolutions of 1917.* Princeton: Van

Nostrand, 1957.

Daniels, Robert V., *A Documentary History of Communism*. New York: Random House (Vintage Books), 1962, 2 volumes.

Gay, Peter, *The Dilemma of Democratic Socialism*. New York: The Crowell-Collier Publishing Co. (Collier Books), 1962.

Gyorgy, Andrew, *Communism in Perspective*. Boston: Allyn and Bacon, 1964.

Hoover, J. Edgar, *A Study of Communism*. New York: Holt, Rinehart & Winston, 1962.

Meyer, Alfred, *Communism*. New York: Random House, 1962.

Mosely, Philip E. (ed.), *The Soviet Union: 1922-1962*. New York: Praeger, 1963.

Rieber, Alfred and Nelson, Robert, *A Study of the USSR and Communism*. Chicago: Scott, Foresman & Company, 1962.

Swearingen, Rodger, *The World of Communism*. Boston: Houghton Mifflin, 1962.

——————, *Focus: World Communism*. Boston: Houghton Mifflin, 1964.

Wilson, Edmund, *To the Finland Station*. New York: Doubleday & Co., 1940.

CHAPTER 5

Review Questions

1. What are the two basic roots of Soviet national policy?
2. What do "security and well-being" mean in terms of Soviet national policy?
3. What is the relation between the Communist Party of the Soviet Union and the government of the USSR?
4. What have been some strategies of Soviet foreign policy?
5. What are some tactics of Communist parties in non-Communist states?

Discussion Questions

1. How is Communist ideology related to Soviet national policy?
2. Why has Soviet foreign policy been so flexible?
3. Why did the cold war pick up in tempo in 1945 and 1946?
4. Why has Khrushchev eased up on the exercise of Soviet controls over Eastern Europe?
5. Why cannot a member of the Communist Party of the United States be a loyal American citizen?

Further Readings

Gyorgy, Andrew, *Communism in Perspective*. Boston: Allyn and

Bacon, 1964.

Hook, Sidney, *World Communism*. Princeton: Van Nostrand, 1962.

Kirkpatrick, Jeane J. (ed.), *The Strategy of Deception: A Study of World-Wide Communist Tactics*. New York: Farrar, Straus & Cudahy, 1963.

Mager, N. H. and Katel, Jacques (ed.), *Conquest Without War*. New York: Pocket Books, 1961.

Ritvo, Herbert (ed.), *The New Soviet Society*. New York: The New Leader, 1962.

Swearingen, Rodger, *The World of Communism*. Boston: Houghton Mifflin, 1962.

CHAPTER 6

Review Questions

1. Why does Khrushchev press for peaceful coexistence today?
2. What is the nature of Khrushchev's peaceful coexistence policies?
3. What problems face the USSR in the area of agriculture?
4. What are some tactics employed by Communist parties which are permitted to function legally in Western nations?
5. How does the Soviet Union seek to promote disunity among Western states?

Discussion Questions

1. Why are Khrushchev's peaceful coexistence policies in conflict with Marx's and Lenin's views about the relation between communism and capitalism?
2. Why is it difficult to label the Soviet economy a Communist system?
3. How does the USSR intend to use the concept of peaceful coexistence in its attempts to penetrate Afro-Asia?
4. Why is a legal Communist party in a Western state more dangerous than one banned by law?
5. Why are Khrushchev's policies in promoting Western disunity more effective than those used by Stalin?

Further Readings

Draper, Theodore, *American Communism and Soviet Russia*. New York: The Viking Press, 1960.

Hoover, J. Edgar, *Masters of Deceit*. New York: Henry Holt, 1958.

Hook, Sidney, *World Communism*. Princeton: Van Nostrand, 1962.

Orwell, George, *1984*. New York: Signet, 1950.

Rossiter, Clinton, *Marxism, the View from America*. New York:

Harcourt, Brace, 1960.

CHAPTER 7

Review Questions

1. Why is the Afro-Asian world of particular importance to the Soviet blueprint for world domination?
2. What are some characteristics of the Afro-Asian states?
3. What advantages does the USSR possess for furthering its policies in Africa and Asia?
4. What obstacles confront Communist efforts in Afro-Asia?
5. How is communism advanced in Afro-Asia?

Discussion Questions

1. Why is nationalism, especially as found in the new Afro-Asian states, difficult to reconcile with Communist doctrine?
2. Can Soviet experience in governing and economic policy be widely adapted to the governments and economies of Afro-Asian states?
3. How are the goals of Communist ideology woven into Soviet foreign-aid programs?
4. What explains differences among Afro-Asian leaders in their policies toward Communist parties within their own states?
5. Why does the USSR place so much stress on propaganda as a key instrument for penetrating the Afro-Asian nations?

Further Readings

Barnett, Doak (ed.), *Communist Strategies in Asia: A Comparative Analysis of Governments and Parties.* Praeger, 1964.

Laqueur, Walter Z., *Communism and Nationalism in the Middle East.* New York: Praeger, 1956.

Whitaker, Urban G., *Propaganda and International Relations.* San Francisco: Chandler Publishing Co., 1960.

CHAPTER 8

Review Questions

1. How did Tito rise to power in Yugoslavia?
2. What is the nature of Tito's "national communism?"
3. What are some aspects of Mao Tse-tung's domestic policies in Communist China?
4. What are some evidences of the "cold war" between Communist China and the USSR?

5. What are some effects of the split between the Soviet Union and Communist China?

Discussion Questions

1. Is the "national communism" of Tito "communism in decline?"
2. Why has the United States extended strong financial support to Communist Yugoslavia since 1948?
3. Why was Mao Tse-tung successful in making China communist?
4. Is Mao more of a Marxist and Leninist than Khrushchev?
5. Why cannot Khrushchev permit any voice other than his own to define the content of Communist ideology?

Further Readings

Crankshaw, Edward, *The New Cold War: Moscow v. Peking.* Baltimore: Penguin Books, 1963.

Daniels, Robert V. (ed.), *A Documentary History of Communism.* New York: Random House (Vintage Books), 1962, Vol. II.

Djilas, Milovan, *The New Class.* New York: Praeger, 1957.

Fremantle, Ann. *Mao Tse-tung: An Anthology of his Writings.* New York: New American Library (Mentor Books), 1962.

Hoffman, George W. and Neal, Fred Warner, *Yugoslavia and the New Communism.* New York: Twentieth Century Fund, 1962.

CHAPTER 9

Review Questions

1. What is the importance of studying right-wing totalitarianism?
2. What is the nature of right-wing totalitarianism?
3. What political philosophers and statesmen have contributed to the theory and practice of right-wing totalitarianism?
4. What were the principal elements of Mussolini's Italian fascism?
5. How did Hitler gain control of Germany?

Discussion Questions

1. In what ways can one distinguish between totalitarianism to the left and totalitarianism to the right?
2. Why is Hegel considered one of the chief architects of modern right-wing totalitarianism?
3. In what ways were Nazi Germany and Fascist Italy "organic" states?

4. Why did so many German people vote for Hitler's National Socialist Party between 1929 and 1933 when clear evidence existed as to the true aims of the nazis?
5. How did Japan gain so much power in Asia down to 1941?

Further Readings

Arendt, Hannah, *The Origins of Totalitarianism*. New York: The World Publishing Co. (Meridian Books), 1958.

Cohen, Carl (ed.), *Communism, Fascism, and Democracy: Their Theoretical Foundations*. New York: Random House, 1961.

Ebenstein, William, *Totalitarianism: New Perspectives*. New York: Holt, Rinehart & Winston, 1962.

Fermi, Laura, *Mussolini*. Chicago: University of Chicago, 1961.

Shirer, William, *The Rise and Fall of the Third Reich*. New York: Fawcett World Library, 1962.

CHAPTER 10

Review Questions

1. What explains Perón's rise to power in Argentina in the 1940's?
2. What role do armies play in Latin American politics?
3. What similarities exist between Franco's Spain and Mussolini's Fascist Italy?
4. How does the Republic of South Africa enforce apartheid?
5. What evidences exist in the Middle East to indicate that racism still has an impact on the official policies of some nations there?

Discussion Questions

1. Are there grounds for believing that national armies in Latin America can be beneficial to the advancement of democracy?
2. Why are there fewer dictatorships in Latin America today than there were after World War II?
3. Why are the regimes of Franco in Spain and Salazar in Portugal hard to define in an ideological sense?
4. Why is democracy as practiced by the white South Africans inconsistent with the ideals of democracy?
5. Why is racism considered to be a manifestation of right-wing totalitarianism?

Further Readings

Eisenhower, Milton, *The Wine Is Bitter*. Garden City, New York: Doubleday & Co., 1963.

Hanke, Lewis, *Continent in Ferment* (Vol. 1, "Mexico and the Caribbean"; Vol. 2, "South America"). Princeton: Van Nostrand, 1959.

Nasser, Gamal Abdel, *The Philosophy of the Egyptian Revolution*. New York: Institute of Current World Affairs, 1954.

Spiro, Herbert, *Politics in Africa*. Englewood Cliffs: Prentice-Hall, 1962 (Chapter IV on South Africa).

Szulc, Tad, *The Winds of Revolution: Latin America Today and Tomorrow*. New York: Praeger, 1963.

CHAPTER 11

Review Questions

1. What is the nature of Afro-Asian authoritarianism?
2. What do Machiavelli's writings and Kemel Atatürk's policies tell us about authoritarianism?
3. What is Sukarno's "guided democracy" in Indonesia?
4. What are the goals of national policy for the Shah of Iran?
5. What are some general patterns of authoritarianism in Africa south of the Sahara?

Discussion Questions

1. Why is authoritarianism a "middle ground" ideology?
2. In what way might it be said that Western democracy emerged from previous patterns of authoritarianism?
3. What is the importance of Ayub Khan's and Bourguiba's views concerning the Islamic faith?
4. Does Nasser's ideology lean more toward communism or toward right-wing totalitarianism?
5. Why are most African states controlled by one or a few men?

Further Readings

Almond, Gabriel, *The Appeals of Communism*. Princeton: Princeton University Press, 1954.

Dean, Vera Micheles, *The Nature of the Non-Western World*. New York: New American Library (Mentor Books), 1957.

Emerson, Rupert, *From Nation to Empire*. Boston: Beacon, 1960.

Heilbroner, Robert L., *The Great Ascent*. New York: Harper & Row, 1963.

Kautsky, John (ed.), *Political Change in Underdeveloped Countries.* John Wiley & Sons, 1962.

Mboya, Tom, *Freedom and After.* Boston: Little, Brown, 1963.

Sigmund, Paul (ed.), *The Ideologies of the Developing Nations.* New York: Praeger, 1963.

CHAPTER 12

Review Questions

1. What are the alternatives if the democracies do not seek to advance the democratic ideology in world affairs?
2. What is a possible timetable for furthering democracy in the Afro-Asian world?
3. What are some obstacles facing democracy in Africa, Asia, and Latin America?
4. What are some things which should be understood before undertaking the task of even promoting democracy in Afro-Asia?
5. What is the importance of propaganda in seeking to further democracy in world affairs?

Discussion Questions

1. Is it too idealistic to believe that democracy can make steady progress in the Afro-Asian world?
2. Why is the authoritarian leader in Africa and Asia so important to the advancement of democracy in those areas of the world?
3. Why might many in Africa and Asia question the sincerity of Western nations in the latters' attempt to promote freedom and social progress as aims of their foreign policies?
4. Why is foreign aid important to advancing the democratic way of life in the non-Western world?
5. How can propaganda serve as a two-edged sword in advancing democracy in world affairs?

Further Readings

Galbraith, John K., *Economic Development in Perspective.* Cambridge: Harvard University Press, 1962.

Millikan, Max F., and Blackmer, Donald L. M. (ed.), *The Emerging Nations: Their Growth and United States Policy.* Boston: Little, Brown, 1961.

Rostow, W. W., *The Stages of Economic Growth: A Non-Communist Manifesto.* New York: Cambridge University Press, 1960.

Scott, John, *Democracy Is Not Enough.* New York: Harcourt, Brace, 1960.

Ward, Barbara, *The Rich Nations and the Poor Nations*. New York: Norton, 1962.

CHAPTER 13

Review Questions

1. What democratic practices can be found in the United Nations?
2. What has the United Nations done to contribute toward the cause of democracy in world affairs?
3. How has the United Nations hindered the goals of international communism?
4. How does NATO protect and advance democracy?
5. What are some distinctively positive aspects of NATO?

Discussion Questions

1. In what ways do positive international organizations support the theory and practice of democracy?
2. Why did the United Nations fail to live up to the expectations of its founders following 1945?
3. Can the policies of President de Gaulle of France be reconciled with the democratic attributes of NATO?
4. In what ways can it be said that NATO provides some degree of security for non-Communist states in world affairs?
5. Why can one naturally expect stresses and strains among the member states of the North Atlantic Treaty Organization?

Further Readings

Gatzke, Hans W., *The Present in Perspective: A Look at the World Since 1945*. Chicago: Rand McNally, 1960.

Osgood, Robert E., *NATO: The Entangling Alliance*. Chicago: University of Chicago Press, 1962.

Rostow, W. W., *The United States in the World Arena: An Essay in Recent History*. New York: Harper, 1960.

Salvadori, Massimo, *NATO, A Twentieth Century Community of Nations*. Princeton: Van Nostrand, 1957.

CHAPTER 14

Review Questions

1. What are some scars in the American practice of democracy?

2. What can an American say to the questioning foreigner about some of these scars?
3. What is the importance of altruism in the American democracy?
4. What are some problems affecting the democratic way of governing in the United States?
5. What is the importance of the positive approach to democracy?

Discussion Questions

1. Why is the statement "democracy begins at home" of particular importance to the future of democracy in world affairs?
2. What is the importance of *e pluribus unum* to the theory and practice of democracy?
3. Why are racial prejudice and discrimination particularly damaging to the possibility of extending democracy in world affairs?
4. How is the democratic principle of "governing by consent of the governed" related to the necessity of civic enlightenment and political participation in a democracy?
5. Can the practice of democracy attain the ideals of democracy?

Further Readings

Chambers, William N. and Salisbury, Robert H. (eds.), *Democracy Today*. New York: Collier Books, 1962.

Daniels, Robert, *Understanding Communism*. Syracuse, New York: The L. W. Singer Company, 1964.

Frankel, Charles, *The Democratic Prospect*. New York: Harper & Row, 1962.

Goals for Americans: Programs for Action in the Sixties. Englewood Cliffs: Prentice-Hall, 1960.

Handlin, Oscar and Mary, *The Dimensions of Liberty*. Cambridge: Harvard University Press, 1961.

Mahoney, John J., *For Us the Living*. New York: Harper, 1945.

Smith, Bradford, *A Dangerous Freedom*. New York: Dell, 1963.

CHAPTER 15

Review Questions

1. What lessons for today's democracies emerge from the Nazi-Fascist clash with democracy in the 1930's?
2. What are some possible responses the democracies can make to the totalitarian challenge confronting them today?
3. Do the democracies "coexist" today with totalitarian states other than those in the Communist bloc?

4. What are some possible areas of cooperation between the democratic nations and the Soviet bloc?
5. What role can the United Nations play in resolving ideological disputes among nations?

Discussion Questions

1. Why is a close study of the 1930's so important to understanding the nature of the cold war of today?
2. Why have many of the greatest statements about the democratic ideology been conceived during periods of peril for democratic peoples?
3. What grounds are there for optimism that future generations of Russians will not subscribe to imperialism as an attribute of Soviet foreign policy?
4. Why are mutual exchanges of people between the Soviet Union and the democracies of particular importance in breaking down Russian suspicion of the West?
5. Is genuine peaceful coexistence among states with differing ideological systems possible?

Further Readings

Bloomfield, Lincoln, *The United Nations and United States Foreign Policy.* Boston: Little, Brown, 1960.

Churchill, Winston, *The Gathering Storm.* Boston: Houghton Mifflin, 1948.

Gyorgy, Andrew and Gibbs, Hubert (eds.), *Problems in International Relations.* Englewood Cliffs: Prentice-Hall, 1962, 2nd edition.

Perkins, Dexter, *America's Quest for Peace.* Bloomington, Indiana: Indiana University Press, 1961.

Index

Afghanistan. *See* Authoritarian states

Africa: authoritarianism in, 274-277; tribal life, 274-275, 289. *See also* Afro-Asia; Authoritarianism; Republic of South Africa.

Afrikaners, 245-246. *See also* Republic of South Africa

Afro-Asia: alliance of states, 144; and USSR, 144-158; characteristics, 143; communism in, 153, 154-155, 158-166; cultural environment, 288-290; nationalism, 7, 146, 294; neutralism, 292-293; promotion of democracy in, 286-287, 291-308; socio-economic problems, 290-291. *See also* Africa; Asia; Authoritarianism; Capitalism; Colonialism; Racism; SEATO

Agriculture: importance of unregimented, 156; in USSR, 131-132

Algeria. *See* Authoritarian states

All-Union Party Congress, 102

Alliance for Progress, 301-302

Alliances. *See* defensive alliances

Anti-Israeli sentiment, 248-249. *See also* Anti-Semitism; Racism

Anti-Semitism: as form of totalitarianism, 202, 211-212; under nazism, 221. *See also* Racism

Anti-Western policies of USSR, 137-142, 163-164

Apartheid, 246-248. *See also* Racism

Arab Socialism, 269

Arab Socialist Renaissance. *See* Ba'ath

Arab states: hostility toward Israel, 248-249. *See also* Authoritarianism

Argentina, 231-233, 237-238

Aristocratic authoritarianism, 257-258

Aristotle: view of democracy, 256

Armed force: as instrument of Soviet policy, 121-122

Army: importance in Latin America, 232, 233, 234-238, 240

Asia: authoritarianism in, 263-265. *See also* Afro-Asia; Authoritarianism; Communist China; Japan

Atatürk. *See* Authoritarian leaders

Atlantic Charter, 311-312. *See also* United Nations

Authoritarian leaders: Atatürk, 259-260; Ayub Khan, 252; Ben Bella, 272-273, 283-284; Bourgiba, 272; goals of, 253-254; Hassan II, 273; Hussein, 271; importance of, 295; Mboya, 253; Nasser, 269-271; Ne Win, 265; Nkrumah, 252; Nyerere, 253; Reza Shah Pahlavi, 268-269; Saud, 271; Sukarno, 252; Thanarat, 264-265; Touré, 252; U Nu, 265; Zahir, 267. *See also* Authoritarian states; Authoritarianism

Authoritarian states: Afghanistan, 267; Algeria, 272-273, 283-284; Burma, 265; characteristics of, 262-265, 273-275; Ghana, 153, 154-155, 275-276; Guinea, 276-277; Indonesia, 263-264; Iran, 268-269; Jordan, 271; Morocco, 273; Pakistan, 266-267; Saudi Arabia, 271; Thailand, 264-265; Tunisia, 272; Turkey under Atatürk, 259-260; United Arab Republic, 269-271. *See also* Afro-Asia; Authoritarian leaders; Authoritarianism

Authoritarianism: aristocratic, 257-258; background of, 255-262; benevolent, 268; cultural environment of, 288-290; democratic support of, 294-299; in Afro-Asia, 143, 263-277; in Latin America, 277; military, 264-265; nature of, 2-3, 5, 251-252; relation to totalitarianism, 151-152; variations in, 254-255. *See also* Authoritarian leaders; Authoritarian states; Ba'ath movement; Democracy; Ideology; Nationalism; Tests to determine ideological trends; Totalitarianism

Ayub Khan. *See* Authoritarian leaders

Ba'ath movement, 271-272, 273

Ben Bella. *See* Authoritarian leaders

Benevolent authoritarianism, 268

"Bloody Sunday," 75

Bolivia, 233-234